Asia-Pacific Economies

The Asia-Pacific region is often described as a 'miracle economy' flourishing in the 'Pacific Century'. With one exception, the economies of the area have deservedly earned a reputation as fast-growing and dynamic. *Asia-Pacific Economies* considers the countries first together and then individually, thus giving a uniquely full picture of the diversity and possibilities of the region.

Part I provides an insight into the core issues, highlighting success stories as well as prospective weaknesses. Topics discussed include:

- macroeconomic management
- financial systems and domestic resources
- environmental issues
- growth, poverty and income distribution
- third-wave democratisation
- globalisation and regional integration
- public policy and political economy
- labour market institutions and human resources

Part II concentrates on individual countries: Hong Kong, Singapore, Taiwan, South Korea, Indonesia, Malaysia, the Philippines, Thailand and China. For each country, a brief history is followed by a political and economic analysis of the situation, with an emphasis placed on recent developments.

Clearly written, this book contains a non-technical but rigorous discussion of public policy and political economy. Supplemented by substantial references, it will be a useful guide to students of this fast-changing region.

Iyanatul Islam is Associate Professor in the Faculty of Asian and International Studies, Griffith University, Brisbane. **Anis Chowdhury** is Senior Lecturer in Economics at the University of Western Sydney, Macarthur, Australia. Both are founding editors of the *Journal of Asia Pacific Economy*. They have published widely and have extensive research experience in this area.

Asia-Pacific Economies

A survey

Iyanatul Islam and Anis Chowdhury

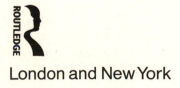

London and New York

First published 1997
by Routledge
11 New Fetter Lane, London EC4P 4EE

Simultaneously published in the USA and Canada
by Routledge
29 West 35th Street, New York, NY 10001

Typeset in Garamond by Pure Tech India Ltd, Pondicherry

Printed and bound in Great Britain by Redwood Books, Trowbridge, Wiltshire

British Library Cataloguing in Publication Data
A catalogue record for this book is available from the British Library

Library of Congress Cataloging-in-Publication Data
Chowdhury, Anis, 1954–
    Asia-Pacific Economies: a survey/Anis Chowdhury
and Iyanatul Islam.
        p. cm.
    Includes bibliographical references and index.
    1. East Asia—Economic conditions—Case studies.   2. East
Asia—Economic policy—Case studies.   3. Asia, Southeastern—
Economic conditions—Case studies.   4. Asia, Southeastern—
Economic policy—Case studies.   I. Islam, Iyanatul, 1953–.   II. Title.
HC460.5.C478 1996
330.95′ 0429—dc20   96–13403
                                                            CIP

ISBN 0–415–10765–2
ISBN 0–415–10766–0 (pbk)

Contents

Figures

Tables

Preface

The Asia-Pacific region is often described in such terms as 'miracle economies' and the 'Pacific Century'. The region is, however, rather diverse and complex, and the aforementioned descriptions do not always apply to all the economies that populate this particular part of the world. This book follows convention by offering a selective perspective on the region and focuses on a group of economies that, with one conspicuous exception, have deservedly earned their reputation as fast-growing, dynamic societies. This group includes: the two city-states of Hong Kong and Singapore, the East Asian economies of South Korea and Taiwan, the People's Republic of China, and Indonesia, Malaysia, Thailand and the Philippines of the Association of South East Asian Nations (ASEAN).

The emphasis is on a non-technical, but rigorous and comprehensive, exposition of key debates in public policy and political economy that permits a greater understanding of contemporary developments in newly industrialised and industrialising economies of the region. The book highlights economic success stories as well as prospective weaknesses – such as environmental degradation – that could constrain future growth. It combines breadth of coverage with country-specific details. Hence, a review of core analytical issues in Part I is supplemented in Part II by sketches of individual countries that focus briefly on their history and recent economic and political developments.

The book is a result of our continued research interest in the region. In writing the book, we have gained from discussions and interactions with friends and colleagues. We thank all of them, especially Dr Bing Zhao of the University of Western Sydney, Macarthur who provided us with key information on the People's Republic of China. The Australian Research Council (ARC) Small Grant (UWS-Macarthur) provided to one of the authors was extremely helpful. The final version of the book was written while we spent our respective sabbaticals at Rutgers University (Department of International Business and Business Environment) and the University of Manitoba (Department of Economics). We owe our gratitude to all these organisations.

We dedicate this book to our families who bore the burden of isolation and deprivation. They remain, of course, our central source of inspiration.

A reader's guide

This book represents a survey of a group of Asia-Pacific economies – Hong Kong, Singapore, South Korea, Taiwan, Indonesia, Malaysia, the Philippines, Thailand and the People's Republic of China. The emphasis is on a rigorous, but non-technical, exposition of central debates in both public policy and political economy of newly industrialised and industrialising economies and the way such debates permit an understanding of contemporary developments in one of the most dynamic regions in the world.

The book is built in two parts. Part I of this book offers a thematic treatment of selected, but salient and highly topical issues facing the Asia-Pacific region. Part I has eight chapters. Part II concentrates on brief country profiles with an emphasis on recent developments. Thus, this is a 'two-in-one' book and should appeal to a diverse readership. A brief description of each chapter follows.

The focus in Chapter 1 is to describe and analyse the extent to which one is witnessing the emergence of an integrated Asia-Pacific economy. The chapter defines the region, illustrates recent economic performance, and discusses trends in globalisation and regional integration. It reflects on such concepts as 'open regionalism' and the evolving institutional framework of regional co-operation.

Chapter 2 deals with the disparate and complex literature on explaining Asia-Pacific dynamism within a political economy framework. The chapter starts with the notion that, to be effective, growth-oriented public policy needs a conducive political environment and considers the extent to which such an environment varies across different countries of the region. There are also normative prescriptions for good governance.

Chapter 3 (entitled 'Macroeconomic stabilisation and economic performance') examines the importance of sound macroeconomic management for providing a conducive environment for sustained, internationally oriented economic growth. It interprets the recent macroeconomic experience of the economies of the region against this fundamental consideration.

Chapter 4 (entitled 'The financial system and economic development) starts with the point that Asia-Pacific dynamism has been characterised by high savings and investments and considers to what extent this can be linked to the nature of the countries' financial systems. This inevitably entails a discussion of financial liberalisation and financial repression and a discussion of the recent experience with a deregulated financial system in the various economies of the region.

Chapter 5 (entitled 'Labour market institutions, human resources and economic performance') critically examines the conventional wisdom that underpinning the success of the Asia-Pacific economies is the central fact that the regulatory framework allowed labour markets to function competitively. This thesis is often combined with the notion that Pacific Asia is a case of 'human-resources-led' development in the sense that aggressive investments were made by national governments in human capital formation.

Chapter 6 (entitled 'Managing the environment in rapidly industrialising economies') deals with the highly topical issue of environmental degradation in the region. Many observers now argue that the economies in the region have a disappointing record of environmental management. There is a discussion of policy options for 'sustainable development'.

The concept of 'shared' growth entails a look at issues in the distribution of the benefits of growth and forms the basis of Chapter 7 (entitled 'Poverty, inequality and economic development'). While it is universally acknowledged that the economies of the region have been spectacularly successful in reducing poverty, the chapter raises the point as to whether it is necessary to look beyond poverty reduction and consider the impact and implications of relative income inequality.

Finally, Chapter 8 rounds up Part I by offering a brief reflection on 'Democracy and development in the Asia-Pacific region'. It discusses the 'third wave' of democratisation and considers the extent to which a durable transition to democratic governance has taken place in the region. There is a debate on 'Asian values' and a reflection on the extent to which such a value-system is incompatible with liberal democracy. The chapter concludes by offering the case for democracy by appealing to its economic rationale.

As noted, Part II of this book encompasses a series of country studies. The primary purpose is to develop statistical profiles of individual countries that are submerged under the weight of comparative analysis in Part I, and to highlight recent developments. Such developments can be better appreciated if they are set within a historical and cultural context. In fulfilling such a task, a particular source, *The Far East and Australasia*, published by Europa Publications, was heavily utilised. The country profiles are arranged as follows: Korea (South), Taiwan, Hong Kong and Singapore are covered in Chapters 9 to 12; the economies that form ASEAN-4 (Indonesia, Malaysia, the Philippines, Thailand) are discussed in Chapters 13 to 16; China – labelled as a 'premier transition economy' because of its rapid transition to a market system – is discussed in Chapter 17.

Part I

Asia-Pacific economic development: selected issues and themes

Chapter 1

The emergence of an integrated Asia-Pacific economy

Overview

INTRODUCTION: DEFINING THE ASIA-PACIFIC REGION

'The economies of East and South East Asia are becoming integrated into a broad Pacific Asia region', proclaim Dixon and Drakakis-Smith (1993: 1). They note:

> This new regional grouping has emerged as the most dynamic component of the global economy. While the region is increasingly dominated by Japan, it has over the last twenty years contained most of the world's fastest growing economies.

Kahn (1979) has drawn attention to the epochal shifts in the centres of economic power that have occurred throughout history. Thus, the centre of international economic dynamism that used to be in the Mediterranean in the distant past was overtaken by the Atlantic in the past two hundred years, but seems to have moved to the Asia-Pacific region since the mid-1960s. Indeed, the term the 'Pacific Century' has become one of the contemporary buzz-words (McCord, 1991; Linder, 1986; Gibney, 1992).

In a recent study, the World Bank (1993a) has emphasised that most of the so-called 'miracle economies' of the world are concentrated in this region. If one compiles a league table of the 'top twenty' (as measured in terms of per capita real GDP growth rate over 1965–85), all the major economies of East and South East Asia are represented in this coveted list.

While one never seems to run short of superlatives in describing the ascendancy of the Asia-Pacific region, commentators vary considerably when it comes to defining the region, a lack of consensus that has prevailed ever since a Japanese economist (Kojima) 'discovered' this geographical entity. What constitutes the Asia-Pacific region? 'Regional definitions', as Dixon and Drakakis-Smith (1993: 1) aptly remark, 'are notoriously difficult to establish', largely because their essential characters do not always neatly coincide with physical boundaries. It would be useful, therefore, to reflect on the way various studies and institutions have tried to define the region.

A premier journal dedicated to a study of the region (*Asian-Pacific Economic Literature: APEL*) defines it to include the developing economies of East and South East Asia and the Pacific islands. The World Bank (1995a: 248) defines 'East Asia and the Pacific' to mean a list which entails a total of 34 'low', 'middle' and 'high' income economies. The Asian Development Bank (ADB: 1994), whose purview includes South Asia, emphasises a subset of developing economies in the region. Dixon and Drakakis-Smith (1993) include Myanmar (Burma) in their definition of 'Pacific Asia'. The present study adopts a more selective definition and one that emphasises analytical, rather than merely geographical, categories and one that focuses on the industrialising and developing economies. These categories are also consistent with the work – and hence the statistical compilations – of the major multilateral agencies as well as some major independent studies (e.g. James *et al.*, 1989; Noland, 1990).

Table 1.1 specifies the analytical boundaries of the Asia-Pacific region as perceived by our study and contrasts it with the geographical limits of the region. As can be seen, this study omits significant chunks of South East Asia as well as all the Pacific islands. It also excludes Australia and New Zealand. Japan is considered, but primarily in terms of its impact on the newly industrialised and industrialising economies of East and South East Asia.

Table 1.1 Defining the Asia-Pacific region

Geographical reach of the 'developing' Asia-Pacific region	'Industrialising' Asia-Pacific region as defined in this study
East Asia	*Newly Industrialised Economies (NIEs)*
Taiwan, Korea (North and South), China, Hong Kong	Taiwan, South Korea, Hong Kong, Singapore
South East Asia	*ASEAN*
Brunei, Lao People's Democratic Republic, Cambodia, Socialist Republic of Vietnam, Malaysia, Indonesia, Singapore, Philippines, Thailand	Malaysia, Indonesia, Philippines, Thailand
Pacific Islands	*The Premier 'Transition' Economy of East Asia*
Fiji, Papua New Guinea, other Pacific islands	People's Republic of China

What is the rationale for the fairly selective grouping used in this study? If one maintains the geographical reach of the Asia-Pacific region, then it affects the image of the region as a new growth pole because it includes island economies in the Pacific and 'transition economies' (such as Cambodia and Laos) that cannot be classified as rapidly industrialising ones. If one really intends to analyse and understand the sources of the dynamism of the Asia-Pacific region, then it would be useful to focus on the 'core' group of economies that are prime examples of such dynamism. Some diversity is, however, introduced in this sample by incorporating the Philippines – an economic laggard.

As can be seen from Table 1.1, the region as defined in this study includes several subgroups: the 'Newly Industrialised Economies' (NIEs), consisting of Korea, Taiwan and the two city-states of Hong Kong and Singapore; the 'ASEAN-4', comprising the four relatively large economies of Indonesia, Malaysia, the Philippines and Thailand that form part of the 'Association of South East Asian Nations'; finally, the People's Republic of China (PRC) is treated separately as a prime example of a 'transition' economy.

As noted, these analytical categories are in line with standard practice. Admittedly, such categories do not coincide neatly with the geographical boundaries of the region. Thus, Singapore, which is part of South East Asia, is lumped with some East Asian economies (e.g. Taiwan). At the same time, the PRC, which is part of East Asia, is treated separately from other economies in this group. The purpose of this sub-classification is to highlight both similarities and differences that exist between economies in this region, and in particular to highlight countries at different stages of economic development. The PRC deserves separate treatment because it still remains the prime example of an economy that has engaged in a transition from a centrally planned to a market-oriented system with remarkable success, and will inevitably be the bench-mark against which other 'transition' economies in Asia and Eastern Europe will be judged.

THE ASIA-PACIFIC ECONOMIES: RELATIVE SIZE AND DIVERSITY

Table 1.2 provides an indication of the diversity of the Asia-Pacific economies by focusing on per capita GNP, a 'market share' measure of GDP (expressed both in terms of regional and world GDP), land-mass and population size. For comparative purposes, corresponding indicators for Japan are also included.

Judged from some perspectives, the Asia-Pacific economies represent a study in contrast. Thus, at one extreme are the rather populous economies of the PRC and Indonesia, accounting for 86 per cent of the regional population. At the other extreme are the two tiny city-states of Singapore and Hong Kong. There is also conspicuous variation in land-mass and topography. Most countries reviewed in this study are contiguous entities, the main exceptions being Indonesia and the Philippines, which are archipelagos containing a total of well over 20,000 islands of considerable diversity.

The economies analysed in this study also encompass a wide range of cultures, religions, ethnic groups and languages. Korea and Taiwan are ethnically largely homogeneous societies while the ASEAN-4 and the two city states are pluralistic and multi-cultural. They bear the imprint of different historical circumstances. Thus, Korea and Taiwan had been

Table 1.2 Relative size of the Asia-Pacific economies

Economy	Area (000 sq km)	Population (million) mid-1993	Per capita GNP (US$) 1993	% of total regional GDP 1990	%of world GDP 1989
NIEs					
Korea	41.1	44.1	7,660	5.4	1.1
Taiwan	19.1	21	10,215	3.3	0.8
Singapore	2.6	2.6	19,850	0.8	0.2
Hong Kong	5.4	5.4	18,060	1.3	0.4
ASEAN-4					
Indonesia	1,919	187.2	740	2.4	0.6
Malaysia	330	19.0	3,140	0.9	1.0
Thailand	300	58.1	2,110	1.8	0.3
Philippines	542	64.8	850	1.0	0.4
PRC	9,561	1,178.4	490	8.2	2.3
Japan	269	124.5	31,490	66.8	17.7

Sources and Notes: World Bank, World Development Report, 1995a; James et al., 1989: 8; ADB, Asian Development Outlook, 1994; International Economic Data Bank, Australian National University (ANU). Data on Taiwan from national statistical sources. The regional shares – drawn from the International Data Bank, ANU – are based on a definition of the Asia-Pacific region that includes Australia and New Zealand.

Japanese colonies, the two city states and Malaysia were British colonies, Indonesia was a Dutch colony, while Thailand was never really colonised. In political terms, there has been significant change and evolution. Starting with rather authoritarian political structures, Taiwan and the Philippines have made significant progress towards democratisation. Singapore and Malaysia may be classified as 'semi-democracies' (Case, 1994; Crouch, 1993), while the PRC, Indonesia and Thailand have yet to make significant progress towards a more open political system.

As can be seen from Table 1.2, the two city states of Singapore and Hong Kong represent the richest economies, with per capita GNP (in US$ at 1990 prices) in excess of $15,000. They are followed by Taiwan and Korea, while Malaysia and Thailand represent the third tier (GNP per capita ranging from $2,000 to $10,000). The low-income economies of this region are represented by Indonesia, the Philippines and the PRC (GNP per capita below $1,000). In general, the relative difference in living standards (as measured by per capita GNP) between the NIEs and the ASEAN-4, and between the former two groups and PRC can be clearly seen from Table 1.2.

The relative size of the Asia-Pacific economies can be measured by using a 'market share' approach, that is, by the proportion of each economy's share in regional and world GDP. Taken together, these economies account for 7.1 per cent of world output (in 1989 prices). This represents a remarkable improvement since 1970, when the share of world output of the Asia-Pacific economies was a mere 3.1 per cent. This, in turn, provides a rough indication of the notion of an emerging centre of world economic power.

Finally, the dominant position of Japan in the regional economy can be easily discerned from the fact that it accounts for 67 per cent of regional GDP and 18 per cent of world output. Its regional impact will be the subject of further consideration in a subsequent section.

ECONOMIC GROWTH AND STRUCTURAL CHANGE: RECENT PERFORMANCE

This study will aim to chart the growth of the Asia-Pacific economies by emphasising recent developments, in particular in the 1980s and early 1990s. This does not mean that the 1960s and 1970s are unimportant, but past studies have covered those periods rather well (e.g. James *et al.*, 1989).

As a group, the Asia-Pacific economies have grown well above the world average – thus confirming the popular perception of the dynamism of the region. Over 1971–92, the NIEs, ASEAN-4 and PRC taken as a collective entity grew at 7.7 per cent, while the growth rate for the world economy over the same period was 2.9 per cent (Kwan, 1993: 3). As noted, the World Bank (1993a) has compiled a list of the twenty fastest growing economies in the world using per capita GDP growth rate over the 1965–85 period. All of the Asia-Pacific economies, with the conspicuous exception of the Philippines, belong to this exclusive list of the 'top twenty'.

Table 1.3 disaggregates recent growth performance by the various subgroups – NIEs, ASEAN-4, PRC – and includes provisional estimates for 1994 and 1995. As can be seen, there has been some slowing down of growth between the 1970s and the 1980s for the NIEs – from 9 per cent in the 1971–80 period to 8.3 per cent in the 1981–90 period. This is also the case for the ASEAN economies. The case of the Philippines is particularly striking, with a sharp deceleration in the average growth rate from 6 per cent to 1 per cent. The PRC provides a conspicuous exception, with average GDP growth surging to 10.4 per cent from 7.9 per cent over the relevant periods. Provisional estimates for 1994 and 1995 suggest that the NIEs will maintain their growth rate around 6.5 per cent, the ASEAN economies around 7 per cent and the PRC will maintain its robust performance of approximately 10 per cent growth. Projections to the year 2000 by Noland (1990: appendix, table A2) show slightly higher growth rates, ranging from 5.9 per cent to 8.5 per cent in ASEAN and between 7.5 per cent and 7.9 per cent in the NIEs.

In sum, it appears that if one compares the 1970s to the 1980s and the early 1990s, then the PRC has easily overtaken the NIEs in terms of rapidity of growth. This is to be expected as the NIEs approach economic maturity. It must be noted too that the slower growth of the ASEAN economies relative to both the NIEs and the PRC is partly influenced by the experience of the Philippines, which suffered a recesson in 1990 and could only manage rather sluggish growth between 1992 and 1993. A sharp

Table 1.3 Growth rate of GDP (per cent per annum): 1971–95

Economy	1971–80 (ave)	1981–90 (ave)	1990–93 (ave)	1994	1995
NIEs	9.0	8.3	6.3	6.5	6.6
Korea	9.0	8.8	6.8	5.7	5.9
Taiwan	9.3	8.5	6.2	6.4	6.6
Hong Kong	9.3	7.2	4.5	5.7	5.9
Singapore	7.9	6.3	7.7	7.0	6.0
ASEAN-4	7.4	4.9	6.3	7.1	7.5
Indonesia	7.7	5.5	6.7	6.7	7.0
Malaysia	7.8	5.2	8.6	8.6	8.4
Philippines	6.0	1.0	1.0	4.0	5.5
Thailand	7.9	7.9	8.8	8.2	8.5
PRC	7.9	10.4	9.6	10.0	9.0

Source: Adapted from ADB, *Asian Development Outlook 1994*, table A1, p. 231
Note: 1994 and 1995 are projected estimates

contrast is provided by Thailand which experienced double-digit growth in 1988–90 and seems to be growing in the mid-1990s above the growth rate of the NIEs.

Table 1.4 charts the structural change in the Asia-Pacific economies by providing some information on sectoral shares of GDP between 1970 and 1993. Consider first the case of the NIEs. How well do they fit the general pattern of sectoral shifts as economies approach maturity? To start with, the well-known Chenery–Syrquin view (Chenery and Syrquin, 1975) that the agricultural sector shrinks with progressive stages of development is certainly borne out in the case of Korea and Taiwan, while the virtually non-existent agricultural sector in the two city states is more a reflection of their urbanised nature than stages of development.

One also observes the progressive dominance of the service sector, and a corresponding decline in the relative size of industry – a process sometimes

Table 1.4 Structural change: sectoral share of GDP (%), 1970–93

Economy	Agriculture			Industry			Services		
	1970	1980	1993	1970	1980	1993	1970	1980	1993
NIEs									
Korea	29.8	14.2	6.4	23.8	37.8	46.1	46.4	48.1	47.6
Taiwan	—	7.9	3.4	—	46.0	41.8	—	46.1	54.8
Hong Kong	—	0.9	0.2	—	32.0	22.6	—	67.2	77.2
Singapore	2.2	1.1	0.2	36.4	38.8	36.5	61.4	60.0	63.3
ASEAN									
Indonesia	35.0	24.4	17.6	28.0	41.3	42.1	37.0	34.3	40.3
Malaysia	—	22.9	15.8	—	35.8	44.2	—	41.3	40.0
Philippines	28.2	23.5	22.7	33.7	40.5	34.4	38.1	36.0	42.9
Thailand	30.2	20.2	12.2	25.7	30.1	40.9	44.1	49.7	46.9
PRC	42.2	25.6	22.6	44.6	51.7	52.0	13.2	22.7	25.4

Source: Extracted from table A6, p. 236, ADB, 1994

referred to (a bit pejoratively) as 'de-industrialisation'. Chow and Kellman (1993: 156), drawing on another source, has highlighted the point – based on cross-country analysis – that as an economy reaches the threshold of $5,000 'de-industrialisation' sets in. Korea seems to deviate from this trend significantly, with the relative size of the industrial sector actually rising between 1980 and 1993 (from 37.8 per cent to 46.1 per cent) and the size of the service sector remaining stable at around 48 per cent.

Despite being at lower income levels, the degree of industrialisation, as measured by the relative size of the industrial sector, in the ASEAN economies and the PRC is by no means smaller than in the NIEs. Indeed, by 1993 the PRC had the largest industrial sector among the Asia-Pacific economies (52 per cent of GDP).

The rapid growth of the Asia-Pacific economies has been underpinned by very high savings and investment ratios (Tables 1.5 and 1.6). The average

Table 1.5 Gross domestic saving rates (per cent of GDP), 1971–95

Economy	1971–80	1981–90	1991–93	1994	1995
NIEs
Korea	22.3	32.0	35.7	34.5	34.3
Taiwan	32.1	32.9	27.3	27.3	27.6
Hong Kong	28.4	31.0	31.4	29.6	29.6
Singapore	30.0	42.6	46.6	45.0	45.0
ASEAN-4
Indonesia	21.6	31.8	36.8	38.7	40.4
Malaysia	29.1	33.0	34.6	39.4	38.7
Philippines	26.5	22.3	16.0	15.0	16.0
Thailand	22.2	27.2	35.5	38.9	40.1
PRC	35.8	34.4	34.5	35.2	35.5

Source: Adapted from ADB, Asian Development Outlook, 1994, table A7
Note: 1994 and 1995 are projected estimates

Table 1.6 Gross domestic investment rates (per cent of GDP), 1971–95

Economy	1971–80	1981–90	1991–93	1994	1995
NIEs
Korea	28.9	30.5	36.6	33.8	33.0
Taiwan	30.5	22.6	23.6	26.1	26.6
Hong Kong	27.8	28.2	28.9	29.5	30.3
Singapore	41.2	42.2	40.1	41.5	42.0
ASEAN-4
Indonesia	19.3	30.4	35.2	35.5	36.0
Malaysia	24.9	34.7	33.9	34.5	35.0
Philippines	27.8	21.9	22.3	25.0	26.4
Thailand	25.3	30.6	41.7	44.1	45.1
PRC	33.9	32.1	35.7	36.2	36.0

Source: Adapted from ADB, Asian Development Outlook, 1994, table A8

savings rate in the 1980s ranged from 31 per cent in Hong Kong to 43 per cent in Singapore, while the corresponding average investment rate ranged from 23 per cent (Taiwan) to 42 per cent (Singapore). In the ASEAN-4, the average savings rate is as high as 33 per cent (Malaysia), with the Philippines falling well below this norm (22 per cent). The PRC is also characterised by rather high savings and investment ratios (over 30 per cent). In general, savings and investment rates for the Asia-Pacific economies are well above the world norm.

Provisional estimates for 1994 and 1995 suggest that this exemplary performance is likely to be maintained in the case of the NIEs and the PRC, although there are some minor exceptions. For the ASEAN economies, the tentative estimates for the mid-1990s suggest rather dramatic improvements in savings and investment performance compared with the 1970s (approaching 40–45 per cent in some cases). Once again, the Philippines provides a conspicuous exception to this salutary trend, with savings rate in fact falling (to as low as 16 per cent) compared with the 1970s, and with average investment rates no higher than in the 1970s.

TRENDS AND PATTERNS IN 'GLOBALISATION' AND REGIONAL INTEGRATION

Globalisation became one of the clichés of the 1980s, but, as Duncan (1995) notes, there is no clear consensus on what it means. Commentators have reflected on the notion of a 'borderless world' (Ohmae, 1990) and predicted the 'end of geography' (O'Brien, 1992). This study will eschew such grand scenarios and define 'globalisation' to describe the progressive integration of national economies through spatial movements in goods and services, finance, technology and international migration. The empirical depiction of the evolution of the Asia-Pacific economies will remain crucially incomplete unless one is able to appreciate how effectively these economies have penetrated international markets, and how, particularly in recent years, they have forged closer regional linkages through trade, foreign direct investment and migration.

International trade

Over a period of twenty-five years (1965–89), the export-orientation of the Asia-Pacific region has gone up quite markedly. In the case of the NIEs, exports as a proportion of GDP have gone up from 26 per cent to 72.1 per cent; in the ASEAN-4, they have risen from 27 per cent to 35.8 per cent, while in China they have gone up from 6.8 per cent to 15 per cent (International Economic Data Bank, ANU).

Exports from the Asia-Pacific region have grown above the world norm over the same period. Export growth rates ranged from 15.5 per cent in the

NIEs to 7 per cent in ASEAN. The world average over that period was 6 per cent (International Economic Data Bank, ANU).

The remarkable ability of the Asia-Pacific economies to integrate with the world economy through international trade can be best illustrated by examining their 'world share' of exports and imports. As Kwan (1993: 11) puts it: 'The Asia-Pacific region has emerged as one of the world's top trading regions, with its share of world trade increasing from 14.6 per cent in 1980 to 22.3 per cent in 1992.' Tables 1.7, 1.8 and 1.9 provide some relevant details. The first table provides an ordinal rank of the Asia-Pacific

Table 1.7 Relative position (in terms of ordinal ranks) of the Asia-Pacific economies in the 'top forty' exporters and importers in the world, 1980 and 1990

Economy	Exporter 1980	Exporter 1990	Importer 1980	Importer 1990
NIEs				
Korea	32	13	20	14
Taiwan	23	12	23	16
Hong Kong	24	11	18	12
Singapore	26	18	17	15
ASEAN-4				
Indonesia	19	28	39	32
Malaysia	40	26	40	24
Thailand	48	31	47	22
PRC	31	15	22	18
Japan	3	3	3	3

Source: Adapted from Beamish et al., 1994, Exhibit 2–2, p. 26
Note: Ranks (1 = highest) assigned on the basis of share of each economy in world exports and imports

Table 1.8 Share of the Asia-Pacific economies in world trade (%), 1980–92

Region	Exports (% of world share)			
	1980	1985	1989	1992
Asian NIEs	4.0	6.3	8.5	9.4
ASEAN-4	2.5	2.5	2.6	3.1
PRC	1.0	1.5	1.8	2.2
USA	11.6	11.8	12.5	12.3
EU	36.5	35.9	38.9	39.8
Japan	6.9	9.8	9.4	9.3

Region	Imports (% of world share)			
	1980	1985	1989	1992
Asian NIEs	4.5	5.7	7.9	9.3
ASEAN-4	2.0	2.0	2.5	3.3
PRC	1.0	2.2	1.9	2.0
USA	13.2	19.1	15.1	14.7
EU	39.7	35.1	38.8	40.3
Japan	7.3	6.9	6.9	6.2

Source: Adapted from Kwan, 1993, table 1.1 which in turn draws on IMF Financial Statistics

Table 1.9 Share of Asia-Pacific economies in world
exports of manufactures (%), 1970–90

Region	1970	1980	1990
Asian NIEs	2.3	5.2	7.9
ASEAN-4	0.2	0.6	2.0
PRC	0.4	0.8	2.7
Japan	9.9	11.3	11.6

Source: International Economic Data Bank, Australian
National University, Canberra

economies in terms of the top forty exporters and importers for 1980 and
1990, while the second provide some comparative data on the world share
of exports and imports for different regional groups in the world economy.
Table 1.9 tracks the world share of manufactured exports of the Asia-Pacific
economies between 1970 and 1990.

As expected, most of the Asia-Pacific economies improved their relative
position – sometimes quite dramatically – among the 'top forty' trading
nations between 1980 and 1990, and this is also reflected in the more
detailed trends in world share of exports and imports of different regional
groups. As expected too, the Asia-Pacific economies show a significant
improvement in their world share of manufactured exports. All this has
occurred against a background of either stagnant or at best rather moderate
improvements in the relative shares of major regional groups in the world
economy, such as the USA and the member countries of the European
Union. This provides another effective illustration of the changing balance
of power in the global economy.

Foreign direct investment

While the openness and international orientation of specific economies can
be described and analysed in terms of their engagement in foreign trade,
another route of globalisation is provided by foreign direct investment
(FDI). Two sets of indicators are used to describe the globalisation of
Asia-Pacific economies: the share of the Asia-Pacific economies in world
FDI inflows and outflows for two points in time, 1985 and 1990.

What strikes one in Table 1.10 is the rather significant increase in Japan's
share of FDI outflows, reflecting Japan's emergence as a major investor in
the world economy in the mid-1980s. This trend is even more pronounced
when one tracks the relative size of Japanese outward FDI (that is, as a
proportion of world total) since the mid-1970s. Data provided by Ramstetter (1993) suggests that in the 1976–80 period, Japan's share of world FDI
outflows was a mere 5.4 per cent; it jumped to 11.3 per cent in the 1981–85
period and reached a peak of 22 per cent in 1990 before declining to 16.6 per
cent in 1991. Commentators generally agree (see, for example Petri, 1993a;

Kwan, 1993; Ravenhill, 1994; Urata, 1994) that this shift in Japanese investment propensities was triggered by large-scale adjustments in the major currencies of the world leading to a very significant appreciation of the yen – an event often referred to as the Plaza Accord of 1985. The result was a predictable loss of competitiveness of Japanese industries, leading to the need to seek off-shore production in low-cost sites (as one element in a range of strategies to deal with deteriorating competitiveness). The discussion at a subsequent juncture returns to this theme and asks whether one is observing the formation of a so-called 'yen bloc' in the Asia-Pacific region.

Table 1.10 also confirms that the NIEs are also playing an important role in both outward and inward flows of FDI. The NIEs' global share of FDI outflows increased from 0.7 per cent in 1985 to 3 per cent in 1990. All the relevant subgroups in Pacific Asia attracted substantial amounts of FDI in the later half of the 1980s. Inward FDI for the NIEs and ASEAN increased by as much as 5.7 times during the 1985–90 period – a particularly noteworthy achievement when one considers the sombre fact that the developing countries' share of inward FDI actually declined over this period (Urata, 1994: 270).

China too became a major recipient of inward FDI: the magnitude of such inflows doubled between 1985 and 1990. In fact, recent developments (1994) suggest intensified competition between China and other subgroups within Pacific Asia. This has led in some cases to dramatic declines in foreign commitments in ASEAN and attempts by such countries to implement policy initiatives to arrest this decline (Lim and Fong, 1994: 27).

Table 1.10 Shares of Asia-Pacific economies in world FDI inflows and outflows, 1985–90

Economy	% share of FDI inflows 1985	% share of FDI inflows 1990	% share of FDI outflows 1985	% share of FDI outflows 1990
NIEs	3.3	4.3	0.7	3.0
	(1.6 mill)	(6.9 mill)	(0.7 mill)	(6.6 mill)
ASEAN-4	2.5	4.3	0.0	0.0
	(1.2 mill)	(6.8 mill)		
PRC	3.5	2.2	1.0	0.4
	(1.7 mill)	(3.5 mill)	(0.6 mill)	(0.8 mill)
Japan	1.2	1.1	11.1	22.1
	(0.6 mill)	(1.8 mill)	(6.4 mill)	(48.0 mill)
World	100.0	100.0	100.0	100.0
	(57.4 mill)	(217.2 mill)	(48.3 mill)	(159.2 mill)

Source: Adapted from Urata, 1994, Table 21.1, p. 271, which in turn draws on IMF, International Financial Statistics, various issues

Regional integration

The issue of regional integration has recently become the subject of considerable discussion – see, for example, Garnaut and Drysdale (1994),

Bergsten and Noland (1993), Frankel and Kahler (1993). Fears have been expressed that the prospect of the world economy breaking into fractious regional blocs would be fundamentally incompatible with multilateralism and globalism. There is, however, an optimistic view that sees the spate of new regional integration arrangements (RIAs) as providing the basis for an integrated global system (e.g. Krugman, 1991; Summers, 1991; Frankel *et al.*, 1994), although some prominent economists continue to treat this view with suspicion (Bhagwati, 1994).

The position taken by this study is that RIAs are compatible with globalism provided there is adherence to the central principle of 'open regionalism', the latter defined to encompass 'integrative processes that contain no element of exclusion or discrimination against outsiders' (Garnaut and Drysdale, 1994: 2).

The conventional wisdom appears to be that one is witnessing the emergence of an integrated Pacific Asia, but that it is different from other regional blocs, such as the European Union, in the sense that the process of regional integration is 'market-driven' – an issue that is re-visited at a subsequent juncture. Has regional integration really deepened in the Asia-Pacific region in recent years?

Kwan (1993) appears to be one of the most ardent advocates of an integrated Pacific Asia, although others have made similar observations (e.g. Yamazawa, 1994; Yamazawa and Lo, 1993; ADB, 1994; Goto and Hamada, 1994). The available data seem to suggest that:

- The Asia-Pacific region reduced its dependence on the US market in the later part of the 1980s.
- The share of intra-regional trade rose significantly after 1985.

A widely accepted way of describing trends in intra-regional trade is to construct so-called 'intensity of trade' indices, that is, a group's share of intra-regional trade is divided by that region's share of worldwide trade. Thus, if the ratio increases over time, one could argue that there is increasing 'regional bias' in international trade. The trends in trade intensity indices are reported separately for imports and exports. Certainly, the integration of the Asian NIEs with other Asian economies seems to have increased between 1970 and 1992, but it is through the route of 'non-Japan' Asia that it has occurred rather than Japan. Thus, for example, the trade intensity of imports has fallen from 2.36 in 1970 to 1.47 in 1992 in the case of Japan, as against an increase in the value of the index from 1.27 to 1.74 for 'non-Japan' Asia. Trade intensity indices for exports tell a similar story. It also needs to be emphasised that, despite evidence of regional integration, North America remains a major trading partner for East Asia (see Table 1.11).

Engaging in international trade, of course, provides a principal mechanism for intra-regional linkages. Other routes include FDI and labour migration. The former has been studied much more extensively than the latter.

Table 1.11 Trends in regional integration as measured by trade intensity
indices: 1970–92

From		N. America	Europe	Asia (except Japan)	Japan
			Import (Ratios: regional share as a proportion of world share)		
Japan	1970	1.11	0.34	0.45	
	1980	0.48	0.16	0.51	
	1985	0.69	0.25	1.31	
	1992	1.21	0.75	1.41	
Asian NIEs	1970	1.46	1.26	1.27	2.36
	1980	0.94	0.59	0.82	1.19
	1985	1.02	0.75	1.17	1.30
	1992	1.07	0.71	1.74	1.47
ASEAN	1970	1.85	2.19	1.00	2.70
	1980	0.88	0.79	0.88	1.19
	1985	1.15	1.15	1.47	1.54
	1992	0.85	0.79	1.46	1.49
From		N. America	Europe	Asia (except Japan)	Japan
			Exports (Ratios: regional share as a proportion of world share)		
Japan	1970	1.49	0.67	0.45	
	1980	0.95	0.61	0.51	
	1985	2.27	0.82	1.31	
	1992	2.36	1.64	1.41	
Asian NIEs	1970	2.27	1.25	0.69	0.81
	1980	1.61	1.14	0.91	0.60
	1985	3.13	1.02	1.38	0.78
	1992	1.62	0.84	1.46	0.57
ASEAN	1970	2.34	1.98	2.55	3.13
	1980	1.85	1.40	1.89	3.34
	1985	1.95	1.29	2.37	2.04
	1992	3.52	2.27	4.44	3.36

Source: Calculated from data in Cohen and Guerrieri, 1994, table 3

Consider the role that FDI has played in forging greater linkages among
Asia-Pacific economies. A popular perception is that the spurt of Japanese
FDI in the mid-1980s has been associated with a greater regionalisation of
such outflows. Frankel (1993: 237) warns against such a perception, declar-
ing with cogent logic: 'If one scales the FDI figures by the host region's role
in world trade, one finds that Japan's investment in Asia ... is almost exactly
in proportion to their size. There is no regional bias.'

If one uses the 1987–90 period as a reference point (Urata, 1994: table
21.3, p. 277), a cursory examination of the regional distribution of FDI
inflows among the Asia-Pacific economies in fact suggests that:

• The share of Japanese FDI fell in all the ASEAN economies (except the
Philippines) and China.

- The shares of NIEs' FDI in ASEAN (once again the Philippines is an exception) and China were, by 1990, higher than the share of Japanese FDI – in some cases by large margins.

It thus appears that, while Japan is an important source of FDI for industrialising Asia-Pacific economies, more recent developments suggest that the NIEs are probably playing an even greater role in moulding the process of greater regional integration through FDI.

As noted, labour migration as a means of integrating regional economies has received relatively less attention compared to FDI and trade flows. There is, however, an emerging view that globalisation is being accompanied by a 'global labour market' (World Bank, 1995a). One can also make the claim of an emerging 'Asia-Pacific labour market'. Intra-regional labour migration in Pacific Asia appears to have reached significant levels, inspiring some observers (OECD, 1992; Salt, 1992) to refer to this phenomenon as the world's 'newest international migration system'. Goto and Hamada (1994: 381) also emphasise 'the high degree of labour mobility among East Asian nations'. The patchy information and disparate literature pertaining to this phenomenon has been carefully synthesised in a comprehensive survey by Athukorala (1993: 50). As he notes:

In the last four decades new and complex patterns of international migration have been emerging, often with startling rapidity, in the Asian-Pacific region...There are at least one million migrant workers in the four Asian NIEs, Japan and Malaysia. As the region becomes more economically integrated through the flow of capital and technology, pressure will grow in both the sending and receiving country for large international flows of labour.

One can, based on current trends and patterns, classify the Asia-Pacific economies into the following groups: 'pure' labour-importing countries (Japan, Hong Kong, Singapore and Taiwan); countries that both import and export labour (Thailand, Malaysia, South Korea), and three 'pure' labour exporters (Indonesia, the Philippines and the PRC). Hong Kong has long been a major recipient of immigrants from mainland China. The flow of migrant labour rose to 500,000 during the 1970s (Abella, 1991: 5).

The macroeconomic linkages forged by labour migration in the Asia-Pacific region – and the implications that follow from such linkages – are as yet not fully documented, but some general observations may be made. From the perspective of the labour-importing countries, the demand for migrant labour is likely to continue unabated as sustained industrialisation creates labour shortages, particularly in the non-tradable sectors (such as services and construction), and among small and medium-sized producers in the tradable sector who are constrained in their ability to engage in off-shore production as a means of coping with declining competitiveness induced by domestic labour shortages.

From the perspective of labour-exporting countries, the need to supply migrant labour will continue as long actual and perceived differentials in living standards persist in the Asia-Pacific region. Furthermore, remittances from labour migration loom large in the total flows of external resources in the case of some economies, such as the Philippines where remittances accounted for 12 per cent of total exports in the early 1990s (Athukorala, 1993: 48). This, in itself, serves as a powerful incentive to maintain the export of labour. Thus, the realities embodied in the demand for, and supply of, migrant labour mean that such forces will continue to mould regional linkages among Asia-Pacific economies, despite restrictive immigration polices and despite understandable social and political concerns pertaining to spatial labour movements in both receiving and sending countries.

UNDERSTANDING THE EMERGENCE OF AN INTEGRATED ASIA-PACIFIC ECONOMY: HISTORY, ECONOMIC DETERMINANTS AND IMPLICATIONS

The discussion in the previous section suggests that the progressive emergence of the Asia-Pacific region as a new centre of economic power in the global scene is being accompanied by closer regional interdependence. This trend towards regionalisation – which apparently seems more pronounced in the later part of the 1980s – is part of a general pattern of regionalisation of the world economy. One needs to understand the historical context of this process, the extent to which it is 'market-driven', and the implications that follow from such analyses.

The historical context

The phenomenon of Asia-Pacific regional interdependence needs to be set in an appropriate historical context. Dixon and Drakakis-Smith (1993: 4), as well as Dixon (1993), trace the integration of Pacific Asia into the world economy to the spread of mercantile capital into the region in the early sixteenth century. Petrie (1993a, 1993b: 121) interprets the emergence of an 'East Asian bloc' in the world economy as the 'product of historical accidents'. These 'historical accidents' pertain to: (a) the 'treaty port system' under Western imperialism; (b) the role that Japan played in East Asia during its imperialist period; (c) the importance of the United States in post-war Pacific relations.

Factors (a) and (b) led to the developing Asia-Pacific economies (referred to as 'East Asia' by Petri) to become one of the most interdependent geographical zones in the world prior to the Second World War. The high degree of regionalisation was subsequently diluted by US hegemonic influence. This trend towards diversification was in turn compounded by the spectacular growth of the East Asian economies in the 1960s and 1970s that appeared to depend significantly on access to US (and, in general, OECD) markets. Since 1985, one is probably witnessing a re-emergence of greater regionalisation that is primarily 'market-driven'.

Petrie (1993a: 110) argues that the middle of the nineteenth century coincided with the emergence of 'co-operative' imperialism that entailed the European powers (Britain, Russia, Prussia, Portugal, Denmark, the Netherlands, Spain, Belgium, Italy) and the USA signing treaties guaranteeing access to Chinese and other ports. A surge of trade ensued, leading to competition for new ports. This provided the basis of the so-called 'treaty port system' which saw a vast amount of regional trade being mediated through the great ports of Hong Kong, Manila, Shanghai and Singapore. Data for the early part of the twentieth century suggest that the engagement of the Asia-Pacific economies in international trade took on a distinct regional dimension. Thus, the share of intra-regional trade rose from 42 per cent in 1913 to 59 per cent in 1938 – figures that are comparable to ones that prevail today (Petrie, 1993a: table 10.1).

The role that Japan played during its imperial phase in creating an integrated regional economy, particularly in terms of linkages between Taiwan, Korea and China, is well documented (Petrie, 1993a; Ho, 1984; Cumings, 1987). The primary mechanisms for forging such regionalism entailed large-scale investments in transport and communication, basic education and manufacturing with the central purpose of developing complementarities of the colonies with the Japanese economy. As the Second World War approached, Japan sought to expand its hegemonic influence on the region through the so-called Greater East Asia Co-Prosperity Sphere (GEACS) and developed strategies to incorporate South East Asia as part of the East Asian regional bloc. The central outcome was a surge in Japan's regional trade which rose to 73 per cent of its total trade by 1940 (Petrie, 1993a: 116).

The outbreak of the Second World War and its aftermath led to large-scale, long-term, changes in the nature of trade and investment flows in the Asia-Pacific region. Although the regional pattern of international trade persisted until the mid-1950s, the defeat of Japan in the Second World War and the emergence of the USA as the pre-eminent economic and political power had wide-ranging repercussions. Haggard (1988: 265) offers a clear expression of this view:

> International political conditions...have had an important bearing on East Asia's economic development. Japan's defeat in the Second World War made the United States the pre-eminent political power in the region. The outbreak of conflict in the Korean peninsula extended the Cold War to Asia, altering the United States' strategic perception of the region... The growth of the regional economy in the Pacific Basin cannot be understood without reference to this underlying strategic context.

The immediate outcome of this 'strategic context' was a massive influx of US aid to Korea and Taiwan, countries that were part of the 'core' of GEACS prior to the war. The liberalisation of the world economy that followed in the 1960s was partly driven by changes in transport and communications technology, but also bore the significant political imprint of US leadership through a multilateral agenda of economic openness. These global developments in turn moulded the regional nature of Asia-Pacific trade and investment flows and re-oriented them towards the US.

The historical context of the evolution of the Asia-Pacific region in the world economy is particularly useful because it highlights two fundamental points. First, it make clear the fact that the perceived regionalisation of Pacific Asia in the later part of the 1980s is by no means a novel phenomenon. Second, it allows one to appreciate the underlying apprehension about Japan's current and prospective role in the regional economy.

While the history of Asia-Pacific regionalism is certainly informative, how well does it allow one to understand the dynamism of individual economies? Here, the answer is much less certain. One could argue that regional trade patterns, if they occur 'naturally' (in the sense of creating trade linkages through exploitation of country-specific comparative advantage and complementarities), are compatible with national economic dynamism. The point is that regional trade patterns in the pre-war period bore the substantial imprint of colonial compulsion rather than carefully articulated domestic policy choices. Ho (1984: 368–9) has made the telling observation that industries that were built during Japanese colonialism were not built on the principle of comparative advantage but to serve specific Japanese needs.

One could argue that the two city-states had a head start relative to other developing economies because of their historically entrenched advantage in enterpreneurship and commercial enterprise arising from their entrepôt past. But Manila and Shanghai were also part of the 'great ports' under the treaty port system. The Philippines had never seemed – at least until now – to consolidate on the head start that such historical circumstances provided. Rapid and sustained growth in China never seemed to spring naturally from its initial conditions, but had to await the market-oriented reforms of the 1970s.

Much has been said about the role that US aid has played in the rapid development of East Asia. Admittedly, such aid, driven by strategic considerations, has played a fundamental role in stabilising the regional economy in the wake of post-war dislocation, but it is easy to exaggerate its long-term impact, as Little (1981) and Reidel (1988) have emphasised.

In sum, while it is important to trace the historical roots of modern economic growth in Asia, such analyses must also be dynamic and forward-looking, attempting to explain how favourable historical circumstances and geographical proximity can be exploited into a phase of sustained economic dynamism.

Analysing the process of market-driven integration: economic determinants

It is commonplace to assert that the process of integration in the Asia-Pacific region is 'market-driven', that is, it has emerged in the absence of a formal framework of regional cooperation. In this respect, it differs markedly from the pre-war pattern of regionalisation which was, at least in part, driven by colonial compulsion.

Commentators seem to agree that, starting in the 1960s and proceeding until the mid-1980s, trade and investment flows in the region were oriented towards the US. The period 1985–86 appears to be a watershed in the evolution of the Asia-Pacific region in the world economy. As noted, the Plaza Accord of 1985 led to massive exchange rate adjustments. The yen was appreciated by 50 per cent, thus allowing the US dollar to adjust downward from its unusually high real value. Petrie (1993a: 119) explains the immediate impact of the exchange rate adjustments rather well:

> Initially, the appreciation of the yen was not matched by other East Asian currencies; thus, other countries became more competitive against Japan in both US and Japanese markets...East Asian [exports] surged in both markets. These export surges also led to accelerating imports from Japan and Singapore. As a result East Asian interdependence intensified; intra-regional trade expanded.

As noted at a previous juncture, the aftermath of the Plaza Accord was also a sharp increase in regional investment flows reinforcing intra-regional linkages. While Japan has played an important role in such flows, the East Asian NIEs have also emerged as major investors in the region. The latter phenomenon was partly driven by their inevitable loss of competitiveness in labour-intensive industries and partly triggered by their appreciation of the exchange rate as a lagged response to the Plaza Accord of 1985.

Several issues and implications need to be addressed regarding such developments. Is one witnessing a long-term shift away from the dependence of the Asia-Pacific economies on the US and a move towards a Japan-led bloc, the so-called 'yen bloc'? What are the tangible and intangible variables that make up the process of market-driven integration in Pacific Asia? How important are such variables? How should one interpret recent policy initiatives in formalising regional interdependence among Asia-Pacific economies?

As noted, Kwan (1993), based on his analysis and evidence, confidently claims that a durable 'yen bloc' is in the process of being formed. Others are not so sure. Frankel (1993) and Frankel et al. (1994) have employed a 'gravity model' to explore this issue in addition to the various determinants of Asia-Pacific regionalism. This statistical technique has also been employed by others (Blomqvist, 1994; Amelung, 1994), though in the latter cases, the gravity model has not been specifically directed to test the role of Japan in East and South East Asia.

The basic premise of a gravity model is that (Frankel *et al.*, 1994: 8): 'trade between two countries is proportionate to the product of their GNPs and inversely related to the distance between them, by analogy to the formula for gravitational attraction between two masses'. Why should bilateral trade flows be related to the GNPs of the participating countries and the distance between them? The central argument is that trade expands to exploit expansions in market size (the latter proxied by GNP), but is deterred by freight and transport costs that are embodied in distance. These, then, are the 'natural' determinants of bilateral trade. If intra-regional trade expands primarily due to these factors rather than through explicit preferential arrangements struck by inter-governmental structures, one could argue that this supports the hypothesis of 'market-driven' integration.

It is possible to expand the notion of 'market-driven' integration beyond the basic variables of country-specific GNPs and geographical proximity. The literature has made a number of extensions. First, one could argue that trade between nations is driven by the need to minimise transactions costs (TC). The contribution by Amelung (1994) is part of the TC-theoretic tradition. The transactions of goods and services across different countries and legal systems entail costs that extend beyond transport costs and frictions associated with legal trade barriers. Prime examples include: costs of contract-making, costs of monitoring contracts, costs of information collection on foreign markets and so forth. Even in the absence of trade barriers and transport costs, high TC may act as natural barriers to trade, so that firms participating in international markets need to circumvent such barriers by minimising TC.

While theoretically identifiable, it is not easy to construct empirical analogues of TC. Amelung (1994) suggests a number of proxies: cultural homogeneity, historical trade links, 'sovereign risk', and exchange rate fluctuations. The last two are intended to measure the degree of uncertainty prevailing in international transactions, with low 'sovereign risk' and low exchange rate fluctuations suggesting greater predictability. Caves (1971) and others have made the point that information costs tend to be higher among trading partners with vastly different cultural backgrounds. Amelung (1994: 65) has also argued, based on some empirical studies, that:

> exporters may be...inclined to intensify existing trading relations in countries in which they have already been exporting rather than enter new markets. The resulting inertia element in international trade can be proxied by using historical trade relations as an explanatory variable.

Amelung (1994) classifies distance and the presence (or lack of) a common border as variables that represent the effect of transport costs on international trade. Petrie (1993a: 108), however, argues that 'the importance of distance is most likely not to distance itself, but to factors correlated with distance'. In other words, distance is probably a proxy for TC and captures such effects as cultural similarity and historical trade links.

The TC-theoretic approach provides a basis for understanding the dynamics of regional integration. Consider, for example, the case of a relatively loosely connected group of economies that become more intertwined as a result of an economic or non-economic shock (as in the case of the 1985 exchange rate re-alignments reported above). The intensified bilateral relations that ensue create the incentive to invest in furthering such links. Bilateral TC fall as a result of such investments and intra-regional trade and investment expands even more.

Amelung (1994) and Blomqvist (1994) have extended the basic gravity model to take account of the fact that trade is also driven by standard 'neo-classical' factors. In other words, two countries trade with each other because of differences in relative factor endowments. Balassa (1977) has extended this framework into a dynamic context. As trade proceeds between a poor, labour-surplus country and a rich, capital-abundant country, it leads over time to a point where the former loses its comparative advantage in labour-intensive activities due to rising wages and living standards. Thus, one observes an intertemporal shift in the product composition of exports (as measured in terms of factor intensities) for a typical developing economy.

An off-shoot of this framework is the 'flying-geese' pattern of economic integration in the Asia-Pacific region, a concept first developed by Akamatsu (1960). The flying-geese model conceptualises Japan as the 'leader' followed by the NIEs which are in turn being followed by the next-tier NIEs in ASEAN. Underlying this flying-geese pattern is the notion of intertemporal shifts in comparative advantage among economies in the region. It also clearly advocates the idea that Japan is being emulated as a model by other East Asian economies. Although the analysis of 'neo-classical' factors by Blomqvist (1994) is clearly driven by such considerations, these ideas have also been explored by others using different statistical and analytical techniques – see, for example, Kwan (1993) and Chow and Kellman (1993). Thus, these contributions can be seen as a complement to the basic gravity model.

The gravity model estimated for the Asia-Pacific economies also incorporates the effect of trade policy in influencing intra-regional trade. Both Amelung (1994) and Blomqvist (1994) rely on a 1987 World Bank study to classify economies in their sample into two basic groups based on their trade regime: strongly/moderately outward-oriented, strongly/moderately inward-oriented. The key proposition is that an outward-oriented trade regime reinforces the 'natural' determinants of bilateral trade. The role that public policy in general plays in influencing the dual phenomena of Asia-Pacific dynamism and regionalism is discussed at greater length at a subsequent juncture.

In sum, intra-regional trade can be explained by such variables as country-specific GNPs, distance, common borders, other TC variables, relative factor endowments and trade policy. To this list, one can add 'dummy' variables to represent the impact of preferential trading arrangements, or more generally to represent cases where two countries in a given pair belong to the same regional grouping. 'The goal', as Frankel *et al.* (1994: 8–9) put it, 'is to see how much of the high level of trade within [a] region can be explained by simple economic factors...and how much is left over to be attributed to a special regional effect'. Thus, the gravity model can be amended to simultaneously test the validity of the market-driven hypothesis of integration and the role that regional grouping plays in such integration. This means that, in its amended version, the gravity model allows one to test the 'yen-bloc' hypothesis.

One can summarise the (statistical) significance of a range of explanatory variables that have influenced the evolution of Asia-Pacific regionalism based on the sample of studies that has been reviewed above in the following way. Clearly, country-specific GNPs, distance, common border and other TC variables are important in explaining the process of regional integration in Pacific Asia. The results also suggest that an outward-oriented trade policy reinforces the 'natural' determinants of bilateral trade.

The role that relative factor endowments or comparative-based advantage variables play is somewhat mixed. Blomqvist (1994) maintains that relative factor endowments play a role in regional integration only in a specific sense: differences in human capital endowments (measured by country-specific differences in education levels) are statistically significant as an explanatory variable, but other measures of relative factor endowment are not.

While some gravity-model-based estimates do not seem to ascribe central significance to comparative-advantage-based variables, other studies utilising alternative statistical techniques tend to do so. Chow and Kellman (1993), for example, rely heavily on the 'revealed comparative advantage' (RCA) method and 'export similarity index' (ESI) to test the relevance of the flying-geese hypothesis. The RCA method, developed by Balassa (1977), focuses on a particular ratio: the market share of product A of country X to any importing country, adjusted by the market share of country X of all imports in the importing country. RCA will be greater than 1 in cases where country X has a comparative advantage; otherwise, it will be less than 1. The ESI tries to track the changing composition of exports of country X by relating it to the past composition of exports of country Y. This application can be done in a context where X is the 'follower' (e.g. Korea) and Y is the 'leader' (e.g. Japan).

Chow and Kellman (1993) arrive at the following conclusions. First, the NIEs have exhibited a tendency to emulate Japan, while the ASEAN economies have tended to emulate the NIEs. This process is, however, complementary rather than competitive. Second, the East Asian NIEs have gradually (over 1965–90) shifted their RCAs from traditional labour-intensive products to more high-tech products, although one conspicuous exception persists: the NIEs still continue to dominate the world market for the labour-intensive products of footwear and clothing. Third, while the ASEAN-4 are trying to emulate the NIEs, only Malaysia and Thailand appear to have the immediate potential of becoming next-tier NIEs. Even then, the path of 'catch-up' is likely to be a rather long one. MacIntyre (1994a) has noted, that, if current growth rates are maintained, it will take Thailand well over twenty years to reach Korean living standards (as proxied by GNP per capita at 1989 prices).

If a flying-geese pattern does indeed prevail as part of Asia-Pacific dynamism, does this create an incentive for Japan to try and cultivate a conscious regional bias in its trade, aid and investment flows? The answer appears to be 'no'. As Frankel (1993: 245) put it: 'there is no evidence of a special Japan effect within Asia'. Frankel (1993: 246) does concede that there is some evidence of Japanese influence in East Asian financial markets and a growing role for the yen in invoicing of trade and finance in the region. Even such evidence does not allow one to conclude that 'Japan is undertaking deliberate policy measures to increase its monetary and financial role.... Gradually increasing role of the yen is primarily the outcome of private decisions by importers, exporters, borrowers and lenders.'

While there may not, as yet, be any discernible 'yen-bloc' effect, it does appear to be the case that if East Asia is treated as a regional or trade bloc, then the dummy variable representing that regional configuration is statistically significant. On the other hand, ASEAN is not. Interestingly, the currently popular APEC – Asia-Pacific Economic Cooperation – appears to have a special regional effect on bilateral trade flows.

APEC AND BEYOND: CONCLUDING COMMENTS

What do these results imply about the recent flurry of policy initiatives to enhance regional co-operation in the Asia-Pacific region? To start with, if members of ASEAN try to create a degree of regionalisation à la EU, it is likely to be self-defeating and welfare-reducing. The leaders of ASEAN have committed themselves to the setting up of AFTA (an ASEAN Free Trade Area), but, to be effective, it needs to be consistent with the principle of 'open regionalism' and the process of market-driven integration. It seems that APEC – consisting of North America, East Asia, South East Asia, Australia, New Zealand – is regarded by some observers as perhaps the most promising forum for inter-governmental co-operation in Pacific Asia (Soesastro, 1994). Started under Australian intiative, it appeared in late 1993 to receive the political support of the US for its guiding principle of 'open regionalism' at the meeting of APEC leaders in Seattle. But since then uncertainties have emerged.

The problem probably lies in the different conceptions of 'open region-alism' among members of APEC, principally US and others. As one recent review of these issues put it: 'Cornered by commitments...to "open re-gionalism", the Americans say that the arrangements will be open to any economy that will make reciprocal commitments (Australian National University, 1994: 22).' Such an interpretation of 'open regionalism' militates against its original conception and is not shared by other members of APEC. The point is that the centre of gravity of the world economy has shifted from the mid-North Atlantic to mid-Pacific and powerful domestic interests in the US seems to blame others for not playing the free-trade game. If APEC has to emerge as a key forum for 'open regionalism', mechanisms must somehow be found to ensure that the US participates in it fully by moving away from its emphasis on reciprocity.

Beyond APEC and other inter-governmental initiatives, Asia-Pacific regionalism is also being characterised by attempts to develop informal and sub-regional 'growth triangles' – see, for example, Yue and Yuan (1994) and Rodan (1994). Yamazawa (1994: 207) has noted a number of such zones that seem to have cropped up: the 'Growth Triangle', centred on Singapore and incorporating Johor State in Malaysia and Batam Island in Indonesia; the 'Baht Zone' in the border area of Thailand, Laos, Cambodia and Vietnam; the 'Greater South China Zone', centred on Hong Kong and including China's Guandong and Fujian provinces and Taiwan; the 'Yellow Sea Economic Zone' which includes the coastal areas facing the Yellow Sea of north and north-east China, North and South Korea, and Japan; and, finally, the Japan Sea Economic Zone, which includes the coastal areas of north-east China, Far East Russia, South and North Korea, and Japan.

It remains to be seen how these informal sub-regions will evolve over time. If such regions are the product of market-driven interactions, then their official designations represent no more than an ex post recognition of an evolving economic fact. If, on the other hand, deliberate policy efforts are taken to generate closer integration within those sub-regions, then the outcome is uncertain. Ultimately, as Krugman (1991) suggests, the number of 'natural' or efficient regional groupings (in the sense of enhanced net trade creation) in the world economy may actually be quite small, suggest-ing that the proliferation of regional zones may well be welfare-reducing. One must not lose sight of the fact that the dynamism of regional inter-dependence among Asia-Pacific economies is largely, though not solely, the result of market forces. Future policy initiatives should, therefore, be con-structed to help, rather than hinder, such market-led interdependence.

Chapter 2

Public policy and political economy

INTRODUCTION: PRELUDE TO EAST ASIAN POLITICAL ECONOMY

The spectacular growth record of the Asia-Pacific economies has spawned a large literature that is endeavouring to explain such dynamism. To some extent, there is an inevitable 'catch-up' effect. There is a well-documented tendency for poor nations to grow faster than richer nations and converge toward the per capita income levels of the latter. Heliwell (1994) offers a lucid survey of the 'convergence' literature and notes that convergence is not inevitable. Indeed, for the economies of South Asia, it does not seem to hold even in the 'conditional' sense (that is, on the strict assumption that such economies are on their 'steady-state' growth path). This implies that one must seek to identify variables that have played a central role in Asia-Pacific dynamism.

One view is to debunk attempts at complex explanations and to argue that the mechanics of development in the region is rather simple: rapid growth in these economies was the product of rapid capital accumulation (e.g. Krugman, 1994). The general view, however, is that policy variables have made an important contribution to the evolution of Pacific Asia in the global economy. The early literature on the Asia-Pacific economies appeared to emphasise this point primarily in the form of trade policy. It became commonplace to assert that outward-oriented policies were central to national economic success (Little, 1981, 1982; Balassa, 1981; Krueger, 1980; Lal and Rajapatirana, 1987). Because such a view was primarily articulated by neo-classical economists, the story of Asia-Pacific dynamism became part of the neo-classical resurgence in development economics.

The neo-classical school that placed primacy on trade policy built its case primarily on the experience of the East Asian NIEs who experienced the 'take-off' to sustained economic growth around the mid-1960s on the basis of 'export-oriented industrialisation'. It would be fair to say that the conviction and certainty that was reflected in this literature is now vulnerable to a 'revisionist' revolution. This is due to at least two factors: (a) recent

strands in the literature that express uncertainty about the causal relationship between the trade regime and economic growth (e.g. Findlay, 1995;
Bardhan, 1995); (b) the literature on statist political economy (Haggard,
1990, 1994; Wade, 1990; Amsden, 1989; Johnson, 1987).

It is now recognised that traditional trade theory, with its emphasis on
static allocative efficiency analyses, could not really serve as the basis for a
dynamic theory of growth. So-called 'new' growth theories have, however,
formalised the way trade policy influences economic growth through such
mechanisms as research and development, learning by doing and technological diffusion. This implies that trade influences economic growth through
the route of productivity growth. Unfortunately, 'the evidence of the link
between trade and productivity growth remains both sparse and mixed'
(Quibria, 1995: 15). In fact, Findlay (1995: 245) has drawn attention to
recent growth accounting exercises by Young (1992) which show that there
was hardly any technical progress in the NIEs, the much-cited exemplars of
export-oriented growth. More than 80 per cent of the growth can be
explained by physical capital accumulation alone and that the 'technology
gap' between the US and the NIEs has apparently widened.

The literature on statist political economy drew attention to the various
kinds of interventionist policies that existed in East Asia that appeared to be
at odds with the stylised fact of outward-oriented policies. It would be more
appropriate to regard the policy framework in NIEs such as South Korea
and Taiwan, as displaying elements of dualistic trade policy that protected
domestic producers while simultaneously allowing access to essential inputs
at world prices. More generally, this literature drew attention to the central
role that the state played in the economic transformation of the NIEs.

It is now widely recognised that the focus on trade policy, although
important, is probably too narrow. The relevant variable is public policy
in general and the way it is shaped in a particular political context – see, for
example, Chowdhury and Islam (1993), Islam (1992, 1996). In other words,
an understanding of the political economy of public policy is crucial in
appreciating the globalisation and dynamism of individual economies.

The World Bank – often regarded as the bastion of neo-classical economics – has sought (1993a) to develop a 'functional approach' to the study
of the 'East Asian miracle' which synthesises the early neo-classical literature with the more recent strand of political economy. This functional
approach has a number of elements:

- 'policy fundamentals' that led to rapid capital accumulation, aggressive
  investments in human capital, and improvements in factor productivity
  that inevitably fed into rapid growth within a framework of sound
  macroeconomic management;
- 'selective intervention' (such as targeted export incentives, selective credit
  allocation) that were generally carefully monitored and incentive-
  compatible;

- the institutional framework that supported the implementation of policy fundamentals and selective intervention.

Lim (1996) expresses a similar idea when he argues how one could develop explanations of Asian economic success that operate at different levels of complexity. The first is a 'production function' approach that is primarily an accounting framework for identifying the various inputs – investments in physical and human capital, factor productivity – that feed into the growth process. One could then extend this 'production function' approach into a 'back-tracking', recursive method that tries to disentangle the more complex variables that underpin the proximate sources of economic growth. This inevitably leads one into an exploration of the complex interplay between policy and politics.

THE INSTITUTIONAL FRAMEWORK OF INTERNATIONALLY ORIENTED ECONOMIC GROWTH: THE CASE OF THE EAST ASIAN NIEs

What kind of political structure or institutional framework facilitates the globalisation of individual economies and the corresponding outcome of rapid growth? This question can be best understood by tracing it to first principles. Parkin (1993: 13) makes the point that 'there are two ... obstacles to prosperity: rent-seeking and policy uncertainty and variability'. The latter – which primarily affect monetary and fiscal policy – in turn are the product of 'a political process'. Parkin has characterised a problem that is often called 'government failure' in the development literature (e.g. Krueger, 1980).

Islam (1992) has suggested a broader conceptualisation of the 'obstacles to prosperity'. Any economy is always subject to the twin pressures of government failure and market failure. Market failure – a state of affairs where privately optimal decisions based on utility-maximising behaviour of individual economic agents diverges from social optimality – has several sources: monopoly imperfections, externalities, public goods, imperfect information and transactions costs. In addition, it is often claimed that the market system does not typically produce a 'fair' distribution of income.

The rectification of market failure and the need to attain an equitable distribution of income represent the primary intellectual case for government intervention; such intervention can paradoxically sow the seeds of government failure. The latter has several sources. First, a public-interest-driven policy agenda can, as suggested at a previous juncture, be subverted by the rent-seeking propensities of the private sector. Second, the predatory behaviour of state officials can lead to a degree of state intervention that is in excess of the socially optimal level. Third, vote-maximising politicians in majoritarian democracies can generate inefficient 'political' business cycles (the notion of policy variability and uncertainty noted above). Another plausible source of government failure is represented by administrative incompetence. One could argue that even if a polity is well endowed with bureaucrats motivated by the need to serve the public interest, lack of sufficient training can lead to a limited capacity to interpret and enforce rules. It is necessary to emphasise that administrative incompetence represents a transient source of government failure on the ground that such incompetence can be alleviated by the provision of appropriate training programmes.

The importance of highlighting the twin problems of government and market failure is that it suggests that any government seeking to promote prosperity through the route of globalisation must be able to mitigate both problems. Scholars specialising on East Asian NIEs have consistently argued that the institutional framework of such economies managed to mitigate market failure without the corresponding burden of government failure. More specifically, East-Asian-style governance has embodied the following distinctive features:

1 An elite bureaucracy (such as the Economic Planning Board in South Korea) staffed by the best managerial talent in the system.
2 A political system that has allowed what the World Bank (1993a: chapter 4) has called 'technocratic insulation'. In other words, key bureaucratic agencies have been given sufficient scope to take policy initiatives.
3 Relatively close government–big-business interactions.

These features protected East Asian policy-makers from the ravages of rent-seeking groups, while at the same time they limited the predatory behaviour of state officials through the inculcation of a coherent development vision. Thus, as a political system it represented a relatively rare species. Some authors, such as Deyo (1989), have highlighted its authoritarian features and focused on its 'exclusionary' politics in the sense that it excluded– or at least significantly constrained – access to the political process by such groups as labour unions.

The model of governance sketched here has been influential in bringing about a re-interpretation of the economic success of the East Asian NIEs. There are, however, some analytical limitations of this model that need to be highlighted.

First, the policy outcomes of the East Asian political system are not independent of the trade regime. Statist writers have to accept the standard neoclassical refrain that the discipline of international competition has limited the incidence of government failure in East Asia (Islam, 1992, 1996; Chowdhury and Islam, 1993: chapter 3). In other words, East Asian political systems do not represent a truly exogenous variable in explaining the economic success of East Asia.

Second, in the presence of human fallibility, societal performance in an authoritarian political system becomes unusually sensitive to the particular abilities of benevolent dictators rather than to the resilience of broad-based political institutions (Sah, 1991).

Third, in highlighting the fact that East Asian political systems represent a rare species, the relevant literature conveys the profoundly pessimistic message that national success stories are not really replaceable and sustainable. As Romer (1993: 88) puts it: 'strong, authoritarian government...require a configuration of bureaucratic competence and ruthless dedication to national economic success that is relatively rare and may be impossible to sustain'.

The East Asian model also conveys the distressing implication that international competitiveness may well be incompatible with democratic institutions. One has to accept that East Asian political systems have, until the recent movements towards democratisation, been authoritarian. In trying to attain 'technocratic insulation', attenuation of human rights and the political exclusion of the labour movement have been quite conspicuous. Admittedly, rapid growth in such economies provided durable political legitimacy even in the absence of democratic institutions (World Bank, 1993a: chapter 4; Garnaut, 1989: 44). Unfortunately, such justifications of the authoritarian features of East-Asian-style governance have inhibited the exploration of alternative institutional configurations for mitigating the twin problems of market and government failure. The implications of this point are spelt out in fuller detail at a subsequent juncture.

THE INSTITUTIONAL FRAMEWORK OF INTERNATIONALLY ORIENTED ECONOMIC GROWTH: SOUTH EAST ASIAN COMPARISONS

How relevant is the institutional framework derived from the experience of the East Asian NIEs in explaining the recent economic transformations taking place in the ASEAN-4? The World Bank (1993a, chapter 4) tries to argue, not really convincingly, that this framework is applicable to both the East Asian NIEs and ASEAN-4. Scholars specialising in South East Asian political economy have maintained, for quite some time, that the relatively straightforward relationship that appears to exist between political structures and rapid, internationally oriented economic growth in the case of the NIEs, cannot be extrapolated to interpret the experiences of South East Asian economic development. As Mackie (1988: 291) notes: the 'differences...turn out to be more significant than the similarities'. What are these differences?

To start with, scholars of South East Asian political economy readily agree that the economies of ASEAN-4 lack the bureaucratic competence and 'technocratic insulation' of their NIE counterparts. MacIntyre (1994b: 7) has emphasised the 'pervasive importance of patrimonial and clientalistic links between government figures and business people'. Such clientalistic links have been particularly influenced by the fact that the local business community is dominated by people of Chinese descent. The implication of this 'ethnic factor' is stressed by MacIntyre (1994b: 8):

> In the period since the Second World War there have been many instances of popular and ocial harassment of Chinese minorities in these countries... Vulnerability to periodically violent and destructive outbursts of indigenous resentment has traditionally led Chinese business people to avoid high profile collective political action and to rely instead upon a more covert form of political representation – clientalism. In return for protection and policy favours, Chinese business people would provide cash, stocks, company directorships to powerful members of the indigenous political elite.

The economies of ASEAN-4 are also well endowed in terms of natural resources relative to the NIEs. It has been argued that resource-rich economies have a tendency to rely on export income from primary commodities to finance inefficient domestic manufacturing industries (Ranis, 1981) – an argument that may help explain why the move towards trade liberalisation occurred at a later stage in South East Asia compared with the NIEs.

One would expect that a combination of limited bureaucratic competence, inadequate 'technocratic insulation', political clientalism and dependence on primary commodities would limit the growth potential of South East Asia. Yet, with the exception of the Philippines, this is manifestly not the case. How does one explain such an apparent paradox?

One possible explanation lies in the 'crisis imperative' that was engendered by the external economic shocks in 1982–86: falling oil prices followed by sharp downturns in other commodity prices. Indonesia, Malaysia and Thailand responded fairly rapidly to restore macroeconomic imbalances (Warr, 1992; Horton et al., 1994) and, within such a framework, created incentives for export-oriented, FDI-dependent industrialisation. These domestic policy initiatives were supported by influential financial institutions such as the World Bank and IMF and coincided happily with the burst of Japan- and NIE-led FDI that followed the exchange rate re-alignments of the mid-1980s.

What were the political forces that led to such responses to the external shocks of the mid-1980s? One line of argument is that, despite a tradition of clientalism, the 1980s saw the emergence of assertive business associations which played an important part in the economic reform agenda of the mid-1980s. This development is apparently particularly evident in Thailand, but can also be detected in Indonesia. They were able to form alliances with reform-minded technocrats in the economic ministries, an alliance that prevailed in domestic policy debates – see, for example, Laothamatas (1988, 1992), Doner (1991a, 1991b, 1992). MacIntyre (1990, 1994a; MacIntyre and Jayasuriya, 1992) has also supported such an interpretation, although he is now doubtful about the sustainability of such a political configuration (MacIntyre, 1994b: 16–17).

As noted, this view of South East Asian political economy is derived mainly from the experiences of Indonesia and Thailand. It is generally acknowledged that the Philippines represents the exception, where 'crony capitalism' under the Marcos regime (Hawes 1987; Hutchcroft, 1991, 1994) has given way to a 'weak' state in a democratic setting as reflected in the reduced momentum for policy reform after 1987 (Dohner and Intal, 1989; Lindsey, 1992).

Doner (1991a, 1992), who is perhaps the most eloquent advocate of this 'new view' of South East Asian political economy, argues that it is a representative example of the analytical framework of 'inclusionary institutionalism'. The essence of the argument seems to be that one should focus on how extra-state institutions – business conglomerates, networks, business interest associations, private-sector–public-sector consultations – as well as the state, resolve market-failure problems. Doner (1991a: 839) emphasises the utility of this approach in the following way:

> Southeast Asianists ... can illustrate the potential utility of an inclusionary rather than a statist form of institutionalism. In drawing attention to the activities of business groups, business associations and public–private sector bodies, Southeast Asianists can clarify nonstatist sources of growth in the region. They can also help to develop an inclusionary model that is relevant for the broad majority of LDCs whose states are much weaker than those of the East Asian [NIEs].

While one does detect a notable difference between the political economy of the East Asian NIEs and South East Asian political economy, this difference should be put into proper perspective. To start with, a post-statist current is evident even within the literature on the NIEs. Noble (1987) has drawn attention to internal conflicts in policy making in Taiwan. Moon (1988, 1990) and Haggard and Moon (1990) have raised questions about the ability of South Korean policy-makers to sustain policy implementation over time. These questions are likely to become even more significant in the more democratised environment of the 1990s.

Studies of South East Asian political economy show up significant similarities with the institutional features of the East Asian NIEs. As Laothamatas (1992), a strong advocate of the distinctive nature of South East Asian political economy, concedes, there are important areas of economic policy-making in Thailand in which one can detect a significant degree of 'technocratic insulation'. These include macroeconomic management and prudential regulation of the financial sector. As Hewison (1985) emphasises and as Laothamatas (1992) also admits, Thailand exhibits elements of exclusionary politics similar to the East Asian NIEs. Thus, interest representation from the farming community and urban labour is carefully managed by the state at the same time as peak business associations are allowed easy access to the policy-making process. MacIntyre (1990) has raised similar caveats in the context of Indonesia.

It is not always easy to separate cause and effect in the policy reform process in South East Asia – especially in the areas of trade and industry. Hill's study of the Indonesian experience (Hill, 1992: 223–6), suggests a sequential interaction of cause and effect: first, technocrats (e.g. in the Ministry of Finance and in the Planning Ministry) circumvented internal opposition from other parts of the bureaucracy to initiate a package of reforms; then, once export success became evident, this created a powerful export lobby in the private sector seeking the consolidation of a commercial environment conducive to the maintenance of international competitiveness.

THE INSTITUTIONAL FRAMEWORK OF INTERNATIONALLY ORIENTED ECONOMIC GROWTH: THE CASE OF THE PRC

The political economy of the PRC is, in many respects, more complex than either South East Asia or the NIEs. A simple transplant of the notion of 'technocratic insulation' – derived from the experience of the East Asian NIEs – is not useful. In the case of China, the politics of policy-making is compounded by the constant tension between socialist ideology and the transition to a market-oriented economy.

The transition to a market-oriented economy and China's progressive integration with its regional neighbours and the world at large have, in recent years, spawned a significant literature. Useful surveys have been conducted by Sung and Chan (1987) and Lin (1988). These have been followed by an admirably lucid up-dated survey by Watson (1994). Other contributions that provide valuable insights into different aspects of policy-making in the PRC include Watson (1992), Findlay *et al.* (1993), Wu (1993), Garnaut and Liu (1992), Goodman (1992), Lardy (1992) and Byrd (1991). The comparatively nascent nature of this literature is driven partly by easier access to data. It is worthwhile to remember, as Wu (1993: 58) notes, that China imposed a 'statistical blackout' in 1960 that persisted until 1979 when it formally adopted its 'open door' policy. It is, however, not just a matter of easier access to data. The processes at work in China today are fascinating and have generated spectacular results. As previously cited statistics amply demonstrate, contemporary China is one of the most buoyant economies in the world and is an emerging giant in the Asia-Pacific region. 'Purchasing power parity' estimates suggest that the size of the Chinese economy is approximately 45 per cent of that of the US economy (Garnaut and Ma, 1993a).

What are the political forces that have driven this well-documented and successful transition to a market economy? The reform process has been characterised by experiments, pragmatic adjustments, and debates over what to do next... This strongly pragmatic focus has contributed to the relative success of China's reforms and must be seen as a strategic choice by the reformist forces. It has enabled old orthodoxies to be set aside or reconstructed and created the space for innovative experiments... It has also accommodated the changing balance of political forces in China.

(Watson, 1994: 49)

Underpinning this pragmatism is the successful alliance that apparently seems to have been forged between the 'technocrats' and party political leaders, but it is an alliance that encompasses different levels and layers of the bureaucracy, academia and the media (Watson, 1994: 50). Against such an institutional setting, considerable debate and consensus-building goes on before broad policy-directions are set. In this respect, the notion of 'technocratic insulation' is rather more complex than suggested by the literature on the NIEs.

China's experiment with market-oriented reforms and efforts at globalisation within a framework of socialist ideology has spawned considerable discussions and speculations as to its sustainability. The events after Tiananmen Square 1989 have shown how one can sharply oscillate between the need to maintain the status quo and the need to align the political system with a rapidly evolving market-oriented system. For the time being at least, it appears that the separation between the political system – driven by socialist ideology and the one-party state – and the economic system will be maintained. The underlying logic for such separation is that continuity, stability and strong political leadership are prerequisites for sustaining rapid growth.

The political economy of public policy in China has also brought to the fore the perennial debate on the costs and benefits of 'gradualism' vs the 'big bang' approach in economic reform. Should one go for a decisive, one-step and sweeping move towards a market economy, as was advocated and attempted in the case of Russia, or should one proceed in a pragmatic, incremental manner, as in the case of China? Russia's dismal experience with the 'big bang' approach and the more successful Chinese experience would appear to suggest the appropriateness of 'gradualism' as a reform strategy. But gradualism has its costs. It has been partly responsible for the 'stop–go' cycles that have characterised recent Chinese economic growth: periods of rapid growth offset by bouts of macroeconomic austerity. It has also sustained the co-existence of profit-driven, relatively efficient 'market' sectors and subsidised, relatively inefficient 'plan' or 'state' sectors. Byrd (1991) has highlighted that such co-existence spawns rent-seeking opportunities and engenders microeconomic distortions, although Liew (1993) offers a more optimistic interpretation (see discussion below).

The future of the reform process in China will continue to be the subject of much debate and speculation, but one can at least predict that sustained growth itself will sow the seeds of further change. Those who gain least from change, such as the workers and managers of state-owned enterprises, are progressively becoming less dominant. Recent evidence suggests that the bulk of industrial production, for both domestic and export markets, in rural areas were generated outside the state sector (Findlay and Watson, 1992). Goodman (1992) has highlighted how an emerging middle class in urban areas is shaping up as a force for consumerism and social change. Regional tensions are also being generated as new growth areas relegate others into 'rustbelts'.

It remains to be seen how such growth-induced changes will be managed. In conclusion, one could argue that the political economy of China appears to be rather distinctive compared with its regional neighbours. One could argue, however, that Chinese political economy shares one common, fundamental trait with the NIEs and, to some extent, South East Asia. This may be called the 'logic of authoritarian politics'. Such a logic manifests itself in the notion that strong, centralised leadership and 'top-down' management of social and economic change is the relevant institutional framework for sustaining the growth process. This in turn leads, as in the Chinese context, to separation between the economic and political systems. The next section will argue that this logic is flawed and suggest that rapid, sustainable, internationally oriented growth is compatible with a more 'open' participatory political system.

THE INSTITUTIONAL FRAMEWORK OF INTERNATIONALLY ORIENTED ECONOMIC GROWTH: SOME NORMATIVE PRESCRIPTIONS

The discussion has so far noted that a model of governance that builds on the experience of the East Asian NIEs is perhaps not so useful in understanding the experience of South East Asia and China, although they are bound together by the common logic of authoritarian politics. This section proposes an alternative perspective on the institutional framework of internationally oriented economic growth and is based on Islam (1996).

The normative prescriptions proffered here on the institutional framework of internationally oriented economic growth is fundamentally linked to the enunciation of the neo-classical principles of 'good' governance. Such principles have an ancient lineage (they go back to Adam Smith) and their application in real-world contexts is independent of the political system. This means that they can be made compatible with democratic institutions. What are these principles of good governance?

There is a broad consensus that the adherence to the following principles is central to the evolution of internationally competitive economies:

1 The state should primarily allow market-based, private-sector-driven, initiatives in the mobilisation and allocation of resources to growth-promoting activities.

2 It should intervene only in cases of clearly established market failure (i.e. in cases where private-sector operations do not correspond to societal interests).

3 In cases of proven market failure, attempts should be made to implement workable and incentive-compatible policies.

4 The state should provide 'pure public goods' (law and order, national defence, public infrastructure) including the proper assignment and enforcement of property rights.

5 The state should provide a stable and predictable macroeconomic environment through appropriate co-ordination of fiscal, monetary and exchange rate policies – a principle that is increasingly being referred to as 'time-consistent' policies (ADB, 1994).

6 The state should enforce a free-trade (or almost free-trade) regime on the ground that such a 'neutral' policy regime restrains the government from making sector-specific interventions (Krugman, 1987; Lal and Rajapatirana, 1987).

If the state broadly conforms to the limits set by the aforementioned prescriptions, then society can realise a range of benefits: reduction in the information burden placed on policy-makers, conservation of scarce administrative and managerial talents, restraints on predatory behaviour, and a reduction in the risk that state officials will be prone to 'capture' by special-interest groups. If, on the other hand, the state progressively exceeds the limits set out above, then eventually government failure will occur which will more than offset the alleged inadequacies of the private sector.

Admittedly, the principles are compatible with authoritarian political systems. What is insufficiently emphasised is that they are also compatible with democratic institutions. The latter entails an elaboration of two issues:

(a) the need to build constitutional safeguards to enforce the prescriptions of good governance;

(b) the need to apply the principle of compensation for creating a constituency for good governance.

Proposition (a) is inspired by the contributions of Brenan and Buchanan (1980). They have suggested in the context of mature democracies that, given the imperfect constraints of competitive politics on inefficient, *dirigiste* states, constitutional restraints may well be necessary on the fiscal, debt and money-creation capacities of the government. Niskanen (1992) has restated the case for this view through the idea of formal adoption of a 'fiscal constitution' for the US.

As part of adopting a fiscal constitution, one could start with the extreme position that all unfunded spending programmes be made constitutionally illegal, thus creating a balanced budget as the only constitutionally admissible possibility. The problem, of course, is that such a rule could lead to debilitating inflexibility. Governments, for example, would be unable to vary their fiscal policy to respond to internal and external shocks. In addition, it could lead to an excessive reliance on monetary (or exchange rate) policy as a tool of macro-management. A more moderate position is that limits on either the tax-raising or debt-creating capacity of the government can only be varied through a super-majority in the legislature, subject to the stipulation that the super-majority rule will not apply in times of national emergencies (e.g. the onset of a war). This practice is not unknown – see, for example, Niskanen (1992).

Switzerland has also been cited as a case where it is legislatively very difficult to increase spending levels (Niskanen, 1992: 17; Alt and Chrystal, 1983: 50). Moreover, there are examples of some European countries (former West Germany) where even the strict version of the fiscal constitution (constitutional illegality of fiscal deficits) operated for a period (Alt and Chrystal, 1983: 50).

There are critics of a fiscal constitution (in terms of the super-majority rule) (e.g. Schultze, 1992) as a prescription for good governance, but even such commentators are acutely aware of the need for a general reform of the budgetary process. They have also endorsed Buchanan's (1963) idea of 'earmarked taxes', that is, specific spending proposals should be tied to specific taxes for financing them. This may well create the incentive for the community to restrain the indiscriminate expansion of publicly provided goods (particularly those with the characteristics of private goods) once it is confronted with the necessity to raise taxes to support such expansion.

A central assumption underlying the case for a fiscal constitution – or, more generally, reform of the budgetary process – is that deficit financing often creates unsustainable monetary expansion, causing bouts of destructive inflation and loss of competitiveness. This in turn suggests another way of restraining macroeconomic instability. Recent research has shown that if the central bank can be made independent from other parts of the government and granted a mandate for maintaining price stability, then a government can strengthen its commitment to price stability and the maintenance of international competitiveness. Thus, central bank independence provides the necessary institutional limits on unsustainable monetary creation that could accompany persistent budget deficits. Cukierman et al. (1992) have assembled evidence that suggests that central bank independence does indeed contribute to low inflation in industrial countries. A more recent study by Cukierman and Webb (1995) assembles evidence from more than 40 countries to show that if the central bank is vulnerable to political instability (as reflected in the frequency of changes in political regimes), then the outcomes are quite adverse: high and variable inflation and slower growth.

In sum, the twin concepts of a fiscal constitution and central bank independence have been advocated as laying the foundations of good governance, primarily in the context of industrial countries with well-established democratic traditions. The cynical observer may well scoff at the suggestion of such ideas being relevant to economies in the Asia-Pacific region on the ground that the political systems of many of these countries have little regard for constitutional principles.

One can respond to this position in a number of ways. First, the objective of intellectual discourse is to rise above cynicism and to suggest constructive options for good governance. Second, if the principle of building in constitutional safeguards for protecting macroeconomic stability are dismissed as being unrealistic, then one cannot escape from the dilemma that development requires a benevolent dictator with the discretion and authority to pursue good policies. Third, there is evidence to suggest that economies in the Asia-Pacific region are capable of pursuing the principles of a fiscal constitution and central bank independence. Indonesia and Thailand, for example, may be cited as cases where a semblance of a fiscal constitution has apparently been followed (Pangestu, 1991; Woo and Nasution, 1989; World Bank, 1993a) with a correspondingly good record of macroeconomic stability. The aforementioned study by Cukierman *et al.* (1992) found that in cases where there was actual (rather than legal or nominal) independence of the central bank (as measured in terms of turnover of central bank governors), this institutional arrangement did indeed contribute to price stability in developing countries.

While constitutional safeguards for protecting macroeconomic stability represent important conditions for the creation and maintenance of international competitiveness, it is ultimately in the realm of trade policy that the issue of competitiveness needs to be located. The orthodox neo-classical position is that free trade is the most effective means of achieving globalisation. The belief in this orthodox position has been shaken by the demonstration that in the presence of market imperfections, some degree of intervention may Pareto-dominate free trade. However, prominent trade theorists argue that this 'new' view of interventionist trade policy is subject to the standard risk of rent-seeking behaviour. Hence, in a world of imperfect politics, free trade is a very useful rule of thumb (Krugman, 1987). The acceptance of this logic implies that there may well be a case for implementing institutional safeguards for protecting the principle of free trade. Thus, one could argue the case for applying the super-majority rule on proposals entailing restraints on free trade. In addition, one could create watchdog bodies (e.g. a GATT-style 'Commission for Free Trade') that make it binding on protectionist proposals to proffer publicly available documentation on the costs and benefits of protection. Such attempts at making the process of trade policy transparent may create the incentive for special-interest groups to reduce their propensity to engage in lobbying activities that seek restraints on free trade.

One could extend this line of reasoning to take account of the notion of 'open regionalism' discussed at a previous juncture. At a time when there is a trend towards the regionalisation of the world economy, the espousal of the notion of 'open regionalism' as part of the mandate of the aforementioned watchdog body seems important in buttressing the capacity of such a body to protect the cause of free trade.

Proposition (b) is built on the premise that the political transition to good governance is rather difficult. As Landes-Mills and Serageldin (1992: 319) note: 'good governance is a fragile plant that will need constant nourishing. It will require a fundamental change in mentality and social expectations.' Not surprisingly the transition to good governance is likely to meet entrenched political opposition from those seeking to maintain the status quo. How does one create an admissible coalition for change in such an environment? The positive theory of government failure does not offer any obvious clue. In a world populated by rent-seekers and predatory political authorities, it is difficult to see how the momentum for reform will voluntarily develop. However, there is an emerging view – shared by economists and political scientists – that one could build a feasible political context for reform based on the principle of compensation. This view conceptualises the community in terms of gainers and losers from a given policy reform. Such disaggregation allows one to delineate the role that the state can play in mediating the conflicts that inevitably accompany institutional and economic policy reform from a previously *dirigiste* regime. Policy reform efforts may be blocked if gainers cannot compensate losers. Such compensation may not occur voluntarily, given high transactions costs and free-rider problems. It is here that the state can step in by implementing a variety of non-distortive compensatory measures (Mosley *et al.*, 1991; Rausser, 1992). Examples of such measures include special worker adjustment compensation for industries facing international competition, privatisation with compensation for adversely affected public-sector employees and so forth. The importance of such measures are highlighted by Rausser (1992: 150) in the following manner: 'since productive policies may harm members of special interest groups, compensation...may actually be politically necessary if society is to approach the optimal configuration of productive policies'.

There is some evidence that some economies in the Asia-Pacific region – encompassing both democratic and non-democratic political systems – have espoused the message inherent in the principle of compensation. Thus Malaysia's vigorous privatisation programme has been underpinned by

public assurances about security of jobs and protection of current benefits, and the promise of more, such as opportunities to own shares in the newly privatised company and to make capital gains from appreciation in the value of these shares...As the experience in Malaysia has shown, once workers are convinced they gain rather than lose, they will most likely support privatisation.

(Yuen and Woon, 1992: 59)

In the case of mainland China, Liew (1993) has argued that the successful management of market-oriented reform has to be related to the fact that safeguards were provided for risk-averse social groups participating in the non-market sector, thus creating a constituency for market-oriented reform.

More generally, a recent survey by Haggard and Webb (1993: 162) on the political economy of policy reform suggests that 'the evidence from the case studies points to the conclusion that compensation measures are usually necessary to sustain political support for adjustment'.

CONCLUDING OBSERVATIONS

This chapter has argued that one needs to understand the internal political factors that have shaped the dual phenomena of Asia-Pacific economic dynamism and regional interdependence. This, in turn, entails an understanding of the political context in which outward-oriented policies were adopted in the various economies of the region. Although one can detect an 'East Asian model' of governance that has been primarily influenced by the experience of the East Asian NIEs, the chapter has suggested that it is important to take account of the distinctive features of the political economy of public policy in South East Asia and the PRC. In the case of the former, bureaucratic competence and 'technocratic insulation' appeared less evident than in the NIEs, and yet the economies of Indonesia, Malaysia and Thailand appeared to have made the successful transition to internationally oriented growth in the 1980s. In the case of the PRC, the transition to a market economy has re-opened debates on the pros and cons of 'gradualism' vs a 'big bang' approach to economic reforms as well as the sustainability of an institutional framework that has aimed to make a separation between a socialist political creed and a market-oriented economic system. The PRC's experience so far suggests that such a formula has worked.

The chapter has noted that despite obvious differences in the political economy of public policy across the various sub-regions of Pacific Asia, the economies of the region are bound together by the logic of authoritarian politics. In other words, a strong, centralised political leadership is seen as a prerequisite for sustaining economic growth even if it entails some attenuation of human rights. The chapter has argued against such a logic and pleaded the case for the adoption of broad principles of governance (derived from the tradition of neoclassical economics) that facilitate globalisation and rapid growth within a political framework that respects democratic traditions. Such a message is highly topical as countries in this region (most notably Korea and Taiwan) try to break away from a historically entrenched authoritarian political tradition and seek to democratise their political systems.

Chapter 3

Macroeconomic stabilisation and economic performance

INTRODUCTION

Development economics has conventionally been conceived as a study of supply-side issues: designing policies and institutions that enhance capital formation and lead to sustained improvements in factor productivity and finding measures for improving the living conditions of the poor beyond the general mechanisms provided by economic growth. In other words, development economics represents the study of long-run structural issues. The role that traditional policy instruments – most notably fiscal, monetary and exchange rate policies – play in demand management (restoring internal and external balance in the presence of disequilibrium situations) has, until recently, not been a major feature of research on developing economies. The turbulent events of the 1970s and 1980s have, however, brought macroeconomic stabilisation issues to the fore. The period has seen the two oil shocks (1973, 1979), a historically unprecedented access to borrowing on world capital markets, spending booms in many countries spurred by ease of access to external finance and the terms-of-trade shifts, OECD recession (mid-1970s, early 1980s) and the debt crisis of 1981/82. For developing countries in general, the period is best seen as attempts to re-establish internal and external balance in a context of external shocks, and implementing a policy package that would allow the resumption of a sustainable, long-run growth path. Out of the diverse macroeconomic experiences of these countries has grown the firm conviction that successful macroeconomic stabilisation is a key element of sustainable economic growth.

The burgeoning literature on the macroeconomic experiences of developing countries during the 1970s and 1980s – an excellent example of which is Little *et al.* (1993) – seems to substantiate the general perception that the successful economies of the Asia-Pacific region have adjusted better than others to the turbulent era of the 1970s and 1980s primarily because they have been able to restore internal and external balance relatively quickly. This chapter reviews this claim in terms of broad analytical issues that impinge on the use of monetary, fiscal and exchange rate policies as key ingredients in macroeconomic stabilisation exercises.

MACROECONOMIC STABILISATION: GOALS AND POLICY INSTRUMENTS

From the perspective of macroeconomic stabilisation, *internal balance* refers to the maintenance of price stability without compromising the objective of long-term, sustainable growth. *External balance* pertains to the attainment of a sustainable balance-of-payments position without, once again, compromising the objective of long-term, sustainable growth. Defined in this way, the conventional notions of internal and external balance are intertwined with long-run growth.

Internal and external balance can be disturbed into disequilibrium (a mismatch of aggregate demand and aggregate supply) either by unanticipated, exogenous shocks or by policy-induced errors. The oil shocks of the 1970s represent a classic example of the former; 'macroeconomic populism' (Dornbusch and Edwards, 1990) whereby governments run unsustainable fiscal deficits to meet politically determined social objectives, represent a notorious example of the latter. The extent to which a macro-stabilisation using conventional tools of demand management needs to be implemented to restore internal and external balance depends upon the nature of the disequilibrium: whether it is temporary and reversible (as in the case of a drought-induced reduction in food supply) or permanent and irreversible (as in the case of the oil shocks of the 1970s). As Joshi and Little (1994: 205) have clarified, in the case of temporary shocks, 'there is no obvious role for demand management policy of the conventional kind'. The best response, in the previously cited case of a reversible agricultural supply shock, is to smooth the path of consumption by drawing down on past stocks of food and foreign reserves. In the case of a permanent shock, some degree of stabilisation through a combination of *expenditure reduction* (through fiscal and monetary contractions) and *expenditure switching* (through exchange rate adjustments) represents an appropriate response. While the former method seeks to reduce aggregate demand to bring it in line with available capacity, the latter seeks to improve capacity utilisation by switching resources from the non-tradable to the tradable sector. This is the key message that flows from the so-called 'dependent economy' or 'Australian model' derived from the seminal contributions by Salter (1959) and Swan (1960).

The normative prescriptions of macroeconomic stabilisation appear to be deceptively simple. A number of complications need to be highlighted. First, policy-makers can easily go astray in their stabilisation efforts if they ignore some well-known rules: there must be as many effective policy instruments as there are objectives; the assignment of instruments to objectives should maximise the effectiveness of the instruments employed (e.g. circumstances may require the use of exchange rate policy to control inflation and fiscal policy to deal with external balance). It is possible to fall into the trap of using one policy instrument to influence multiple and conflicting objectives. This has sometimes been referred to as the 'assignment problem'.

Second, monetary, fiscal and exchange rate policies are closely inter-linked. This interlinkage is particularly important in the presence of capital mobility and in industrialising economies with insufficiently developed money markets as well as limited revenue-raising capacities. The current literature on macroeconomic management in developing economies regards the interdependence of policy instruments – and hence their optimal design in a context of interdependence – as a central issue.

Third, the so-called rational expectations revolution in macroeconomics (e.g. see the volume of essays in Sargent, 1986) has highlighted the role that expectations-formation by economic agents plays in policy design and effectiveness. A central message of this literature is that attempts to use discretionary fiscal and monetary policy to attain predetermined targets can be nullified because, in an expectations-driven economy, workers and pro-ducers can anticipate their outcomes and accordingly alter their behaviour. It is now recognised that the underlying assumptions of the rational ex-pectations literature were rather stringent (e.g. full and efficient utilisation of macroeconomic information by private agents, perfect price/wage flex-ibility). Despite this, the literature has rightly emphasised the need to move away from an uncritical reliance on discretionary demand-management policies to the need to make a credible commitment to simple, transparent policy rules (e.g. commitment to monetary growth targets). One could argue that such a prescription has considerable relevance for industrialising economies, given their limited administrative capacities and given the fact that policies have to be conceived in a political context (see below).

Fourth, as with economic policy formulation in general, political economy considerations cannot be ignored – a central fact discussed at some length in a previous chapter. Political forces may lead to the adoption of monetary, fiscal and exchange rate policies that are sub-optimal. Furthermore, political forces may generate wage and relative price rigidities. Hence, macroeconomic management needs to be buttressed by appropriate institutional arrange-ments in order to facilitate the credible commitment to policy rules.

MONETARY, FISCAL AND EXCHANGE RATE POLICIES: ISSUES AND OPTIONS

The purpose of this section is to expand on two themes noted above: the 'assignment problem' and the interlinkage of policy instruments.

Monetary policy pertains to the determination and allocation of mone-tary aggregates (usually referred to as 'high-powered', 'reserve' or 'base' money) and the price at which such aggregates are transacted, that is, the interest rate. Textbook analysis suggests that one can control either price (the interest rate) or quantity (monetary aggregates), but not both. Further-more, the capacity of policy-makers to control monetary aggregates de-pends on the nature of the exchange rate regime – on which more later.

Fiscal policy pertains to the determination and allocation of government expenditures and the way they are financed. Joshi and Little (1994) have observed that the primary issue confronting industrialising economies is the 'fiscal problem' – on which more later.

The exchange rate (or, more accurately, a weighted average of bilateral rates) represent the ratio of domestic and foreign currencies, either defined as, say, number of bahts per US dollar, or as its reciprocal. The first definition is adopted here. When adjustments are made for domestic and foreign price levels (or inflation rates – if the aim is to gauge movements rather than levels) one arrives at the real exchange rate. Thus,

$$R = P/(e \times Pf) \tag{1}$$

where R is the real exchange rate, P is domestic price level (measured in baht), Pf is the foreign price level measured in dollars, and e is the nominal exchange rate. It follows that an appreciation of R (or a rise in R) implies a loss of competitiveness (it takes more units of foreign goods in order to obtain a unit of domestic good). Conversely, a depreciation (or a fall in R) implies an increase in a country's external competitiveness. Exchange rate regimes can vary from a fully fixed rate to fully unified ones. Intermediate cases include managed floats and a discretionary crawling peg. Issues in exchange rate policy currently seem to focus on its role as a 'nominal anchor' as distinct from its role in influencing external competitiveness. These issues are re-visited at a subsequent stage.

The interlinkage of policy instruments can be effectively illustrated by introducing some macroeconomic identities. As Bruno (1993: 21) has emphasised, one can write the total money supply (M) as:

$$M = \text{Domestic Credit (DC)} + \text{Net Foreign Assets (NFA)} \tag{2}$$

where DC = Central Credit to government (CC) + Bank Credit to public (BC).

Equation (2) shows that one can create Money (M) in a number of ways: either through increases in the components of DC or through the sale of foreign exchange to the central bank (which will increase NFA). The inclusion of NFA in the definition clearly shows the close connection between monetary policy and the exchange rate regime. A commitment to maintain fixed exchange rate means that changes in NFA will dominate changes in M, unless full sterilisation is possible. Thus, the government will lose its capacity to undertake independent monetary policy.

Consider now the central role that fiscal policy plays in macro-management and the linkage between fiscal and monetary policies. This can be highlighted by the following 'public financing identity' (Easterly and Schmidt-Hebbel, 1993: 213):

Fiscal/public Deficit Financing (FDF) = Money Financing (MF) + Domestic Debt Financing (DDF) + External Debt Financing (EDF) (3)

Note that the fiscal deficit is defined to include the central government, state and local governments, state enterprises and the central bank.

This identity shows that the government can finance deficits by seignorage ('printing money' – MF above), borrowing at home (DDF), or borrowing abroad (EDF). Easterly and Schmidt-Hebbel (1993: 213) highlight the macroeconomic implications that follow from the above identity:

> Each...type of financing, if used excessively, results in a specific macroeconomic imbalance. Money creation leads to inflation. Domestic borrowing leads to a credit squeeze...and the crowding out of private investment and consumption. External borrowing leads to a current account deficit and the appreciation of the real exchange rate and sometimes to a balance of payments crisis...or an external debt crisis.

Equation (3) also suggests that if MF is the dominant mode of financing, then monetary policy clearly becomes subservient to the needs of the fiscal authorities. There is a general presumption that, given the underdeveloped nature of bond and financial markets in industrialising economies, monetisation of fiscal deficits is significant. Furthermore, despite the easy availability of external finance in the 1970s, developing countries have quickly learned that the tap of external finance cannot be turned on and off at will.

Evidence suggests that the typical developing country finances approximately 50 per cent of the public deficit through the banking system (Little *et al.*, 1993: chapter 10). More direct estimates of seignorage suggest that for developing economies (for a sample of 35 countries), it amounts to 2 per cent of GNP compared with 1 per cent for industrial economies (sample size: 15) (Easterly and Schmidt-Hebbel, 1993: 221). It follows that assuming monetary control entails assuming control over the government's budgetary position.

There is, as noted above, a close link between fiscal policy and external balance. This can be highlighted in a convenient way by introducing the following macroeconomic identity:

Current Account Deficit (CAD) = [Private Savings (PS) – Private Investment (PI)] + Fiscal Deficit (FD) (4)

PS less PI is sometimes referred to as 'the private-sector balance'. Assuming that it remains constant, increases in FD will be directly reflected in increases in CAD (a proposition that, for obvious reasons, is referred to as the 'twin deficit hypothesis'). There is, in addition, the standard proposition that, in the presence of a high degree of capital mobility, fiscal expansion appreciates the real exchange rate and 'crowds out' net exports (Mundell/Fleming). This in turn worsens CAD. It thus follows that improvements in the external balance require fiscal adjustments.

The foregoing discussion has also suggested the central role that fiscal policy can play in influencing private investment and consumption. Hence, one cannot assume that the private-sector balance in equation (4) will remain constant in the face of persistent and unsustainable fiscal deficits. Such deficits can crowd out private investment through an increase in the real interest rate. In addition, elements of public expenditure, such as the expansion of state enterprises, can directly compete with the private sector. Of course, public investment can complement private investment (such as investment in infrastructure), implying that one needs to take account of both the overall volume of fiscal expansion as well as its composition.

It is thus clear that when one takes account of the repercussions of persistent and unsustainable fiscal deficits on monetary policy, the external balance and the private sector balance, macroeconomic stabilisation must entail fiscal adjustment as a central ingredient. The resolution of the 'fiscal problem' is, at the same time, the resolution of the 'assignment problem'.

So far, the discussion has focused on fiscal and monetary policy. It is necessary to deal with the design of an appropriate exchange rate regime. Traditionally, the focus has been on the polar cases of fixed and flexible exchange rates. The conventional argument is that unified, fully flexible exchange rates impart a high degree of volatility, given the 'thin' nature of the exchange rate market in industrialising countries. Thus, such countries should stick to a fixed exchange rate regime. The modern version of this view focuses on the efficacy of a fixed exchange regime on the ground that it serves as a 'nominal anchor': that is, as a bulwark against inflation – see, for example, Aghevli *et al.* (1991), Corden (1991) and Garnaut (1991). In practice the nominal anchor approach can take several forms: pegging the domestic currency to the currency of a country with a history of stable prices; using foreign exchange as legal tender; or making a firm commitment to a pre-announced rate of nominal devaluation, an arrangement referred to as a *tablita* regime.

What is the rationale behind the nominal anchor approach? Bruno (1993: 28–9) offers a clear, compact statement:

> In a small, open economy the relationship between the general price level and the exchange rate is considerably tighter than between money and prices, primarily because import prices play a large role in the input–output system. Any increase in the cost of imports (say, through a devaluation) quickly feeds into the general price level, which is further enhanced when there is some formal linkage between ... wages ... and the price level. For this reason there is an advantage in anchoring the price level to the exchange rate.

If the exchange rate becomes in effect an anti-inflation tool (in preference to monetary policy), how does one resolve the other functions of the exchange rate, namely, in dealing with external balance and competitiveness? The answer is to use 'incomes policy to keep a wage level that is consistent, given the nominal exchange rate, with the required real exchange rates determining international competitiveness and the current account' (Bruno, 1993: 28–9).

Dornbusch and Reynoso (1993) have re-visited the fixed vs flexible exchange rate regime to advocate a 'dual rate' approach, which they claim is a pragmatic device in cases of high degree of capital mobility which cannot be effectively controlled. The basic premise is that exchange rate shifts reflect changes in economic fundamentals as well as transient factors that could lead to speculative attacks (in the form of capital inflows and outflows) on the domestic currency. If stringent controls on the capital account are not possible, then one needs a device which allows policy-makers to insulate the exchange rate from transitory disturbances trans-mitted via the capital account. Thus, the need for a dual rate: 'an "official" rate that applies to most, if not all, trade transactions and a .. . "free" rate at which all other transactions take place' (Dornbusch and Reynoso, 1993: 119). The official rate will thus serve as a nominal anchor, while the unregulated rate will reflect the volatility of capital flows. The caveat is that, to be effective, a dual rate system needs to be 'well managed'. This in essence means the size of the premium between the two rates should be modest – in the order of 15–20 per cent. Large and persistent increases in the premium beyond this threshold range will then serve as a signal that the official rate needs to be re-aligned.

Despite the theoretical appeal of the nominal anchor approach and its modified version in the presence of capital mobility (the dual rate system), and despite the fact that it is practised by some countries, there is a growing tendency to adopt an adjustable peg or a managed float. Under such an arrangement, there is government intervention in the foreign exchange market, but there is no commitment to a particular rate and frequent adjustments are made. Whatever the merits of this approach relative to the previous cases, an appropriate exchange rate regime must follow simple, stable rules that avoid cumulative overvaluations. Both theory and evidence suggest that when exchange rates are distorted and misaligned, they can cause serious consequences: wasteful allocation of resources, capital flight, rent-seeking, red tape and corruption.

So far, the discussion has proceeded on the assumption that monetary, fiscal and exchange rate policies are used solely to attain macroeconomic targets of internal and external balance. The assignment problem then became primarily one of designing an optimal policy mix (should one, for example, use monetary or exchange rate policy as an anti-inflation tool?). Unfortunately, the recent macroeconomic history of developing economies is littered with cases where the assignment problem has been compounded by the fact that such macro-policy instruments have been used to pursue multiple, microeconomic objectives. Selective credit allocation at preferential rates has been the norm rather than the exception. Extensive interventions have occurred in the foreign exchange market, generating multiple rates, controls on foreign exchange transactions and so forth. Inevitably, such interventions compromise the capacity of monetary authorities to use monetary and exchange rate policy to cope with the objectives of internal and external balance.

Given that policy objectives have both macro-and microeconomic counterparts, the assignment problem is best solved by disentangling microeconomic, supply-side issues from macroeconomic instruments and targets. Thus, for example, the objective of developing particular industries or activities in which the perceived social rate of return is higher than the corresponding private rate of retune is best handled through other measures, such as strengthening property rights, rather than through selective credit allocation.

Finally, the point needs to be reiterated that the conduct of stable macropolicies may well require the need to devise institutional arrangements that facilitate credible commitments by the government to the maintenance of internal and external balance. After all, 'good policies' are not voluntarily spurned, nor are they ignored because of lack of knowledge. The capacity to engage in stable macroeconomic management needs to be nourished by improving the political economy framework within which public policy is conducted. As a previous chapter has noted, such devices as a fiscal constitution and central bank independence (actual rather than nominal) have played a role in contributing to the superior macroeconomic performance of some of the economies of the Asia-Pacific region.

MACROECONOMIC STABILITY AND LONG-RUN ECONOMIC PERFORMANCE: CLOSING THE LOOP

What is the relationship between macroeconomic stability and long-run economic performance (defined, albeit arbitrarily, as a time-period at least as long as a decade)? Several clues have been offered so far, particularly in terms of the adverse consequences that follow from the incidence of unsustainable fiscal deficits and exchange rate misalignments. It would be useful at this juncture to provide a sharper focus on the central and highly topical question of the relationship between macroeconomic stability and long-run trends in economic performance.

As noted, macroeconomic stability represents the maintenance of internal and external balance by minimising or avoiding boom–bust or stop–go cycles even in the face of exogenous shocks (whether favourable or unfavourable). Long-run economic performance can be proxied in several ways. Given the thrust of the discussion, it is desirable to identify performance indicators that reflect notions of sustainable internal balance and external balance. Given these considerations, obvious candidates include long-term trends in per capita GNP, inflation (representing internal balance) and current-account deficits/surpluses (representing external balance). These in turn need to be related to long-term trends in the government's fiscal position, seignorage (as an indication of money-financed fiscal deficits), and the exchange rate regime. Thus, one may formulate the following testable hypothesis: countries which maintain a sustainable fiscal position (implying also control over monetary aggregates) and a competitive exchange rate regime are rewarded with superior performance in terms of good growth, moderate inflation and a sustainable balance-of-payments position. This probably is a fair reflection of the emerging conventional wisdom on the link between macro-policy and economic performance. As Summers and Thomas (1993: 248) put it: 'Sound macroeconomic policies with sustainable fiscal deficits and realistic exchange rates are a prerequisite to progress'.

In operationalising the hypothesis that 'sound macroeconomic policies' are systematically linked to good economic growth, Little *et al.* (1993: chapter 11), adopt a framework that is both tractable and intellectually appealing. Recognising that economic growth reflects the confluence of a complex set of variables (natural resources and the availability of public goods, such as health and basic education, etc.) which may not be easily linked to macroeconomic policy, the Little *et al.* study focuses on the behaviour of the average investment ratio (and, as a corollary, the average savings ratio), in terms of both its stability and productivity. Stability is measured in terms of the coefficient of variance, while a measure of 'apparent productivity' (growth in GNP per head divided by the average investment ratio) is employed.

The focus on the behaviour of investment can, of course, be justified given the proposition that fiscal imbalances 'crowd out' private investment. In addition, the macroeconomic experience of many developing economies tends to suggest that, during the era of easily available external finance, they engaged in a public-sector-led investment boom, only to engage in a drastic retrenchment once the macroeconomic crunch came towards the early 1980s. This boom–bust cycle can be captured in the volatility of the average investment ratio. One could argue that this in turn has deleterious effects on the aggregate volume of investment by undermining the confidence of the private sector about future demand.

Why will a public-sector-induced boom–bust cycle in investment affect the productivity of aggregate investment? The answer lies in the fact that when large-scale public investments are undertaken in haste and are propelled by euphoric expectations about the external environment, mistakes may be made in project selection and proper cost–benefit analysis may well be jettisoned (Little and Mirlees, 1991). Thus, the portfolio of investments would be dominated by inefficient, poorly selected projects. The implication is that the overall productivity of investment is likely to be adversely affected. These considerations imply the following testable hypotheses: countries following sound and stable macroeconomic policies are likely to have high average investment ratio, low volatility and high productivity of investment. All these in turn produce superior economic performance in terms of growth.

The Little *et al.* study performs some 'growth regressions' on a sample of eighteen countries over a twenty-year period (1970–89), three of them being the high-growth economies of the Asia-Pacific region: Indonesia, Korea and Thailand. The authors find some support for the hypothesised link between per capita GNP growth, average investment and savings ratio, the volatility of aggregate investment and its efficiency as measured by apparent productivity. These empirical regularities will be re-visited at a later stage, but it is worth noting that the estimated equations 'explain' no more than 29 per cent of the variations in growth rates across countries. This is perhaps not surprising as it merely reflects the fact that growth is a complex process and is the product of a diverse range of tangible and intangible variables. The point is that macroeconomic policy does seem to exert some influence through the investment channel.

MACROECONOMIC STABILISATION AND ECONOMIC PERFORMANCE: THE EXPERIENCE OF THE ECONOMIES OF THE ASIA-PACIFIC REGION

The foregoing analytical discussion has provided the basis for interpreting some broad empirical regularities on the link between macroeconomic policy and economic performance in the Asia-Pacific region. This section draws heavily on a range of sources. The Little *et al.* study has already been extensively cited at several stages in this chapter and elsewhere. A good survey on macroeconomic management in the region can be found in Treadgold (1990) and Garnaut (1991), although the latter has a more specific focus on exchange rate management. Good individual country studies include Thorbecke (1991), Ahmed (1993), Woo and Nasution (1989), Woo *et al.* (1994) on Indonesia; Warr and Bhanupongse (1994) on Thailand; Demery and Demery (1991), Nam (1991) and Dornbusch and Park (1987) on Korea; Harrold *et al.* (1993) on China. Other sources include Chowdhury and Islam (1993), World Bank (1993a, 1995a, 1995b), ADB (1994), Petrie (1993b), Leipziger and Thomas (1993), the country studies underpinning these sources, and James *et al.* (1989). All these sources will not be specifically cited at every juncture; sometimes they will.

The empirical discussion proceeds in several stages. First, there is a brief reflection on the impact of the external shocks on the Asia-Pacific economies during the 1979–82 period and the way they responded to such shocks. This is followed by an attempt to provide some empirical substance to the analytical framework developed in the previous section, namely, the link between performance indicators of internal and external balance and the behaviour of macro-policy instruments; and the impact of macro-policy on economic growth via the investment channel. Finally, a parsimonious and selective case-study of specific country experiences will be offered. The sample is chosen such that they offer a fair representation of the region (Singapore, Thailand, Korea, Indonesia, Malaysia, China).

Table 3.1 provides some estimates of the size of the external shocks experienced by the economies of the region during the 1974–82 period and also includes South Asia as a comparator. The estimates are averages for the period as a proportion of GNP. If one excludes Indonesia and Malaysia, which are resource-rich (Indonesia is a net oil exporter) and hence gained from the external shocks of the period, then the picture that emerges is one where the East Asian NIEs were most vulnerable to such shocks – the magnitude being −24.8 per cent for this group of economies compared with −15.9 per cent for ASEAN and −14.2 per cent for South Asia.

Table 3.1 Relative size of external shocks: 1974–82

Region/economy	Ratio of external shocks (% GNP)
NIEs	−24.8
Hong Kong	−26.7
Korea	−13.3
Singapore	−46.3
Taiwan	−12.7
ASEAN-4	−14.9
Indonesia	23.6
Malaysia	6.4
Philippines	−14.5
Thailand	−15.3
South Asia	−14.2

Source: Selectively extracted from James *et al.*, 1989: table 4.9: 115
Note: The average for ASEAN-4 includes only Philippines and Thailand

James *et al.* (1989: chapter 4) employ a decomposition framework that allows them to disentangle the various types of adjustment measures, including conventional stabilisation policies, that were undertaken by the various countries. One can write aggregate direct adjustments to the exogenous disturbances as:

DA (Direct Adjustment) = Expenditure Switching (ES) + Expenditure Reduction (ER)   (5)

This is line with the 'dependent economy/Australian model' noted at a previous juncture. Note that in the James *et al.* study ES is specifically measured in terms of export market penetration and import substitution, while expenditure is shown as import reduction through lower GNP. Any difference between DA and the size of the external shocks is shown as 'net external finance'. In other words, the 'resource gap between exports and imports created by the external shocks and offset by direct adjustments must be filled by additional net financial inflows' (James *et al.*, 1989: 118).

Using this framework, the James *et al.* study finds that the economies of the region – in particular the NIEs – relied heavily on ES (particularly in the form of export market penetration) supplemented by conventional demand-management policies. Several economies in the region, such as Singapore, the Philippines and Thailand, also relied significantly on net external finance. The important role that external finance can play in the adjustment process has been noted by several authors, see for example Summers and Pritchett (1993), Bourguignon *et al.* (1991).

External funds – whether from public or private sources – can enhance the capacity of policy-makers in cushioning the possible adverse income-distribution and social consequences of traditional expenditure-reduction policy responses to exogenous disturbances – see chapter 7. However, the risk is that a reliance on external finance – particularly if it is in the form of concessional grants from multilateral agencies – can delay the need to take prompt and sizeable adjustment measures. This is best exemplified by the different experiences of Singapore and the Philippines. Export market penetration amounted to 67 per cent of the adjustment component of external shocks in Singapore, while it amounted to only 17.5 per cent in the Philippines (James *et al.*, 1989: table 4.10, p. 117).

Chowdhury and Islam (1993, chapter 11: 210) also adopt a similar decomposition framework to that employed by the James *et al.* study, apply it to the East Asian NIEs and arrive at the following conclusions:

> The East Asian NIEs responded to external shocks with [expenditure] reducing and switching…policies with varying degrees. The [expenditure] reduction was achieved mainly through public sector savings. The main switching device, devaluation…enhanced export expansions and import substitutions.

The Chowdhury and Islam study is thus in line with the conclusions of James *et al.* (1989). More importantly, it validates the basic thrust of the orthodox theory of stabilisation-cum-adjustment to exogenous disturbances in order to restore internal and external balance. In other words, expenditure reduction needs to be combined with expenditure-switching. In more concrete terms, this entails fiscal control as a prerequisite for control over monetary aggregates and a realistic exchange rate policy that entails prompt devaluations to shift resources to the tradable goods sector. Countries which followed these injunctions prospered; those which did not or delayed necessary action were faced with full-blown macroeconomic crises.

The central role of fiscal prudence in influencing macro-stability in the Asia-Pacific economies is emphasised by Leipziger and Thomas (1993: 9) in the following terms:

East Asia's governments exercised macro-economic discipline, ensuring that fiscal and external deficits were kept in control...Over the past quarter century the fiscal deficit and the current account deficit in developing East Asia were less than half the average for other developing countries.

Table 3.2 re-examines this view by attempting to establish some empirical regularities between selected performance indicators and the behaviour of the fiscal deficit, by focusing on the 1980s for the economies of the Asia-Pacific region. This is done by comparing the country-averages of the Asia-Pacific region by using the averages for all 'low- and middle-income countries' (LMIC) as a comparator. This allows one to establish the extent to which these economies represent an 'outlier', given their record of fiscal prudence.

The striking feature of Table 3.2 is the extent to which the economies of the Asia-Pacific region represent an outlier when judged against the chosen

Table 3.2 Growth, inflation, external indebtedness and fiscal deficit, 1980–93

Economy	Growth (GNP per capita: %) Above LIMC ave?: Yes/No	Inflation (%) Below LIMC ave?: Yes/No	NPV estimate of External Debt/ Export (%) Improvement?: Yes/No 1993 vs 1980	Fiscal deficit/ surplus(% GNP) Improvement?: Yes/No 1993 vs 1980
East Asian NIEs				
Hong Kong	yes	yes	yes	no, as at '93 slight deterioration
Singapore	yes	yes	yes	yes, surplus increased
Korea	yes	yes	yes	yes, in surplus
Taiwan	yes	yes	yes	no, as at '93 significantly deficit higher
ASEAN-4				
Indonesia	yes	yes	no, above LMIC average	yes, in surplus
Malaysia	yes	yes	yes	yes, in surplus
Philippines	no, -ve growth	yes	no, above LMIC average	no, as at '93 deficit constant
Thailand	yes	yes	yes	yes, in surplus
China	yes	yes	yes	n.a., but deficit below LMIC average

Sources: World Bank, 1995a: Table 1, Table 11, Table 23; Kaji, 1994: Table 1, Table 20
Notes: External debt ratio defined as discounted value of future debt service to exports of goods and services. Fiscal deficit pertains only to the gap between revenue and expenditure of central government only. LMIC average is 0.9% for growth, 72.8% for inflation, 127% (1980), 136.2% (1993) for external/export ratio.

comparator for the 1980–93 period. Apart from the conspicuous case of the Philippines, which has experienced negative growth (–0.6 per cent), all the economies have grown well above the LMIC average of 0.9 per cent, in most cases six times higher! Inflation has generally been of single-digit magnitudes compared with the LMIC average of 72.8 per cent.

The behaviour of external balance – as proxied by a relative measure of external indebtedness – also shows that they are below international norms. The interesting exception is Indonesia. The net present value (NPV) of external debts averaged above 190 per cent as against comparator values of 127 per cent (1980) and 136 per cent (1993). This high figure, however, does not reflect lack of control of the external deficit. Its record of macro-performance and its projected oil revenues have, so far at least, enabled it to remain credit-worthy in international capital markets. Nevertheless, Indonesia needs to remain vigilant about the medium-term behaviour of its external indebtedness.

Table 3.2 shows that fiscal deficits have in fact moved into a surplus in a large number of cases in East Asia, while in LMICS as a group, the general trend has been toward a widening fiscal deficit. Thus, the broad pattern is one where fiscal prudence is linked to superior economic performance. Nevertheless, some interesting deviations emerge. The case of the Philippines is expected, but the experience of Taiwan deserves more comment. Estimates compiled by the ADB (1994: table A23; also pp. 75–9) show that the central government's fiscal position shifted from a surplus of 1.9 per cent of GDP to a deficit of 5.8 per cent in 1993. This largely reflects the high level of government expenditure on infrastructure projects. The fact that inflation has been contained below 5 per cent clearly suggests that the government has engaged in non-inflationary financing of the deficit. While the deficit appears affordable, given the presence of net private-sector savings, Taiwan needs to be vigilant about the future behaviour of its fiscal position.

Table 3.3 seeks to shed some light on the impact of macroeconomic stability on economic growth through the investment channel for selected economies of the region – Korea, Indonesia, Thailand. The sample size is appropriate in the sense that it covers both first- and second-generation NIEs. The comparators are represented by the mean values for a group of 'intermediate' and 'bad' performers (defined in terms of per capita GNP growth rates and inflation rates for the 1970–89 period).

It is clear that the three economies had higher average investment ratio than both the 'intermediate' and 'bad' performers (27 per cent in the three Asia-Pacific economies vs 22 per cent and 20 per cent for the comparators). The difference in the efficiency of investment is even more conspicuous. However, the instability of investment as measured by the coefficient of variance is not necessarily lower in the three economies relative to the 'intermediate performers' largely because of the relatively high degree of

Table 3.3 The impact of macro-stability on growth, saving and investment performance

Economy	Growth per capita 1970–89	Investment ratio (%)	Investment efficiency	Investment instability	Saving ratio (%)
Korea	6.5	29	21	0.13	25
Indonesia	4.2	26	16	0.20	26
Thailand	4.1	22	20	0.09	22
Group ave. 'inter'	1.9	22	8	0.13	17
Group ave. 'bad'	−2.3	20	−2	0.24	16

Source: Adapted from Little et al., 1993, p. 347, table 11.1
Notes: 'inter' Group ave. = average value for six countries classified as 'intermediate' performers.
'bad' Group ave. = average value for six countries classified as 'bad' performers

volatility in the aggregate volume of investment in Indonesia. The evidence presented here is only suggestive as the average investment ratio and its efficiency is only one of a complex set of influences on the process of capital formation.

What role has the exchange rate played in macroeconomic stabilisation-cum-adjustment in the Asia-Pacific region? As noted, this is often identified as a crucial factor in influencing macroeconomic performance in the region. To start with, the notion of a 'nominal anchor' does not receive strong support as most economies of the region appear to have moved to some form of exchange rate flexibility in the 1980s and, in many cases, have been able to sustain real depreciations that aided their outward-oriented policies (Dean et al., 1995). A possible exception is Singapore, as it appears to have exchange rate targeting as official policy (Chowdhury and Islam, 1993: chapter 10; Lim et al., 1988). As will be noted later, even in such a well managed economy, exchange rate targeting did not always work smoothly.

The role that exchange rate policy has played in the macroeconomic performance of East Asia is summarised by Petrie (1993b: 14) as follows:

> Realistic exchange rates were a hallmark of East Asian macroeconomic policy. Several of miracles began with major exchange rate reforms, which included devaluations, the unification of multiple exchange rates, and commitments to keeping real exchange rates competitive. Some of the region's economies even kept exchange rates undervalued (Taiwan in the 1960s and all of the NICs in the 1980s). While these aggressive exchange rate policies were initially adopted to solve some balance of payments problems...they proved so successful in generating export growth that they became the centrepiece of East Asian policy.

Another way of establishing the effectiveness of exchange rate policies in East Asia is to relate their performance against selected comparators. Thus, the World Bank (1993a: chapter 3) focuses on real exchange rate variability in the selected economies of the region – Korea, Malaysia, Thailand – and compares them with some Latin American economies – Argentina, Mexico,

Peru – for the 1970–88 period. The difference is quite striking: real exchange rate variability was in the order of 10 per cent in the East Asian economies, but was as high as 150 per cent in the Latin American economies.

With increased globalisation and financial deregulation, the 1990s have witnessed a surge in capital flows (Spiegel, 1995). Although the East Asian countries traditionally received a large flow of direct foreign investment (DFI), the flow of short-term portfolio investment was very negligible in the 1970s and early 1980s. In almost all Asia-Pacific countries the flow of both DFI and portfolio investment has increased dramatically since the late 1980s (see Das, 1996). During 1990–94, the Asia-Pacific countries received a net capital inflow of US$ 170 billion. This represents nearly half the total inflows of capital to developing countries during the same period. What is more interesting is a sharp rise in portfolio investment from about US$2 billion in 1990 to about US$42 billion during the period 1991–94. This large surge in capital inflows presents several problems for the receiving countries.

To begin with, inflows of capital create problems for the countries following a fixed or pegged exchange rate regime. It leads to increases in domestic money supply unless sterilised. Sterilisation has its costs and limits if the financial sector is not well developed. If the sterilisation is done through open market operations, the central banks are forced to invest in low-yield foreign reserves while at the same time issuing domestic debt at high enough yields to attract commercial banks and private citizens away from private loans and investments. The differential between the domestic and foreign yields is the 'quasi-fiscal' costs which are estimated at almost one-half per cent of GDP in Latin America (Kiguel and Leiderman, 1993, quoted in Dean, 1996). Furthermore, sterilisation prevents domestic interest rates equalising with the foreign rate and thereby prolongs capital inflows. If the sterilisation is done through raising the reserve requirement, the quasi-fiscal cost is transferred to the customers of commercial banks as the spread between loan and deposit rates widens due to the fact that the reserve money does not earn interest. However, it is claimed to have the advantage that by curbing the credit-creation capacity of banks, it induces prudence.

If capital flows are not sterilised, there will be real appreciation of domestic currency via inflation as money supply increases as the central banks accumulate foreign reserves. In the flexible exchange rate system the real appreciation occurs through nominal appreciation. In either case, it has the same effect on the country's tradable sector as in the case of 'Dutch disease' syndrome. The real appreciation can pose a serious problem particularly for the liberalising countries as it effectively negates the impact of depreciation which is an important element of liberalisation programmes.

When the current account developments are driven by capital account then large capital flows can lead to an unsustainable current-account deficit. This is especially so, if the inflow is in response to a consumption boom.

To the extent the inflow is dominated by short-term portfolio investment, commonly referred to as 'hot money', it is very volatile, and the receiving country's exchange rate can potentially come under speculative attacks. Moreno (1995) has identified 126 episodes of speculative attacks on Asia-Pacific currencies during 1980–94 in the sense of pressure to either depreciate or appreciate. However, the Asia-Pacific countries successfully countered the speculative attacks on their currencies (Moreno, 1995).

Second, rapid reversals of these flows can cause domestic liquidity problems while large increases in inflows may jeopardise the safety of the banking system. Furthermore, if the government perceives that these inflows are largely temporary and reflect the private sector's optimal decision, it may avoid the adjustment process entirely.

Corbo and Hernandez (1996) reviewed the experience of Latin American and Asian countries and listed eight measures to deal with large capital inflows. They are: (a) move towards a more flexible exchange rate, (b) fiscal restraint, (c) sterilisation by open market operations, (d) sterilisation by other means (reserve requirement), (e) restrictions on capital inflows, (f) liberalising the current account, (g) selective liberalisation of the capital account, and (h) strengthening the domestic financial system.

The study highlights the fiscal restraint that accompanied other measures in Asia-Pacific countries. Fiscal restraint lowers aggregate demand and reduces the inflationary pressure. Both Corbo and Hernandez 1996 and Dean (1996) find that the sterilisation either by open market operations or by raising reserve requirements have been used widely in the Asia-Pacific region. Singapore, Malaysia, Indonesia and Thailand have also tried to sterilise via shifting government deposits (such as provident funds) from commercial banks to central banks. This, however, means that the central bank's quasi-fiscal costs are being transferred to pensioners or to the government. It can also create cash management problems for banks as was experienced in Indonesia.

Sterilisation by any means was less effective in either preventing capital flows or reducing the pressure on exchange rates. Thus, there are now moves towards greater flexibility of exchange rates. Glick *et al.* (1995) also find that greater flexibility will insulate these countries better from external shocks or inflation than the current pegging system.

DEALING WITH MACROECONOMIC IMABALANCES: SOME CASES

The impression that could be easily created by the discussion so far is that macroeconomic policy was error-free and consistently applied in East Asia. This section seeks to clarify that such a generalisation is obviously rather facile. Indeed, the thrust of recent research is not that policy mistakes were not made, but that they were identified quickly and decisive action taken with corresponding speed. The emerging conventional wisdom is that at the core of macroeconomic success in East Asia lies 'pragmatic policy-making' meaning the 'willingness to repudiate failed policies' (Leipziger and Thomas, 1993: 4). While this proposition can be illustrated relatively easily in the market-oriented economies of the Asia-Pacific region, the case of the transition economy of China is more complex and will be treated separately.

Indonesia experienced a recession in the 1980–82 period in conjunction with a real exchange rate appreciation that was fed by a classic primary commodity and oil boom. Then, in 1986 it experienced an external shock with an unanticipated decline in oil prices. Yet, at the end of the 1980s, Indonesia managed to sustain an impressive growth rate, reduced its dependence on the oil sector, and carried out an impressive array of reforms entailing the financial, trade and tax regimes within a framework of macroeconomic stability. How did Indonesia manage such an enviable outcome despite the fact that, at least to a transient degree, it appeared to be suffering from macroeconomic imbalances that can, to some extent, be related to an episodic policy failure (the real exchange rate appreciation)?

Part of the answer lies in the fact that Indonesia never really lost fiscal control. It has flexibly operated a 'balanced budget rule' since 1967 which does not allow the government to finance deficits by borrowing from the central bank. The budget is defined as revenue from foreign loans. This means that the reduction of the latter entails an inevitable fiscal contraction. Guided by this balanced budget rule, the government managed to reduce government expenditure primarily in the form of a postponement of public investment projects. In addition, as a result of various fiscal reforms that were implemented in 1983, non-oil tax revenue rose by more than 2 per cent of GDP. The 1983 and 1986 nominal devaluations (that translated into real devaluations) in conjunction with trade reforms also played a crucial role in bringing about a boom in non-oil exports. Finally, Indonesia had recourse to external finance. While this in itself was a reflection of its credit-worthiness, such access to finance helped cushion the adverse effects of the adjustment process. There also seems to be almost unanimous agreement that macroeconomic management in Indonesia has benefited from the maintenance of an open capital account. This meant that macroeconomic imbalances were quickly reflected in capital flight. This, in turn, created pressures on policy-makers to re-assert macroeconomic control. Further details on the Indonesian experience can be found in Ahmed (1993), Woo and Nasution (1989), Woo *et al.* (1994), Bhattacharya and Pangestu (1993), Thorbecke (1991).

Malaysia is another case which experienced a classic primary commodities boom, starting in 1979. This fed into a real exchange rate appreciation and was accompanied by an ambitious fiscal expansion that was partly domestically financed, but external debt played a significant role. Yet, when by 1982, the terms of trade shifted against Malaysia, the authorities did not depreciate the currency and bring expenditure in line with income. One could argue that the fiscal expansion was justified at the time because the deteriorating external situation was thought to be temporary and because of the easy availability of external finance. Nevertheless, the authorities reacted relatively quickly to the growing macroeconomic imbalance. Expenditure-switching policy in the form of devaluation was instituted in 1984 and continued until 1987. Fiscal control was regained and the degree of external indebtedness was sharply reduced – from 86.5 per cent of GNP in the peak year (1985/86) to 47.6 per cent in 1991. Thus, at the beginning of the 1990s, Malaysia was able to exhibit an enviable combination of low inflation, moderate external indebtedness, a budget surplus and sustained, export-led growth. For further details on the Malaysian experience, see Salleh and Mayanathan (1993), Demery and Demery (1991), World Bank (1993a).

Korea represents an interesting case-study in regaining macroeconomic control. The authorities began an anti-inflation programme in 1979, but it was derailed by a series of internal and external shocks: the 1979 oil price increase, the exceptionally bad harvest of 1980 and the world recession of 1982 that impeded the buoyancy of Korean exports. In 1980, Korea experienced a steep recession (–5 per cent GDP growth) – the first since the 1950s – in combination with an inflation rate of 29 per cent. Initially, the authorities tried to cope with it through expansionary fiscal and monetary policy and a devaluation of the won in 1980. By 1982, the stance was reversed and the government engaged in a series of fiscal retrenchment as well as curbs on credit expansion. This was accompanied by a wage freeze in the public sector and restrictive wage guidelines for the private sector. Inflation came down to single-digit levels by the mid-1980s, aided by an improvement in the terms of trade and recovery in the domestic production of cereals. The Korean government also followed an aggressive policy of external debt-reduction by drawing on burgeoning international reserves generated by exports to make payments ahead of schedule. The external debt–GNP ratio fell from a peak of 52.5 per cent in 1985–86 to 15 per cent by 1991. For further details on the Korean experience, see Dornbusch and Park (1987), Collins and Park (1989), Kim and Leipziger (1993).

Singapore is widely recognised as one of the most well-managed economies in the world. Yet, in 1985 it suffered a steep recession – the first in two decades. There was a real exchange rate appreciation combined with sluggish external demand. While a multiplicity of factors were responsible for this outcome, lack of policy co-ordination between exchange rate and wages policy was an important reason. It would be useful to remember at this stage that if exchange rate targeting is employed to serve as a nominal anchor, then wages policy should be used to deal with external competitiveness. The Singapore government did not observe this rule between 1979 and 1985. In 1979, a regime of 'high wages' was instituted in order to shift resources away from labour-intensive activities towards more 'high-tech', capital-intensive activities as part of the country's 'industrial restructuring programme'. There was simultaneously a nominal appreciation of the exchange rate. Thus, the real exchange rate appreciation was compounded by this confluence of the nominal rate appreciation and 'high' wages policy. This caused a deterioration of external competitiveness and, in a context of sluggish external demand, contributed to the 1985 recession. The authorities quickly abandoned the high wages policy and ensured greater co-ordination between the exchange rate and domestic wage movements. Further details on the case of Singapore can be found in Lim *et al.* (1988) and Soon and Tam (1993).

Thailand presents an interesting case. Between 1974 and 1985, the cumulative deterioration of its terms of trade stood at 36 per cent of GDP. The real resource balance during 1974–89 was 9.3 per cent of GDP. Thailand received Structural Adjustment Loans (SAL) of US$596.6 million from the IMF/World Bank. As part of SAL conditionality Thailand followed restrictionist fiscal and monetary policies. The budget deficit was brought down to 3.6 per cent of GDP during the mid-1980s and the tightening of monetary policy saw the rise in interest rates, control on credit expansion and the decline in M1 growth rate. During 1988–91 Thailand managed to change its fiscal deficit to a surplus of 4.9 per cent of GDP. The exchange rate was also devalued: 8.7 per cent in 1981 and then 17.4 per cent in 1984. Between 1980 and 1986, the baht–dollar rate depreciated by 30 per cent. As a result of these structural programmes, Thailand was able to turn its real resource balance into a surplus, and raise its GDP growth rate from less than 5 per cent in the early 1980s to around 12 per cent in the second half of the decade. According to the IMF, Thailand is 'an excellent example of successful development, combining adjustment with growth' (Robinson *et al.*, 1991). However, Thailand's real resource balance reverted to negative figures and the current-account deficit has soared to more than 5 per cent of GDP in recent years. The inflation rate is also edging up. What has gone wrong? A detailed analysis (Chowdhury and Islam, 1996) shows that the resource-switching impact of devaluation/depreciation did not work in Thailand as upward adjustments in minimum wages followed exchange rate adjustments. The nominal monthly wages in manufacturing rose by 59.3 per cent between 1983 and 1984. This is in stark contrast to what has happened in Korea. Furthermore, the fiscal deficit was contained mainly by cuts in infrastructure investment which are now causing strains in the economy. Thus, the lesson to be learned from the Thai and Korean experiences is that the adjusting countries must resist wage claims and should not choose the softer option of cuts in infrastructure investment.

China is one of the most successful 'transition economies'. A gradual, pragmatic approach to market-oriented reforms, started in 1978, has been one of the hallmarks of recent Chinese economic development. There has been a tendency, however, for the authorities to generate 'stop–go' cycles. One can detect periods of overheating and inflation in 1985–86, 1988–89 and at present (whose origins go back to 1993). It is generally acknowledged that the fundamental cause of these cycles is the insufficient development of appropriate macro-policy tools. In addition, the authorities have found it difficult to disengage from their political commitment to support ailing industries. This is reflected in a consolidated government deficit estimated to be as high as 8 per cent of GNP. Not surprisingly, this has become an important source of inflationary pressures.

Reform-minded Chinese economists have argued that old instruments – representing remnants of the planning system, such as price and investment controls – continue to be exercised, but with minimal effect. These controls, they argue, should be abandoned and much more attention given to fiscal, monetary and exchange rate policy. Others have noted that the financial sector has a tendency to lead to an overexpansion of credit and an excessive reliance of enterprises on bank credit. The central government's share in national revenue is also too low, impeding its ability to manage the economy. In response to such growing macroeconomic challenges and imbalances, the third plenum adopted far-reaching fiscal and financial-sector reforms. These include: simplification of tax structure, tax-sharing between central and provincial units, gradual development of indirect monetary instruments, separation of policy from commercial lending, development of domestic capital markets, a system of prudential regulation and supervision, and the introduction of a central bank law which specifically precludes central bank finance of government budget deficits. The announced reform of state enterprises through corporation and commercialisation should also enable the central government to reduce its political commitment to aiding ailing state enterprises. Further details on the Chinese experience can be found in World Bank (1995b) and Harrold *et al.* (1993).

CONCLUDING REMARKS

Macroeconomic stability is a key ingredient of national economic success. Recent research has revealed that a combination of fiscal control and competitive real exchange rate policy represents the hallmark of successful macroeconomic stabilisation. This is in line with the so-called 'dependent economy' model which recommends a combination of expenditure reduction (through fiscal and monetary contraction) and expenditure switching (through devaluation) to deal with macroeconomic imbalances.

Given the imperfectly developed bond and capital markets in developing economies and the fact that one cannot rely on an unlimited supply of external finance, macroeconomic stabilisation inevitably has to rely on fiscal control as a prerequisite for monetary control. Another way of instituting monetary discipline is to use the exchange rate regime as a nominal anchor, but it appears that apart from one case (Singapore), this approach has generally not been followed. The emphasis has been on timely adjustments of the nominal exchange rate in order to avoid protracted overvaluations in real terms. This conclusion is reinforced when one considers the implications for managing the macroeconomy in a context of high degree of capital mobility.

A considerable body of evidence has now accumulated that corroborates the fact that economies of the Asia-Pacific region have successfully managed to maintain macro-stability, despite a rather turbulent period of external shocks. One can generally correlate indicators of macro-policy – notably fiscal discipline and exchange rate policy – with indicators of long-run economic performance. There is also suggestive evidence that macro-stability has led to a rapid rate of capital accumulation and investment efficiency.

Such stylised evidence does not, of course, imply that macro-policies were consistently pursued. Policy mistakes were made, but they were quickly identified and corrective decisions taken with corresponding speed. A brief and selective review of the experiences of some of the economies of the region substantiate this emerging conventional wisdom. The case of China is, however, more complex. There has been a tendency in China to generate 'stop–go' cycles that is fundamentally a reflection of insufficiently developed macro-policy tools and a political commitment to supporting deficits created by ailing state enterprises. More recent developments suggest that the Chinese authorities have realised the macroeconomic challenges that they face and are in the process of implementing wide-ranging reforms. Such reforms in turn should boost the capacity of policy-makers in their quest for macro-stability.

A final point. Successful macroeconomic management in the Asia-Pacific region has benefited not only from the foresight of its policy-makers, but also from appropriate institutional arrangements. One can detect a semblance of a fiscal constitution in Indonesia, Thailand and Taiwan (before 1987), while China is currently experimenting with similar legislation. The importance of such institutional arrangements in strengthening the capacity of policy-makers to engage in appropriate management is increasingly being highlighted in the burgeoning literature on the subject.

Chapter 4

The financial system and economic development

INTRODUCTION

What role do financial systems play in the economic development of nations? Until the seminal contributions by Shaw (1973) and McKinnon (1973), there was hardly any clearly articulated position on this issue. Development economics appeared to be preoccupied with real sector issues. The correspondence between real-sector development (particularly in terms of saving, investment and their productivity) and the prevailing financial system was not analysed in any depth.

The Shaw-McKinnon contributions generated a new orthodoxy: financial 'deepening' or development is an essential ingredient of the process of capital accumulation as reflected in savings and investment ratios and their productivity. This in turn contributes to economic growth. Financial deepening is best facilitated by a competitive financial system in which interest rates are market-determined and in which there is an absence (or at least insignificance) of administratively driven selective credit allocation. The converse of this view is the hypothesis of 'financial repression': interest rates that are held below market-clearing rates and selective credit allocation that follow administrative, rather than commercial criteria. Other symptoms of financially repressed economies include: segmentation of the financial system into regulated and unregulated segments; disintermediation in the regulated segment; scarcity of saving and investment and low capital productivity. The policy message that follow from this paradigm is clear. Both financial and real-sector development require a comprehensive package of financial liberalisation that frees up interest rates to their market-clearing levels and eliminates administratively determined selective credit allocation.

The hypothesis of financial liberalisation appeared to exert quite a considerable influence on policy developments in industrialising nations. As Hanna (1994: 1) notes:

> Theories of the link between financial performance and economic growth, particularly as advanced by McKinnon (1973) and Shaw

(1973), have been the basis for a series of financial reforms around the world, most prominently in the Southern Cone of Latin America, but also in Turkey, parts of Africa and East Asia.

In the Asia-Pacific region, Korea and Taiwan appear to be among the first cases of 'high-interest policy' instituted in the mid-1960s. Certainly, in the case of Korea, interest rate reform in 1965 was adopted as a result of the recommendations by Shaw, Gurley and Patrick – see Cole and Park (1983). Indonesia built upon the experience of Korea to institute attempts to revive the financial sector in 1968, although this was subsequently reversed after the oil-price shock of 1973 (Cole and Slade, 1992). Korea, too, reversed its early efforts at interest rate reform during the 'heavy and chemical industries' (HCI) drive of the 1970s. Both these economies have subsequently renewed their quest for financial-sector reform. Taiwan was also one of the early cases of 'high-interest-rate policy', although in subsequent periods, the Taiwanese financial system evolved as a heavily regulated one. As far as the other economies of the region are concerned, Singapore and Hong Kong have long been known as international financial centres. Financial reform in Malaysia and the Philippines started in 1978 and 1980 respectively (World Bank, 1993b), while China is experimenting with this process (World Bank, 1995). Thailand has generally been noted for its modest distortions in financial markets (Agarwala, 1983; World Bank, 1989). The available data also suggest that, compared with other regions, financial repression has been moderate and that real interest rates have exhibited less variability (World Bank, 1993a).

To what extent has the financial liberalisation hypothesis been vindicated by the experience of these economies? What are the lessons of experience? These issues form the substance of this chapter.

The enthusiasm that greeted the financial liberalisation hypothesis has turned out to be overly optimistic and somewhat naive. The empirical foundation of the Shaw–McKinnon paradigm appears less robust than was anticipated – for example, the evidence on the interest-rate–savings link is quite ambivalent. It now appears that too much attention was given to the allocative aspects of the financial system and too little to prudential, organisational and protective regulation – an issue of central significance when one takes account of market failures that characterise financial systems (Stiglitz, 1989). Furthermore, the disastrous results of financial reform in the 1970s in the Southern Cone countries highlighted the need to avoid severe macro-imbalances as a precondition for realising the beneficial effects of financial liberalisation and to pay more careful attention to the sequencing of reforms – see Edwards (1984) for a review. Advocates of the early version of the financial liberalisation hypothesis have themselves modified their position and have lent support to a more nuanced version of this view – see McKinnon (1982, 1984, 1988).

One can also detect a trend in the recent literature to question the analytical foundations of the financial liberalisation hypothesis by arguing that what is apparently perceived to be financial repression is really a case of efficient internal capital markets (Lee, 1992). Variants of this argument can be found in Wade (1988) and Amsden (1989). The Korean experience of the 1970s and that of Japan in the early phase of its industrialisation are often marshalled as evidence in favour of this intriguing view. The present chapter focuses on this debate by offering a critical evaluation of the 'internal capital market hypothesis' and its variants.

Finally, the early writers on the role of finance did not pay much attention to the different components of the financial system, in particular the distinction between short-term money-market instruments and other long-term debt instruments. The chapter notes recent developments in this area by drawing on the work of Cole *et al.* (1995).

FINANCIAL LIBERALISATION: THE TRADITIONAL VIEW

It would be useful at this juncture to re-visit the Shaw–McKinnon paradigm. The purpose is to provide a fuller statement of this well-known view of the role of finance in economic development.

If one adopts a historical perspective on the evolution of financial regulation, as Long and Vittas (1992: 45–6) do, then it is understandable why financial repression in the 1950s and 1960s became the norm rather than the exception. The newly independent countries of Asia and Africa inherited a financial system which was dominated by foreign-owned banks with a concentration of branch networks in major metropolitan areas. Such banks specialised primarily in short-term finance and much of it went to foreign-owned firms. In Latin America and southern Europe, foreign ownership was less conspicuous, but the financial system was geared towards short-term finance.

The governments of the developing nations decided that sweeping changes in financial practices were necessary to re-orient the extant system as a tool of development policy. Thus, nationalisation of major commercial banks in Africa and South Asia became a common practice. Specialised industrial and agricultural banks were set up under public control; financial institutions were directed to lend to selected industries under preferential terms; interest rates were usually held below inflation rates. As Long and Vittas (1992: 45) observe: 'Given the financial systems then in place, and the models of development prevailing in the 1960s, the approach taken was quite understandable.'

It is in such a context that the documentation of the deleterious effects of financial repression by McKinnon and others appeared so novel and revolutionary. The consequences of financial repression on saving and investment are well known: the flow of saving falls when the real return on deposits declines; the portfolio of investment projects is dominated by low-risk/low-productivity ventures, because banks try to minimise risks by selecting only safe and secure projects. In sum, both the volume and the productivity of capital formation are adversely affected.

Financial repression also causes segmentation of credit markets. Firms that do not have preferential access to bank credit are then forced to resort to informal sources of finance. Thus, an unregulated or curb market develops. To the extent that such markets cannot realise the benefits of financial intermediation, the interest rates prevailing in the informal segment may well be excessive in real terms.

The model of financial repression sketched above lends itself to a simple, seductive policy proposal: liberalise domestic financial markets through interest rate reform and elimination of selective credit allocation. The predicted outcomes include financial deepening and an enhanced degree of capital formation. How robust, in both empirical and analytical terms, is this basic tenet of financial liberalisation? This is the subject of the subsequent sections.

FINANCIAL LIBERALISATION: SOME COMPLICATIONS

Cottani and Cavallo (1993: 48) have noted that the '1970s literature on financial repression and liberalisation emphasised certain aspects of the problem while ignoring others'. This has understandably created some complications for the naive version of the financial liberalisation hypothesis. The purpose of this section is to highlight these complications, starting with some basic points of clarification.

The argument that financial development promotes real-sector development assumes a unidirectional causality: the former causes the latter. As Patrick (1966) noted nearly three decades ago, causality runs both ways. Economic growth creates demands for financial services (so-called 'demand-following' expansion of the financial system); economic growth is also preceded by financial development (so-called 'supply-leading' evolution of the financial system). Disentangling this two-way causality is not an easy task, although Jung's (1986) analysis of fifty-six countries (which include some of the Asia-Pacific economies) suggests that causality changes over the course of economic development. In other words, in the initial stages of development, supply-leading forces are dominant, while in later stages demand-following forces are at work. What is the relevance of this finding for the Shaw–McKinnon hypothesis? One possible interpretation is that it is supportive of the paradigm in the sense that the benefits of financial liberalisation accrue most at the early stages of development, while progressive affluence provides a built-in mechanism for the evolution of the financial system.

A central element of the financial liberalisation hypothesis – the saving–interest-rate link has not received robust empirical support. Giovannini's

(1985) study that pools time-series and cross-section data for eighteen developing countries, including some of the Asia-Pacific economies, finds little support for the proposition that the elasticity of saving with respect to the real interest rate is high. This conclusion is similar in spirit to the ones reached by Leff and Sato (1980), Fry (1984, 1985), Hanna (1994), de Melo and Tybout (1986) and Barandiaran (1987). Not surprisingly, the World Bank (1989: 27), in a major review of the role of finance in economic development concludes: 'whether financial variables affect the saving rate is still an open question...'.

In retrospect, the weak (and even non-existent) support for the interest-rate–saving link is understandable. Basic theory suggests that the ambiguity in the relationship between real interest rate and saving can be analysed by decomposing the interest rate effect into income and substitution effects. While an increase in real interest rate encourages savings through the substitution effect (i.e. savers substitute present consumption with future consumption), it discourages savings through the income effect (i.e. as savers become better off with the rise in their interest income, they tend to spend more). Thus, substitution and income effects work in opposite directions and the savings rate responds positively to a rise in real interest rates, only if the former outweighs the latter.

One should also distinguish between the 'composition' and 'volume' effects on saving of interest rate reform. As Schmidt-Hebbel and Webb (1992) note, changes in real interest rates can cause a change in the composition of assets – a shift into financial assets and out of physical assets – without affecting the overall volume of private saving. Given these considerations, one can appreciate the following remarks by Cottani and Cavallo (1993: 45): 'Although those countries that have liberalised have witnessed a rapid re-orientation of savings...to the deregulated sector, the effect on total saving has been less noticeable.'

A variation of the above argument is the so-called 'Cavallo effect' (Cavallo, 1977). The diversion of funds from the informal market as a result of financial liberalisation will reduce the supply of loanable funds as bank deposits require reserves. As a result, there will be a credit squeeze and a rise in working capital cost. If one assumes that firms in developing countries depend on borrowing for their working capital, one could argue the case that financial liberalisation will have recessionary consequences (Bruno, 1979; Taylor, 1983). The validity of this argument hinges on the substitutability between time deposits and informal market loans. In other words, there will be a large portfolio shift from the informal to the formal market following the rise in real deposit rates if time deposits and informal loans are close substitutes.

It must be emphasised that the real interest rate is one of many variables that affect saving behaviour. Fry (1991), for example, identifies several variables, apart from the real interest rate, that influence national saving ratios of industrialising Asian economies: the government's fiscal position (improvements in the fiscal deficit improve national saving ratios); external indebtedness (high external indebtedness reduces national saving ratios); inflation rates (high inflation is inimical to high saving); population dependency ratios (increases in such ratios decrease national saving ratios). Other factors that have been known to influence saving behaviour include public saving schemes and the expansion of banking in rural areas (James et al., 1989: chapter 3). The implication that follows from this discussion is that a focus on interest rate policy alone without regard to other supporting variables is rather partial and misleading. One also appreciates why, in the presence of a multiplicity of variables, the explanatory significance of the real interest rate in affecting saving behaviour in developing countries has generally been weak in econometric studies.

Shaw (1973) has made the important point that 'financial repression is part of a package'. Such a package entails distortions in foreign exchange markets, in the trade regime, in labour and product markets in general, and macroeconomic instability. This observation has an important implication that was not sufficiently emphasised by the early writers on financial repression. The removal of distortions in the financial system without corresponding reform of distortions in other markets and the restoration of macroeconomic stability is a ratification of the classic 'theory of the second best': the removal of one source of distortion while leaving others intact does not necessarily constitute a welfare-improving move. This issue will be re-visited at a later stage.

The naive version of the financial liberalisation hypothesis generally abstracts from problems of market failure that could afflict financial systems. One now has a clearer understanding of the implications of market failure. Such failure stems from a number of sources, such as externalities, the exercise of monopoly power by dominant banks, and information asymmetries between borrowers and lenders (Kay and Vickers, 1988). Examples of externalities include the risk of systematic failure (that is, the notion that bank failures may be correlated, with actual or threatened failure in one case raising the risk of failure of another) and the so-called 'infection effect' (lowering of product and price standards through excessive competition). Concern has also been expressed that financial liberalisation could unleash dominant firms that could exercise monopoly power (through excessive price–cost margins and erection of entry barriers) to the detriment of dynamic and static efficiency – see Vittas (1992a) for a fuller exposition of these ideas.

Stiglitz (1989) has emphasised the central role that information asymmetries play in the market failure of financial systems. In essence, the argument is that banks do not have perfect information about the credit-worthiness of borrowers. In such a context moral hazard and adverse selection problems could emerge: borrowers have an incentive to assume more risky projects when the cost of credit increases; the banks' reliable clients may be replaced by less solvent debtors because the former are indistinguishable from the latter. In such a context, interest rate 'overshooting' could occur (that is, rising to excessive levels to cover default risk), thus crowding out low-risk projects with high, ex ante social rates of return. It is plausible that in the early stages of development information asymmetries are more acute, partly because of the lack of institutions that collect and disseminate credit information.

Macroeconomic instability could exacerbate problems of moral hazard, as a key advocate of financial liberalisation, McKinnon (1984) has recognised. This consideration also represents a sophisticated variant of the fallacy of the second best alluded to at a previous juncture. Macroeconomic instability exacerbates the moral hazard problem because of the risk of systematic failure. This makes it difficult for the monetary authorities to sanction the imprudence of a particular bank, thus creating incentives for interest rate 'overshooting'. In a significant departure from his original position, McKinnon (1988) has suggested the need to impose controls on interest rates to cope with cases of moral hazard and argues that the failure of the authorities to recognise the problem of interest rate 'overshooting' was partially responsible for the financial collapse that characterised the Southern Cone countries in the 1970s.

In another attempt to provide a more nuanced version of the original financial liberalisation hypothesis, McKinnon (1982) has argued the need to pay attention to the sequencing of reforms. This is a significant departure from the 'big bang' approach advocated by Shaw (1973), that is, the notion that all microeconomic reforms should be attempted simultaneously. The revisionist view seems to be that the deregulation of the financial system should follow a sequential path – see Edwards (1984). Reform should start with the trade and exchange rate regime, followed by financial-sector reform. Once domestic financial liberalisation is complete, liberalisation of the capital account can be implemented. The World Bank (1989: 127–8) has re-affirmed this dogma by observing that 'until [domestic financial] reforms are well underway, it will probably be necessary to maintain controls on the movement of [foreign] capital'.

The logic of the sequencing approach is driven by the concern that a country undergoing domestic financial liberalisation could be vulnerable to destabilising capital flows, a concern that grew out of the experience (once again!) of the Southern Cone countries. It is not clear how relevant the sequencing approach is today, given that the days of easy and cheap external credit are over. One can also identify at least one case (Indonesia) where this sequencing was not followed without any deleterious effects (Cole and Slade, 1992).

The discussion so far has raised a number of complications that afflict the naive version of the financial liberalisation hypothesis. Its advocates have been acutely aware of some of these complications and have sought to revamp the basic theory to fit with the changing context of developing economies. Despite these modifications, there are those who believe that, under conditions of market failure, financial liberalisation is an untenable proposition. More importantly, what is construed as financial repression can in fact be re-interpreted as a mechanism that is able to resolve market failure and thus facilitate growth. This topic forms the substance of the subsequent section.

CAN FINANCIAL REPRESSION BE GOOD FOR GROWTH?

Can a repressed financial system actually facilitate rapid economic growth? Lee (1992) provides the most comprehensive rationale in favour of this hypothesis. Variants can be found in Wade (1988) and Amsden (1989, 1991) – see also Amsden and Euh (1993). In developing this argument, it would be useful to start with the distinction that Zysman (1983) makes between a capital-market-based and credit-based financial system. In a capital-market-based financial system, securities (stocks and bonds) are the main sources of long-term business finance. Borrowers can choose from a broad spectrum of capital-and money-market instruments offered competitively through a large number of specialised financial institutions.

In a credit-based system, the capital market is weak and firms rely heavily on credit to finance investment. This makes them heavily dependent on banks – to the extent that banks are the main suppliers of credit. However, if banks are themselves dependent on the government, then firms become heavily dependent on the government. One thus has a case of a state-controlled, credit-based financial system. In such an institutional environment, financial repression (in the form of control of credit allocation by the government) becomes the norm, and firms exhibit high debt–equity ratios.

Wade (1988: 133) maintains that Korea and Taiwan can be characterised as exhibiting the classic features of government-dominated credit-based systems. During the 1970s, debt–equity ratios were 300–400 per cent in Korea and 100–200 per cent in Taiwan. The corresponding figures in such Latin American countries as Brazil and Mexico were 100–120 per cent. In the industrialised countries, the figures were below 100 per cent. Furthermore, in Taiwan, virtually the entire banking system has, until very recently, been government-owned. In Korea the same was true until 1980–83 and even after the financial deregulation of the mid-1980s, the government exercises de facto control of the banking system through personnel policies, appointment of senior managers, range of services and the like.

There are, according to the advocates of this view, distinct advantages that flow from the operation of a state-dominated, credit-based system. Wade (1988: 134), for example, identifies the following alleged advantages. First, 'a credit-based system permits faster investment in developing country conditions than would be possible if investment depended on the growth of firms' own profits or on the inevitably slow development of securities market'. More importantly, productive investment is less affected by speculative stock market booms and busts.

Second, a credit-based system tends to avoid the bias towards short-term profitability that often appears to be associated with a stock market system. This stems from the argument that lenders of long-term finance are interested in the ability of borrowers to repay the loans over the long-term. Hence, long-term performance becomes the dominant consideration entailing a focus on such issues as the ability of organisations to develop new products, cost-competitiveness and so on. These therefore become the criteria that managers are concerned with rather than short-run performance in the stock market.

Finally, a state-dominated financial system provides the government with the necessary political clout to implement its industrial strategy. As Wade (1988: 134) puts it: 'firms are dissuaded from opposing the government by knowledge that opponents may find credit difficult to obtain'.

The notion that a credit-based financial system can be seen as a political device to assist governments in the implementation of industrial strategy is the crux of Amsden's (1989, 1991) argument that financial repression is an essential feature of 'late industrialisation' (of which Korea and Taiwan are classic examples). In her model of late industrialisation, governments deliberately use selective credit allocation in order to speed up the process of industrialisation. However, industrialising nations run the risk that costs of financial repression can outweigh its alleged benefits in the sense that it can provoke a subsidy mentality and induce wasteful rent-seeking behaviour. Yet, governments in late industrialisation can circumvent this difficulty by ensuring that abuse of preferential credit allocation is minimised through the imposition of strict performance standards. If such standards are based on good approximations of exante social rates of return, then politically determined credit allocation will lead to socially profitable investments in 'desirable' industries and sectors. Hence, financial repression will lead to rapid growth.

A more sophisticated argument in favour of financial repression stems from transactions cost economics which in turn relies heavily on the notion of information asymmetries. This view is closely associated with the work of Lee (1992) and can be characterised as the 'internal capital market hypothesis'.

As noted at a previous juncture, when information asymmetries between borrowers and lenders are high and pervasive, they can be a potent source of market failure. Under such circumstances, reliance on the 'internal capital market' (reliance on finance generated through retained earnings or out of depreciation charges) can resolve market failure by reducing or eliminating the incidence of information asymmetries.

Lee (1992) has tried to adapt this argument to the East Asian case by suggesting that a state-dominated credit-based system operates as a de facto internal capital market. The state cultivates a long-term and close relationship with borrowing firms. The atmosphere of trust and co-operation created as a result of this close relationship allows 'lender monitoring' to be carried out effectively and efficiently. The outcome is that information asymmetries (and transactions costs) are minimised. Hence, what is apparently considered a phenomenon of financial repression is in effect a de facto internal capital market that is more efficient than private capital markets – an interpretation that is endorsed by Dalla and Khatkhate (1995) in their evaluation of Korean financial reforms in the 1980s and 1990s.

While the above arguments are suggestive and interesting, one can construct cogent counter-arguments. First, one should be careful not to confuse a credit-based system with a state- controlled credit-based system. Financial repression is a necessary feature of the latter, not the former. More importantly, the major advantages of a credit-based system as identified by Wade do not require the existence of state control (and hence financial repression). The only way in which financial repression can contribute to economic growth in this framework is to presuppose that a strong-willed government has the capacity to overcome the inadequacies of private capital markets without the corresponding risk of government failure.

The hypothesis of the superiority of 'lender monitoring' in a state-controlled financial system is also questionable when one takes account of the interactions between formal and informal credit markets. This point can be developed using an argument expounded by Cole and Patrick (1986). When formal financial institutions are regulated, informal credit markets expand. Such markets provide funds to those who cannot obtain credit from formal sources. In addition, privileged borrowers in regulated markets have an incentive to re-lend to users in unregulated markets (and hence profit from arbitrage). The net outcome is that informal credit markets act as a channel for diverting official (regulated) credit to more profitable investment opportunities, thus invalidating the notion that the state can effectively monitor the behaviour of borrowers. Some evidence can be offered to substantiate these arguments by focusing on the Korean experience. Thus, in 1972, approximately 50 per cent of commercial firms in Korea financed their investment needs through the informal credit market. In addition, credit diversion was quite extensive (Cole and Patrick, 1986).

A final point. The notion that financial repression facilitates economic growth can be seen as a reaction to the popular perception that financial liberalisation is synonymous with a *laissez-faire* approach. However, current developments in the literature suggest that the choice is not between a *laissez-faire* approach and a *dirigiste* system. The focus is now on a competitive financial sector within an appropriate regulatory framework – an issue that is expanded in the following section.

MANAGING THE FINANCIAL SYSTEM DURING THE PROCESS OF DEVELOPMENT: TOWARDS AN APPROPRIATE REGULATORY FRAMEWORK

Both the naive version of the financial liberalisation hypothesis and strident advocates of (East Asian-style) financial repression pay insufficient attention to the fact that the resolution of market failure that afflicts financial systems needs an appropriate regulatory framework. An internal capital market – or, more generally, financial repression – can, in theory, resolve the problem of market failure, but the emerging conventional wisdom is that prudential and other regulations are essential for a stable, efficient and fair financial system. Table 4.1 – which draws heavily on Vittas (1992c) – provides a simple framework that allows one to locate the importance of prudential and related regulations in the efficient management of financial systems.

Although Table 4.1 has set up the different types of financial regulation as seemingly mutually exclusive categories, in reality the different regulations

Table 4.1 Types of financial regulation – objectives and key policy instruments

Type of regulation	Objectives	Examples of key policy instruments
Macroeconomic	To maintain control over aggregate economic activity and maintain external and internal balance	Reserve requirements, direct credit and deposit ceilings, interest rate controls, restrictions on foreign capital
Allocative	To influence the allocation of financial resources in favour of priority activities	Selective credit allocation, compulsory investment requirements, preferential interest rates
Structural	To control the possible abuse of monopoly power by dominant firms	Entry and merger controls, geographic and functional restrictions
Prudential	To preserve the safety and soundness of individual financial institutions and sustain public confidence in systemic stability	Authorisation criteria, minimum capital requirements, limits on the concentration of risks, reporting requirements
Organisational	To ensure smooth functioning and integrity of financial markets and information exchanges	Disclosure of market information, minimum technical standards, rule of market-making and participation
Protective	To provide protection to users of financial services, especially consumers and non-professional investors	Information disclosure to consumers, compensation funds, ombudsmen to investigate and resolve disputes

Source: Adapted from Vittas, 1992c: 63

have effects that cut across their designated domains. Thus, global credit controls that stem from macroeconomic objectives also fulfil a prudential function to the extent that they restrain banks from imprudent expansion of credit. Despite this caveat, it would be fair to maintain that the central purpose of prudential and organisational regulation is to deal with market failure associated with information asymmetries, while protective regulation focuses on the need to design a 'fair' financial system that protects the interests of users of financial services. The table also makes it clear that the liberalisation/repression debate has focused primarily on the allocative aspects of the financial system. This in turn reflects the stylised fact that in developing countries prudential, organisational and protective regulations were hardly considered largely because information problems were given insufficient attention. However, this is beginning to change. As Vittas (1992c: 79) puts it:

> In both developed and developing countries financial regulation is now moving toward the elimination or substantial reduction of macroeconomic, allocative, and structural controls and toward the adoption and substantial strengthening of prudential, organisational and protective controls.

FINANCIAL SYSTEMS AND ECONOMIC DEVELOPMENT: SOME EVIDENCE FROM THE ASIA-PACIFIC REGION

This section attempts to establish some broad empirical regularities by focusing on the relationship between the interest rate regime, financial deepening and real sector developments (as proxied by saving ratios and the efficiency of investment) in the Asia-Pacific economies. The section also briefly deals with the development of the short-term money market in East Asia – a component of the financial system that has generally been neglected in previous studies.

Good reviews of the process of financial deepening in East Asia can be found in Arndt (1983), Cole and Patrick (1986), Cole (1988). Researchers have generally relied on the ratio of broad money (M2) to gross domestic product (GDP) as a general measure of financial deepending or development for cross-country analysis. M2 is typically defined to include currency in circulation plus demand, time and savings deposits. Table 4.2 provides a rough indication of financial deepening (M2/GDP) and its relationship to the interest rate regime (as a crude proxy for the existence or absence of financial repression) in selected economies of the Asia-Pacific region.

As can be seen in Table 4.2, there is evidence of substantial financial deepening in the Asia-Pacific economies between 1971–90. The Philippines and China are not included in the table as comparable data could not be compiled for the relevant period. Nevertheless, some illustrative information may be provided. The M2/GDP ratio increased moderately, from 26 per cent in 1980 to 38 per cent in 1993 in the Philippines, but rose rather sharply in China, from 34 per cent to 80 per cent over the same period (World Bank, 1995a: World Development Indicators, table 12).

Table 4.2 Financial deepening (M2/GDP:%) and the interest rate regime in selected Asia-Pacific economies, 1971–80 vs 1980–90

Economy	M2/GDP (%) 1971–80	M2/GDP (%) 1981–90	Interest rate regime (real rate: +ve/−ve)
Hong Kong	85.7	155.0	−ve (1973–91)
Korea	33.7	36.8	+ve (1971–90), but protracted period (1973–79, 81–83) when −ve
Singapore	61.7	78.8	+ve (1977–91)
Taiwan	58.1	110.2	+ve (1974–91)
Indonesia	16.1	24.3	+ve (1970–90), but some period (1973–76) when −ve
Malaysia	44.2	88.2	+ve (1976–91)
Thailand	35.8	57.6	+ve (1977–90)

Sources: M2/GDP ratios from Chowdhury and Islam, 1993, table 8.2, p. 133. Interest rate regimes from World Bank, 1993a: chapter 5; Cole and Slade, 1992; Fry, 1985.

The empirical pattern depicted in Table 4.2 tends to suggest some relationship between the nature of the interest rate regime and the process of financial development in line with the Shaw–McKinnon hypothesis. In general, the sample of economies covered in the table operated an interest rate regime where real interest rates were held above the relevant inflation rate. In cases where there were distinct periods of financial repression (as in Korea and Indonesia), financial deepening appeared to languish. The case of Korea is particularly conspicuous in having a 'shallow' financial system relative to the other NIEs. There was a heavy reliance on non-bank financial intermediaries during the period of financial repression.

It must be emphasised that the nexus between financial deepening and the interest rate regime is only suggestive. As Gurley (1967) established many years ago, there is a systematic positive correlation between M2/GDP and per capita income, reflecting so-called demand-led expansion of the financial system. Hence, financial deepening in the Asia-Pacific region reflects demand-led expansion through economic growth independently of any effect imparted by a given interest rate regime. This is best seen in a comparison of the experiences of China and the Philippines. Financial development in China has apparently reached a level comparable to Singapore in 1990, while in the Philippines the degree of financial development has been modest. Per capita income growth in the latter has been negative in the 1980s, while China has been one of the fastest growing economies in the world over the last decade.

One must also highlight the fact that Hong Kong appears to be an 'outlier' in the sample of countries represented in Table 4.2. Thus, despite the fact that Hong Kong is the only country in the sample where the real interest rate has been negative over the relevant period, its degree of financial deepening appears to be the highest. To some extent, the case of Hong Kong represents its particular institutional characteristics as an off-shore financial centre. As Cole (1988: 28) notes, the exceptionally high M2/GDP ratio in Hong Kong may well reflect the fact that it does not distin-guish between local residents' and non-residents' bank deposits, a practice that does not prevail in Singapore – a competing offshore financial centre in the region. The fact that foreigners are (or were) prepared to hold bank deposits in Hong Kong despite an unfavourable interest rate regime pre-sumably implies the presence of compensating factors – better facilities and services, perception of a sound, secure and confidential financial transac-tions system, etc.

Table 4.3 tries to trace some empirical regularities between the interest rate regime, the incidence of financial-sector reform and real-sector devel-opments. Proxies used for the real-sector variables entail saving and ratios as well as a crude measure of investment efficiency. The latter is best captured by the incremental capital–output ratio, but in its absence one can generate a surrogate measure that entails adjusting the growth of per capita output by the average investment ratio – a measure that is sometimes referred to as the 'apparent productivity of investment' (see chapter 3). Table 4.3 suppresses

Table 4.3 Interest rate regime, incidence of financial reform and the behaviour of saving and investment efficiency: 1971–80 (period 1) vs 1981–1990 (period 2)

Economy	Increase in saving ratio: Yes/No (period 1 vs period 2)	Increase in investment efficiency: Yes/No (period 1 vs period 2)	Interest rate regime (real rate: +ve/–ve for relevant period	Financial reform initiated: Yes/No/ Not applicable
Hong Kong	Yes	No	–ve	Not applicable
Korea	Yes	No	+ve, with periods when –ve	Yes
Singapore	Yes	No	+ve	Not applicable
Taiwan	Yes	Yes	+ve	Yes
China	No	Yes	+ve in recent years	Yes, but of very recent origin ('94–'95)
Indonesia	Yes	No	+ve, but distinct subperiod when –ve	
Malaysia	Yes	No	+ve	Yes
Philippines	No	No	+ve, but significant volatility	Yes

Sources: Saving and investment calculated from data provided in World Bank, 1995a; ADB, 1994. For sources on interest rate regime and financial sector reform, see Table 4.2 and text.

precise numerical details in favour of ordinal magnitudes as a means of exploring the extent to which the selected real-sector variables shift between two sub-periods (1971–80, 1981–90) given the prevailing interest rate regime and the incidence of financial-sector reform.

As noted, most of the major financial reforms in the Asia-Pacific region started at the end of the 1970s. Hence, Table 4.3 considers movements in real-sector variables in the 1980s relative to the 1970s. The information provided in the table does allow one to shed some light on the central proposition of the basic model of financial liberalisation that one would expect a systematic relationship between saving, investment efficiency and the financial regime – with reform in the regime leading, after some lags, to improvements in capital formation. In most cases, saving ratios shift in the expected direction.

What the table does not support is the notion that investment efficiency would improve with the onset of financial reform. In the majority of cases, the 'apparent productivity of investment' actually declined, despite nearly a decade of financial reforms. Such a finding is inconsistent with Fry's (1991) conclusion based on a cross-country comparison of Asian economies that investment efficiency is positively correlated with financial liberalisation.

As noted at a previous juncture, there are a host of factors that influence the process of capital formation in developing economies. In fact, econometric studies typically find that non-financial variables play a more important role than financial variables in influencing saving behaviour. This pattern is replicated in the case of the Asia-Pacific region. Fry (1984) concludes that the expansion of bank branches in rural areas played a more important role than interest rates in raising national saving rates in Taiwan and Korea. Scitovsky (1985) cites low population growth rates, the inadequacy of social security benefits, the limited availability of consumer credit and mortgage loans, the high proportion of individual proprietorship and the existence of a bonus component in the compensation system as central variables influencing saving rates in the NIEs. Other observers have noted the existence of compulsory savings scheme in Singapore and Malaysia as exerting a favourable influence on domestic resource mobilisation (World Bank, 1993a: chapter 5).

A previous chapter (chapter 3) has noted how the degree of macroeconomic stability, particularly in the form of fiscal prudence, can have salutary effects on domestic saving and investment ratios, including efficient utilisation of the capital stock. The validity of this view in the case of the Asia-Pacific economies is supported by the stylised fact that fiscal deficits have been contained and, in many cases, turned into a surplus in the various economies of the region – see chapter 3 for further details. An important implication follows from this observation. Financial-sector reform without a corresponding degree of macroeconomic stability is likely to be self-defeating. On the other hand, the deleterious effects of (mild) financial repression can be at least partly offset by stable macroeconomic policies.

MONEY MARKETS AS DISTINCT COMPONENTS OF THE FINANCIAL SYSTEM IN THE ASIA-PACIFIC REGION: ISSUES AND EVIDENCE

Money markets – meaning transactions primarily in assets and debt instruments with less than one year's maturity generated by public, non-public, bank and non-bank entities – have been ignored in previous studies. This is conspicuous in the seminal contributions of Shaw (1973) and McKinnon (1973) which focused on the formal banking system, but is also evident in such studies as Fry (1988), Drake (1980), Coats and Khatkhate (1980) and the World Bank (1989). However, this is beginning to change with the emergence of such contributions as Emery (1991) and Cole *et al*. (1995). The latter, which forms the basis of this section, focuses on Japan, Hong Kong, Singapore, Indonesia, Malaysia and the Philippines.

Why should one be concerned with money markets as distinct components of the financial system? As Cole *et al*. (1995: 10) observe, this stems from some important functions of money market instruments. To start with, government or central bank instruments (such as bonds and bills) serve as tools of monetary policy. Second, interest rates on money market instruments serve as a reference rate for the rest of the financial system. Third, money market instruments facilitate liquidity management by households and firms. Finally, they facilitate long-term lending.

Trends in the 1980s suggest that private money markets grew in tandem with the rest of the financial system in Hong Kong, Singapore and Malaysia. Laggards in the sample include Korea, Indonesia and the Philippines. The nature of government policy played a key role in influencing these different patterns of growth. Singapore and Malaysia represent cases of a broad and continuous commitment to the growth of money markets. Korea represents a story of neglect (induced by its legacy of financial repression in the 1970s). The sluggish development of private money markets in Indonesia bears the imprint of erratic, stop–go policies. Finally, the Philippines, where the private domestic money markets/GDP ratio actually fell between 1980 and 1988, is conspicuous for a confused approach that stemmed from basic tension between the need to relax financial controls and the historical legacy of a *dirigiste* regime.

The development of a market for government instruments (such as bonds and bills) can facilitate the operation of monetary policy. Indeed, the general perception is that the lack of such a market means that monetary policy often has to depend on quantitative macroeconomic controls, such as direct controls on domestic credit expansion. Such direct controls can in turn inhibit the degree of competition in the financial system. A related proposition is that fiscal deficits create enormous pressures on governments of industrialising nations to monetise such deficits because of the non-existent or inadequate nature of the bond market. What is the status of the market for government instruments in the Asia-Pacific region? With the possible exception of Malaysia, government policy in the 1980s seems to have inhibited the development of a short-term government securities market from serving the functions that they perform in developed countries. This partly reflects a combination of institutional arrangements (prohibition of debt-financing in Indonesia), fiscal conservatism (reflected in a reluctance to borrow to finance debts as in Hong Kong, or a lack of need to borrow, as in Singapore), and failure to use competitive pricing for government debt instruments (as in Korea).

In sum, the development of short-term money market instruments has not been particularly buoyant in many economies of the Asia-Pacific region – although there are some notable exceptions. Economic growth alone cannot expect to tackle this problem. Appropriate government policy is required for this purpose. Competitive and healthy money markets should be seen as part of the broader agenda of developing a stable and sound financial system.

TOWARDS AN APPROPRIATE REGULATORY FRAMEWORK FOR MANAGING THE FINANCIAL SYSTEM IN ASIA-PACIFIC ECONOMIES: SOME CONCLUDING REMARKS

This chapter has tried to argue that the key challenge facing developing economies is to nurture an appropriate regulatory framework for managing the financial system. In extending this conclusion to the specific case of the Asia-Pacific economies, it would be useful to set the context by summarising the core issues raised so far.

The starting point in any discussion of financial systems in industrialising economies is the notion that removal of policy-induced distortions in financial markets will generate sustained real effects by enhancing the national saving rate and improving investment efficiency. The core ideas were developed by Shaw and McKinnon and appeared both radical and refreshing in an intellectual environment when *dirigisme* in development economics was still fashionable. In retrospect, the 'first-generation' version of the financial liberalisation hypothesis appeared somewhat naive. Critics were able to point out that the interest-rate–saving link – a key element of the Shaw–McKinnon framework – lacked a robust empirical and analytical foundation. A crucial issue – market failure – was also ignored. Some have gone even further and argued that financial repression can actually be seen as a mechanism for facilitating growth, an argument that can be rationalised by appealing to information asymmetries that in turn sow the seeds of market failure.

The chapter has tried to interpret the experience with the operation of the financial regime in the Asia-Pacific economies in light of these cross-currents in the literature. Although some of the economies in the region –

Korea, Taiwan, Indonesia – experimented with a 'high-interest-rate policy' in the mid-to-late 1960s, these experiments were subsequently reversed. Large-scale, systematic changes in the interest rate regime and credit allocation policies really started in earnest towards the end of the 1970s. Thus, the Asia-Pacific economies had more than ten years of experience with financial-sector reforms. In general, interest rates have been held above the inflation rate and the degree of volatility in real rates has been lower than in other regions. Deviations from the pattern of positive real interest rates include Hong Kong, Korea (in the 1970s) and Indonesia (in the mid-1970s).

The broad evidence suggests quite impressive financial deepening in the region, and in cases where it did not occur to the expected degree, such as Korea, one can plausibly blame it on the interest rate regime. However, one cannot discount the simultaneous occurrence of demand-led expansion of the financial system that stems from the growth in per capita income. An attempt to provide a rough indication of the relationship between saving, investment efficiency and the financial regime in the Asia-Pacific economies produced mixed results. Saving ratios appeared to move in the predicted direction, but no systematic correlation emerged between investment efficiency and the incidence of financial-sector reforms. Even in the case of saving ratios, one cannot ignore the significance of a host of other variables, such as macroeconomic stability, compulsory saving schemes and so forth.

The early writers on the financial system in developing economies also ignored the money market, particularly in terms of transactions in short-term debt instruments generated by public, non-public, bank and non-bank entities. Money markets fulfil some important functions – such as facilitating the development of indirect tools of aggregate demand management – and hence their growth has to be seen as part of the broader agenda of nurturing a healthy financial system. One can detect buoyant growth of private money-market instruments in Hong Kong, Singapore and Malaysia, but not elsewhere. The development of a market for short-term government securities too has been neglected, although there are some notable exceptions. In both cases, the outcomes reflect the nature of government policy.

What can one say about the future evolution of financial systems in the Asia-Pacific economies and what can one say about the normative criteria for managing such systems? As noted, the economies of the region have, in general, been able to cope with the transition to a policy regime where interest rate determination and credit allocation policies follow market-driven, rather than administrative, criteria. Even Korea, the most controversial case of heavy intervention in financial markets, has virtually moved away from such an approach. Seen from this perspective, the financial liberalisation-repression debate seems to have outgrown its topicality. Recent concerns with information asymmetries and moral hazard problems suggest that the choice is not between a *laissez-faire* approach and financial *dirigisme* but the development of an efficient, sound and fair system within a regulatory framework that builds on prudential, organisational and protective regulations.

It would be fair to maintain that the initial thrust of financial-sector reforms in East Asia was on allocative aspects. Not much attention was given to the need for developing prudential and related regulations. To take one example, financial reforms in Indonesia, which started in 1983 and are regarded to be among the most comprehensive in the region, entailed attempts to improve prudential supervision only in 1989. The most comprehensive measures in this area were announced as recently as 1991, that is, nearly a decade after the onset of reforms (Hanna, 1994: 27).

The concern about improving prudential supervision stems in large part from the fact that the onset of a more liberal financial regime in East Asia has been characterised by bank failures and financial fraudulence – see Fry (1990) for some comparative data, Lau (1990b) on Taiwan, Sheng (1992) on Malaysia, Hanna (1994) on Indonesia. The precise nature of these problems varied from country to country, but common elements entailed large-scale accumulation of non-performing loans and downright corruption through insider trading. In many cases, the problems assumed proportions that jeopardised public confidence in the banking system (Lau, 1990b: 207). These are problems that one would anticipate from market failure theory, but they also motivated governments to pay much greater attention to improving the regulatory framework of financial markets.

Chapter 5

Labour market institutions, human resources and economic performance

INTRODUCTION

What is the role of labour market institutions and policies in the evolution of internationally competitive economies? Does Pacific Asia represent a case of competitive labour markets? Is there such a phenomenon as 'human-re-source-led development'? Is this a valid interpretation of East Asian economic ascendancy? These are the central questions that are explored in this chapter.

THE LABOUR MARKET AND ECONOMIC DEVELOPMENT: TWO VIEWS

Freeman (1993) identifies two views on the role of the labour market in economic development. There is the 'distortionist view' typically associated with the work of the World Bank – although in more recent contributions the Bank has offered a more nuanced view of its position (World Bank, 1995a: chapter 12). The alternative is the 'institutionalist' view associated with the work of the ILO. In the case of the latter, such labour market interventions as minimum wage legislation, mandated contributions to social security, job security legislations, large-scale unionisation and collective bargaining impair the growth process through a variety of routes. These interventions, while 'intended to raise welfare and reduce exploitation...actually work to reduce the cost of labour...and reduce labour demand...and labour incomes where most of the poor are found' (World Bank, 1990: 63). ILO (1991b: 5), on the other hand, claims that 'over the long run suppression of free industrial relations jeopardises prospects for economic development', and that there is a 'need to re-regulate the labour market' (ILO, 1991a: 65).

THE 'DISTORTIONIST VIEW' IN A CONTEXT OF 'LABOUR SUBORDINATION'

In order to appreciate the significance of this debate and its relevance to Pacific Asia, it is necessary to offer a more detailed exposition of the alternative perspectives noted above. Consider first the 'distortionist' view which interprets organised labour as the source of both market failure and government failure. Trade unions represent monopoly imperfections in labour markets. They also form part of protection-seeking distributional coalitions. Indeed, recent models of trade union behaviour perceive them as 'insiders' primarily interested in seeking benefits for employed members and unconcerned about the interests of 'outsiders' (unemployed, new job-seekers) (Carruth and Oswald, 1987).

Apart from unions, minimum wage legislation and job security regulations may also cause unemployment by creating wage rigidities. In the context of developing economies, such institutional variables are primarily responsible for the existence of entrenched 'dualism': a 'fix-wage' formal sector consisting of a 'labour aristocracy' and a 'flex-wage' informal sector consisting of casual, low-paid jobs. In other words, sectoral wage differentials would be higher in the presence, rather than the absence, of labour market institutions.

It is also alleged that organised labour leads to restrictive practices that impede job flexibility, constrain the capacity of management to cope with external shocks, and retard technological innovation. The net effect is to impede dynamic efficiency.

It also follows that labour market rigidities impair international competitiveness. By increasing labour costs above market-clearing levels, and by retarding productivity, high union density, minimum wage legislation and related regulations lead to adverse shifts in 'unit labour costs' (nominal wages adjusted by productivity) – a standard measure of trends in international competitiveness. More importantly, 'pro-labour' legislation can offset the salutary effects on export competitiveness that can be generated by exchange rate policy. Thus, for example, devaluations typically enhance export competitiveness by engineering a fall in real wages. This presupposes the absence of real wage resistance by workers – an assumption that may not be valid in the presence of strong unions and wage indexation.

If the regulatory framework does not allow the unfettered operation of the labour market and leads to adverse consequences on competitiveness through multiple channels, does this mean that coercive labour legislation (ban on unions, organised industrial action, minimum wage legislation, job security regulations, etc.) is the necessary price that industrialising economies have to pay? Seen from a historical perspective, even governments in mature industrialised countries appear to have been motivated by such a view. As Lee (1989: 13), drawing on the work of Fisher (1961), notes: 'the pioneer industrialised countries such as England, France, the United States and Germany delayed the emergence of effective unions during their ... take-off stages ... mainly through anti-union legislation'.

One also detects an intriguing, but unintended, convergence of views between scholars who are advocates of the 'distortionist' model and radical scholars who oppose coercive legislation – or 'labour subordination' as they prefer to call it – on ideological grounds but accept the economic logic behind it. Representative examples include Deyo (1987b) and Frobel *et al.* (1980), although it must be noted that in a later contribution Deyo (1989) adopts a rather more circumspect view on the labour subordination hypothesis. Despite this caveat, the observation that 'foreign and local investors have an especially strong interest in low wages,…in labour peace and a minimum of union interference in managerial autonomy' (Deyo, 1987b: 46), captures the spirit of the radical position which maintains that state-imposed labour discipline is vital to the success of export-oriented industrialisation.

Such an argument is largely inseparable from the position taken by Bhagwati (1986) – an eminent economist steeped in the neo-classical tradition and presumably a natural ally of the 'distortionist' model. Bhagwati (1986: 100), drawing on the experience of the East Asian NIEs, accepts the point that 'authoritarian methods to keep trade union wage demands under control' can pay substantial dividends in the form of low inflation and general macroeconomic stability.

LABOUR MARKET INSTITUTIONS AND POLICIES: THE INSTITUTIONALIST VIEW, POLITICAL ECONOMY CONSIDERATIONS AND A MORE ECLECTIC PARADIGM

One problem with the distortionist model is that it represents selective use of economic theory and ignores, or abstracts from, the point that unemployment or an inefficiently low volume of employment (relative to the full employment norm) may emerge even in the absence of labour market distortions. Thus, it is well known that employers may pay workers 'efficiency wages' that are above the market-clearing norm in order to reduce labour turnover and enhance labour productivity. It is also well known that monopoly imperfections in the product market would reduce the demand for labour below the full employment norm even in the presence of a perfectly competitive labour market.

It is worth remembering too that in developing economies with labour surplus conditions, interventionist labour market policies probably have limited impact. It is difficult to sustain the argument that non-union and union labour would be imperfect substitutes in the presence of an abundant supply of low-skilled workers. This would in turn act as a 'natural constraint' on the market power of organised labour. Similar considerations allow one to understand why it is relatively easy to circumvent minimum wage and other employment regulations in labour surplus economies.

The institutionalist view does not simply rely on a critique of the 'distortionist' model. It tries to go beyond this position and develop an alternative framework for analysing the appropriate role of the labour market in economic development. The institutionalist view has probably not enjoyed much popularity among the community of economists and academic scholars. It deserves greater attention. Standing (1992: 327) depicts this as a school of thought that interprets 'unions as a source of "dynamic efficiency", obliging enterprises to pay efficiency wages rather than "market clearing" wages and inducing management to raise productivity by technological innovations and cost-saving practices rather than reliance on low-cost labour'. Sengenberger (1991: 249) makes a very similar point when he argues that labour standards and other legally mandated benefits create pressures on employers to 'overcome the misguided preoccupation with cost-cutting ... and [focus] attention to the strengthening of productive power (via training, technical innovation etc.)'.

One could also invoke the notion of market failure in justifying labour market interventions. Such interventions – in the form of, say, mandated benefits or minimum standards for labour training – could be seen as producing positive externalities that cannot be 'internalised' by firms. Hence, profit-maximising employers do not provide such socially desirable benefits. Labour market interventions in such a situation could be regarded as one possible response to market failure rather than undesirable microeconomic distortions.

The argument that key labour market institutions, such as unions, can play a productive role in economic development is not merely confined to the work of the ILO. A variant of the institutionalist hypothesis is the voice/exit model of Freeman and Medoff (1984). Unions can provide a 'voice' through which workers can air any grievances. The weakness or absence of unions may induce workers to take the 'exit' option, leading to an increase in labour turnover. Higher labour turnover in turn impedes firm productivity.

Pencavel (1995: 23), in a careful review of the role of unions in economic development, reaches a conclusion that is similar in spirit to the institutionalist perspective:

> Unions have the potential to help raise productivity in the workplace by participating with management in search of better ways of organising production. It is important for workers also not to feel alienated from the economic and social system and to believe they have a stake in it. Process matters: even if outcomes were identical, employees value the fact that they or their agents help to shape their working environment.

Nelson (1991) has emphasised that if trade unions are structured as peak associations within a framework of democratic corporatism, then evidence from Europe shows that one can achieve the twin blessings of low inflation and low unemployment. A theoretical rationale can be provided in terms of game theory. A well-known result from such an analytical framework is that if bargaining partners – the government, peak employers and workers' associations – have long-term time-horizons induced by repeated strategic interaction, then they may arrive at 'co-operative' solutions (e.g. collective wage restraint in the face of external shocks) that are able to take account of societal interest at the expense of sectional interests. Such a rationale resonates with Axelrod's (1984) theory of the evolution of co-operation in a context of repeated 'prisoner's dilemma' games. Empirical evidence supporting the corporatist thesis can be found in Chowdhury (1994).

One should, as Freeman (1993: 135–9) emphasises, take account of a range of political economy considerations when interpreting the appropriate role of the labour market in economic development. The concept of corporatism noted above is part of this repertoire of political economy arguments. The point is that the exercise of 'inclusive' politics where organised labour is given access to the policy-making process as part of a tripartite dialogue between government, business and labour may breed responsible unionism. Beyond this, there are other ways in which organised labour can play a productive role in the political management of economic policies.

It is now widely recognised that policy-makers trying to implement a structural adjustment package (trade liberalisation, macroeconomic stabilisation, etc.) need political support to sustain this programme. One way of engendering such support is to provide compensatory labour market measures, such as severance pay, job re-training, etc. in order to enhance the capacity of workers to cope in the post-reform phase. Other possibilities include ownership rights of workers through profit-sharing in public-sector enterprises undergoing privatisation as a means of reducing resistance to privatisation. Finally, organised labour can contribute to the effective implementation of a structural adjustment package by offering feedback to the government on their social and income distribution effects – a point emphasised by Birdsall (1995: 442).

LABOUR MARKET INSTITUTIONS AND POLICIES IN PACIFIC ASIA

The distortionist model appears to have been influential in the interpretation of the role of the labour market in the Asia-Pacific region. Thus, Adams and Davis (1994: 22), drawing on the work of Nugent (1991), Balassa (1988) and Fields and Wan (1989), uphold the conventional wisdom that:

> Asian labour markets are generally less regulated than in Latin America. While Latin American governments have often used wage regulations to promote different economic sectors, even when the result is wages above their market-clearing levels, East Asia has generally relied on market-determined wages and consequently kept costs down...and avoided the formation of entrenched labour groups.

The message that follows from Adams and Davis (1994) is clear. East Asia epitomises the prescriptions of the 'distortionist model'. The presence of a labour market relatively free of distortions constitutes one important reason why East Asia has consistently exhibited a superior performance to economies in other parts of the world.

How valid is such a characterisation of labour markets in the Asia-Pacific region? To start with, the Philippines represents a conspicuous exception to this generalisation. Banuri (1991: 176) characterises the Philippine labour market as exhibiting typical Latin American features. Furthermore, China, with the elements of a centrally planned economy still remaining intact, does not easily fit the competitive labour market model.

Both Korea and Taiwan have witnessed waves of industrial unrest following the political liberalisation of the late 1980s, breaking away from a historically entrenched tradition of strict controls on the labour movement. The role and power of unions in the two countries have now seen substantially enhanced (Galenson, 1992). In ASEAN, Malaysia has been conspicuous for banning unions in the export-oriented, FDI-dependent electronics sector, but agreed to allow unionisation in 1988 (Standing, 1992: 329). Minimum wage legislations exist in Thailand and Indonesia and have recently been increased – see the chapters on individual countries in Part II.

Union densities are not necessarily lower in East Asia compared with other developing countries. Frenkel (1993), for example, estimates union densities at 17 per cent in Singapore, 19 per cent in Hong Kong, 33 per cent in Taiwan, 24 per cent in South Korea, 14 per cent in Malaysia and 6 per cent in Thailand. In Pakistan and India union densities are below 10 per cent (World Bank 1995a: 82). If one considers union–union wage differentials as an indicator of a regulated labour market, East Asia does not turn out to be an 'outlier'. Thus, in Malaysia the union wage premium is in the order of 15–20 per cent compared with 10 per cent in Mexico and 5–20 per cent in developed economies – USA, UK, Germany (World Bank, 1995a: 81).

In sum, the cosy picture of a deregulated labour market in Pacific Asia is at odds with the stylised facts, particularly in terms of recent developments. Despite this, one could argue with some validity that attempts have been made to curtail or suppress unionisation in the countries of this region on the ground that unregulated union activities deter the growth process. The 15-year ban on unions in the electronics sector in Malaysia, for example, was motivated by the argument that the presence of such organisations deter foreign investment (Standing, 1992: 329).

The attempt to control the labour movement in the Asia-Pacific region has also been reinforced by political motives – a point highlighted by Deyo (1989). Certainly, in the East Asian NIEs, the initial phase of coercive legislation had political origins because of the perceived association of organised labour with communist dissidents.

Several commentators (e.g. Lee, 1984; Manning and Fong, 1990; Addison and Demery, 1987) have noted that there is no evidence that the East Asian economies have deliberately tried to suppress wages in the export-oriented sectors in order to maintain and prolong their competitive advantage in labour-intensive manufacturing. While the commentators were motivated to marshall this evidence against the 'labour subordination' hypothesis, such evidence does not really constitute a robust test of the distortionist model. Wage suppression may, in fact, be a short-sighted strategy because it impairs the long-term capacity of developing, labour-surplus economies to develop comparative advantage in more capital-intensive, skill-intensive goods and services. This is an argument that would certainly be approved by the institutionalist view.

A more direct empirical test of the distortionist–institutionalist debate has been offered by Freeman (1993) and Standing (1992). The former study assembles cross-country evidence to arrive at the following conclusions:

- The alleged fatal inefficiencies of labour market distortions are not borne across a range of countries with a record of interventionist policies. Real wages have been variable and minimum wages in real terms fell precipitously in many countries. Intersectoral wage differentials appear to be lower – rather than higher – in interventionist regimes.
- 'Extant studies reject the claim that unions are a general impediment to macroadjustments or to enterprise performance in developing countries, although they may be so in particular cases' (Freeman, 1993: 134).

Standing (1992) represents one of the very few studies that tries to test the role of unions in affecting enterprise performance using firm-level data. The data were generated from a large-scale 1988 survey of Malaysian establishments. He arrives at the following conclusions on the relationship between unionisation and labour market outcomes.

- Unionised firms were more likely to engage in training and thus improve worker productivity.
- Product innovations and work re-organisation were much more prevalent in unionised firms.
- There appears to be a positive correlation between the unionisation and labour productivity.
- There is no clear-cut evidence that unions represent a source of employment rigidity.

In sum, it is difficult to be dogmatic about the distortionist model. It represents selective use of economic theory. Its empirical foundation is shaky. The institutionalist view and political economy arguments suggest ways in which labour market institutions can play a productive role in economic development and thus provide the basis for a more eclectic paradigm that could, in turn, serve as a bench-mark in appraising labour market developments in Pacific Asia. In particular, there is a case for revising the view that coercive labour legislation to remove or alleviate microeconomic distortions is the necessary price to pay for rapid industrialisation. Such legislation probably represents an avoidable infringement of human rights. These emerging ideas are now ratified by the World Bank (1995a: 86) which is often perceived to be an advocate of the 'distortionist' view:

> Denial of workers' rights is not necessary to achieve growth of incomes. It is possible to identify the conditions and policies under which free trade unions can advance rather than impede development. Unions are likely to have positive effects on efficiency and equity and their potential negative effects are likely to be minimised, when they operate in an environment when product markets are competitive, collective bargaining occurs at the enterprise or plant level, and labour laws protect the rights of individual workers to join the union of their choosing, or none at all.

THE ROLE OF HUMAN RESOURCES IN ECONOMIC DEVELOPMENT: SOME ANALYTICAL PROPOSITIONS

There is a well-entrenched view that the superior performance of the economies of Pacific Asia relative to other economies has to do with their human resources in the form of an abundant supply of skilled workers. The Asian Development Bank (1989: 153–4) represents a good example of this view:

> An examination of the postwar economic record of the ... NIEs and the more advanced South East Asian countries reveals that human capital formation has been a crucial underlying factor in these countries' growth ... Even though it is difficult to quantify the contribution of human capital to economic growth, there is virtual unanimity regarding its critical role.

Perceptions on the role of human resources in economic development bear the imprint of human capital theory which posits a direct link between a person's endowment of education and productivity. In addition, it is typically assumed that higher earnings reflect higher productivity. Much of the current enthusiasm with human resources can be traced to so-called endogenous growth theories expounded by such practitioners as Romer (1986, 1990), Lucas (1988, 1990) and Grossman and Helpman (1990). Indeed, one recent book on human resources in the Pacific Rim (Ogawa et al., 1993) claims to have been inspired by the relevance of these so-called 'new' growth theories.

The recent wave of growth theories broke away from the Solow–Denison approach which treated technical progress as exogenous and incorporated human capital in the production function. Human capital became an endogenous variable that drove the growth process. In both Romer (1986) and Lucas (1988), for example, human capital accumulation has externally inducing effects. Thus, the average level of human capital in a community has a favourable impact on the productivity of a typical worker in addition to his/her endowment of human capital. The advocates of the new growth theory emphasise the knowledge spillover effects due to learning-by-doing. There could also be a close interaction between formal education and training and learning-by-doing, to the extent that the capacity to engage in the latter is enhanced by the former. The assumption in new growth theories of externalities in human capital are typically combined with the assumption of increasing returns to scale in production.

The analysis of the externally inducing effects of human capital is not only limited to the advocates of new growth theories. Those who are not explicitly linked to this analytical tradition have also reflected on this issue. Thus, Colcough (1982) and Schultz (1988) have drawn attention to the external effects of education in the form of reduced fertility, better health and nutrition and so forth.

If human-resource-led development simply means the role that human capital formation plays in economic development à la human capital theory and recent growth theories, then it appears to be a relatively non-controversial proposition. One ventures into more contentious terrain when the proposition becomes prescriptive: that through deliberate and aggressive investments in education and training one can change the comparative advantage of an economy from low-skill, labour-intensive products to more skill-intensive goods and services, thus attaining rapid, internationally oriented growth. The answer is not as clear-cut as it appears.

In the case of the conventional human capital theory, the returns to education and training are appropriated by individuals through higher earnings. Thus, to the extent that both the formal education and training system and the labour market operate efficiently, utility-maximising decisions at the individual level will lead to socially optimal investments in human capital. It is not obvious that a case can be made for interventionist public policy in terms of traditional human capital theory.

In the case of new growth theories, externalities and increasing returns to scale will cause the social rate of return to investments in human resources to exceed the private rate of return and thus create market failure. This in turn creates a role for more active public policy: various measures could be designed to rectify such market failure.

The productive role that human resources play in economic development has been challenged by the screening hypothesis which maintains that education merely serves as a screen or sieve through which able and trainable workers are allocated to different jobs in society (e.g. Thurow, 1974, 1976). The education and training system has social value to the extent that it can fulfil its screening function efficiently. Some radical critics have taken

this critique a step further. The schooling system, such radical critics maintain, essentially entails an inter-generation reproduction of the class structure; those receiving education come from favoured backgrounds and the
primary function of the schooling system is to install a sense of diligence
and a respect for authority. Such arguments imply radical reform of the
social and economic system as a prerequisite for any conceivable reform of
the school system in a market economy.

It is clear that, while conventional human capital theory and the recent
growth theories, ascribe a central role to human capital formation as a
source of growth, alternative perspectives paint a less optimistic picture.
Moreover, as Stern's (1991) survey of the proximate determinants of growth
has shown, human capital (including learning-by-doing) is one of a complex
list of such determinants. Other major proximate causes of growth include:
physical capital accumulation; research and innovation; quality of infrastructure; intersectoral shifts of resources; management and organisation.
Not surprisingly, the Asian Development Bank (1989: 170), an ardent
advocate of human-resource-driven development, tempers its position by
injecting a note of caution:

> Human resources alone...are not sufficient. Sustained economic growth
> depends crucially on how well these resources are developed and how
> efficiently land, capital and technology are mobilized...Educated man-
> power may be wasted if capital and raw materials are lacking, if econom-
> ic policies are inappropriate, if enterpreneurship is lacking, or if political
> structures are unstable.

HUMAN RESOURCES AND ECONOMIC DEVELOPMENT: A CRITICAL INTERPRETATION OF THE EVIDENCE, WITH SPECIAL REFERENCE TO THE ASIA-PACIFIC REGION

Ultimately, it is at the level of empirical evidence that one can form some
judgement on the role of human resources in economic development. The
discussion at this juncture will draw on selected aspects of the available
evidence: rate-of-return studies and cross-country evidence as well as studies of specific countries, experiences in the Asia-Pacific region.

Behrman (1990: 89) offers a careful review of the evidence and arrives at
the following conclusion:

> There appears to be some evidence about the *association* between human
> resource investments...But there is surprisingly little systematic quanti-
> tative evidence for the proposition that human resource investments
> cause substantial development or that the usual types of market failures
> warrant much higher human resource investments than would occur
> without activist policy interventions.

The present study upholds Behrman's position as a review of some of the evidence will illustrate.

Gannicott (1990: 49) compiles evidence on rate of returns to investment in education in Pacific Asia from a range of sources and compares it with the cross-country patterns compiled by Psacharopoulos (1985). He notes:

> The results for [the Asia-Pacific region] conform broadly to the general pattern of international evidence: returns (both private and social) are highest in primary education and lowest for higher education; private returns exceed social returns; and returns to education are generally above the 10 percent rule-of- thumb often used as the opportunity cost of capital.

There are some exceptions. Rate of return seems to be highest in higher education in Malaysia; social rate of returns exceeds private rate of returns in Thailand; private rate of returns are strikingly low in China (and is below the 10 per cent rule-of-thumb) – a point that is also endorsed by Byron and Manaloto (1990). Despite these exceptions to the general pattern, what is important is the finding that social rates do not usually exceed the private rate of return. In fact, it is usually the reverse, suggesting 'overinvestment' rather than 'underinvestment' in education. Furthermore, the strikingly low rate of returns in education sit uncomfortably with the stated commitment by the authorities in China to bring about substantial expansions in both vocational and higher education at the expense of basic education. This has prompted Gannicott (1990: 59) to warn that 'the country has almost certainly embarked on a misconceived pattern of resource allocation in education'.

Critics of run-of-the-mill studies on returns to education question whether even the high private rates are reliable estimates. This critique is not unfounded when one takes account of the poor quality of the education and training system in many developing countries, the effect of family background, the influence of ability and motivation, and inefficient policy management. Representative examples of such views can be found in Behrman and Birdsall (1983), Heyneman and Etienne (1989), Behrman and Wolfe (1984) and Mehmet (1988).

What about the association – rather than causality – between human resources and countries with different growth records and different stages of development? Booth (1994: 77–8), in a review of Ogawa et al. (1993) and Asian Development Bank (1990), expresses 'nagging doubts' about this association and focuses on two 'outliers': the Philippines and Thailand. In the case of the former, human capital endowments have historically been one of the best in South East Asia and yet it remains an economic laggard. Thailand has lagged behind, especially in post-primary education. Yet, Thailand has been one of the most rapidly growing economies in ASEAN.

One could argue that the existence of a few exceptions and outliers do not prove that critics of human-resource-driven strategy are right. Hence, it would be useful to consider econometric tests of the causal relationship between human resources and economic growth based on large-scale cross-country data. Two good examples are Otani and Villaneuva (1989) and Azariadies and Drazen (1990). The former considers annual average data for the 1970–85 period for 55 developing countries. The study finds that investment in human capital, measured by the ratio of government educational expenditure to GNP, had a significant impact on economic growth. But in quantitative terms this was less than the corresponding effects flowing from the rate of export growth and the domestic savings rate. The study then tries to qualify this conclusion by arguing that if one takes into account private-sector investments in education and the entire economy's investments in health, nutritional intake, and on-the-job training, the financing of investment in human capital would probably be a much more significant contributing factor to long-term economic growth.

Azariadies and Drazen (1990) is a study that is very much in the spirit of the new growth theories. They use a formal model to capture the point that for countries with the same per capita income, those with higher endowments of human resources would have higher (future) growth. This idea is then econometrically tested using a sample of 32 countries which includes some Asian economies. The evidence in favour of their hypothesis is limited and, as Behrman (1990: 79) argues, sensitive to statistical estimation problems. Romer (1989), who has also tried to test new growth theories using cross-country data, readily concedes that the evidence is 'tenuous at best' (as cited in Behrman, 1990: 81).

Sengupta (1991, 1993) represent some recent examples that seek to test the validity of new growth theories by focusing exclusively on the experience of the NIEs. The conclusion, based largely on the experience of Korea, is that investment in human capital, increasing returns to scale and the impact of openness in international trade are the key determinants of the growth process in the NIEs – see Sengupta (1993).

Such a conclusion has to be interpreted with care. One could readily argue that it is really a test of the benefits that flow from an outward-oriented trade regime rather than human resources *per se*. If a country rich in human capital endowments combines this with a *dirigiste* regime, then this may offset the growth potential of human resources – as the experience of Cuba, Sir Lanka and the Philippine testify. Furthermore, the indicator that Sengupta (1993: 348) uses for measuring human capital (lagged output per worker) is really a measure of learning-by-doing rather than formal education. This leaves open the question of public policy in human resource development because one could argue that it is an issue best left to the private sector.

CONCLUDING COMMENTS

This chapter has dealt with two themes: labour market institutions and policies and the role of human resources in economic development. A typical characterisation of the dynamism of Pacific Asia is that it is the product of competitive labour markets buttressed by coercive labour legislation and rapid accumulation of human capital.

The chapter has offered a critical appraisal of such themes. The competitive labour market model derives its intellectual inspiration from the 'distortionist' view of the role of the labour market in economic development. Labour market performance in East Asia has been epitomised by rapid employment expansion and growth of real wages. While this negates the more radical 'labour subordination' hypothesis, it does not invalidate the prescriptions of the 'institutionalist' view of the labour market. The latter has argued that the 'distortionist' view has simply overlooked the productive role that such key institutions as unions can play in the growth process. Moreover, political economy considerations reinforce the position of the institutionalists.

In many respects, this represents a profoundly optimistic message for such countries as Taiwan and Korea as they try and negotiate a future within a framework of an incipient, but assertive, labour movement. The institutionalist literature also provides the basis for an eclectic paradigm that South East Asian policy-makers can use as a useful bench-mark to evaluate labour market performance. The extant tradition in certain countries of South East Asia reflect what Pencavel (1995: 3) has called an 'obstructionist regime' whose primary purpose is 'to strictly regulate if not suppress collective bargaining'. Such a tradition needs to change as there is no compelling rationale behind it.

The chapter has highlighted the fact that there has been a ready inclination to accept the notion of human-resource-led development in understanding the dynamism of the Asia-Pacific region. But finding robust evidence to support this proposition has proven to be more difficult. Even an apparently simple task of establishing an association between human capital endowment and economic growth is afflicted by outliers. More rigorous econometric tests using the framework of new growth theories do not fare much better as their results are open to a range of interpretations. This does not mean that human resources are unimportant. It possibly does mean that the role of human resources in economic development has been exaggerated. It is best to perceive human capital as one proximate determinant of economic growth that reaches its full potential when supporting factors are present.

Where does one go from here in terms of the role of public policy in managing human resources? Certainly, the government should continue to play a fundamental role in the provision of basic education and health, but beyond this the case for public subsidisation of education to rectify alleged market failure problems is probably dubious. It may well be, as Jimenez (1986, 1990), Psacharopoulos and Jimenez (1989) and others have argued, that the national interest is best served by a greater reliance on cost-recovery schemes and private-sector initiatives in managing post-primary education.

Chapter 6

Managing the environment in rapidly industrialising economies

INTRODUCTION

A topical issue that is going to impinge on the prospects of sustaining rapid and shared growth in the Asia-Pacific region pertains to environmental degradation. Does rapid, internationally oriented growth lead to the destruction of the environment to the point where 'sustainable development' is not possible? What is the record on environmental protection and management in East Asia? The answers to these questions are contentious. While the World Bank Policy (1993b: 1) maintains that 'fast growing economies with liberal trade policies ... have experienced less pollution-intensive growth than closed economies', it also concedes (World Bank, 1993c: 40) that East Asia's environmental record is 'in some respects ... about the worst among the developing regions'. Carter (1994) and Kaji (1994) also consider the rising environmental threat as one of the greatest development challenges facing East Asia and one that will test the innovative capacities of its leaders.

Against such a stark scenario is the more optimistic notion that there are built-in mechanisms that will cause the problem of environmental degradation to be mitigated in the long run. One could argue that the income elasticity of demand for environmental quality is high. This implies that with progressive affluence, the economies of Pacific Asia will experience political pressures from an assertive middle class seeking a cleaner environment within the framework of a global movement towards an ecologically friendly development paradigm. This interpretation is compatible with the cross-country evidence that pollution levels rise up to a certain income (GDP) level, and then taper off – a phenomenon referred to as the 'environmental Kuznets curve' (World Bank, 1992). At the same time, one could argue that particular groups who suffer most from environmental degradation, such as indigenous tribal communities, may lack the political clout to protect their interests. How minority interests and middle-class-based demands for a cleaner environment are articulated and managed will play an important role in the 'greening' of Pacific Asia's development. Furthermore, as the subsequent discussion will highlight, market failures and inappropriate public policies – which lie at the root of environmental problems – will not automatically go away without properly designed policies.

DEVELOPMENT, INTERNATIONAL TRADE AND THE ENVIRONMENT: THE ISSUES

The environmental impact of economic development is slowly being recognised – see, for example, the World Bank (1992), OECD (1991), Pearce and Warford (1992), Dasgupta and Maler (1992), Dasgupta (1995), Repetto (1995), Munasinghe and Cruz (1995). Within this broad framework, the impact on the environment of trade liberalisation – and hence globalisation – has gained prominence (e.g. Anderson and Blackhurst, 1992; Pearce, 1993).

The current concerns about the environmental consequences of economic growth are by no means new. One can, as Trisoglio (1993) has argued, detect a logical continuity between the 'limits to growth' debate of the early 1970s (Meadows *et al.*, 1972), which focused on the depletion of natural resources, to the current discussions on the ability of the environment to absorb waste and maintain its life-sustaining functions. 'Sustainable development', a term that owes its popularity to the World Commission on Environment and Development (1987) – often referred to as the Brundtland Report – has now become a dominant paradigm. Although the World Bank (1992) has complained that 'sustainable development' is a concept that is not easy to operationalise, it is best interpreted to mean that 'economic activity should not degrade the natural resource base on which it depends' (Trisoglio, 1993: 87). Meadows *et al.* (1992), who pioneered the 'limits to growth' debate, also emphasise this notion of sustainability by arguing that environmental trends since the early 1970s suggest natural resource depletion and the production of urban and industrial pollution at a rate that exceeds environmental limits.

Can one reconcile the paradigm of sustainable development with the economist's preoccupation with a global economy propelled by free trade? Pearce (1993: 56), one of the leading academic practitioners in the field of environmental economics, arrives at the following conclusion: 'trade liberalisation is likely to give rise to negative environmental externalities, but also to some environmental gains'. In other words, the answer is by no means clear-cut. One can think of reasons that could lead to a situation in which a truly liberal international trading system would impose environmental costs; equally, one can think of circumstances in which a policy of protection will degrade the environment.

Free trade or a more liberal trading system on a worldwide basis is a time-honoured means to secure improvements in living standards. Thus, the primary purpose of free trade is the expansion of consumption and output. This will inevitably generate greater demands on natural resources and land.

Pearce (1993) refers to this as the 'growth effects' of free trade. Whether this will inevitably contribute to environmental degradation depends on the energy-intensity of free-trade-led growth and industrialisation. If energy-intensity goes up, then enhanced economic activity generated by trade liberalisation will increase energy consumption. Evidence compiled by UNIDO (1991) suggests that the energy-intensity of industrialisation has gone down in the developed economies, partly as a result of the adoption of 'clean technology' by the corporate sector, but it seems to have gone up in developing economies. The study by Lucas *et al.* (1992) reinforces this position by their conclusion that the intensity of pollution is beginning to taper off in developed countries, but appears to be increasing in developing countries.

The environmental impact of free trade is also influenced by the so-called 'specialisation effect' and 'industrial migration'. Trade liberalisation leads to increased specialisation along the lines of comparative advantage, with developing economies specialising in traditional, labour-intensive products. At the same time, industrial migration could occur, as traditional industries in the developed economies seek low labour costs in the developing economies in order to maintain their competitiveness. Thus, both the specialisation effect and industrial migration provide the basis of the restructuring of the world economy (or international division of labour). The environmental implications of such restructuring follow from the possible link between pollution-intensity and a developing country's comparative advantage in traditional, labour-intensive industries.

In an insightful contribution, Low and Yeats (1992) examine trade flow data to examine the environmental implications of specialisation and industrial migration. They demonstrate that while the share of 'dirty' industries in world trade has fallen between 1965 and 1988, the share of such industries in the exports of many developing countries has actually increased over the same period. This is consistent with the authors' analysis based on the 'revealed comparative advantage' (RCA) method. The latter suggests a disproportionate increase in the RCAs of pollution-intensive industries of developing economies over the period under study. In sum, there is evidence of a correlation between pollution-intensity and a developing country's comparative advantage. Free trade could thus cause environmental degradation by encouraging specialisation according to comparative advantage.

Perhaps the fundamental element that underpins the free-trade-environment nexus is the issue of 'market failure'. As Pearce (1993: 55) puts it:

Free trade neglects the environment in the same way that domestic markets fail to take account for environmental losses. In other words, trade liberalization can be expected to increase ... 'market failure' – the environmental damage that comes with the workings of the free market economy.

A range of 'environmental externalities' – linked to both production and consumption' – could emerge as a result of international transactions in goods and services. Such externalities could affect two types of common property resources – 'local commons' and 'global commons' (Dasgupta and Maler, 1992). An example of the former is represented by the case of unsustainable deforestation generated by the production of timber for exports. Perhaps the most contentious element of market failure pertains to the externalities that impinge on 'global commons'. They arise when the pollution generated by an exporting nation degrades a common resource – the ozone layer, the atmosphere, the oceans. The problem with environmental externalities – whether they impinge on local or global common property resources – is that there is no self-correcting mechanism for private consumers and firms engaged in the use and production of traded goods and services to take account of such externalities and compensate the affected parties for the damage and welfare losses that are inflicted. Hence, free trade has the potential to degrade the environment and contributes to market failure independently of domestic sources of market failure.

A recent analysis by Chichilnisky (1994) has made the important point that market failures associated with international trade stem from differences in the specification of property rights across countries. In the relatively rich 'North', specification of property rights over local commons is considerably more stringent than in the relatively poor 'South'. As Chichilnisky (1994: 853–4) puts it:

> Today many environmental resources are unregulated common property in developing countries...Examples are rainforests...grazing land, fisheries and aquifers...Industrial countries have much better defined property rights for their resources than do developing countries. The United States has property rights regimes for petroleum...Japan is well known for its protection of property rights in environmental resource, including even sunlight. Germany recently initiated a parallel system of national accounts which records the depreciation of environmental assets, effectively treating the accounting of national property on the same basis as that of private property.

Given that unregulated environmental resources in the South serve as inputs in the production of traded goods and services, private producers in that region have a comparative cost advantage for such producers and services over private producers in developed countries. This provides the basis for trade between the North and the South and generates the problem of the commons in the international arena: the North overconsumes underpriced resource-intensive products imported from the South. Thus the Chichilnisky model provides one with a new perspective on the topical issue of the alleged comparative advantage of developing countries in 'dirty industries' – see discussion at a previous juncture.

If there is a link between free trade and environmental degradation, does this imply that a policy of protection is the answer? This is by no means obvious. One could argue persuasively that trade barriers lead to the over-production of protected goods and services (compared with the free trade case) and thus contributes to environmental degradation. The European Union's Common Agricultural Policy which encourages over-intensive use of the land is a striking example. In this case, one could in fact argue that the movement to free trade will reduce overproduction and may benefit the environment. Yet another example of the negative environmental consequences entailed in preferential trading arrangements comes from the European Union (EU). Veenendaal and Opschoor (1986) have drawn attention to the fact that the EU's favoured treatment of Botswana beef exports is partly responsible for over-grazing and desertification in Botswana. Finally, a series of World-Bank-sponsored studies have shown that less open economies have a bad environmental record. The case of Eastern Europe is by now notorious (Radetzki, 1992). Countries of the former East European bloc are conspicuous for the profound neglect of the environment. Birdsall and Wheeler (1992) show that the less open economies of Latin America are, in fact, 'pollution havens'. They also argue that open economies have greater opportunities to acquire 'clean' and 'green' technologies from abroad. Smil (1984) has shown that, in the years prior to economic reform, the PRC experienced severe environmental degradation.

The clear message from the above discussion is that one should not revert to the cause of old-fashioned protectionism under the guise of environmental concerns. Neither theory nor evidence can be marshalled to argue that *dirigiste*, protectionist regimes enhance environmental quality. Equally, free trade could lead to environmental degradation in the absence of countervailing measures and political mobilisation of concern for the environment. These points deserve further amplification.

Dasgupta and Maler (1992) and Dasgupta (1995) have forcefully argued that one step towards ensuring that environmental concerns are fully reflected in the policy-making process and at the level of the community is to make them an integral part of the national accounting system and project appraisal procedures. This means calculating the losses from the unsustainable use of local common property resources – soil, fuelwood, water and so forth – and incorporating them in estimates of real net national product (NNP) – see the German example noted above.

Such a view is theoretically impeccable and morally appealing. One could argue, as Dasgupta and Maler (1992) do, that local commons represent vital resources for the poor. When a combination of market failures and inappropriate policies (such as subsidisation of energy-intensive industrialisation) threaten the quality and preservation of local commons, the poor are likely to suffer most. They are also, as Brandon (1994: 23) emphasises 'disproportionately the victims of pollution because they are less buffered

than the nonpoor from water pollution, toxic wastes, solid wastes, conges-
tive traffic and air and noise pollution'. Thus an approach that makes
explicit the costs of environmental degradation will promote both economic
efficiency and equity.

While one can appreciate the robust logic of 'environmental accounting',
the practical constraints of implementing this approach have been the
source of concern among some observers (e.g. Munasinghe, 1992). Many
developing economies may simply lack the technical capacity to engage in
'environmental accounting'. One counter-argument to this pessimism is that
such technical expertise can either be acquired from abroad or can be freely
obtained through international development agencies such as the World
Bank.

'Environmental accounting' is the first – albeit fundamental – step in the
development of an ecologically friendly development paradigm. One still
has to develop appropriate pollution-abatement measures. These measures
can be broadly grouped into two types: command-and-control measures
and market-oriented, incentive-driven measures. An example of the former
would be the articulation of environmental standards that are then enforced
by an administrative agency. Examples of the latter would include pollution
taxes and tradable pollution permits and, more generally, policies that
improve the specification and implementation of property rights over the
use of environmental resources. The consensus seems to be that it is more
cost-effective to implement market-oriented pollution-abatement measures
than command-and-control-type schemes. The latter are administratively
costly to manage and require competent and committed bureaucrats.

In trying to choose between different types of market-oriented pollution-
abatement measures, one can draw on the contribution by Chichilnisky
(1994) which formalises an insightful observation by the World Bank (1992)
about the efficacy of environmental or 'green' taxation. Suppose that the
countries of the South levy a tax on the use of environmental resources in
order to raise the producer's costs and thus deter its use of environmental
resources. Chichilnisky (1994) shows that such taxes could have perverse
effects and lead to more extraction of environmental resources. The essence
of the argument is that taxes will reduce the demand for resources. This in
turn will mean that harvesters will receive lower prices for their products.
In order to compensate for this price effect, harvesters may work harder and
extract more rather than less environmental resources. Such an argument
leads Chichilnisky (1994) to make the case for property-rights policies as
the central strategy for coping with environmental degradation. The author
(1994: 865) concludes that:

Property rights change slowly because they require expensive legal infrastructure and enforcement. Poor countries may find themselves unable to
implement such policies quickly. The improvement of property rights of

indigenous populations in developing countries . . . should nevertheless be considered a major policy goal. There is a small but apparently growing trend of this type in Brazil, Bolivia, Colombia, Ecuador, French Guiana, and Venezuela.

Various types of microeconomic reforms – such as removal of subsidies and raising prices for infrastructure-related services (e.g. energy, water, garbage, sewage, transport, etc.) – that are primarily driven by other motives (such as public-sector reform), also have an important role to play because of their environmental implications. In other words, given that such micro-economic distortions as energy subsidies contribute to pollution-intensive development, their removal contributes to the amelioration of environmental degradation.

Measures for pollution abatement that have been proposed at the domestic level have also been extended to deal with the case of global commons. Thus, harmonisation of environmental standards across countries is a much-noted proposal. The typical critique is that harmonisation would be administratively costly to manage, particularly given enforcement problems stemming from the well-known 'free-rider' syndrome (country X has the incentive to 'cheat' by free-riding on the international community's observance of environmental standards). This suggests that a market-oriented approach may be more appropriate. Dasgupta and Maler (1992) have argued for the application of tradable pollution permits at the international level – which, in effect, is a version of property-rights policies applied at global levels.

Despite the theoretical appeal of this proposal, one has to concede that engendering global co-operation in managing the environment is probably more complex and contentious than engendering such co-operation at the domestic level. Thus, the thrust of the discussion so far is that dealing with environmental degradation at the domestic level is probably more feasible than dealing with it at a global level. Nevertheless, developed countries should facilitate this process by seeking ways and means for persuading developing countries to pay much greater attention to property-rights policies, pursuing microeconomic reforms that generate environmentally friendly side-effects and for providing technical assistance for policy formulation along such lines.

THE ENVIRONMENT AND INTERNATIONALLY ORIENTED ECONOMIC GROWTH: SOME EAST ASIAN EVIDENCE

The discussion so far has revealed how, in the absence of appropriate policies, internationally oriented economic growth can lead to market failure in the form of environmental degradation. How has East Asia, as an exemplary case of rapid growth, fared in terms of managing the environment? This section aims to focus on this issue.

Kaji (1994: 210) notes:

> East Asian countries have made progress in many environmentally im-
> portant areas, including rural sanitation and the availability of drinking
> water. The region's accumulated problems, however, in some respects are
> about the worst among the developing regions. These are in the areas of
> soil erosion, water logging, and salinization; urban environmental degra-
> dation; industrial pollution and energy sector emissions; and deforesta-
> tion and loss of habitat.

Focusing on a specific country in the region – Indonesia – Petrick and
Quinn (1994: 41) observe:

> The deforestation and degradation of Indonesia's tropical forests is inter-
> nationally recognised as a serious, multi-facted problem...Studies indi-
> cate that Indonesia is being deforested at an accelerating rate from 5,500
> square kilometers annually in 1980 to 7,000 by the mid-1980s, and now
> stands around 12,000 square kilometres per year...This is more defor-
> estation than any other single country except Brazil.

Table 6.1 compiles a range of environmental indicators (energy intensity,
carbon dioxide emissions, incremental carbon dioxide emissions, deforestation) for East Asia and compares them with other regions of the world. The
comparative data reveals that the East Asian region has a poor record in
terms of a range of environmental indicators. Carbon dioxide emissions (as
at 1989) appear to be three times the level of Latin America, while energy
intensity is nearly double. Projections until the year 2000 suggest that East
Asia will continue to generate the highest amount of carbon dioxide emissions. Compared with the other regions noted in the table (South Asia, Sub-
Saharan Africa, Latin America), deforestation has occurred at a higher rate
in East Asia.

Table 6.1 Environmental indicators: East Asia and other regions

Region	Energy intensity 1989	Carbon dioxide emissions, 1989	Deforestation, 1981–90	Incremental Carbon dioxide emissions, 1990–2000
East Asia	1.05	934	1.4	703
South Asia	0.61	567	0.6	222
Sub-Saharan Africa	0.56	376	0.8	42
Latin America & Caribbean	0.60	278	0.9	36

Source: Based on World Bank, 1993b, figures 3.1, 3.2, pp. 42–4
Notes: Energy intensity = kg of oil equivalent per $ GDP; carbon dioxide emissions = tons of carbon
per mill. $ GDP; deforestation = annual %. Note that East Asia includes Vietnam, Myanmar, Laos,
Cambodia.

City-level data collected across countries in 1980–84 reveal that nine of the fifteen cities in the world with the highest levels of suspended particulate matter (SPM) are located in East Asia (Kingsley *et al.*, 1994: 21; Hammer and Shetty, 1995: 5).

The social costs of environmental degradation are enormous. World Bank estimates suggest that the annual cost of air pollution is as high as US$3.1 billion in Bangkok, US$1.6 billion in Kuala Lumpur, US$800 million in Jakarta. These estimates would be as much as 40 per cent higher if one includes additional costs due to congestion (Brandon, 1994: 22).

What are the factors that have shaped this sorry evidence of environmental degradation? One can anticipate the answer, given the analytical discussion at a previous juncture. To some extent, the degradation reflects the by-products of rapid economic growth: energy-intensive industrialisation and urbanisation. To a considerable extent the evidence reflects more deep-seated problems: the lack of political will and governance to tackle environmental problems; widespread market failures compounded by inefficient policies, such as sub-optimal pricing of infrastructural services. Hammer and Shetty (1995: 11) highlight the inadequate nature of property rights in parts of East Asia as a major source of market failure. They observe:

In China, unsustainable forestry practices for obtaining fuelwood and building materials can be directly linked to the lack of clear property rights. In Indonesia and Malaysia, encroachment by illegal loggers and conflicts over the use of public lands are also a product of unclear or unenforced property rights.

The countries of the Asia-Pacific region are slowly beginning to recognise the need for much greater vigilance with respect to monitoring and maintaining environmental standards. This is also being driven by an assertive middle class as it increasingly demands reduced air, water and noise pollution. Almost all the countries in the region have legislated protection of their air, land and water. Many have created specialised agencies and environmental ministries and have drawn up (or are in the process of drawing up) guidelines and standards to enforce legislation. City-specific experiences (China, Indonesia, Korea, the Philippines, Thailand) suggest the evolution of multi-pronged approaches to vehicle congestion and air pollution, such as: aggressive vehicle inspection; reduction in diesel and two-stroke in urban fleets; taxes aimed at vehicles, parking or road use; upgrading technologies or fuels; fuel switching from pollution-intensive sources to cleaner varieties (World Bank, 1993c). In most of East Asia, one can also detect a phasing out of energy subsidies (Hammer and Shetty, 1995: 3).

Despite progress in the area of environmental management, it is recognised that a lot more needs to be done through the development of an integrated approach (Brandon, 1994; World Bank 1993b). The principles of good environmental management are well known and need only be briefly repeated here. First, it has be emphasised that anti-growth, protectionist policies are not the answer. It is easier to control degradation in a growing rather than in a stagnant economy. Economic growth creates more public revenues that could be fruitfully invested in environmental programmes; it facilitates rapid turnover of ageing technology and restructuring of industry and its product mix. Policies that promote economic openness provide greater opportunities for attracting foreign expertise in 'green' technology. Hence, the customary emphasis on rapid, internationally oriented economic growth in the Asia-Pacific region would have to remain a fundamental element of environmental management.

Second, US and European experiences have shown that 'command-and-control' measures for dealing with the environment generate relatively high administrative costs and are inefficient. Hence, countries of the Asia-Pacific region would be better served by a more cost-effective, market-oriented approach. This does not mean an abdication of the responsibilities of the government with respect to environmental management. In fact, the reverse is true: public institutions charged with environmental policy-making and enforcement need to be re-oriented towards the fundamental notion that environmental resources are not unregulated commons, but precious national endowments buttressed by appropriate property rights. This also entails environmental accounting, at least at the project-appraisal level, raising prices for infrastructural services (e.g. energy, water, garbage, sewage and transport), privatisation or at least commercialisation of certain aspects of infrastructural services, forging partnerships with industry so that it has an incentive for self-regulation, boosting public and media attention about the environment as a way of inducing informal 'social regulation' through informed public participation.

CONCLUDING OBSERVATIONS

Recent evidence suggests that, while the economies of the Asia-Pacific region have attained remarkable success in fostering rapid, internationally oriented growth, their record in terms of coping with environmental degradation has been quite poor. Market failures associated with environmental externalities have been at the root of this problem but they have also been compounded by inappropriate policies.

It is possible to argue that environmental degradation is a transitional problem. One could, for example, argue that an 'environmental Kuznets curve' is at work, given that the cross-section patterns show that at higher income levels pollution levels tend to be lower (World Bank, 1992; Panayotou, 1992). But, as Dasgupta (1995: 167) has emphasised, the so-called environmental Kuznets curve is 'something of a mirage'. Not all environmental damages are reversible and they adversely affect the poor most.

Prevention of environmental damage, rather than a subsequent clean-up, is less costly. Market failures and inappropriate public policies – which lie at the root of environmental externalities – will not automatically go away without properly designed policies. This will require political will and commitment and a fundamental reorientation away from treating the environment as unregulated common resources to considering it as a precious national endowment that needs to be carefully managed and monitored. Thus the central message of this chapter is that policy-makers in this region can no longer ignore issues pertaining to environmental degradation.

Chapter 7

Poverty, inequality and economic development

INTRODUCTION

The World Bank (1993a) regards the 'miracle economies' of East Asia as spectacular examples of 'shared growth'. This concept has two dimensions: changes in absolute poverty and trends in relative income inequality. Certainly, there has been a rapid and sustained reduction in poverty in a short period of time in the Asia-Pacific region. The experiences of China and Indonesia, two of the most populous and low-income economies of the region, illustrate this claim rather well. Rural poverty (as measured by the proportion living below a given poverty line) in China fell from 33 per cent in 1978 to 11.5 per cent in 1990, while in Indonesia, rural poverty declined from 33.9 per cent to 14.3 per cent over the same period (Asian Development Bank, 1994: table 3.3, p. 190).

The Asian Development Bank (1994: 35) expresses the conventional wisdom when it notes that: a 'remarkable feature of economic growth in East Asia is that it has been accompanied by a reduction in income inequality'. The World Bank (1993a: 3) offers an identical observation about the 'high performing East Asian Economies' (HPAEs): the 'HPAEs' low and declining levels of inequality are...a remarkable exception to historical experience and contemporary evidence in other regions'. Fields (1995: 84) observes: 'The most outstanding examples of broad-based economic improvements over a sustained period of time are the...NIEs...Their income distribution experiences...present a picture of extraordinary improvements.'

More recent trends in inequality, however, suggest a complex picture, with inequality rising in some cases. One could argue that what matters to the concept of shared growth is the reduction in absolute poverty. But one could also argue that adverse perceptions about relative income inequality could affect the social and political cohesion that has been the hallmark of the rapidly growing economies of the region. Indeed, Alesina and Rodrik (1994) argue – and provide evidence – that inequality in land and income ownership is negatively correlated with subsequent growth.

It thus appears that the concept of 'shared growth' needs to be carefully scrutinised. This requires an understanding of the broad forces that led to the reduction in absolute poverty in the region and a greater focus on recent trends in income inequality. This in turn entails a brief reflection on the contemporary relevance of well-known paradigms on the growth–equity nexus, such as the 'Kuznets hypothesis' (Kuznets, 1955) and Sen's 'entitlement approach' (Sen, 1981).

INEQUALITY, POVERTY AND ECONOMIC DEVELOPMENT: THE ISSUES

This chapter started with the notion of 'shared growth' – a notion advocated by the World Bank. As noted, shared growth has two elements: inequality and poverty alleviation. The conventional wisdom is that the countries of the Asia-Pacific region exhibit the rare case of rapid growth with sustained reductions in income inequality and absolute poverty. What do available theories say about the mechanisms that lead to such an outcome? To what extent are these theories and general propositions ratified by the experience of Pacific Asia? These are the central questions that form the substance of the rest of the chapter.

It would be useful to commence the discussion in this section by making a distinction between the structural determinants of poverty and inequality and policy-induced effects on these variables. The distinction is, of course, artificial, given that structure and policy interact concurrently and continuously. Nevertheless, the development literature typically takes as its point of reference the hypothesis, first developed by Kuznets (1955), that there are inevitable trends in income distribution during the course of development which occur independently of policy interventions. At the same time, the development literature in the 1970s was replete with attempts to identify appropriate policy measures to reduce poverty and to bring about a more equal distribution of income (Ahluwalia et al., 1979; Streeten et al., 1981). In the 1980s, this preoccupation changed in form but not in substance. The concern of the 1980s – which received insufficient attention in the 1970s – was with the impact of macroeconomic stabilisation measures and World Bank/IMF-led structural adjustment programmes on the poor (World Bank, 1990; Heller, 1988; Demery and Addison, 1987; Bourguinon et al., 1991; Summers and Pritchett, 1993). Thus, the distinction between structure and policy, which will be consistently maintained in this chapter, is meant to capture cross-currents in the development literature.

As noted earlier, in a classic paper, Kuznets (1955) noted a systematic link between inequality and development. He hypothesised a secular trend in inequality for nations undergoing development – with an increase in inequality in the early stages followed by a decrease in the later stages. Although Kuznets adopted a time-series perspective, the revival of interest in the U-shaped hypothesis in the development literature in the 1970s has been dominated by a cross-section view and analysis. Practitioners working with cross-country data have generally tended to support the U-shaped hypothesis (Adelman and Morris, 1973; Paukert, 1973; Ahluwalia, 1976; Lydall, 1977; Cromwell, 1977; Ahluwalia et al., 1979). This has prompted at least one practitioner to note that the U-shaped hypothesis has 'acquired the force of economic law' (Robinson, 1976).

The U-shaped hypothesis however, has its critics (Beckerman, 1977; Lee, 1977; Paukert, 1973; Anand and Kanbur, 1981; Fields, 1995). The critique highlights a number of points: the hypothesis, as resurrected in the development literature, is based on cross-country data which are not comparable; the database encompasses countries with different policy and political environments, and hence is not relevant to an examination of a hypothesis pertaining to the 'natural' history of the development/growth process; cross-section data cannot be used to make time-series inferences; and finally, the hypothesis is highly sensitive to the data set and the functional form used (Anand and Kanbur, 1981).

Although imaginative attempts have been made to formalise the Kuznets model (see, for example, Anand and Kanbur, 1981, 1984), the fact remains that it is essentially devoid of analytical and policy content. Given that the Kuznets framework inevitably abstracts from the complex array of other structural factors which influence movements in inequality and poverty, can one think of alternative approaches?

As a starting point, some practitioners, such as Bigsten (1989) and Sundrum (1990), attempt to provide a checklist of structural factors (e.g. intersectoral labour allocation, population pressure, asset distribution, technology, factor-market performance) which affect income distribution. However, as Lal (1976) has warned, it is not enough to have a checklist. It is necessary to show how the various structural factors interact. It would be fair to maintain that a robust and general model of income distribution is yet to be constructed. Sen (1981), however, has made an ambitious attempt in this direction in his 'entitlements approach'. In a subsequent contribution, Sen (1985) has focused on conceptualising poverty as the lack of certain basic capabilities. Prime examples include the ability to avoid hunger and illiteracy, which is rather different from income-based approaches to poverty. As will be argued in greater detail at a later stage, the advantage of Sen's work lies in the fact that it allows the prevailing policy environment to be easily incorporated as a major influence on income distribution.

As Sen (1981: 308) puts it:

Each economic and political system produces a set of entitlement relations governing who can have what in that system. For a market economy, the determining variables of entitlements can be broadly split into:
(i) ownership vector...
(ii) exchange entitlement mapping...

The former pertains to the portfolio of physical and human capital assets which a person owns. The latter pertains to the ability of an individual to acquire, given his or her ownership bundle, the alternative bundles of commodities through production or trade.

Sen maintains (1981: 311) that:

> Poverty removal ... is ultimately dependent on a wide distribution of effective entitlements, and this – for any given level of per capita income – would tend to be reflected in the low level of inequality in the distribution of income.

What causes a 'wide distribution of effective entitlements'? There are two generic forces corresponding to the distinction that Sen makes between ownership vector and exchange entitlement mapping. Thus, any factor or set of factors which affect the ownership vector would directly influence both poverty and inequality. Common examples include a sustained increase in the overall volume of assets and asset redistribution, such as land reform. Similarly, any factor or set of factors which influence the exchange entitlement mapping will in turn affect poverty and inequality. Examples include the shifts in terms of trade faced by poor peasants, the availability of employment opportunities for semi-skilled and unskilled workers and the direct provision of 'basic needs' (primary education, basic health-care services, low-cost housing, etc.) by the state.

As should be obvious, the 'entitlement approach' does not make neat predictions concerning the time-path of inequality and poverty during the course of development as do models that belong to the Kuznets genre. All that it suggests is that the key structural determinant of inequality in a market economy is the set of entitlement relations. Any market economy at any stage of development will experience either a decline or a rise in poverty and inequality depending upon the nature of changes in its set of entitlement relations.

Critics of the 'entitlement approach' may seize upon its lack of predictive capacity as a weakness. One could also argue that the distinction between ownership vector and exchange entitlement mapping is rather stylised and is not always helpful. Thus, to take one example, rapid expansion of primary education affects both the exchange entitlement mapping and the ownership vector. The position maintained by this chapter is that, despite these alleged limitations, the 'Entitlement Approach' represents a marked improvement on Kuznets-type views on income distribution in developing economies. The simplicity of the Kuznets model is gained at the expense of analytical content. More importantly, the prevailing policy environment does not seem to play any explicit and important role in the determination of income distribution. The advantage of the 'Entitlement Approach' is that it assigns an explicit and significant role to public policy in terms of its impact on poverty and inequality. Public policy thus becomes the subject of discussion at this juncture.

Policy measures which influence both the ownership vector and the exchange entitlement mapping will in turn influence outcomes on poverty and inequality. This seems to be the key message of the 'Entitlement Approach'. One obvious example of a policy measure which directly affects the ownership vector in a developing economy is asset redistribution through land reform. Since land is a key asset in many, if not most developing countries, land reform has understandably been the subject of much discussion in the development literature. However, as is well known, land reform is a politically costly exercise and is thus not a readily useful policy option in most cases. This suggests the need to consider more feasible policy alternatives which have poverty-alleviating potential.

There are two broad policy measures which have considerable relevance in influencing the set of entitlement relations in a market economy: employment creation and direct provision of basic needs by the state. Consider first the case of employment creation. One could argue that it affects both the ownership vector and the exchange entitlement mapping. Thus, the principal asset of the poor is their labour services. Employment creation, by enhancing the value of this asset, would influence the prevailing ownership vector. At the same time, the enhanced purchasing power of the poor generated by employment creation allows them to acquire the preferred bundle of alternative commodities – thus affecting the exchange entitlement mapping. Given that employment creation works through both channels, it is a powerful redistributive tool.

What is the most effective way to create employment of the labour services of the poor on a sustainable basis? It is at this juncture that the notion of export-oriented industrialisation becomes highly relevant to the discussion. As is well known, export-oriented industrialisation provides the opportunity for developing economies to intensively utilise a key resource which is in plentiful supply: semi-skilled and unskilled workers. Given that such workers are typically represented in poverty groups, the enhanced purchasing power of such groups reduces poverty. At the same time, this strategy has an equalising influence on income distribution by increasing the income share of poorer groups in society. To this familiar point, Fields (1995) has added the important observation that, to generate favourable income distribution effects, export-oriented industrialisation needs to operate in the context of relatively undistorted labour markets, free of institutional impediments that raise wages above the market-clearing level.

It is worth pointing out that, according to Sen, the key issue is labour-intensive industrialisation rather than export-oriented industrialisation. Employment creation is a means of entitlement raising and whether this is generated via the domestic market or the export market is a secondary issue – see Sen (1981: 299). This point has some appeal but it should be treated with caution. While large economies may rely on domestic markets to foster labour-intensive industrialisation, this is unlikely to be a feasible option for economies with a limited domestic market size. Furthermore, monopoly imperfections which inhibit the growth of labour demand are more likely to crop up in narrow domestic markets than in the global terrain of export markets.

Employment creation may be seen as an indirect means of entitlement raising. It operates through the labour market to enhance the purchasing power of the poor who then acquire their preferred bundle of commodities. A more direct method of entitlement raising is the selective provision of 'basic needs' to the poor by the state (Streeten *et al.*, 1981). Thus, public investments in primary education, basic health delivery systems, low-cost housing, sanitation facilities may all be seen as basic needs which enhance the endowments of the poor as well as their exchange entitlement mapping. Advocates of basic needs would emphasise that as a strategy it is consumption-oriented in appearance but productivity-enhancing in substance. In other words, there are large human capital components in the various basic needs items. The productivity-enhancing effect of education is, of course, well known but it has also been argued that improved nutritional standards and better health facilities raise the productive potential of an individual, have beneficial effects in reducing fertility, and generally enhance a person's adaptability and capacity to change. Thus, the basic needs strategy alleviates poverty both by boosting the current consumption bundle of the poor and by raising their productivity.

Recent strands in the literature have gone beyond the claim that public spending on basic needs is an essential component of poverty alleviation to analysing ways of designing well-targeted spending programmes that have maximum impact in reducing poverty. Such a literature has yielded some reasonably robust conclusions (de Walle, 1995):

- Spending on basic services – in particular primary and secondary education and basic health care – almost universally reaches the poor. This implies that the case for expanding the share of public spending on basic needs – so-called 'broad targeting' – is well substantiated, although vigilance is still necessary in ensuring that the benefits of such spending programmes do not go disproportionately to the better-off.
- Certain interventionist public policies – such as food subsidies, public employment schemes, etc. – have at times been quite pro-poor, but there have also been many cases of dismal failures.
- When poverty is widespread and administrative capacity for monitoring public spending programmes is low, broad targeting is desirable.
- Generally, what is needed is a combination of universalism on certain spending categories (usually of a basic-needs type) and finer targeting in others (for providing safety nets, for example). Such a two-pronged approach provides a good basis for policy design.

Finally, it would be useful to round up the discussion by asking: which strategy – employment creation or basic needs provisions (or 'broad targeting') – is more effective in alleviating poverty and generating a more equal distribution of income? It is best to regard the two as complementary rather than competing strategies. As the World Bank puts it (1990: 51):

> Both elements are essential. The first provides the poor with opportunities to use their most abundant asset – labour. The second improves their immediate well-being and increases their capacity to take advantage of the newly created possibilities. Together, they can improve the lives of . . . the poor.

While employment creation and basic needs provisions were core policy issues in the 1970s and they continue to be so today, the 1980s added a new dimension to the debate on the impact of the policy environment on poverty and income distribution. This stems from the fact that a number of developing economies have experienced serious macroeconomic imbalances manifested in unsustainable fiscal deficits, rising external indebtedness, balance-of-payments problems and rampant inflation. This has prompted the governments of these countries to implement orthodox stabilisation measures – fiscal restraints, tight credit controls, etc. – in order to restore macroeconomic equilibrium. In addition, many developing economies have followed structural adjustment policies recommended by key multilateral institutions – the World Bank and the International Monetary Fund – as the condition for loans to deal with their macroeconomic disequilibrium. These structural adjustment policies usually entail efforts to implement policy reform as a means of boosting aggregate supply. The intention is not only to offset the aggregate demand reduction caused by orthodox stabilisation measures but to provide the basis for future growth. The typical elements in structural adjustment measures entail minimising distortions in the relative price structure through trade liberalisation, deregulation of product and factor markets as well as privatisation. The primary objective is to achieve a more internationalised, private-sector-driven economy. While sound in principle, the practice of macroeconomic stabilisation-cum-structural-adjustment has, according to some critics, led to unanticipated adverse consequences on poverty and income distribution. This has prompted many development observers to seek macroeconomic adjustment 'with a human face' (Cornia *et al.*, 1988).

Summers and Pritchett (1993: 385) have responded to this critique by offering qualified support IMF/World Bank-led adjustment programmes. As they put it:

> Evidence suggests that the poor fared better on average in adjusting nations though they are often hurt in the stabilization phase when recession is unavoidable. There is also no evidence that social indicators (e.g., infant mortality) have deteriorated in adjusting countries.

Why should these stabilisation-cum-adjustment measures lead to adverse income-distribution consequences? The reduction in aggregate demand engenders a rise in unemployment and this, in turn, directly affects the living standards of the poor. More ominously, faced with the exigencies of restoring macroeconomic equilibrium, many developing countries cut back public expenditure on essential social services, many of which are critical in maintaining the well-being of the poor. The long-term implications are adverse, as these developments can be seen as de facto divestment of human capital.

It is important, in making an assessment of the link between adjustment measures and poverty, that a number of factors be taken into account. First, the adverse impact of adjustment measures on poverty is essentially of a short-run nature. In principle, adjustment measures should boost output growth in the medium-to-long run and thus create sustainable employment opportunities for the poor. Second, there are important components of adjustment measures, such as exchange rate depreciation, which have distributional consequences. Exchange rate depreciation typically boosts demand for labour-intensive exports in the manufacturing sector and also assists small farmers who produce exportable goods. Third, the income distribution consequences are in many cases quite complex, creating a diverse range of gainers and losers so that the net effect is not always clear. Thus, for example, deregulating controls on food prices – a favourite item in the adjustment agenda – will boost living standards of small farmers who are net producers of food, but hurt landless rural workers and the urban poor.

Despite the above qualifications, the fact remains that adjustment measures can, under certain circumstances, cause at least a transitional increase in poverty. Thus the current policy challenge is to find means of cushioning these unfavourable effects of adjustment. The World Bank (1990: chapter 7) has called for attempts to protect public expenditure on basic-needs-type services through a temporary pause in investment and, more importantly, through a restructuring of the government's fiscal position – a conclusion that is endorsed by Summers and Pritchett (1993). This would entail, as Sundrum (1990: 282) puts it 'increasing public revenue mainly by taxes falling on the upper income-groups, and by reducing public expenditure on services whose benefits accrue mainly to these groups'. Several studies of country-specific experiences have in fact shown that countries which have been able to adopt measures similar to the ones mentioned were successful in offsetting the adverse effects of stabilisation-cum-adjustment policies on the poor – as will be demonstrated later in a more detailed case study of two Asia-Pacific nations (Malaysia and Indonesia).

There is a more fundamental lesson which one learns from the discussion so far. Efficient macroeconomic management and correspondingly efficient microeconomic policies may not always be seen as poverty-alleviating and redistributive strategies in the same spirit that such measures as, say, land reform are. However, macro-cum-micro policies, taken in their entirety, are critical in creating an environment in which equitable growth can take place.

INEQUALITY, POVERTY AND ECONOMIC DEVELOPMENT: ASIA-PACIFIC EXPERIENCE

This section provides a broad sketch of medium-term trends in inequality and poverty in the economies of the Asia-Pacific region. Two measures are used – the Gini ratio for income inequality and the head-count ratio as a measure of poverty (that is, the proportion of the population lying below a given poverty line). The latter is also supplemented by a 'social indicator' (infant mortality). While the Gini ratio is an acceptable measure of income inequality, it has been recognised for some time that the head-count ratio is a theoretically inadequate measure of poverty (e.g. Sen, 1976). Nevertheless, when it is not possible to use more robust, 'distribution-sensitive' poverty measures, 'it is better to use the...Headcount Ratio than to use no index at all' (Asian Development Bank, 1994: 191).

Before delving into details, the reader needs to be reminded about problems of access to reliable data – a problem that is particularly acute in the case of income distribution statistics. As Fields (1995) has correctly emphasised, such statistics are simply not published regularly anywhere, and the international agencies, such as the World Bank, have been notoriously reticent about providing data through their regular published sources. When attempts are made to construct such data sets, not many countries meet the test of reliability – see Fields (forthcoming). These observations should be borne in mind when interpreting the information provided in the following tables.

Table 7.1 shows head-count ratios for regional aggregates – East Asia vs other regions of the world for a particular year (1990) and we follow this up with more country-specific details (Table 7.2). As can be seen, East Asia has a considerably lower level of poverty (11 per cent) compared with the average for other developing countries (30 per cent). Another popular mea-

Table 7.1 Poverty indices: East Asia vs other regions, 1990, 1992

Region	Head-count index (%) 1990	Infant mortality (per 1,000) 1990	Human development index (HDI) 1992
East Asia	11	34	0.636 (0.874 excluding PRC)
Latin America	25	47	0.822
Middle East and N. Africa	33	80	0.644
Sub-Saharan Africa	48	107	0.389
South Asia	49	92	0.453
Aggregate	30	63	0.570

Sources: Adapted from Squire, 1993: table 1, p. 378 for head-count index and infant mortality. The human development index (HDI) is adapted from UNDP, 1995, table 39, p. 214.
Notes: HDI is a composite index made up of life expectancy, educational enrolments at different levels and per capita real GDP measured in terms of purchasing power parity (PPP). HDI has a maximum value of 1.00, indicating the highest level of achievement in human development. The head-count index is based on a poverty line in 1985 purchasing power parity dollars (PPP) of $370 per person per year.

sure of social progress (infant mortality) shows that the index of infant mortality in East Asia (28 per 1,000) is well below the developing country average (63 per 1,000). The UNDP's human development index (HDI) also depicts a story of success. What is even more germane to the discussion here is that East Asian performance in terms of these basic indices is significantly better than that of Latin America – a region at a similar income level to the economies of East Asia.

Table 7.2 provides more country-specific details and charts medium-term trends in poverty (as measured by head-count ratios for rural and urban areas) covering, in some cases, a thirty-year time-span (from the 1960s to the 1990s). The story that one can tell from Table 7.2 is one of unmitigated success as far as poverty alleviation is concerned. Poverty has apparently been virtually eliminated in the two city-states of Hong Kong and Singapore. Even in the large, populous economies of the region – such as China and Indonesia – there have been rapid and sustained reductions in both rural and urban poverty over two decades. The sorry exception, once again, is the Philippines. Although poverty fell between 1961 and 1991, the rate of progress was slow and the incidence of poverty remains rather high compared with other economies of the region. The cases of Indonesia and the Philippines are worth noting. Both are island economies and at similar income levels: US$670 GNP per capita for Indonesia vs US$770 GNP per capita for the Philippines (in 1992 prices). Yet, rural poverty was 18.5 per cent

Table 7.2 Medium-term trends in absolute poverty (head-count ratios): Asia-Pacific experience

Country (year)		Urban (%)	Rural (%)
China	1978		33.0
	1985	1.9	11.9
	1990	0.4	11.5
Indonesia	1970	50.7	58.5
	1980	19.7	44.6
	1987	8.3	18.5
Philippines	1961	50.5	64.1
	1971	40.6	57.3
	1991	36.7	52.4
Korea	1965	54.9	35.8
	1980	10.4	9.0
	1984	4.6	4.4
Hong Kong	1963/64	35.6	
	1973/74	3.5	
Singapore	1972/73	7.0	
	1977/78	1.5	
	1982/83	0.3	

Sources and Notes: Selectively extracted from ADB, 1994, table 3.3, p. 190. Hong Kong and Singapore estimates from Rao, 1988: 38. See Rao and ADB for details on methodology and original sources.

in Indonesia in 1987 and a staggering 52.4 per cent in the Philippines as recently as 1991. Even allowing for different methodologies and data, the comparison is quite striking.

Table 7.3 charts medium-term trends in inequality for a number of Asia-Pacific economies. It would be useful to discuss the two groups – the Asian NIEs (Hong Kong, Singapore, Korea, Taiwan) and the ASEAN-4 (Indonesia, Malaysia, the Philippines, Thailand) – separately. In the case of the former, the general trend seems to be a fall in inequality for a certain period followed by a perceptible shift towards greater inequality – particularly in the 1980s. The only exception seems to be Taiwan where the sharp decline in inequality between 1964 and 1970 apparently seems to be followed by a phase (1976–90) of relative constancy in the value of the Gini ratio. These conclusions seem to be at variance with the trends reported in Fields (1995, see especially p. 103).

In the case of the ASEAN-4, Thailand stands out as a case where there has been a rather sharp increase in inequality between 1975 and 1990. In Indonesia, a moderate fall in the value of the Gini ratio between 1976 and 1980 has been offset by an equally moderate increase in inequality between 1990 and 1993. The Philippines and Malaysia represent cases where inequality was lower in the 1980s than they were in the 1960s and 1970s – but then the initial values of the Gini ratio were rather high.

It thus appears that one can no longer maintain the conventional wisdom that the Asia-Pacific economies represent rare cases of rapid, egalitarian

Table 7.3 Trends in income distribution (as measured by Gini ratio) in eight Asia-Pacific economies, 1961–93

Hong Kong Year and value of Gini ratio	Korea Year and value of Gini ratio	Singapore Year and value of Gini ratio	Taiwan Year and value of Gini ratio	Indonesia Year and value of Gini ratio	Philippines Year and value of Gini ratio	Malaysia Year and value of Gini ratio	Thailand Year and value of Gini ratio
1966 0.49	1964 0.34	1966 0.50	1964 0.36	1976 0.34	1961 0.49	1968 0.50	1965 0.41
1971 0.44	1970 0.33	1973 0.46	1970 0.30	1980 0.34	1965 0.49	1970 0.51	1968 0.43
1976 0.44	1976 0.39	1980 0.41	1976 0.31	1987 0.32	1971 0.48	1976 0.53	1975 0.45
1980 0.37	1980 0.39	1986 0.46	1980 0.31	1990 0.32	1986 0.45	1979 0.49	1981 0.47
1986 0.42	1988 0.40	1989 0.49	1985 0.32	1993 0.34	1989 0.45	1988 0.46	1986 0.50
1991 0.45			1990 0.31				1990 0.50

Sources and Notes: Selectively extracted from Medhi, 1994, table 1, p. 61. See Medhi (1994) for details on original sources.

growth. It was probably a valid proposition from the vantage point of the 1960s and 1970s, but more recent trends suggest a different story.

How should one interpret these patterns of poverty and inequality, given the analytical discussion of the previous section? To start with, how do these cases relate to the standard bench-mark in international comparisons of income distribution, namely, the Kuznets hypothesis or the Kuznets curve? The first-generation literature on the East Asian NIEs often noted that this group of economies defied the pessimistic predictions of the Kuznets curve. Ironically, they still defy the predictions of the Kuznets curve, but in a rather different fashion.

As Medhi (1994: 70) concludes:

The available data indicate that the distribution of income in the... Asian NIEs... has shown a tendency to become more unequal in recent years. This is in contrast to the earlier periods of their development where income inequality declined as the economies grew... It suggests the reverse of the Kuznets hypothesis, according to which the income distribution gets worse... before it gets better later.

The stylised facts that need to be explained are thus the following: reduction in inequality in the early stages of growth followed by an increase later in the case of the NIEs; cases of growing inequality in some of the ASEAN economies, especially Thailand; sustained and rapid reductions in poverty across all the Asia-Pacific economies.

At this stage one can resurrect the entitlements approach which considers distributional changes as the product of changes in the ownership vector and changes in exchange entitlement mapping. Changes in a key ownership vector – land ownership in the rural areas of Taiwan and South Korea – have been influenced by historical circumstances. In both these countries, land reform programmes were implemented at the end of the 1940s – often under foreign (American) supervision. In the case of South Korea, land reforms were instituted between 1947 and 1949, with the net outcome being a redistribution of land owned by big farmers and absentee landlords. The effect on the size of distribution of land ownership can be gleaned from the following statistics. In the late 1930s, 3 per cent of all farm households had owned over 66 per cent of all land, whereas by the end of the 1940s, less than 7 per cent of all households were landless (Amsden, 1989: 38). In addition, it must be noted that the destruction caused by the Korean War had a levelling effect on asset distribution (Choo, 1975).

In the case of Taiwan, land reform entailed the following elements: rent reduction, sale of public land and the 'land to the tillers programme'. The net effect was that between 1949 and 1957, owner–farmers as a proportion of all farmers increased from 36 to 60 per cent (Kuo, 1975). Thus, in both the cases of Taiwan and South Korea, early land reforms played an important role in generating a relatively equitable distribution of income in the initial stages of their rapid economic growth.

While asset redistribution in South Korea and Taiwan explains the trend towards less equality in the early stages of their rapid economic growth, the same analysis cannot be applied to the cases of Singapore and Hong Kong. Moreover, even in the cases of South Korea and Taiwan, one has to consider durable factors – rather than one-shot asset redistribution – in explaining long-term trends in inequality and poverty. As the entitlement approach emphasises, in a developing, labour-surplus economy, the utilisation and returns to labour services represent the major mechanisms for reducing poverty and generating more equitable growth. Seen from this perspective, labour-intensive industrialisation – entailing the utilisation of semi-skilled and unskilled workers – represents the key route to the reduction of poverty. All the four NIEs are, of course, characterised by labour-intensive industrialisation fostered by an export-oriented regime. This produced full employment and rapid growth of real wages within the span of a decade.

Labour-intensive industrialisation loses some of its explanatory significance in the light of recent increases in inequality in East Asian NIEs. The very success of export-oriented industrialisation in eliminating labour-surplus conditions in East Asia provided the momentum for a policy shift emphasising industrial restructuring. A growing phase of labour scarcity entailed an inevitable upward pressure on labour costs which, without a compensating increase in productivity, posed an inevitable threat to sustained competitive advantage in labour-intensive products. This was the common driving force towards the adoption of restructuring policies in East Asia during the 1970s. The precise timing, scale and intensity of these policies varied across the countries. In Singapore, the restructuring policies were pursued vigorously between 1979 and 1984; in Korea, these policies were particularly evident between 1973 and 1979. Restructuring efforts in Taiwan and Hong Kong have been less intensive and vigorous, with such policies being primarily effective in the financial sector in Hong Kong.

The impact of restructuring on income distribution works primarily via income adjustments in the labour market. Incentives to guide resources in capital- and skill-intensive sectors tend to increase the demand for skilled and professional workers at the expense of semi-skilled and unskilled workers. At the same time, efforts to increase the supply of skills through the education and training system take time to catch up with the changes in labour demand patterns. Thus, one probable outcome is that income distribution turns unfavourably against workers with lower human capital endowments. Suggestive evidence supporting this proposition can be found in Chowdhury and Islam (1993: chapter 12).

Specific policies associated with the restructuring process and the transition to a labour-scarce phase probably contributed to the worsening inequality in South Korea and Singapore. In the former, the government explicitly tried to favour large firms – and in particular the chaebols (large diversified business groups) – by offering them preferential credit so that they could play a leading role in moving the economy towards heavy, capital-intensive industries. This led to a sharp increase in industrial concentration and offset the relatively equitable asset distribution which Korea had in the 1950s (Amsden, 1989; Kim, 1986). In the case of Singapore, it was noted that a selective immigration policy caused labour market segmentation and contributed to rising inequality. It is necessary to add to this observation that the selective immigration policy was pursued as an adjunct to the process of industrial restructuring.

In the case of Hong Kong, Lin (1985) has noted that the worsening income distribution between 1976 and 1981 coincided with an increase in the size of the service sector, particularly financial services. In a subsequent contribution, Lin (1994) has made the point that that shift of resources towards the service sector (so-called 'de-industrialisation') has been accompanied by a shift of the most labour-intensive industries from Hong Kong to China, reducing the demand for low-income workers and depressing wage levels.

An important aspect of inequality in the NIEs that has been insufficiently studied pertains to the implications that follow from the demographic transition that occurs in tandem with the transition to a labour-scarce phase. One can witness an irreversible decline in fertility, implying that, over time, such societies will have a relatively high cohort of older people. Deaton (1995) has shown that, in such situations, inequality tends to increase primarily because consumption and income among the old are more unequally distributed (the so-called 'within-cohort effect'), but also because inequality between age groups tends to go up (the so-called between-cohort effect'). Deaton provides evidence from Taiwan to support these propositions.

Consider now the case of the ASEAN-4. At least three of the economies (Indonesia, Malaysia, Thailand) are widely regarded to be the most recent examples of export-oriented, labour-intensive industrialisation. Rapid and sustained reductions in poverty in those economies may thus be attributed to this general factor. The impact on income distribution is, however, more complex. While inequality in Malaysia has fallen, the case of Thailand represents an opposite extreme, with a sustained phase of growing inequality. This contrast could be partly explained by the fact that Malaysia has had, ever since 1969, a strong commitment to redistributive policies in the form of the New Economic Policy (NEP) whose purpose was to improve the economic well-being of the Malay population (the ethnically dominant and politically powerful group in Malaysia). Commentators generally agree that this redistributive strategy at least partially explains the improvement in income distribution (Medhi, 1994; World Bank, 1993a) – primarily because it was conceived as a 'positive-sum game': improvement in the economic well-being of the Malays, but not at the expense of others and in the context of a growing economy.

Thailand stands out as a case of successful labour-intensive industrialisation which, while responsible for reductions in overall poverty, has not apparently had a commensurate impact on income inequality. Medhi (1994), drawing on the contributions of Atchana and Teerana (1989) and Pranee (forthcoming), maintains that relative income standards of workers and households in the industrial and service sectors grew more rapidly relative to workers and households in the agricultural sector. This presumably reflects benign neglect of the agricultural sector which, incidentally, is the reverse of what happened in Indonesia – see Thorbecke (1991).

The entitlement approach also emphasises that the direct provision of basic needs by the state is an effective mechanism for reducing poverty and inequality. Dreze and Sen (1990) are strong advocates of the view that economic growth may not lead to broad-based improvement in standards of health and education as reflected in such indicators as life expectancy, child mortality, primary enrolment rates and adult literacy unless they are accompanied by deliberate public provision of basic services. Dreze and Sen approvingly cite the case of particular countries (such as Sri Lanka) and particular states (such as Kerala in India) to substantiate their case.

The common perception is that the mechanism of basic needs provision was less important in East Asia. The process of acquiring basic needs by the poor occurred through the market rather than through deliberate public action. In other words, the higher income generated through labour-intensive industrialisation to large segments of the population provided them with the necessary purchasing power to acquire basic needs.

This view is certainly not valid when one extends the sample of Asia-Pacific economies to include China. Given its political ideology, China has a commitment to an interventionist basic needs strategy – see, for example, Ahmad and Wang (1991), World Bank (1992). The Asian Development Bank (1994: 198) summarises the Chinese experience in the following manner:

> Through its efforts to provide improved health, education, disability and retirement benefits, China has achieved a much lower rate of poverty than would be expected given its level of national income. China has also attained levels of social indicators which exceed those of much wealthier countries.

Even in the case of the market economies of Pacific Asia, elements of both 'broad targeting' (the universal provision of basic services) and 'narrow targeting' (income transfers focusing on particular services and particular segments of the population) can be found. Thus, in the case of Hong Kong, apparently the epitome of *laissez-faire* policies, Lin and Ho (1984: 50) note:

> the government spends something approaching one-fourth of the national income providing various sorts of physical infrastructure...compulsory primary education, extensive medical and health services,

subventions for numerous social welfare agencies, and public low-cost housing for well over 40 per cent of the population.

An ambitious low-cost public housing programme is also a key feature of Singapore (Lim *et al.*, 1988). In addition, it is well known that in all the East Asian NIEs, large-scale public investment in education and training ranging from basic levels to tertiary levels was made. Thus, in many respects, the NIEs followed a 'basic needs' strategy that not only improved social well-being but was also investment-oriented in the sense of augmenting the productivity of human resources. This aspect of public policy is also being replicated in the emerging NIEs of South East Asia.

While labour-intensive industrialisation, the transition to a labour-scarce phase in the NIEs, and public spending on basic needs have been the key driving forces in moulding medium-term trends in income distribution in Pacific Asia, to what extent have short-term changes in inequality and poverty in the economies of the region borne the brunt of the macroeconomic stabilisation and structural adjustment of the 1980s? As noted, this is a topical and somewhat contentious issue, given the view of some critics who believe that the macroeconomic stabilisation and structural adjustment of the 1980s have, in many cases, worsened inequality and poverty. Have the economies of the region suffered a similar fate? Brief case studies of Indonesia and Malaysia are offered followed by broad reflections on the NIEs.

Table 7.4 Macro-stabilisation, structural adjustment and income distribution: Malaysia, Indonesia, 1978–89

Country	Year/origin of crisis	Particular characteristics	Main macro policies	Poverty indicators
Malaysia (1978–87)	1982–83 OECD recession Expansionary fiscal policy Deteriorating terms of key primary commodities (rubber, tin, oil)	No recourse to IMF NEP during 1970s Foreign borrowing till 1984 Persistent large fiscal deficits	Devaluation (1984) Cuts in public expenditure	Urban poverty up slightly, rural down Distributional shift to Malays maintained During adjustment period, annual increases in education (5.7%), health (3.7%)
Indonesia (1979–89)	1982–83 Decline in terms of trade (oil) OECD recession	No recourse to IMF Balanced budget (constitutionally required) Continued access to foreign funds	Devaluation Interest rate liberalisation Trade reform Tax reform Fiscal restraint	Poverty fell, both urban and income distribution stable Cuts in social expenditure (schools, clinics) starting in 1986

Sources: Extracted from Bourguignon *et al.*, 1991: 1493, which, in turn, draws on Demery and Demery, 1991 (Malaysia) and Thorbecke, 1991 (Indonesia)

As can be seen from Table 7.4, both Malaysia and Indonesia experienced unanticipated external shocks in 1982–83: OECD recession and deteriorating terms of trade. Buoyed up by the 1979 commodity and oil price boom, Malaysia entered into a path of unsustainable fiscal expansion, while Indonesia was unable to restructure its economy from its dependence on the oil sector. Yet, faced by the adverse external shocks of the early 1980s, policy-makers in both economies responded swiftly with a combination of macro-stabilisation and structural adjustment measures. Indonesia, in particular, embarked on wide-ranging fiscal, financial and trade reform. What is most germane to the discussion here is that both economies managed to maintain their momentum of poverty alleviation and apparently did not experience any adverse trends in inequality throughout the period of adjustment. Indonesia and Malaysia have thus defied the pessimistic claims of those who maintain that adjustment in the 1980s led to immiserisation in many developing countries.

The information in Table 7.4 provides some clues to this happy outcome. First, both economies had access to foreign funds at a time when such access for many developing economies was denied. This is itself a reflection of the perceived credibility of domestic policies pursued by Malaysia and Indonesia. More importantly, access to foreign funds served as a very significant cushion in dealing with the external shocks of the early 1980s. Second (not shown in the table), both economies had rather favourable initial conditions, namely, rapid investment-driven growth. Third, Malaysia maintained its commitment to social expenditure which grew in real terms during the adjustment phase. Fourth, Indonesia maintained its commitment to rural development even during the difficult period of the 1980s, although it did start cutting down on social expenditure around 1986. Finally, both economies combined fiscal contraction with expenditure-switching policies.

In sum, Indonesia and Malaysia represent clear examples of economies that offset the adverse distributional consequences of macroeconomic austerity through a policy package that is advocated by those who claim that adjustment measures need a 'human face'. Using simulation exercises, Thorbecke (1991) and Demery and Demery (1991) have shown that these economies would not have yielded markedly better outcomes with alternative policy packages.

The case studies of Indonesia and Malaysia also confirm what one knows in general terms about the NIEs. They have been remarkably successful in resuming rapid growth after every recessionary phase. This has primarily occurred because of the fact that policy-makers took quick and decisive action in terms of pushing through macroeconomic stabilisation measures, in ensuring that expenditure on social services was protected during the recessionary phase, and in being able to maintain the momentum of export-oriented policies (e.g. through exchange rate devaluations). Such favourable policy developments ensured that the adverse impact of cyclical factors on poverty was quickly reversed.

CONCLUDING OBSERVATIONS

This chapter has critically evaluated the conventional wisdom that the economies of the region – in particular the NIEs – represent remarkable examples of shared growth. While it is certainly true in terms of poverty reduction, the evidence is less clear when it comes to recent trends in inequality. One can detect episodes of rising inequality in the NIEs and also in some ASEAN economies, such as Thailand. Possible reasons include the effects flowing from the transition to a labour-scarce phase, the dynamics of demography and country-specific factors. The chapter also evaluated the recent debate on the impact of stabilisation-cum-structural-adjustment policies in East Asia and concluded that the countries of the region have been successful in quickly reversing the adverse impact of cyclical factors on income distribution.

Given the remarkable record of sustained and rapid reductions in poverty (primarily the product of basic needs provision and labour-intensive industrialisation), given the ability of policy-makers to successfully manage the stabilisation-cum-adjustment policies with a 'human face', is one 'nit-picking' when the cases of episodic increases in inequality are highlighted?

If one accepts that the NIEs have experienced a full-scale transition to a labour-scarce phase, and that there has been an irreversible decline in fertility, then they have become what Deaton (1995) has called 'ageing and growing economies'. Deaton (using data from Taiwan and selected developed economies) has shown that overall inequality tends to increase in such economies. Thus, both measured and observed inequality are likely to become a significant social concern in the future. This, in turn, could adversely influence the dynamism of these economies through the mechanism of 'distributive politics' (Alesina and Rodrik, 1994). In other words, when inequality becomes a major social concern, it sows the seeds of demands for redistributive measures which in turn retard growth through policy distortions. Indeed, in the case of at least one of the NIEs (Korea), one can detect some evidence of the emergence of 'distributive politics'. As Leipziger *et al.* (1992: xi–xii) put it:

> The perception that the economic gains of Korea's rapid growth have not been fairly enough distributed is causing difficulties in the labour market, where workers...are trying to appropriate a portion of the gains they feel have eluded them in the past...Government has indicated that dealing with this perception is one of the highest priorities because it is complicating the task of economic management.

It thus appears that policy-makers in the 'miracle economies' can no longer seek comfort from the somewhat outmoded knowledge that the problem of inequality has been eliminated through rapid growth.

Chapter 8

Epilogue: Democracy and development in the Asia-Pacific region

INTRODUCTION

The economic dynamism of a select band of economies in the Asia-Pacific region has deservedly attracted international acclaim. As the brief thematic review has shown – and as elaborated in the country profiles in Part II – these economies have exhibited rapid, persistent growth that, at the same time, has led to rapid, sustainable reductions in poverty. Some of them – such as Singapore and Hong Kong – now boast per capita income levels that (when measured in current exchange rates) are above Australia and New Zealand. Others – such as Korea – are poised to join the ranks of the club of industrialised nations through membership of the OECD. Malaysia, Indonesia and Thailand are proudly wearing the badge of the 'next-generation' NIEs. While other transition economies – such as Russia – are still struggling with the trauma of transforming a *dirigiste* economy – China has demonstrated how, within the space of a decade, pragmatic management of market-oriented reforms can fuel the forces of rapid, sustained growth.

Despite such wonderful achievements, the premier group of Asia-Pacific economies have shown some stresses and strains of rapid change and have to negotiate some formidable challenges in the future. Perceptions about growing income disparities, the protection of human rights and environmental degradation are emerging as major social issues. One could argue that these issues are particular manifestations of the central problem of constructing viable forms of democratic governance as growing affluence inevitably unleashes such demands in civil society. Some of these countries – such as Korea and Taiwan – apparently seem to be on the verge of resolving this problem, but many others simply have not come to terms with it.

The economies of the region are now facing an era fraught with tensions and uncertainties. On the one hand, there are those (e.g. Huntingdon, 1991) who maintain that the 1980s witnessed the 'third wave' of democratisation, but there are others who believe that progress towards democracy in the developing world is still disappointingly modest (Kohli, 1993). How much progress towards democracy have the countries of the region made in relation to this alleged 'third wave'? What are the obstacles and constraints to the transition to democratic governance? More importantly, is such a transition even desirable, given a powerful body of entrenched opinion that maintains that liberal-democratic traditions are not fully compatible with core 'Asian values' which in turn are seen as the fundamental intangibles that undergird economic dynamism in the region? These are the key questions that will continue to occupy the energy and attention of policy-makers and political leaders in the region in the medium term. Such issues deserve some reflection.

PROGRESS TOWARDS DEMOCRACY IN THE ASIA-PACIFIC REGION: A DURABLE TRANSITION?

Hungtingdon's much-noted 'third wave' hypothesis has strident supporters. Consider the following observations:

> Men and Women with the courage of their democratic convictions have in a half generation overthrown tyrannies of one stripe or another throughout Latin America, Eastern and Central Europe, the former Soviet Union, parts of Northeast Asia and Southeast Asia and Africa. Now throughout these vast regions civic cultures are evolving, the institutions of constitutional self government are being constructed, the rule of law is taking hold.
>
> (National Endowment for Democracy, 1991: 3)

The editors of the *Journal of Democracy*, the official journal of the National Endowment for Democracy, summarise the democratic transition in the world – and in the Asia-Pacific region – in the following manner:

> Democracy has made great strides in the past five years...Democratic regimes are gradually taking hold...throughout Eastern and Central Europe...In Asia, Nepal and Bangladesh experienced democratic transitions during the [last] five years. Taiwan has virtually completed one... South Korea is moving toward democratic consolidation. Thailand's regime remains more ambiguous, but its massive May 1992 demonstrations against military domination of politics, forcing constitutional changes and new elections, have made a future military coup much less likely.
>
> Apart from the Middle East, Africa remains the region with the most stubborn persistence of authoritarian rule. Yet authoritarian regimes have been destabilised there as never before and vigorous civil societies are emerging.
>
> (*Journal of Democracy*, 1995: 3–4)

Kohli (1986: 684) has warned against the uncritical acceptance of such views. As he puts it:

The so-called democratic revolution in the developing world has run into numerous problems. A majority of developing countries continue to be ruled by authoritarian rulers. Those who have made transitions, as well as some longer-standing ones, are now experiencing chaotic politics and growing centralisation. A well functioning democracy is a rare exception in the contemporary developing world.

Some advocates of the Huntingdon hypothesis agree that 'in many new democracies of the "third wave" – and some that have existed for several decades – political parties and institutions have become less effective and democratic' (*Journal of Democracy*, 1995: 3–4).

It is thus clear that, while there is evidence of democratic transition on a global scale, there is no room for complacency. The various countries of the Asia-Pacific region are certainly part of this global trend, but nagging doubts remain whether such a transition is widespread and durable. Alagappa (1995) has offered a more nuanced account of the nature of progress towards democracy in the Asia-Pacific region. The picture that he paints is one of caution and guarded optimism.

Consider, to start with, the cases of *Taiwan* and *South Korea*, widely regarded to be in a phase of democratic consolidation. The biggest challenge that Taiwan faces is that, in response to domestic demands for ending the country's international isolation, future democratically elected governments may adopt a more aggressive stance against the PRC. This in turn may heighten tensions, generate demands for strengthening national security and provide the basis for a renewed role for the military in Taiwanese politics.

In the case of South Korea, one could argue that the 1992 election of the first civilian President – Kim Young Sam – marks the perpetual termination of military rule in the country. But there are enduring concerns about the durability of the democratic transition. Corruption and bribery afflict the political process, exemplified most recently by the initiation of criminal proceedings against Roh Tae Woo – the military strongman under whose regime South Korea formally emerged as a democracy (*New York Times*, 2 December 1995). Woo faces allegations that – during his regime – he built up a personal 'slush fund' through illegal contributions from the corporate sector. Apart from such scandals, one also has to contend with the fact that the institutionalisation of political parties is yet to be accomplished, there is a concentration of power in the executive, and the rule of law has been slow to develop. As in the case of Taiwan, national security considerations always loom large, in this case driven by the perceived threat of a North Korean invasion. Despite talks and discussions about re-unification, relations with North Korea remain highly uncertain and tense and pose the risk that this could be manipulated by the military to re-assert their role in South Korean politics.

Observers agree that in *Thailand* and the *Philippines*, democratic development has not consolidated itself. Political parties in Thailand are fractured along regional lines, have weak organisational structures and are so numerous that they generate the need for potentially unstable coalition governments. Moreover, the military remains a central force in Thai politics and always casts a shadow on the durability of civilian governance.

Alagappa (1995: 31) maintains that

> in the Philippines, little substantive progress has been made since the restoration of formal democracy in 1986... Most governing elites belong to old political clans, and in recent years there has been a return to pork-barrel and patronage politics. Political parties remain weak; the legal system is inaccessible to most citizens, inefficient and weakened by wide-spread corruption and bribery... violations of civil rights are common.

One could argue that in a formal, nominal sense, *Singapore* and *Malaysia* represent cases of long-standing and well-functioning democracies in the Asia-Pacific region. There are, after all, free elections and the rule of law is well established by regional standards. Political scientists, however, are inclined to treat them as 'semi-democracies'. A dominant party has been in power for a long time; the opposition is weak and the personalities of particular leaders – Mahathir in Malaysia and Lee Kuan Yew in Singapore – are writ large on the body politic. Although Lee Kuan Yew has formally stepped down from Prime Ministership, his legacy of tight political control remains intact, particularly in terms of the way dissidents are treated (Seow, 1994; Lingle, 1995). Lingle (1995: 173) makes the strong claim that 'apart from certain oil-rich countries, Singapore is probably the only society in the world that has achieved consistently high standards of living without developing more recognisably democratic institutions'. Moreover, both Mahathir and Lee Kuan Yew are among the most vocal critics of Western-style liberal-democratic traditions – a key point that will be expanded at a later stage.

Any review of political liberalisation in East Asia must take account of the fact that the 'third wave' has still not reached many countries in the region. The *PRC* and *Indonesia* are prominent examples. The Suharto government in Indonesia – which has remained in power since 1965 – has so far enjoyed a high degree of legitimacy primarily on the basis of the need to maintain political stability and sustaining economic development. On both counts, such needs have been amply met. Yet, as Alagappa (1995: 34) has emphasised, the legitimacy of the Suharto government has been questioned since the mid-1980s, by a loose coalition of intellectuals, human rights organisations, Islamic organisations, Christian minorities and some segments of the armed forces. While such dissent has not reached a scale to spark off a political crisis in the near future, the current government cannot ignore the growing tension that is seeping through the political process; a new formula for political legitimacy will have to be found.

The PRC represents a fascinating case for close observers of the process of democratisation in the Asia-Pacific region. Limited political liberalisation was undertaken in combination with market-oriented reforms by the Chinese Communist Party (CCP) in 1979. A salient feature of this political transformation was the 'self-liberalisation' of the Chinese mass media in the 1980s. In ushering such limited changes, the CCP chose what Pei (1994) has called the 'evolutionary authoritarian route' in which a market-based economy is allowed to consolidate itself before full democratisation sets in. However, as the notorious June 1989 Tiananmen incident has demonstrated, the government is prepared to use massive force to suppress mass-based pro-democracy movements. China at this juncture runs the risk of being stuck at the 'politically disreputable half-way point of market authoritarianism' (Prybala, 1995: 165). However, perpetuating this 'half-way point' is inherently difficult. As Pei (1994: 50) notes:

> reform generates forces that simultaneously strengthen the societal groups and movements that directly challenge the old regime and erode the institutions and legitimating principles...for self-preservation [of that regime].

In a subsequent contribution, Pei (1995: 66) has advanced the notion of 'creeping democratisation' in China. As he puts it:

> endogenous and incremental changes in the political institutions of the authoritarian regime are gradually forming subtle but important checks and balances against the ruling party's monopoly of power, strengthening the rule of law, and cultivating self-government at the grass-roots level. Although China's progress in these areas has been extremely limited...if they are allowed to continue, they will gradually lay the institutional foundation for the eventual democratization of China.

Goldman (1994) has identified some promising developments that could sow the seeds of democracy in China. She analyses how internal demands for political transformation have shifted from a cosy circle of 'democratic elite' led by the establishment *literati* to non-establishment activist intellectuals who emerged on the Chinese political stage towards the end of the Deng era. This nascent group has been characterised by attempts to 'bring together diverse social groups and establish an alternative political organisation' (Goldman, 1994: 351). These attempts could in turn contain the 'seeds for the development of a civil society' (Goldman, 1994: 242). Compounding these long-term developments is the event of May 15 1995 when forty-five prominent Chinese intellectuals petitioned China's leaders to reverse the 'counter-revolutionary' verdict on the 1989 peo-democracy movement and highlighted the need for democratic accountability (Documents on Democracy, 1995a: 182).

Despite such promising developments, one should not be lulled into a false sense of optimism. As Alagappa (1995: 35) has warned:

It is hard to envisage democratic transitions occurring in the near term in China...where independent political organisation...will continue to be...hampered by the intolerance of incumbent governments. A new Tiananmen incident would, at best, speed the pace of political change. At worst, it could result in a strengthening of conservative forces and a corresponding diminution of the likelihood of democratic transition.

Pei (1995: 77), the advocate of 'creeping democratisation', is also acutely aware of the risks that lie ahead and the challenges that China faces in sustaining political liberalisation. Thus, one plausible future scenario is an 'accelerating crisis of governability' if the decay of the pre-reform, communist – authoritarian political institutions is not capably replaced by new, pro-democratic political institutions.

In sum, as this brief review of political change in the Asia-Pacific region has shown, significant transformations have occurred, but there are enduring – and well-founded – concerns about the durability of democratic transitions. The 'third wave' may not as yet prove to be decisive enough in overwhelming non-democratic regimes in the region. This is partly because of a well-entrenched view that Western-style democratic traditions are inimical to core 'Asian values' that undergird economic dynamism. How valid is this view?

DEMOCRACY, 'ASIAN VALUES' AND ECONOMIC DEVELOPMENT

The issue of a 'trade-off' between democracy and development has both an 'old' and a 'new' version. The 'Asian values' argument is part of the new version, but one needs to appreciate its historical lineage.

It used to be argued, as Bhagwati (1966: 204) did, that developing nations faced a 'cruel choice between rapid (self-sustained) expansion and democratic processes'. Bhagwati has since then retracted this position and has re-visited this issue in a recent contribution (Bhagwati, 1995). The 'cruel choice' hypothesis appeared sensible at the time because dominant paradigms on development emphasised that economic growth was driven primarily by capital accumulation. The political implication of this line of thinking was that authoritarian regimes would be better able than democracies to raise investment and saving rates to levels that would promote and sustain economic growth. Why? 'Authoritarian regimes would be able to extract a greater surplus from their populations through taxation and "takings"...than democracies. The latter, after all, [have] to persuade voters to pay the needed taxes and make other necessary sacrifices' (Bhagwati, 1995: 53).

The 'cruel choice' hypothesis, however, never implied that the trade-off between democracy and development would be permanent. Once the initial, and necessarily painful, step towards self-sustained growth was accomplished, progressive affluence would generate demands for political liberalisation and the system would eventually respond to such demands – a proposition that forms part of 'modernisation theory'. Historical evidence tended to support this view (Moore, 1966), while cross-country studies were able to demonstrate a positive correlation between levels of economic development and stable democracies (Lipset, 1959). 'Development first, democracy later' thus became the conventional wisdom.

The new version of these old arguments has a cultural dimension. The emphasis is now on discipline and the need to maintain social cohesion as key ingredients of economic development. As Lee Kuan Yew puts it: 'what a country needs...is discipline more than democracy. The exuberance of democracy leads to indiscipline and disorderly conduct which are inimical to development' (see *Economist*, 27 August 1994; see also Zakaria, 1994). Discipline in turn is the product of core 'Asian values' – a generic term that is used here in preference to 'Confucian' values because its ideological appeal cuts across both 'Confucian' (such as China and Singapore) and 'non-Confucian' societies (such as Malaysia). Note that the Lee Kuan Yew thesis does not even seem to condone the sequential 'development first, democracy later' approach. Instead, it seems to suggest paternalistic authoritarianism (buttressed obviously by nominally democratic institutions, such as free elections) as a durable political system.

Fukuyama (1995a: 12) maintains that Lee Kuan Yew is not alone in pushing this view. Such overt anti-democratic sentiment has also been expounded by Malaysian intellectuals and officials in recent years and in particular by Mahathir and Fukuyama maintains that 'many people in Asian societies have come to share [such] beliefs' (1995b: 20). This has prompted him to warn that 'Asian paternalistic authoritarianism' is the 'most serious new competitor to liberal democracy' (1995a: 11).

It is not clear, however, that one is observing the emergence of a Pan-Asian critique of liberal democracy. Lee Kuan Yew's views have been contested by other political leaders in the region. Consider, for example, the following remarks by You Ching, county magistrate of Taipei:

> Some Asian leaders...have argued that democracy is not suitable to the particular context of Asian culture...But Taiwanese democratisation proves that Western ideas and Asian cultural values are compatible... Ideas of democracy and human rights are not only applicable but absolutely necessary for the development of societies in Asia and elsewhere.
> (Documents on Democracy, 1995a: 185)

There is, in addition, the newly formed Forum of Democratic Leaders in the Asia-Pacific Region (FDL-AP), currently located in Seoul. In its inaugural meeting (1–2 December 1994), FDL-AP adopted, as one of its primary resolutions, the goal that it would commit itself to refuting the 'false judgement that the Asia-Pacific region is devoid of historical legacy and cultural heritage suitable for democracy' (Documents for Democracy, 1995b: 186).

One is thus observing an emerging rift in ideas and opinions about the relationship between 'Asian values' and democracy in the region – a rift that follows the ideological divide between new democracies and their non-democratic or quasi-democratic counterparts. Despite this rift, it would be fair to say that the 'Asian values' hypothesis has attracted considerable attention and, superficially at least, seems to have credibility. Two factors in particular have played a role in its current status. First, some of the most successful economies in contemporary times come from the region in which the spurt towards sustained industrialisation occurred under authoritarian (or at best semi-democractic) regimes. Second, there is the perceived decline of the liberal-democractic West – most notably the USA – as a centre of economic power, but more importantly as a bearer of moral standards. To at least some sections of East Asian society, rampant crime, breakdown of the family, racial tensions and illegal immigration are seen as typically American problems that have tarnished – perhaps for ever – the USA as an exemplar worthy of emulation.

US scholars themselves have added substance to adverse perceptions about liberal-democratic regimes. There is the well-known view of Olson (1982) that mature democracies have built-in mechanisms for stagnation through the institutionalisation of 'distributional coalitions'. A more recent variant of this argument is the hypothesis of 'demosclerosis' that is alleged to be the 'silent killer' of good governance in the USA (Rausch, 1994). Judged against such analyses and the foregoing perceptions of declining economic and moral standards, one can appreciate why the search for an 'Asian alternative' to democratic governance holds such appeal in some quarters. Despite this element of credibility, the 'Asian values' hypothesis has considerable limitations.

To start with, the weight of theory and evidence suggests that Confucianism (or core 'Asian values' as described here) is neither necessary nor sufficient for rapid growth (Chowdhury and Islam, 1993: chapter 2). The lack of progress in imperial China and Korea – quintessential Confucian regimes – bear testimony to this.

Second, Fukuyama (1995b) has made the point that Confucianism is compatible with democratic traditions, once one moves away from its emphasis on discipline and social cohesion. The Confucian emphasis on self-improvement through education, non-discriminatory and meritocratic examination systems encourages social mobility and spawns a middle class that provides a durable basis for democratic transitions. However, once core 'Asian'/Confucian values are diluted to this level of generality, they lose their distinctiveness and become part of universal human values.

Third, it may well be that the 'Asian values' hypothesis is essentially an argument that tries to justify the current political order in parts of East Asia and, like all state-sanctioned ideology, is not really intended to be a care-fully constructed, intellectually rigorous proposition. Indeed Fukuyama (1995b: 28) has made the controversial claim that a Lee Kuan Yew-type hypothesis is simply a weapon of political control because, paradoxically, Sinitic societies exhibit a culturally ingrained distrust of state authority and low level of 'spontaneous citizenship'. This is because of 'intense familism' that is characteristic of Chinese societies and that takes precedence over all other social relations. Hence, social cohesion has to be imposed from the top. As he puts it:

> The weaker Chinese deference to authority creates a greater need for an authoritarian political system in Chinese societies...One is led to sus-pect that the emphasis on political authoritarianism in Singapore and other Southeast Asian societies is less a reflection of those societies' self-discipline...than of their rather low level of spontaneous citizenship and corresponding fear of coming apart in the absence of coercive political authority.

Emmerson (1995) takes a more subtle position. He contends that con-cerns about social cohesion may not simply be the preoccupation of elites. Certain societies may simply have a higher proportion of 'order-valuing, disorder-fearing' citizenry. Thus, the exercise of coercive political authority may be voluntarily accepted by such citizenry, creating a form of govern-ance that may not be recognisably democratic in the Western, liberal sense.

THE CASE FOR DEMOCRATIC GOVERNANCE: SOME CONCLUDING OBSERVATIONS

In disabusing the notion that liberal democracies do not represent a viable and desirable alternative for the Asia-Pacific region, one has to move away from treating democratic governance in abstract, ideological terms. As Olson (1993) emphasises, the economic case for democracies has rarely been systematically and cogently argued. In a region where political legiti-macy is primarily based on economic performance, the pro-democracy case needs to be made in such terms.

To start with, the defects of democratic governance that one associates with the USA conflates the particular and the general. 'Demosclerosis' is not a unique feature of democracies. It is not often noted that Olson's much-cited work (1982) on the growth-retarding effects of entrenched distributional coalitions afflicts any society experiencing long periods of regime stability – for example, the imperial systems of Japan, China and Korea. This implies that it is not inevitable that democracies will spawn growth-inhibiting interest groups. As noted in chapter 2 of this volume, it is possible, in principle at least, to design institutional arrangements that can protect democracies – and political systems in general – from the rapacious effects of both rent-seeking interest groups and interventionist behaviour of state officials.

As the discussion at a previous juncture highlighted, the old version of the trade-off between democracy and development rested on the notion of draconian state action for generating saving and investment. The dominant paradigms on appropriate public policies for economic development now emphasise the protection of property rights and market-based incentives as key ingredients in driving the twin processes of capital accumulation and innovation. There is historical evidence that safeguarding property rights is essential for growth (North and Weingast, 1989; North, 1994). These considerations have also motivated Olson (1993) to construct the economic rationale for democracy because – as a political system – its emphasis on the rule of law enables it to protect property rights more effectively than authoritarian regimes.

The arguments advanced by Elster (1995) in favour of democracy are also similar in spirit to the property rights view of development. It represents a generalisation of the need for fiscal and monetary 'constitutions' for promoting macroeconomic stability – ideas that were explored in chapter 2. Elster (1995: 215) makes the point that economic efficiency can be enhanced if governments can make credible pre-commitments through constitutional mechanisms. This in turn is best achieved in a democracy where civil society is able to exercise effective political rights.

While the theoretical rationale for democracy can be readily made, what about the evidence? There are now more than twenty studies that rely on cross-country regressions to demonstrate that authoritarian regimes do not exhibit superior growth performance relative to democracies – see Kohli (1986), Heliwell (1992, 1994) and Przeworski and Limongi (1993) as representative examples. See Alesina and Perotti (1994) for a survey. Moreover, when finer gradations are used to classify democratic regimes, Przeworski (1995: 230) reports that observed annual per capita growth rates (for the 1950–90 period) are 1.9 per cent for authoritarian regimes, 2.9 per cent for parliamentary democracies and 1.5 per cent for presidential democracies. Thus, the particular form of democratic governance seems to matter for growth.

Several scholars have gone beyond the impact of democracies on per capita growth rates to examine the association between particular aspects of societal performance and the political regime. Sen (1994) has consistently argued that democracies have a much better record of famine-prevention than autocracies. This stems from the role that a free press plays in disseminating information about impending disasters, which creates an incentive for politicians to alleviate and prevent such disasters.

Payne (1995: 41–3) is an advocate of the emerging view that 'democracy is a prerequisite for the achievement of better environmental policies' in large measure because 'democratic governments are less likely to abuse the human rights of environmentalists or suppress their criticisms, and more likely to be accountable and responsive to demands'. These arguments were also made by McCloskey more than a decade ago. As he observed (McCloskey, 1983: 157): 'Many of the important ecological measures that are being implemented are being implemented by democracies ... By contrast ... totalitarian states are among the worst ecological offenders.'

Bhagwati (1995: 55) and Payne (1995: 41) have drawn attention to a growing body of historical scholarship that demonstrates that democratic states have not fought one another. Thus, the spread of democracy may well pave the way for global peace and prosperity, conserve costly dollars that would otherwise go into military expenditure and release resources that would be potentially available for developmental efforts.

In sum, as Bhagwati (1995: 50) notes, the 'new thinking on development' is now that 'democracy does not handicap development, and in the right circumstances can even promote it'. The weight of both theory and evidence repudiate the old version of the 'cruel choice' hypothesis and its current variant, the 'Asian values' argument. While the latter has powerful adherents in the Asia-Pacific region, it is pleasing to note that these views are being contested by democrats in the region. In sustaining development in the future, and in specific areas of highly topical social and economic concerns, such as environmental protection, the spread and consolidation of democratic governance in Pacific Asia will play a crucial role. The much-noted 'Pacific Century' will then truly come of age.

References for Part I

Abella, M.I. (1991) 'Structural Change and Labour Migration within the Asia Region', *Regional Development Dialogue*, 12(3): 3–21

Adams, F.G. and Davis, I. (1994) 'The Role of Policy in Economic Development: East Asia and Latin America', *Asian-Pacific Economic Literature*, 8(1): 8–24

Addison, T. and Demery, L. (eds.) (1987) *Wages and Labour Conditions in the Newly Industrialising Countries of Asia*, London: Overseas Development Institute

Adelman, I. and Morris, C.T. (1973) *Economic Growth and Social Equity in Developing Countries*, Stanford: Stanford University Press

Agarwala, R. (1983) 'Price Distortions and Developing Countries', World Bank Staff Working Papers, No. 575

Aghevli, B., Khan, M.S. and Montiel, P. (1991) *Exchange Rate Policy in Developing Countries: Some Analytical Issues, Occasional Paper* No. 78, Washington, D.C.: International Monetary Fund

Ahluwalia, M. (1976) 'Inequality, Poverty and Development', *Journal of Development Economics*, 3(4): 307–42

Ahluwalia, M., Carter, N.G. and Chenery, H.B. (1979) 'Growth and Poverty in Developing Countries', *Journal of Developing Economes*, 6(3): 299–334

Ahmad, E. and Wang, Y (1991) 'Inequality and Poverty in China', *World Bank Economic Review*, 5(2): 231–58

Ahmed, S. (1993) *Appropriate Macroeconomic Management in Indonesia's Open Economy*, World Bank Discussion Paper No. 191, Washington, D.C.: World Bank

Akamatsu, K. (1960) 'A Theory of Balanced Growth in the World Economy', *Weltwirtschaftliches Archiv*, 86 (2)

Alagappa, M. (1995) 'Democracy's Future: The Asian Spectrum', *Journal of Democracy*, 6(1): 28–36

Alesina, A. and Perotti, R. (1994) 'The Political Economy of Growth: A Critical Survey of the Literature', *The World Bank Economic Review*, 8(3): 351–71

Alesina, A. and Rodrik, D. (1994) 'Distributive Politics and Economic Growth', *Quarterly Journal of Economics*, May: 464–90

Alt, J. and Chrystal, K.A. (1983) *Political Economics*, London: Wheatsheaf Books

Amelung, T. (1994) 'The Impact of Transaction Costs on Trade Flows in the Asia-Pacific', in Garnaut, R. and Drysdale, P. (eds), *Asia-Pacific Regionalism–Readings in International Economic Relations*, Sydney: Harper Collins

Amsden, A. (1989) *Asia's Next Giant: South Korea and Late Industrialization*, New York: Oxford University Press

Amsden, A. (1991) 'Diffusion of Development: The Late Industrializing Model and Greater Asia', *American Economic Review*, Papers and Proceedings, 81(2): 282–6

Amsden, A. and Euh, Y-D. (1993) 'South Korea's 1980s Financial Reforms: Good-bye Financial Repression (Maybe), Hello New Institutional Restraint', *World Development*, March

Anand, S. and Kanbur, S.M. (1981) 'Inequality and Development: Critique', *mimeo*, London: SSRC Development Economics Study Group

Anand, S. and Kanbur, S.M. (1984) 'Poverty under the Kuznets Process', *Economic Journal* Supplement, 95: 42–9

Anderson, K. and Blackhurst, R. (1992) *The Greening of World Trade Issues*, London: Harvester Wheatsheaf

Arndt, H. (1983) 'Financial Development in Asia', *Asian Development Review*, 1(1): 86–100

Asian Development Bank (1989) *Asian Development Outlook*, Manila: Asian Development Bank

Asian Development Bank (1990) *Human Resource Policy and Economic Development – Selected Country Studies*, Manila: Economics and Development Center, Asian Development Bank

Asian Development Bank (1994) *Asian Development Outlook*, Hong Kong: Oxford University Press

Atchana Wattananukit and Teerana Bhongmakapit (1989) 'The Impact of the External Sector on the Thai Economy and its Determinants', *TDRI Annual Conference*, Bangkok: 17–18 December

Athukorala, P. (1993) 'International Migration in the Asian – Pacific Region: Patterns, Policies, and Economic Implications', *Asian-Pacific Economic Literature*, 7 (2): 28–57

Axelrod, R. (1984) *The Evolution of Cooperation*, New York: Oxford University Press

Azariadies, C. and Drazen, A. (1990) 'Threshold Externalities in Economic Development', *Quarterly Journal of Economics*

Balassa, B. (1977) 'A Stages Approach to Comparative Advantage', World Bank Staff Working Paper

Balassa, B. (1981) *The Newly Industrializing Countries in the World Economy*, New York: Pergamon

Balassa, B. (1988) 'The Lessons of East Asian Development: An Overview', *Economic Development and Cultural Change*, 36 (April), S273–91

Banuri, T. (1991) *Economic Liberalization no Panacea: The Experiences of Latin America and Asia*, New York: Oxford University Press

Barandiaran, E. (1987) *Financial Liberalization in LDCs: A Review of Evidence*, Working Paper, Washington, D.C.: World Bank, Finance and Economics Division

Bardhan, P. (1995) 'The Implications of New Growth Theory for Trade and Development', in Quibria, M.G. (ed.) *Critical Issues in Asian Development*, Hong Kong: Oxford University Press

Beamish, P. *et al.* (1994) *International Management: Text and Cases*, Homewood, Ill.: Irwin

Beckerman, W. (1977) 'Some Reflections on Redistribution with Growth', *World Development*, 5(8): 665–76

Behrman, J.R. (1990) *Human Resource Led Development? Review of Issues and Evidence*, New Delhi and Geneva: ILO-ARTEP

Behrman, J.R. and Birdsall, N. (1983) 'The Quality of Schooling: Quantity Alone Is Misleading', *American Economic Review*, 2.

Behrman, J.R. and Wolfe, B.L. (1984) 'The Socioeconomic Impact of Schooling in a Developing Country', *The Review of Economics and Statisics*, 66(2)

Bergsten, C.F. and Noland, M. (1993) *Pacific Dynamism and the International Economic System*, Washington, D.C.: Institute for International Economics

Bhagwati, J. (1966) *The Economics of Underdeveloped Countries*, London: Weidenfeld and Nicolson

Bhagwati, J. (1986), 'Rethinking Trade Strategy' in Lewis, J.P. and Kallab, V. (eds), *Development Strategies Reconsidered*, New York and Oxford: Transaction Books

Bhagwati, J. (1994) 'Regionalism and Multilateralism: An Overview' in Garnaut, R. and Drysdale, P. (eds) *Asia-Pacific Regionalism – Readings in International Economic Relations*, Sydney: HarperCollins

Bhagwati, J. (1995) 'The New Thinking on Development', *Journal of Democracy*, 6(4):

Bhattacharya, A. and Pangestu, M. (1993) 'Indonesia: Development Transformation and Public Policy' in *Lessons of East Asia Series*, Washington, D.C.: World Bank

Bigsten, A. (1989) 'Poverty, Inequality and Development' in Gemmel, N. (ed.) *Surveys in Development Economics*, Oxford: Basil Blackwell

Birdsall, N. (1995) 'Round-table Discussion on Employment and Development: Growth, Inequality and the Labour Market', *Proceedings of the World Bank Annual Conference on Development Economics 1994*, Washington D.C.: World Bank

Birdsall, N. and Wheeler, D. (1992) 'Trade Policy and Industrial Pollution in Latin America: Where are the Pollution Havens?', in Low, P. (ed.) *International Trade and the Environment*, World Bank Discussion Paper No. 159, Washington DC: World Bank

Blomqvist, H. (1994) 'Bilateral Trade Flows in East Asia: A Gravity Approach', in Nguyen, T. and Roy, K.C. (eds) *Economic Reform, Liberalisation and Trade in the Asia-Pacific Region*, Calcutta and London: Wiley-Eastern

Booth, A. (1994) 'Review of Ogawa *et al.*', *Asian-Pacific Economic Literature*, 8(1): 77–9

Bourguinon, F., de Melo, J. and Morrison, C. (1991) 'Poverty and Income Distribution During Adjustment Issues and Evidence', *World Development*, 19(11): 1485–508

Brandon, C. (1994) 'Reversing Pollution Trends in Asia', *Finance and Development*, June: 21–3

Brenan, G. and Buchanan, J.M. (1980) *The Power to Tax: Analytical Foundations of a Fiscal Constitution*, Cambridge: Cambridge University Press

Bruno, M. (1979) 'Stabilization and Stagflation in a Semi-Industrialized Economy', in Dornbusch, R. and Frenkel, J. (eds) *International Economic Policy, Theory and Evidence*, Baltimore: Johns Hopkins University Press

Bruno, M. (1993) 'Monetary Policy Rules for a Small, Open Economy' in Dornbusch, R. (ed.) *Policymaking in the Open Economy: Concepts and Case Studies in Economic Performance*, Washington, D.C.: World Bank, EDI Series in Economic Development

Buchanan, J. (1963) 'The Economics of Earmarked Taxes', *Journal of Political Economy*, 71: 307–30

Byrd, W.A. (1991) *The Market Mechanism and Economic Reform in China*, New York: M.E. Sharpe

Byron, R.P. and Manaloto, E.Q. (1990) 'Returns to Education in China', *Economic Development and Cultural Change*, 38(4): 783–96

Carruth, A. and Oswald, A.J. (1987) 'On Union Preferences and Labour Market Models: Insiders and Outsiders', *The Economic Journal*, 97, 386: 431–45

Carter, B. (1994) 'Reversing Pollution Trends in Asia', *Finance and Development*, June, 21–3

Case, W. (1994) 'Elites and Regimes in Comparative Perspective: Indonesia, Thailand and Malaysia', *Governance*, 7(4): 431–60

Cavallo, D. (1977) *Stagflationary Effects of Monetarist Stabilization Policies*, unpublished Ph.D. Thesis, Harvard University

Caves, R.E. (1971) 'International Cooperation: The Industrial Economics of Foreign Direct Investment', *Economica*, 38: 1–27

Chenery, H. and Syrquin, M. (1975) *Patterns of Development*, New York: Oxford University Press

Chichilnisky, G. (1994) 'North–South Trade and the Global Environment', *American Economic Review*, 84(4): 851–975

Choo, H. (1975) 'Some Sources of Relative Equity in Korean Income Distribution: A Historical Perspective' in *Income Distribution, Employment and Economic Development in Southeast Asia*, Vols I and II, Tokyo and Manila: Japan Research Centre and Asian Council of Manpower Studies

Chow, P.C.Y. and Kellman, M.H. (1993) *Trade: The Engine of Growth in East Asia*, New York: Oxford University Press

Chowdhury, A. (1994) 'Centralised vs Decentralised Wage-Setting Systems and Capital Accumulation – evidence from OECD countries 1960–1990', *The Economic and Labour Relations Review*, 5(2): 84–100

Chowdhury, A. and Islam, I. (1993) *The Newly Industrialising Economies of East Asia*, London and New York: Routledge

Chowdhury, A. and Islam, I. (1996) 'Thailand's Adjustment Experience in the 1980s – What Are the Lessons?', mimeo

Coats, W.L., Jr and Khatkhate, D. (eds) (1980) *Money and Monetary Policy in Less Developed Countries*, London: Pergamon Press

Cohen, S.S. and Guerrieri, P. (1994) 'The Variable Geometry of Asian Trade', in Doherty, E. (ed.) *Japanese Investment in Asia: International Production Strategies in a Rapidly Changing World*, Conference Proceedings, 26–27 September 1994, San Francisco: The Asia Foundation and BRIE

Colcough, C. (1982) 'The Impact of Primary Schooling on Economic Development: A Review of Evidence', *World Development*, 10(3): 167–85

Cole, D. (1988) 'Financial Development in Asia', *Asia Pacific Economic Literature*, 2(2): 26–47

Cole, D. and Park, Y.C. (1983) *Financial Development in Korea, 1945–78*, Cambridge, Mass.: Harvard University Press

Cole, D. and Patrick, H. (1986) 'Financial Development in the Pacific Basin Market Economies', in Tan, A. and Kapur, B. (eds) *Pacific Growth and Financial Interdependence*, Sydney: Allen and Unwin

Cole, D. and Slade, B. (1992) 'Indonesian Financial Development: A Different Sequencing?' in Vittas, D. (ed.) *Financial Regulation: Changing the Rules of the Game*, Washington, D.C: EDI Development Studies, World Bank

Cole, D.C., Scott, H.S. and Wellons, P.A. (eds) (1995) *Asian Money Markets*, New York: Oxford University Press

Collins, S. and Park, W.A. (1989), 'External Debt and Macroeconomic Performance in South Korea' in Sachs, J.D. and Collins, S.M. (eds) *Developing Country Debt and Economic Performance*, Chicago: University of Chicago Press

Corbo, V. and Hernandez, L. (1996) 'Macroeconomic Adjustment to Capital Inflows: Lessons from Recent Latin American and East Asian Experience', *World Bank Research Observer*, 11(1): 61–86

Corden, W.M. (1991) 'Exchange Rate Poicy in Developing Countries', in de Melo, J. and Sapir, A. (eds) *Trade Theory and Economic Reform – North, South and East: Essays in Honour of Bela Balassa*, Oxford: Basil Blackwell

Cornia, G.A., Jolly, R. and Stewart, F. (1988) *Adjustment with a Human Face*, Oxford: Clarendon Press

Cottani, J. and Cavallo, D. (1993) 'Financial Reform and Liberalization' in Dornbusch, R. (ed.) *Policymaking in the Open Economy: Concepts and Case Studies in*

Economic Performance, Washington, D.C.: World Bank, EDI Series in Economic Development

Cromwell, J. (1977) 'The Size Distribution of Income: An International Comparison', *The Review of Income and Wealth*, 23(3): 291–308

Crouch, H. (1993) 'Malaysia: Neither Authoritarian nor Democratic', in Hewison, K., Robinson, R. and Rodan, G. (eds) *Southeast Asia in the 1990s*, Sydney: Allen and Unwin

Cukierman, A. and Webb, S.B. (1995) 'Political Influence on the Central Bank: International Evidence', *World Bank Economic Review*, 9(3): 397–424

Cukierman, A., Webb, S.B. and Neyapati, B. (1992) 'Measuring the Independence of Central Banks and its Effect on Policy Outcomes', *World Bank Economic Review*, 6(1): 353–98

Cumings, B. (1987) 'The Origins and Development of Northeast Asian Political Economy: Industrial Sectors, Product Life Cycles, and Political Consequences' in Deyo, F. (ed.) *The Political Economy of the New Asian Industrialism*, Ithaca and London: Cornell University Press

Dalla, I. and Khatkhate, D. (1995) *Regulated Deregulation of the Financial System in Korea*. World Bank Discussion Papers No. 292, Washington, D.C.: World Bank

Das, D. (1996) 'Energing Markets and Macroeconomic Stabilization: With Special Reference to Asia-Pacific Economies', *Journal of the Asia-Pacific Economy*, 1(3)

Dasgupta, P. (1995) 'Economic Development and the Environment: Issues, Policies, and the Political Economy' in Quibria, M.G. (ed.) *Critical Issues in Asian Development*, Hong Kong: Oxford University Press

Dasgupta, P. and Maler, K.-G. (1992) 'The Environment and Emerging Development Issues', *Proceedings of the World Bank Annual Conference on Development Economics 1991*

Dean, J. (1996) 'Recent Capital Flows to Asia/Pacific Countries: Tradeoffs and Dilemmas', *Journal of the Asia Pacific Economy*, 1(3)

Dean, J.M., Desai, S. and Riedel, J. (1995) *Trade Policy Reform in Developing Countries since 1985*, World Bank Discussion Paper No. 267, Washington, D.C.: World Bank

Deaton, A. (1995) 'Inequality in Aging and Growing Economies' in Quibria, M.G. (ed.) *Critical Issues in Asian Development*, Hong Kong: Oxford University Press

de Melo, J. and Tybout, J. (1986) 'The Effects of Financial Liberalisation on Savings and Investment in Uruguay', *Economic Development and Cultural Change*, 34(3): 607–40

Demery, L. and Addison, T. (1987), *The Alleviation of Poverty under Structural Adjustment*, Washington D.C.: World Bank

Demery, L. and Demery, D. (1991) 'Poverty and Macroeconomic Policy in Malaysia, 1979–1987', *World Development*, 19(11), 1620–30

de Walle, D.V. (1995) *Public Spending and the Poor: What We Know, What We Need to Know*, Policy Research Working Paper 1476

Deyo, F. (ed.) (1987a) *The Political Economy of the New Asian Industrialism*, Ithaca, NY and London: Cornell University Press

Deyo, F. (1987b), 'State and Labor: Modes of Political Exclusion in East Asian Development' in Deyo (1987a)

Deyo, F. (1989) *Beneath the Economic Miracle: Labor Subordination in the New Asian Industrialism*, Berkeley: University of California Press

Dixon, C. (1993) *South East Asia in the World-Economy*, Cambridge: Cambridge University Press

Dixon, C. and Drakakis-Smith, D. (1993) *Economic and Social Development in Pacific Asia*, London and New York: Routledge

Documents on Democracy (1995a) 'China', *Journal of Democracy*, 6 (July): 182–5
Documents on Democracy (1995b) 'The Asia-Pacific Region', *Journal of Democracy*, 6 (January): 186
Dohner, R.S. and Intal, Jr. P. (1989), 'The Marcos Legacy: Economic Policy and Foreign Debt in the Philippines' in Sachs, J.D. and Collins, S.M. (eds) *Developing Country Debt and Economic Performance, Vol. 3*, Chicago and London: University of Chicago Press
Doner, R.F. (1991a) 'Approaches to the Politics of Economic Growth in Southeast Asia', *Journal of Asian Studies*, 50(4): 818–49
Doner, R.F. (1991b) *Driving a Bargain: Automobile Industrialization and Japanese Firms in Southeast Asia*, Berkeley: California University Press
Doner, R.F. (1992) 'Limits of State Strength: Toward an Institutionalist View of Economic Development', *World Politics*, 44(4): 398–431
Dornbusch, R. (ed.) *Policymaking in the Open Economy: Concepts and Case Studies in Economic Performance*, Washington, D.C.: World Bank, EDI Series in Economic Development
Dornbusch, R. and Edwards, S. (1990) *Macroeconomic Populism in Latin America*, Working Paper No. 2986, Cambridge, Mass.: National Bureau of Economic Research
Dornbusch, R. and Park, Y. (1987), 'Korean Growth Policy', *Brookings Papers on Economic Activity*, 2: 389–454
Dornbusch, R. and Reynoso, A. (1993) 'Financial Factors in Economic Development', in Dornbusch, R. (ed.) *Policymaking in the Open Economy: Concepts and Case Studies in Economic Performance*, Washington, D.C.: World Bank, EDI Series in Economic Development
Drake, P.J. (1980) *Money, Finance and Development*, New York: Wiley
Dreze, J. and Sen, A.K. (1990) *Hunger and Public Action*, Oxford: Clarendon Press
Duncan, R. (1995) 'Implications of Globalisation for Transitional and Developing Economies' in *Economic Planning Advisory Commission Globalisation: Issues for Australia, Commission Paper No. 5*, Canberra: Australian Government Publishing Service
Easterly, W. and Schmidt-Hebbel, K. (1993) 'Fiscal Deficits and Macroeconomic Performance in Developing Countries', *The World Bank Research Observer*, 8(2): 211–39
Economist (1994) 27 August, p.15
Edwards, S. (1984) *The Order of Liberalization of the External Sector in Developing Countries*, Essays in International Finance 156, Princeton, NJ: Princeton University Press
Elster, J. (1995) 'The Impact of Constitutions on Economic Performance', *Proceedings of the World Bank Annual Conference on Development Economics 1994*, Washington, D.C.: World Bank
Emery, R.F. (1991) *The Money Markets of Developing East Asia*, New York: Praeger
Emmerson, D.K. (1995) 'Singapore and the "Asian Values" Debate', *Journal of Democracy*, 6(5): 95–105
Fields, G. (1995) 'Income Distribution in Developing Economies: Conceptual, Data, and Policy-Issues in Broad-based Growth', in Quibria, M.G. (ed.) *Critical Issues in Asian Development*, Hong Kong: Oxford University Press
Fields, G. (forthcoming) 'Data for Measuring Poverty and Inequality in Developing Countries', *Journal of Developing Economies*
Fields, G.S. and Wan, H. Jr. (1989) 'Wage Setting Institutions and Economic Growth', *World Development*, 17(9): 1471–83

Findlay, C. and Watson, A. (1992) 'Surrounding the Cities from the Countryside', in Garnaut, R. and Liu, G. (eds) *Economic Reform and Internationalisation: China and the Pacific Region*, Sydney: Allen and Unwin

Findlay, C., Martin, W. and Watson, A. (1993) *Policy Reform, Economic Growth and China's Agriculture*, Paris: OECD

Findlay, R. (1995) 'Recent Advances in Trade and Growth Theory' in Quibria, M.G. (ed.) *Critical Issues in Asian Development*, Hong Kong: Oxford University Press

Fisher, P. (1961) 'The Economic Role of Unions in Less-Developed Areas', *Monthly Labour Review*, September

Frankel, J. (1993) 'Is Japan Creating a Yen Bloc in East Asia and the Pacific' in Frankel, J. and Kahler, M. (eds) *Regionalism and Rivalry: Japan and the U.S. in Pacific Asia*, Chicago: University of Chicago Press. Reprinted in Garnaut, R. and Drysdale, P. (eds) (1994) *Asia-Pacific Regionalism – Readings in International Economic Relations*, Sydney: HarperCollins

Frankel, J. and Kahler, M. (eds) (1993) *Regionalism and Rivalry: Japan and the U.S. in Pacific Asia*, Chicago: University of Chicago Press

Frankel, J.A., Shang-Jin Wei and Stein, E. (1994) *APEC and Other Regional Economic Arrangements in the Pacific*, Working Paper 94–.04, San Francisco: Center for Pacific Basin Monetary and Economic Studies, Economic Research Department, Federal Reserve Bank of San Francisco

Freeman, R.B. (1993) 'Labor Market Institutions and Policies: Help or Hindrance to Economic Development?', *Proceedings of the World Bank Annual Conference on Development Economics 1992*, Washington D.C.: World Bank

Freeman, R.B. and Medoff, J.L. (1984) *What Do Unions Do?* New York: Basic Books

Frenkel, S. (ed.) (1993) *Organized Labor in the Asia-Pacific Region: A Comparative Study of Unionism in Nine Countries*, Cornell International Industrial and Labor Relations Report No. 24, Ithaca, NY: ILR Press

Frobel, F., Heinrichs, J. and Kreye, O. (1980) *The New International Division of Labour: Structural Unemployment in Industrialised Countries and Industrialisation in Developing Countries*, Cambridge: Cambridge University Press

Fry, M. (1984) 'Saving, Financial Intermediation and Economic Growth in Asia', *Asian Development Review*, 2(1): 82–102

Fry, M. (1985) 'Financial Structure, Monetary Policy, and Economic Growth in Hong Kong, Singapore, Taiwan and South Korea, 1960–1983', in Corbo, V., Krueger, A. and Ossa, F. (eds) *Export-Oriented Development Strategies: The Success of Five Newly Industrializing Countries*, Boulder, Colo.: Westview Press.

Fry, M. (1988) *Money, Interest, and Banking in Economic Development*, Baltimore: Johns Hopkins University Press

Fry, M. (1989) 'Financial Development: Theories and Recent Experience', *Oxford Review of Economic Policy*, 5(4): 13–28

Fry, M. (1990) 'Nine Financial Sector Issues in Eleven Asian Developing Countries', *Working Paper, IFGWP–90–09*

Fry, M. (1991) 'Domestic Resource Mobilization in Developing Asia: Four Policy Issues', *Asian Development Review*, 19(1): 14–39

Fukuyama, F. (1995a) 'Democracy's Future: The Primacy of Culture', *Journal of Democracy*, 6(1): 7–14

Fukuyama, F. (1995b) 'Confucianism and Democracy', *Journal of Democracy*, 6(2): 20–33

Galenson, W. (1992) *Labor and Economic Growth in Five Asian Countries: South Korea, Malaysia, Taiwan, Thailand and the Philippines*, New York: Praeger

Gannicott, K. (1990) 'The Economics of Education in Asian-Pacific Developing Countries', *Asian-Pacific Economic Literature*, 4(1): 41–64

Garnaut, R. (1989) *Australia and Northeast Asian Ascendancy*, Canberra: AGPS

Garnaut, R. (1991) 'Exchange Rate Regimes in the Asian-Pacific Region', *Asia Pacific Economic Literature*, 5(1): 5–26

Garnaut, R. and Drysdale, P. (eds) (1994) *Asia-Pacific Regionalism – Readings in International Economic Relations*, Sydney: HarperCollins

Garnaut, R. and Liu, G. (eds) (1992) *Economic Reform and Internationalisation: China and the Pacific Region*, Sydney: Allen and Unwin

Garnaut, R. and Ma, G. (1993) 'How Rich Is China: Evidence from the Food Economy', *The Australian Journal of Chinese Affairs*, July, 30: 122–46

Garnaut, R. and Ma, G. (1993b) 'Economic Growth and Stability in China', *Journal of Asian Economics*, 4(1): 5–24

Gibney, F. (1992) *The Pacific Century*, New York: Maxwell Macmillan International

Giovannini, A. (1985), 'Savings and Real Interest Rate in LDCs', *Journal of Development Economics*, 18(2–3): 195–218

Glick, R., Hutchison, M. and Moreno, R. (1995) 'Is Pegging the Exchange Rate a Cure for Inflation? East Asian Experiences', Center for Pacific Basin Monetary and Economic Studies, Federal Reserve Bank of San Francisco, working paper no. PB95–08

Goldman, M. (1994) *Sowing the Seeds of Democracy in China: Political Reform in the Deng Xiaoping Era*, Cambridge, Mass.: Harvard University Press

Goodman, D. (1992) 'China: The State and Capitalist Revolution', *The Pacific Review*, 5(4): 350–9

Goto, J. and Hamada, K. (1994) 'Economic Preconditions for Asian Regional Integration', in Ito, T. and Krneger, A. (eds) *Macroeconomic Linkage: Savings, Exchange Rates, and Capital Flows*, Chicago and London: University of Chicago Press

Grossman, G.M. and Helpman, E. (1990) 'Trade, Innovation and Growth', *American Economic Review*, No. 2

Gurley, J.G. (1967) 'Financial Structure in Developing Countries' in Krivine, D. (ed.) *Fiscal and Monetary Problems in Developing States*, New York: Praeger

Haggard, S. (1988) 'The Politics of Industrialization in the Republic of Korea and Taiwan', in Hughes, H. (ed.) *Achieving Industrialization in Asia*, Cambridge: Cambridge University Press

Haggard, S. (1990) *Pathways from the Periphery: Politics of Growth in the Newly Industrializing Countries*, Ithaca, NY: Cornell University Press

Haggard, S. (1994) 'Conclusion' in MacIntyre, A.J. (ed.) *Government and Business in Industrializing Asia*, Ithaca, NY: Cornell University Press

Haggard, S. and Moon, C. (1990), 'Institutions and Economic Policy: Theory and a Korean Case Study', *World Politics*, 42, January: 210–37

Haggard, S. and Webb, S.B. (1993) 'What Do We Know about the Political Economy of Economic Policy Reform?', *The World Bank Research Observer*, 8(2): 143–68

Hammer, J.S. and Shetty, S. (1995) *East Asia's Environment: Principles and Priorities for Action*, World Bank Discussion Paper No. 287, Washington DC: World Bank

Hanna, D.P. (1994) *Indonesian Experience with Financial Sector Reform*. World Bank Discussion Paper No. 237, Washington, D.C.: World Bank

Harrold, P., Hwa, E.C. and Jiwei, L. (1993) *Macroeconomic Management in China: Proceedings of a Conference in Dalian*, June 1993, World Bank Discussion Paper No. 222, Washington, D.C.: World Bank

Hawes, G. (1987) *The Philippine State and the Marcos Regime*, Ithaca, NY: Cornell University Press

Heliwell, J. (1992) 'Empirical Linkages between Democracy and Growth', *Working Paper No. 4066*, Cambridge, Mass.: National Bureau of Economic Research

Heliwell, J. (1994) 'Asian Economic Growth', in Dobson, W. and Flatters, F (eds) *Pacific Trade and Investment: Options for the 1990s*, Conference Proceedings, Toronto, 6–8 June 1994, Queens University, Kingston

Heller, P. (1988) 'Fund-Supported Adjustment Programs and the Poor, *Finance and Development*, 25(4) 2–5

Hewison, K.J. (1985) 'The State and Capitalist Development in Thailand', in Higgott, R. and Robison, R. (eds) *Southeast Asia: Essays in the Political Economy of Structural Change*, London: Routledge and Kegan Paul

Heyneman, S.P. and Etienne, B. (1989) 'Higher Education in Developing Countries: What, How and When'? *IDS Bulletin*, 20(2)

Higgott, R., Leaver, R. and Ravenhill, J. (eds) (1994) *Pacific Economic Relations in the 1990s: Conflict or Cooperation?* Sydney: Allen and Unwin

Hill, H. (1992) 'Manufacturing Industry' in Booth, A. (ed.) *The Oil Boom and After*, Singapore: Oxford University Press

Ho, S.P.S. (1984) 'Colonialism and Development: Korea, Taiwan, Kwantung' in Myers, R.H. and Petrie, M.R. (eds) *The Japanese Colonial Empire, 1895–1945*, Princeton, NJ: Princeton University Press

Horton, S., Kanbur, R. and Mazumdar, D. (eds) (1994) *Labour Markets in an Era of Adjustment, Vol. 1, EDI Development Studies*, Washington DC: World Bank

Huntingdon, S.P. (1991) *The Third Wave: Democratization in the Late Twentieth Century*, Norman: University of Oklahoma Press

Hutchroft, P. (1991) 'Oligarchs and Cronies in the Philippine State: The Politics of Patrimonial Plunder', *World Politics*, April: 414–50

Hutchcroft, P. (1994) 'Booty Capitalism: Business–Government Relations in the Philippines', in MacIntyre, A.J. (ed.) *Business and Government in Industrialising Asia*, Sydney: Allen and Unwin; Ithaca, NY: Cornell University Press

ILO (1991a) 'Employment Policies in the Economic Restructuring of Latin America and the Caribbean', *World Employment Program (WEP)* 1–04–07 (Doc. 2), August, Geneva: International Labour Organisation

ILO (1991b) 'Social Protection, Safety Nets and Structural Adjustment', *Governing Body Committee on Employment*, GB. 25111/CE/4/5, November, Geneva: International Labour Organisation

Islam, I. (1992) 'Political Economy and East Asian Economic Development', *Asian-Pacific Economic Literature*, 6(2): 69–101

Islam, I. (1996) 'Governance, International Competitiveness and Economic Development: Some Analytical Considerations', in Kapur, B., Quah, T.E. and Teck, H.H. (eds) *Development, Trade and the Asia-Pacific: Essays in Honour of Lim Chong Yah*, Singapore: Prentice-Hall

James, W., Naya, S. and Meier, G. (1989) *Asian Development: Economic Success and Policy Lessons*, Madison: University of Wisconsin Press

Jimenez, E. (1986) 'The Public Subsidisation of Education and Health in Developing Countries: A Review of Equity and Efficiency', *World Bank Research Observer*, 1(1): 111–29

Jimenez, E. (1990) 'Social Sector Pricing Revisited: A Survey of Some Controversies', *Proceedings of the World Bank Annual Conference on Development Economics 1989*, Washington, D.C.: World Bank

Johnson, C. (1987) 'Political Institutions and Economic Performance: The Government – Business Relations in Japan, South Korea, and Taiwan', in Deyo, F. (ed.) *The Political Economy of the New Asian Industrialism*, Ithaca, NY and London: Cornell University Press

Joshi, V. and Little, I.M.D. (1994) *India: Macroeconomics and political Economy*, Washington, D.C.: World Bank

Journal of Democracy (eds) (1995) 'Democracy's Future', *Journal of Democracy*, 6(1): 3–6

Jung, W. (1986), 'Financial Development and Economic Growth: International Evidence', *Economic Development and Cultural Change*, 34(2) 333–46

Kahn, H. (1979) *World Economic Development: 1979 and Beyond*, London: Croom Helm

Kaji, G. (1994) 'Challenges to the East Asian Environment', *Pacific Review*, 7(2): 205–13

Kay, J. and Vickers, J. (1988) 'Regulatory Reform in Britain', *Economic Policy*, October

Kignel, M. and Leiderman, L. (1994) 'On the Consequence of Stenlized Intervention in Latin America: The Case of Columbia and Chile', Mimeoograph, Tel Aviv: Tel Aviv University

Kim, J. (1986) *Wages, Employment and Income Distribution in South Korea: 1960–83*, Bangkok and Geneva: ILO-ARTEP

Kim, K. and Leipziger, D.M. (1993) 'Korea: A Case of Government-Led Development' in *Lessons of East Asia Series*, Washington, D.C.: World Bank

Kingsley, G.T., Ferguson, B.W., Bower, B.T. and Dice, S.R. (1994) *Managing Urban Environmental Quality in Asia*, Washington, D.C.: World Bank Technical Paper No. 220, Asia Technical Department Series

Kohli, A. (1986) 'Democracy and Development' in Lewis, J. and Kallab, V. (eds) *Development Strategies Reconsidered*, Washington, D.C.: Overseas Development Council

Kohli, A. (1993) 'Democracy amid Economic Orthodoxy: Trends in Developing Countries', *Third World Quarterly*, 14(4): 671–91

Krueger, A. (1980) 'Trade Policy as an Input to Development', *American Economic Review*, 70(2): 288–92

Krugman, P. (1987) 'Is Free Trade Passé?', *Journal of Economic Perspectives*, 1(2): 131–44

Krugman, P. (1991) 'The Move towards Free Trade Zones' in *Policy Implications of Trade and Currency Zones*, A Symposium Sponsored by the Federal Reserve Bank of Kansas City, Wyoming, August: 7–42. Reprinted in Garnaut, R. and Drysdale, P. (eds) (1994) *Asia-Pacific Regionalism – Readings in International Economic Relations*, Sydney: HarperCollins

Krugman, P. (1994) 'Of the Asian Tigers', *Foreign Affairs*, Nov./Dec. Reprinted in *Report on Business Magazine*, May 1995: 73–9

Kuo, S. (1975) 'Income Distribution by Size in Taiwan: Changes and Causes' in *Income Distribution, Employment and Economic Development in Southeast Asia*, Vols I and II, Tokyo and Manila: Japan Research Centre and Asian Council of Manpower Studies

Kuznets, S. (1955) 'Economic Growth and Income Inequality', *American Economic Review*, 45(1): 1–28

Kwan, C.H. (1993) *Economic Interdependence in the Asia-Pacific Region: Towards a Yen Bloc*, London and New York: Routledge

Lal, D. (1976) 'Distribution and Development: A Review Article', *World Development*, 5(9): 725–38

Lal, D. and Rajapatirana, S. (1987) 'Foreign Trade Regime and Economic Growth in Developing Countries', *World Bank Research Observer*, 2(2): 189–218

Landes-Mills, P. and Serageldin, I. (1992) 'Governance and the External Factor', *Proceedings of the World Bank Annual Conference on Development Economics 1991*, World Bank: Washington, D.C.

Laothamatas, A. (1988) 'Business and Politics in Thailand: New Patterns of Influence', *Asian Survey*, 28, April: 451–70

Laothamatas, A. (1992) *Business Associations and the New Political Economy of Thailand: From Bureaucratic Policy to Liberal Corporatism*, Boulder, Colo.: Westview Press

Lardy, N. (1992) *Foreign Trade and Economic Reform in China*, Cambridge: Cambridge University Press

Lau, L. (ed.) (1990a), *Models of Development: A Comparative Study of Economic Growth in South Korea and Taiwan*, San Francisco: ICS Press

Lau, L. (1990b), 'The Economy of Taiwan 1981–1988: A Time of Passages', in Lau (1990a)

Lee, C.H. (1992) 'The Government, Financial System and Large Enterprises in the Economic Development of South Korea', *World Development*, February

Lee, E. (1977) 'Development and Income Distribution – A Case Study of Sri Lanka and Malaysia', *World Development*, 5(4): 279–89

Lee, E. (1984) 'Introduction' in Lee, E. (ed.) *Export Processing Zones and Industrial Employment in Asia*, Bangkok and Geneva: ILO-ARTEP

Lee, J.S. (1989) 'Labour Relations and the Stages of Economic Development', *Industry of Free China*, 71(4): 11–29

Leff, N. and Sato, K. (1980) 'Macroeconomic Adjustment in Developing Countries: Instability, Short-Run Growth and External Dependency', *Review of Economics and Statistics*, 24(63): 11–32

Leipziger, D. *et al.* (1992) *The Distribution of Income and Wealth in Korea*, Washington D.C.: World Bank, EDI Development Studies

Leipziger, D.M. and Thomas, V. (1993) 'An Overview of Country Experiences' in *Lessons of East Asia Series*, Washington, D.C.: World Bank

Liew, L. (1993) 'Gradualism in China's Economic Reforms and the Role of a Strong, Central State', *mimeo*, Faculty of Asian and International Studies, Griffith University, Brisbane, Australia

Lim, C., Chowdhury, A., Islam, I. *et al.* (1988) *Policy Options for the Singapore Economy*, Singapore: McGraw-Hill

Lim, D. (1996) *Explaining Economic Growth: A New Framework*, Cheltenham: Edward Elgar

Lim, L. and Fong, P.E. (1994) 'The Southeast Asian Economies: Resilient Growth and Expanding Linkages', *Southeast Asian Affairs 1994*, Singapore: Institute of Southeast Asian Affairs

Lin, C.Z. (1988) 'China's Economic Reforms II: Western Perspectives', *Asian-Pacific Economic Literature*, 2(1): 1–25

Lin, T.B. (1985) 'Growth Equity and Income Distribution Policies in Hong Kong', *The Developing Economies*, 23(4): 397–411

Lin, T.B. (1994) 'De-industrialisation, Integration and the Great U-Turn in Hong Kong', *mimeo*, Hong Kong: New Asia College, Chinese University of Hong Kong

Lin, T.B. and Ho, Y.P. (1984), *Industrial Restructuring in Hong Kong*, Bangkok and Geneva: ILO-ARTEP

Linder, S.B. (1986) *The Pacific Century*, San Francisco: Stanford University Press

Lindsey, C. (1992) 'The Political Economy of International Economic Policy Reform in the Philippines: Continuity and Restoration', in MacIntyre, A.J. and Jayasuriya, K. (eds) *The Dynamics of Economic Policy Reform in Southeast Asia and the Southwest Pacific*, Singapore: Oxford University Press

Lingle, C. (1995) 'Trouble in Paradise', *Journal of Democracy*, 6 (July): 172–5

Lipset, S.M. (1959) 'Some Social Requisites of Democracy: Economic Development and Political Legitimacy', *American Political Science Review*, 53: 69–105

Little, I.M.D. (1981) 'The Experiences and Causes of Rapid Labour-Intensive Development in Korea, Taiwan Province, Hong Kong and Singapore and the Possibilities of Emulation', in Lee, E. (ed.) *Export-led Industrialization and Development*, Bangkok and Geneva: ILO-ARTEP.

Little, I.M.D. (1982) *Economic Development*, New York: Basic Books

Little, I.M.D. and Mirlees, J.A. (1991) 'Project Appraisal and Planning Twenty Years On', *Proceedings of the World Bank Annual Conference 1990*, Washington, D.C.: World Bank

Little, I.M.D., Cooper, R.N., Corden, W.M. and Rajapatirana, S. (1993) *Boom, Crisis and Adjustment: The Macroeconomic Experience of Developing Countries*, New York: Oxford University Press for the World Bank

Long, M. and Vittas, D. (1992) 'Changing the Rules of the Game' in Vittas, D. (ed.) *Financial Regulation: Changing the Rules of the Game*, Washington, D.C.: EDI Development Studies, World Bank

Low, P. and Yeats, A. (1992) 'Do Dirty Industries Migrate'? in Low, P. (ed.) (1992) *International Trade and the Environment*, Washington, D.C.: World Bank Discussion Paper No. 159

Lucas, R.E. Jr. (1988) 'On the Mechanics of Economic Development', *Journal of Monetary Economics*, 10(1): 3–42

Lucas, R.E. Jr. (1990) 'Why Does not Capital Flow from Rich to Poor Countries?', *American Economic Review*, 10(1)

Lucas, R.E., Wheeler, D. and Hettige, H. (1992) 'Economic Development, Environmental Regulation and the International Migration of Toxic Industrial Pollution: 1960–88' in Low, P. (ed.) (1992) *International Trade and the Environment*, Washington, D.C.: World Bank Discussion Paper No. 159

Lydall, H. (1977) 'Income Distribution during the Process of Development', *ILO Working Paper* No. 52

MacIntyre, A.J. (1990) *Business and Politics in Indonesia*, Sydney: Allen and Unwin.

MacIntyre, A.J. (1994a) 'Indonesia, Thailand and the Northeast Asia Connection' in Higgott, R., Leaver, R. and Ravenhill, J. (eds) *Pacific Economic Relations in the 1990s: Conflict or Cooperation?* Sydney: Allen and Unwin

MacIntyre, A.J. (ed.) (1994b) *Business and Government in Industrialising Asia*, Sydney: Allen and Unwin; Ithaca, NY: Cornell University Press

MacIntyre, A.J. and Jayasuriya, K. (eds) (1992) *The Dynamics of Economic Policy Reform in Southeast Asia and the Southwest Pacific*, Singapore: Oxford University Press

Mackie, J. (1988) 'Economic Growth in the ASEAN Region: The Political Underpinnings' in Hughes, H. (ed.) *Achieving Industrialisation in East Asia*, Cambridge: Cambridge University Press.

Manning, C. and Fong, P.E. (1990) 'Labour Market Structures in ASEAN and the East Asian NIEs', *Asian-Pacific Economic Literature*, 4(2): 59–81

McCloskey, H.J. (1983) *Ecological Ethics and Politics*, Totowa, NJ: Rowman and Littlefield

McCord, W. (1991) *The Dawn of the Pacific Century*, New Brunswick, NJ: Transactions Publishers

McKinnon, R. (1973), *Money and Capital in Economic Development*, Washington, D.C.: Brookings Institution

McKinnon, R. (1982) 'The Order of Economic Liberalisation: Lessons from Chile and Argentina', in Brunner, K. and Metzler, A.H. (eds) *Economic Policy in a World of Change*, Amsterdam: North-Holland

McKinnon, R. (1984) 'Pacific Growth and Financial Interdependence: An Overview of Bank Regulation and Monetary Control', *Pacific Economic Papers*, 117, Research School of Pacific Studies, Australian National University

McKinnon, R. (1988) 'Financial Liberalization in Retrospect: Interest Rate Policies in LDCs', in Ranis, G. and Schultz, P. (eds) *The State of Development Economics*, Oxford: Basil Blackwell

Meadows, D.H. *et al.* (1972) *The Limits to Growth*, New York: Universe Books

Meadows, D.H., Meadows, D. and Randers, J. (1992) *Beyond the Limits*, Vt: Chelsea Green Publishing

Medhi Krongkiew (1994) 'Income Distribution in East Asian Developing Countries', *Asian-Pacific Economic Literature*, 8(2): 58–74

Mehmet, O. (1988) *Human Resource Development in the Third World: Cases of Success and Failures*, Kingston, Ont.: Ronald P. Frye and Co.

Moon, C.I. (1988) 'The Demise of a Developmentalist State?: The Politics of Stabilisation and Structural Change', *Journal of Developing Societies*, 4: 67–84

Moon, C.I. (1990) 'Beyond Statism: Rethinking the Political Economy of South Korea', *International Studies Notes*, 15 (1): 24–7

Moore, B. (1966) *Social Origins of Dictatorship and Democracy*, Boston: Beacon Press

Moreno, R. (1995) 'Macroeconomic Behavior during Periods of Speculative Pressure of Realignment: Evidence from Pacific Basin Economies', *Economic Review, Federal Reserve Bank of San Francisco* no. 3: 3–16

Mosley, P., Harrigan, J. and Toye, J. (1991) *Aid and Power: The World Bank and Policy-based Lending*, Vol. I, London and New York: Routledge

Munasinghe, M. (1992) Discussion on 'The Environment and Emerging Development Issues', *Proceedings of the World Bank Annual Conference on Development Economics 1991*

Munasinghe, M. and Cruz, W. (1995) *Economywide Policies and the Environment*, Washington, D.C.: World Bank Environment Paper No. 10

Myers, R.H. and Petrie, M.R. (eds) (1984) *The Japanese Colonial Empire, 1895–1945*, Princeton, NJ: Princeton University Press

Nam, S.W. (1991) 'The Comprehensive Stabilization Program (1979)', in Cho, L.J. and Kim, Y.H. (eds) *Economic Development in the Republic of Korea: A Policy Perspective*, East–West Center, Hawaii University Press

National Endowment for Democracy (1991) *Anual Report 1991*, Baltimore: Johns Hopkins University Press

Nelson, J. (1991) 'Organised Labour, Politics, and Labour Market Flexibility in Developing Countries', *The World Bank Research Observer*, 6(1): 37–56

Niskanen, W.A. (1992) 'The Case for a New Fiscal Constitution', *Journal of Economic Perspectives*, 6(2): 13–24

Noble, G.W. (1987) 'Contending Forces in Taiwan's Economic Policymaking', *Asian Survey*, 27

Noland, M. (1990) *Pacific Basin Developing Countries: Prospects for the Future*, Washington, D.C.: Institute for International Economics

North, D. (1994) 'Economic Performance through Time', *American Economic Review*, 84: 359–68

North, D. and Weingast, B. (1989) 'Constitutions and Commitment: The Evolution of Institutions Governing Public Choice in Seventeenth-Century England', *Journal of Economic History*, 49: 803–32

Nugent, J.B. (1991) 'The Demise of Economic Development in Latin America and its Implications for other Developing Countries', *Journal of Economic Development*, 16 (June): 7– 35

O'Brien, R. (1992) *Global Financial Integration: The End of Geography*, New York: Chatham House Papers

OECD (1991) *The State of the Environment*, Paris: Organization for Economic Co-operation and Development

OECD (1992) *Trends in International Migration*, Paris: Organization for Economic Co-operation and Development

Ogawa, N., Jones, G.W. and Williamson, J.G. (eds) (1993) *Human Resources in Development along the Asia-Pacific Rim*, Singapore: Oxford University Press

Ohmae, K. (1990) *The Borderless World*, Sydney: Harper Collins

Olson, M. (1982) *The Rise and Decline of Nations*, New Haven, Conn.: Yale University Press

Olson, M. (1993) 'Dictatorship, Democracy and Development', *American Political Science Review*, 87, September: 567–76

Otani, I. and Villanueva, D. (1989) 'Major Determinants of Long-Term Growth in LDCs', *Finance and Development*, September

Panayotou, T. (1992) 'Environmental Kuznets Curve: Empirical Tests and Policy Implications', *mimeo*, Cambridge, Mass.: Harvard Institute for International Development

Pangestu, M. (1991) 'Macroeconomic Management in the ASEAN Countries', in Ariff, M. (ed.) *The Pacific Economy: Growth and External Stability*, Sydney: Allen and Unwin

Parkin, M. (1993) 'The Macroeconomic Requirements for Prosperity', *Australian Economic Review*, 1st Quarter: 11–20

Patrick, H. (1966) 'Financial Development and Economic Growth in Underdeveloped Countries', *Economic Development and Cultural Change*, 14(2): 174–89

Paukert, F. (1973) 'Income Distribution at Different Levels of Development – A Survey of Evidence', *International Labour Review*, 108 (2/3): 97–125

Payne, R.A. (1995) 'Freedom and the Environment', *Journal of Democracy*, 6(3): 41–55

Pearce, D. (1993) 'Can GATT Survive the Environmental Challenge', *Green Globe Yearbook 1993*, Oxford: Oxford University Press

Pearce, D. and Warford, J. (1992) *World without End: Economics, Environment and Sustainable Development*, Oxford: Oxford University Press

Pei, M. (1994) *From Reform to Revolution: The Demise of Communism in China*, Cambridge, Mass.: Harvard University Press

Pei, M. (1995) 'Creeping Democratization in China', *Journal of Democracy*, 6(4): 64–79

Pencavel, J. (1995) *The Role of Labor Unions in Fostering Economic Development*, Policy Research Working Paper No. 1469, Washington D.C.: World Bank

Petrie, P. (1993a) 'The East Asian Trading Bloc: An Analyical History', in Frankel, J. and Kahler, M. (eds) *Regionalism and Rivalry: Japan and the U.S. in Pacific Asia*, Chicago: University of Chicago Press. Reprinted in Garnaut, R. and Drysdale, P. (eds) (1994) *Asia-Pacific Regionalism – Readings in International Economic Relations*, Sydney: Harper Collins

Petrie, P. (1993b) 'Common Foundations of East Asian Success' in *Lessons of East Asia Series*, Washington, D.C.: World Bank

Petrick, J.A. and Quinn, J.F. (1994) 'Deforestation in Indonesia: Policy Framework for Sustainable Development', *Journal of Asian Business*, 10(2): 41–56

Pranee Tinakorn (forthcoming) 'Industrialisation and Welfare: How Poverty and Income Distribution Are Affected' in Mehdi Krongkiew (ed.) *Thailand's Industrialisation and its Consequences*, London: Macmillan

Prezeworski, A. (1995) 'Comments on the Impact of Constitutions on Economic Performance', *Proceedings of the World Bank Annual Conference on Development Economics 1994*, Washington, D.C.: World Bank

Prezeworski, A. and Limongi, F. (1993) 'Political Regimes and Economic Growth', *Journal of Economic Perspectives*, 7: 51–69

Prybala, J. (1995) 'Books in Review: Departures from Communism' [reviews of Pei (1994) and Goldman (1994)], *Journal of Democracy*, 6(4): 164–8

Psacharopoulos, G. (1985) 'Returns to Education: A Further International Update and Implications', *Journal of Human Resources*, 20: 583–97

Psacharopoulos, G. and Jimenez, E. (1989) 'Financing Education in Developing Countries', *IDS Bulletin*, 20(1)

Quibriq, M.G. (ed.) (1995) *Critical Issues in Asian Development*, Hong Kong: Oxford University Press

Radetzki, M. (1992) 'Economic Growth and Environment' in Low, P. (ed.) *International Trade and the Environment*, Washington, D.C.: World Bank Discussion Paper No. 159

Ramstetter, E. (1993) 'Asian Multinationals in the World Economy', *International Economic Insights*, 4(4): 19–22

Ranis, G. (1981) 'Challenge and Opportunities Posed by Asia's Superexporters: Implications for Manufactured Exports from Latin America' in Bower, W. and Collins, M. (eds) *Export Diversification and the New Protectionism: The Experiences of Latin America*, Champaign: University of Illinois

Rao, V. (1988), 'Income Distribution in East Asian Developing Countries', *Asian Pacific Economic Literature*, 2(1): 26–45

Rausch, J. (1994) *Demoscelorsis: The Silent Killer of American Government*, New York: Times Books

Rausser, G. (1992) 'Predatory vs Productive Government: The Case of US Agricultural Policies', *Journal of Economic Perspectives*, 6(3); 133–58

Ravenhill, J. (1994) 'The Japan Problem in Pacific Trade' in Higgott, R., Leaver, R. and Ravenhill, J. (eds) *Pacific Economic Relations in the 1990s: Conflict or Cooperation?* Sydney: Allen and Unwin

Reidel, J. (1988) 'Economic Development in East Asia: Doing What Comes Naturally?', in Hughes, H. (ed.) *Achieving Industrialization in Asia*, Cambridge: Cambridge University Press

Repetto, R. (1995) 'Trade and Sustainable Development' in Quibria, M.G. (ed.) *Critical Issues in Asian Development*, Hong Kong: Oxford University Press

Robinson, D., Byeon, Y. et al. (1991) *Thailand: Adjusting to Success – Current Policy Issues*, Washington, DC: International Monetary Fund

Robinson, S. (1976) 'A Note on the U-Hypothesis Relating Income Inequality and Economic Development', *American Economic Review*, 66(3): 437–40

Rodan, G. (1994) 'Reconstructing Division of Labour: Singapore's New Regional Emphasis' in Higgott, R., Leaver, R. and Ravenhill, J. (eds) *Pacific Economic Relations in the 1990s: Conflict or Cooperation?*, Sydney: Allen and Unwin

Romer, P. (1986) 'Increasing Returns to Long-Run Growth', *Journal of Political Economy*, 94(5): 1002–35

Romer, P. (1990) 'Are Nonconvexities Important for Understanding Growth?', *American Economic Review*, 80(2)

Romer, P. (1993) 'Two Strategies For Economic Development: Using Ideas and Producing Ideas', *Proceedings of the World Bank Annual Conference on Development Economics 1992*, Washington, DC: World Bank

Sah, R.K. (1991) 'Fallibility in Human Organizations and Political Systems', *Journal of Economic Perspectives*, 5(2): 67–88

Salleh, I.M. and Meyanathan, S.D. (1993) 'Malaysia: Growth, Equity and Structural Transformation' in *Lessons of East Asia Series*, Washington, D.C.: World Bank

Salt, J. (1992) 'The Future of International Labour Migration', *International Migration Review, 26(4): 1077– 1111*

Salter, W.E.G. (1959) 'Internal and External Balance: The Role of Price and Expenditure Effects', *Economic Record*, 35: 226–38

Sargent, T.J. (ed.) (1986) *Rational Expectations and Inflation*, New York: Harper and Row

Schmidt-Hebbel, K. and Webb, S.B. (1992) 'Public Policy and Private Saving' in Corbo, V., Fischer, S. and Webb, S.B. (eds) *Adjustment Lending Revisited: Public Policies to Restore Growth*, Washington DC: World Bank

Schultz, T.P. (1988) 'Education Investments and Returns' in Chenery, H. and Srinivasan, T.N. (eds) *Handbook of Development Economics*, Amsterdam: North-Holland

Schultze, C. (1992) 'Is There a Bias towards Excess in U.S. Government Budgets or Deficits', *Journal of Economic Perspectives*, 6(2): 25–43

Scitovsky, T. (1985) 'Economic Development in Taiwan and South Korea: 1965–81', *Food Research Institute Studies*, 19(3): 215–64

Sen, A. (1994) 'Freedoms and Needs', *New Republic*, 31 January: 10–17

Sen, A.K. (1976) 'Poverty; An Ordinal Approach', *Econometrica*, 44(2): 219–31

Sen, A.K. (1981), 'Public Action and the Quality of Life in Developing Countries', *Oxford Bulletin of Economics and Statistics*, 43(4): 287–317

Sen, A.K. (1985) *Commodities and Capabilities*, Amsterdam: North-Holland

Sengenberger, W. (1991) 'The Role of Labour Market Regulation in Industrial Restructuring', in Standing, G. and Tokman, V. (eds) *Towards Social Adjustment*, Geneva: ILO

Sengupta, J.K. (1991) 'Rapid Growth in NICs in Asia: Tests of New Growth Theory for Korea', *Kyklos*, 44(4)

Sengupta, J.K. (1993) 'Growth in NICs in Asia: Some Tests of New Growth Theory', *Journal of Development Studies*, 29(2): 342–57

Seow, F. (1994) *To Catch a Tartar: A Dissident in Lee Kuan Yew's Prison*, New Haven, Conn.: Yale Center for International and Area Studies

Shaw, E. (1973) *Financial Deepening in Economic Development*, New York: Oxford University Press

Sheng, A. (1992) 'Bank Restructuring in Malaysia' in Vittas, D. (ed.) *Financial Regulation: Changing the Rules of the Game*, Washington, D.C.: EDI Development Studies, World Bank

Smil, V. (1984) *The Bad Earth: Environmental Degradation in China*, New York: Sharpe Publishers

Soesastro, H. (1994) 'Pacific Economic Cooperation: The History of an Idea' in Garnaut, R. and Drysdale, P. (eds) *Asia-Pacific Regionalism –Readings in International Economic Relations*, Sydney: HarperCollins

Soon, T-C. and Tam, C.S. (1993) 'Singapore: Public Policy and Economic Development' in *Lessons of East Asia Series*, Washington, D.C.: World Bank

Spiegel, M. (1995) 'Sterilization of Capital Inflows through the Banking Sector: Evidence from Asia', *Economic Review, Federal Reserve Bank of San Francisco*, no. 3: 17–34

Squire, L. (1993) 'Fighting Poverty', *American Economic Review, Papers and Proceedings*, 83(2): 377–83

Standing, G. (1992) 'Do Unions Impede or Accelerate Structural Adjustment? Industrial vs Company Unions in an Industrialising Labour Market', *Cambridge Journal of Economics*, 16 (September): 327–54

Stern, N. (1989) 'The Economics of Development: A Survey', *Economic Journal*, 199(397): 597–685

Stiglitz, J.E. (1989) 'Markets, Market Failure, and Development', *American Economic Review*, May

Streeten, P. *et al.* (1981), *First Things First: Meeting Basic Needs in Developing Countries*, New York: Oxford University Press

Summers, L. (1991) 'Regionalism and the World Trading System' in *Policy Implications of Trade and Currency Zones*, A Symposium Sponsored by the Federal Reserve Bank of Kansas City, Wyoming, August: 7–42

Summers, L.H. and Pritchett, L.H. (1993) 'The Structural-adjustment Debate', *American Economic Review, Papers and Proceedings*, 83(2): 393–389

Summers, L.H. and Thomas, V. (1993) 'Recent Lessons of Development', *The World Bank Research Observer*, 8(2): 235–7

Sundrum, R.M. (1990) *Income Distribution in Less Developed Countries*, London and New York: Routledge

Sung, Y. and Chan, T. (1987) 'China's Economic Reforms I: The Debates in China', *Asian-Pacific Economic Literature*, 1(1): 1–24

Swan, T.W. (1960) 'Economic Control in a Dependent Economy', *Economic Record*, 36 (73): 51–66

Taylor, L. (1983) *Structuralist Macroeconomics: Applicable Models for the Third World*, New York: Basic Books

Thorbecke, E. (1991) 'Adjustment, Growth and Income Distribution in Indonesia', *World Development*, 19(11): 1595–641

Thurow, L. (1979) 'Job Competition Model', in Piore, M. (ed.) *Unemployment and Inflation*, White Plains, N.Y.: M.E. Sharpe

Treadgold, M. (1990) 'Macroeconomic Management in Asia-Pacific Developing Countries', *Asian-Pacific Economic Literature*, 4(1): 3–40

Trisoglio, A. (1993) 'International Business and Sustainable Development', *Green Globe Yearbook 1993*, Oxford: Oxford University Press

UNDP (1995) *Human Development Report*, New York: Oxford University Press

UNIDO (1991) *Industry and Development: Global Report 1990*, Vienna: United Nations Industrial Development Organization

Urata, S. (1994) 'Changing Patterns of Direct Investment and the Implications for Trade and Development' in Garnaut, R. and Drysdale, P. (eds) *Asia-Pacific Regionalism – Readings in International Economic Relations*, Sydney: HarperCollins

Veenendaal, E. and Oopschoor, J. (1986) *Botswana'a Beef Exports to the EEC: Economic Development at the Expense of a Deteriorating Environment*, Amsterdam: Institute for Environmental Studies, Free University of Amsterdam

Vittas, D. (ed.) (1992a) *Financial Regulation: Changing the Rules of the Game*, Washington, D.C.: EDI Development Studies, World Bank

Vittas, D. (1992b) 'Introduction and Overview' in Vittas (1992a)

Vittas, D. (1992c) 'The Impact of Regulation on Financial Intermediation', in Vittas (1992a)

Wade, R. (1988), 'The Role of Government in Overcoming Market Failure: Taiwan, Republic of Korea and Japan' in Hughes, H. (ed.) *Achieving Industrialization in Asia*, Cambridge: Cambridge University Press

Wade, R. (1990), *Governing the Market: Economic Theory and the Role of Government in East Asian Industrialization*, Princeton, NJ: Princeton University Press

Warr, P. (1992) 'Exchange Rate Policy, Petroleum Prices, and the Balance of Payments' in Booth, A. (ed.) *The Oil Boom and After*, Singapore: Oxford University Press

Warr, P.G. and Bhanuprangse Nidhiprabha (1994) *Macroeconomic Policies, Crisis, and Long-Term Growth in Thailand*, Washington, D.C.: World Bank

Watson, A. (ed.) (1992) *Economic Reform and Social Change in China*, London and New York: Routledge

Watson, A. (1994) 'China's Economic Reforms: Growth and Cycles', *Asian-Pacific Economic Literature*

Woo, W.T. and Nasution, A. (1989) 'Indonesian Economic Policies and their Relation to External Debt Management', in Sachs, J.D. and Collins, S.M. (eds) *Developing Country Debt and Economic Performance*, Chicago: University of Chicago Press

Woo, W.T., Glassburner, B. and Nasution, A. (1994) *Macroeconomic Policies, Crisis, and Long-Term Growth in Indonesia*, Washington, D.C.: World Bank

World Bank (1989) *World Development Report 1989: Financial Systems and Development*, New York: Oxford University Press

World Bank (1990), *World Development Report 1990*, New York: Oxford University Press

World Bank (1992) *World Development Report 1992 – Development and the Environment*, New York: Oxford University Press

World Bank (1993a) *The East Asian Miracle: Economic Growth and Public Policy*, New York: Oxford University Press for the World Bank

World Bank (1993b) *World Bank Policy Research Bulletin*, January–February, 4(1)

World Bank (1993c) *Sustaining Rapid Development in East Asia and the Pacific* Washington, D.C.: World Bank

World Bank (1995a) *World Development Report 1995: Workers in an Integrating World*, New York: Oxford University Press

World Bank (1995b) *Trends in Developing Economies*, Washington, D.C.: World Bank

World Commission on Environment and Development (1987) *Our Common Future*, Oxford: Oxford University Press

Wu Yanrui (1993) 'Productive Efficiency in Chinese Industry', *Asian-Pacific Economic Literature*, 7(2): 58–66

Yamazawa, I. (1994) 'On Pacific Economic Integration' in Garnaut, R. and Drysdale, P. (eds) *Asia-Pacific Regionalism – Readings in International Economic Relations*, Sydney: HarperCollins

Yamazawa, I. and Lo, F-C. (eds) (1993) *Evolution of Asia–Pacific Economies: International Trade and Direct Investment*, Kuala Lumpur: Asian and Pacific Development Centre

Young, A. (1992) 'A Tale of Two Cities: Factor Accumulation and Technical Change in Hong Kong and Singapore', *NBER Macroeconomics Annual 1992*, Cambridge: National Bureau & Economic Research

Yue, C.S. and Yuan, L.S. (1994) 'Subregional Economic Zones in Southeast Asia' in Garnaut, R. and Drysdale, P. (eds) *Asia-Pacific Regionalism – Readings in International Economic Relations*, Sydney: HarperCollins

Yuen, N.C. and Woon, T.K. (1992) 'Privatization in the Asian-Pacific Region', *Asian-Pacific Economic Literature*, 6(2): 42–68

Zakaria, F. (1994) 'Interview with Lee Kuan Yew', *Foreign Affairs*, vol. 73, March-April: 109–26

Zysman, J. (1983), *Government, Markets and Growth: Financial Systems and the Politics of Industrial Change*, Ithaca, NY: Cornell University Press

Part II

Country surveys: recent developments

Chapter 9

Republic of Korea (South Korea)

HISTORY AND CULTURE

The name 'Korea' is the English version of Koryo, a kingdom which was established in the central region of the Korean peninsula in AD 918. Korea was subjected to repeated Chinese invasions and intermittent Chinese occupations. The Chinese colonies in the north-western region of Korea, which began in 108 BC, lasted until the 4th century AD. The Chinese influence on Korea reached its height during the Koryo period when its political system became similar to that of China. In the 13th century Korea became a satellite of feudal China, ruled by the Yuan dynasty.

The Koryo dynasty was overthrown by Gen. Yi Song-Gye in 1392 and the Yi dynasty lasted until 1910. Yi renamed the kingdom as Choson, the name of an ancient kingdom believed to have been established by a mythical figure, Tan'gun in 2333 BC. Seoul became new Choson's capital. The Yi dynasty brought the entire Korean peninsula and the island of Cheju under its rule. The kingdom was governed with a Confucian bureaucracy manned by an elite class of scholar-officials chosen through a Chinese-style competitive civil service test. Korea became increasingly Confucianised as a vassal to China, ruled by the Ming dynasty (Nahm, 1995: 450).

Korea was always at the centre of struggle among regional powers. The 16th and early 17th centuries were marked by Japanese and Manzhaou (Manchurian) invasions. In the late 19th century, Japan contested first with China and later with Russia over the control of Korea. Following the Japanese victory in the Sino-Japan War of 1894–95 and the Russo-Japanese War of 1904–05, Korea became a protectorate of Japan. In 1910, Japan annexed Korea, ending the rule of the Yi dynasty.

Although the Japanese colonial rule was highly repressive and exploitative, modern commerce and industry had their foundation during the Japanese occupation (Nahm, 1995: 450). However, the Korean economy was developed to serve the purposes of Japan. Food production was increased to feed the ever-growing population of Japan and an increasing amount of Korean rice was exported to Japan. Likewise, Korean industries were predominantly supplying the Japanese domestic market.

The cultural heritage of the Korean people can be traced to the prehistoric tribal Puyo people. The Tungusic people who migrated into the Korean peninsula in 3000 BC brought shamanistic religion and a palaeolithic culture. The Sinification of Korean culture began during the Chinese occupation. Buddhism came to Korea from China in the 3rd century AD and became the state religion of Koryo. Confucian influence grew stronger in the 7th century and became dominant during the Yi dynasty which adopted Confucianism as the state creed.

The Japanese tried to force the Korean people to adopt Shintoism and to change their names to read like Japanese. However, the Japanese efforts to destroy the Korean language and culture largely failed.

Historically, Korea developed as a society highly stratified into landed gentry (*yangban*) and the toiling masses. The toiling masses were further classified into 'good people' or 'common people' who were engaged in agriculture, and 'the low-born', who were engaged in trade, manufacturing or other 'lesser' occupations. Obviously, the gentry or *yangban* owned the land and formed the educated class which supplied high-ranking government officials during the Yi dynasty.

GEOPOLITICAL DEVELOPMENTS

The liberation of Korea from Japanese occupation was on the agenda of the British and their Second World War allies, in particular the US and China. The leaders of the United Kingdom, the United States and China issued the Cairo Declaration stating that 'in due course Korea shall become free and independent', and this was accepted by the USSR. However, a US proposal led in 1945 to the division of Korea into two military zones on the two sides of the 38th parallel – the south falling under US occupation and the north being under the control of the USSR. Under the proposal the US forces entered Korea from the south and Soviet forces from the north.

Shortly before Japan surrendered to the allies, a prominent left-wing nationalist, Yo Un-Hyong, formed the Committee for the Preparation of the National Construction of Korea (CPNCK). Yo was encouraged by the Japanese Governor-General in Korea to form a political body to maintain law and order when Japanese colonial rule ended. Two days before the arrival of the US forces, the CPNCK called a 'National Assembly' and proclaimed the 'People's Republic of Korea' over the entire country on September 6, 1945.

The USSR, whose forces by then occupied the northern half of Korea, quickly recognised the authority of the 'People's Republic'. However, the US refused to recognise the 'People's Republic'. Instead it established the US Army Military Government in Korea (USAMGIK) which operated until the proclamation of South Korea's independence in August 1948.

The UK, the US and the USSR entered into the Moscow Agreement in December 1945. The agreement provided for a five-year trusteeship for Korea under a four-power regime (China was the fourth power), with the objective of establishing an independent and united Korea. The Korean political leaders greeted the agreement with violent protests. But the communists throughout Korea suddenly changed their stance in favour of the Moscow Agreement.

The US–Soviet commission, which was formed to establish a united Korean government in consultation with the Korean political leaders, met in Seoul in March–May 1946. But the meeting failed as the Soviet delegates insisted that only 'the democratic forces', meaning those who supported the Moscow Agreement could participate in the discussion. The second session of the joint commission, which met in Pyongyang in May 1947, also failed for the same reason and it became clear that the Soviet Union wanted to establish an all-Korean government dominated by the communists.

Thus, the US and the Soviet Union went ahead to establish South and North Korean client states. A South Korean Interim Legislative Assembly was established in May 1947. The formation of an interim government under the nationalists was resented by South Korean politicians from both right and left. There was an upsurge of terrorist activities and a number of prominent politicians were assassinated. The interim government was unable to bring stability and there was extreme economic hardship.

The US finally abandoned the Moscow plan in September 1947 and the Korean issue was raised at the UN General Assembly. The UN Temporary Commission on Korea was formed in November with the mandate to conduct a national election in Korea for an all-Korea government. However, the UN plan was rejected by the Soviet Union and the communist regime in the North.

UN-sponsored elections in the South were held in May 1948. The elected National Assembly in South Korea drew up a democratic constitution for the Republic of Korea and elected Dr Syngman Rhee as the first President of the Republic. The UN recognised the legitimacy of Dr Rhee's government and the Republic of Korea was inaugurated on August 15, 1948, ending the US occupation.

On June 25, 1950, North Korean forces crossed the 38th parallel and four days later captured Seoul. Soon the North Korean forces occupied most of South Korea. At the request of Seoul, the US-led UN multinational forces mounted a counter-attack and drove back the North Korean forces. In October 1950, the UN forces captured Pyongyang. About 200,000 Chinese military personnel were then sent in for the defence of North Korea. The Chinese forces advanced into South Korea, but were later pushed back by the UN troops.

In July 1951, peace negotiations began and hostilities ended two years later with an agreement on July 27, 1953. The ceasefire line, along the 38th parallel, divides the two Koreas with a narrow demilitarised zone separating the two frontiers. The war inflicted enormous damage on South Korea with more than 800,000 casualties. Despite the ceasefire, tensions between two Koreas remain with occasional flare-ups, and there is a permanent US force in South Korea.

However, the question of unification of Korea is still on the agenda. On July 4, 1972 both the Korean governments simultaneously announced the opening of dialogue between the two sides. A North–South Co-ordinating Committee was formed for facilitating peaceful unification without outside intervention.

Internal political developments

The internal politics of South Korea (henceforth Korea) has been marked by repressions and political unrest, often turning into violence and military coups. To begin with, there was a communist-inspired military rebellion in October 1948. Although the rebellion was brutally crushed, political instability and terrorist activities continued. In response, the government of President Rhee became more autocratic. There were widespread repressions of political opponents of President Rhee and his Liberal Party (LP) government.

In July 1952, the National Assembly amended the constitution to allow for a popularly elected President and Dr Rhee won the election which was held under martial law. There were further amendments to the constitution which included the abolition of the post of Prime Minister and of the clause limiting the incumbent President to only two terms. Despite growing unpopularity of the repressive President Rhee's government, which was riddled with widespread corruption, Dr Rhee had easy wins in two consecutive elections in 1956 and 1960. Curiously, his wins were aided on both occasions by the sudden death of the opposition candidate some weeks before the election.

However, popular discontent against the corrupt and repressive government intensified and fierce student riots broke out throughout the country, immediately following the election. President Rhee and his government were forced to resign and a caretaker government was established. In mid-June, the National Assembly amended the constitution and adopted a strong parliamentary system of government, with a President as a figurehead.

On May 16, 1961, a small group of army officers led by Maj. Gen. Park Chung-hee staged a coup and overthrew the government on the pretext that it had failed to bring political and economic stability. The junta dissolved the National Assembly and proclaimed martial law, banning all political activities. In December 1962, a constitutional amendment was passed by national referendum which restored a strong presidential system of government. Gen. Park, who had earlier relinquished his military position and formed the Democratic Republican Party won the presidential election held in October 1963. On December 17, Park was formally inaugurated as President and the newly elected National Assembly was convened, marking the restoration of civilian constitutional rule.

The Park government initiated wide-ranging policy reforms, and substantial economic progress was achieved under the two five-year plans (1962–66 and 1967–71). However, growing political discontent due to the quasi-military nature of the government and alleged corruption of military and government officials caused uneasiness within the government. President Park thus used the opportunity of changed international conditions arising from the Sino-US *détente* and new developments in North–South relations to proclaim martial law and abrogate the constitution in October 1972. Park replaced the National Assembly with the National Conference for Unification (NCU). After the fall of Saigon and the US defeat in Vietnam, Park further tightened his control by proclaiming the Presidential Emergency Measure for Safeguarding National Security.

The partial relaxation of martial law failed to quieten political unrest and the government became increasingly oppressive and autocratic. The unrest culminated in a serious uprising in Pusan and other southern cities in October 1979. On October 26, in the midst of the crisis, President Park was shot and killed by the director of the Korean Central Intelligence Agency, Kim Chae-kyu. President Park's prime minister, Choi Kyu-ha, became the acting President and martial law was imposed once again. Two months later, the NCU elected Choi to become the President of the Republic.

Taking the opportunity of a power struggle within the ruling party and the military, Lt. Gen. Chun Doo-hwan staged a coup and became the new strong-man in Korean politics. Meanwhile, the demand for the immediate adoption of a constitution and the installation of a civilian government intensified. Students and demonstrators clashed with police and paratroopers, and took over the city of Kwangju on May 19, 1980. A week later, the army crushed the rebellion at a cost of 200 lives, but the riots spread to other cities. President Choi stepped down in August, and in the following month Gen. Chun who resigned from active army duty replaced Choi as President.

President Chun immediately initiated investigations into political corruption, bribery and favouritism. This led to the conviction of many prominent figures and enhanced President Chun's popularity. A new constitution was passed by national referendum and Chun was elected President on February 25, 1981 to serve a single seven-year term.

President Chun's initial popularity did not last long. Amidst economic crises arising from the second oil-price shock and the worldwide recession in the early 1980s, the Chun government was rocked by a financial scandal involving relatives of Chun's wife. The demand for more political openness continued, despite relaxation of controls. In March and April 1986 mass rallies were held in Seoul, Pusan, Kwangju and Taegu in demand for constitutional reform and the resignation of Chun. The death of a student, allegedly as a result of police torture, in January 1987 fuelled a new wave of anti-government demonstration. Organised mass rallies and violent confrontations became a daily occurrence.

In July 1987, the government granted amnesty to political prisoners and a month later agreed on the basic outline of a new constitution allowing direct presidential election. In October, it conceded the revision of labour laws, guaranteeing workers' rights to form trade unions and to conduct collective bargaining. The process of democratisation culminated in the adoption of the new constitution through a national referendum and the holding of the direct presidential election on December 16, 1987. Roh Tae-woo was inaugurated as President on February 25, 1988, completing the peaceful transition to democratic civilian rule. In an unprecedented move, Chun appeared on national television to publicly apologise for the misdeeds of his regime. He later retreated with his wife to a Buddhist monastery in Kangwon Province. Despite the democratisation of the political process and the conviction of corrupt former government officials, anti-government demonstrations continued to flare up during President Roh's tenure of office.

Kim Young-sam, who replaced Roh as president of the ruling DLP, won a convincing victory in the 1992 presidential election. Kim's radical social and economic reform agenda and fight against corruption of both politicians and military officials earned him widespread public support. President Kim also moved quickly to limit the power of the military and the security services. The government has changed organisational arrangements to ensure civilian control and to prevent a return to military power.

The general election of April 11, 1996, which came immediately after North Korea's incursion into the demilitarised zone, produced some unexpected results. The main opposition led by Kim Dae-jung lost the balance of power to Kim Jong-pil. Kim Jong-pil's Conservative Party won 50 seats, making it the second largest minority party. Kim Jong-pil actively advocates a parlimentary system of government which would provide checks and balances against 'an irresponsible president'. Although President Kim Yong-sam's party lost its absolute majority in the assembly, it seems the Korean people want stability.

THE ECONOMY

The Republic of Korea is one of the most densely populated countries in Asia. It has an estimated population of 44.5 million which is about twice that of North Korea. While (South) Korea occupies only 45 per cent of the peninsula and is not well endowed with natural resources, it has achieved a remarkable economic growth. The rapid economic expansion that began in 1963, transformed Korea from an underdeveloped, agriculture-based economy into a newly industrialised economy in less than two decades. In 1993, the share of industrial output in GDP stood at more than 43 per cent and manufacturing accounted for nearly 93 per cent of total merchandise exports. Its per capita income is estimated at US$7,466 in 1993. The basic economic and trade indicators of Korea are presented in Tables 9.1–5.

Table 9.1 Key macroeconomic indicators of South Korea

Indicator	1971–80	1981–90	1992	1994
Real GDP growth rate (%)	9.0	8.8	4.8	7.6
Inflation rate (CPI, %)	16.5	6.4	6.2	4.6
Share in GDP (%)				
Gross domestic saving	22.3	30.0	35.2	32.5
Gross domestic investment	28.6	30.5	35.9	33.8
Current account	−8.5[a]	−1.0[b]	−1.5	−2.1
Debt servicing ratio (% export)	14.1[a]	21.6[b]	7.9	5.1

Source: ADB, Outlook (various issues)
Notes: a 1980, b 1990

Growth and structural change

The substantial inflow of foreign aid, following the Korean War, helped Korea achieve a moderate rate of economic growth during 1953–58. However, economic expansion slowed during 1959–62 and the growth rate of per capita income declined to almost zero in the early 1960s. The two five-year plans spanning the period 1962–71 and policy reform had remarkable impacts on Korea's economic performance. Korea managed an average annual growth rate of 8.6 per cent during the 1960s. Despite severe balance of payments shocks due to two oil-price rises in the 1970s, the Korean economy grew by 9 per cent during 1971–80. The resilience of the Korean economy was also displayed in the 1980s when the real GDP grew by 8.8 per cent per annum.

However, the Korean economy was prone to inflation. It seems that the policy-makers were more concerned with growth than with inflation (Park, 1983). Its average annual inflation rate of 16–17 per cent during 1960–80 was well below many Latin American and African countries, but, nonetheless, was higher than other East Asian NIEs. Only in the 1980s, did inflation ease and the annual rise in the consumer price index remained around 5–6 per cent.

The other weak spot in Korea's economic performance is its current account deficit. Despite a substantial increase in gross domestic saving, the gross national saving still falls short of gross domestic investment. The current account turned into a surplus for a brief period during 1986–89, but became negative once again. There was a small surplus of only US$0.5 billion in 1993, but a deficit was recorded in the following year. However,

Korea managed to reduce its debt servicing ratio of more than 21 per cent in 1985 to 5 per cent in 1994.

The structural transformation of the Korean economy since 1960 has been quite extensive. In the early 1960s, Korea was essentially an agricultural economy with agriculture accounting for 37 per cent of GDP and 66 per cent of employment. Manufacturing's contribution to GDP in 1960 was only 14 per cent and to employment was 9 per cent. In 1992, manufacturing accounted for nearly 34 per cent of GDP and 30 per cent of employment.

Table 9.2 Sectoral contributions to Korea's GDP

Sector	1975	1985	1992
Agriculture	24.1	12.8	7.1
Industry	32.5	41.9	46.2
Manufacturing	22.5	30.3	33.8
Services	43.5	45.3	46.7

Source: ADB, *Key Indicators* (various issues)

Korea's manufacturing sector itself has undergone significant structural changes. In the 1960s, light and labour-intensive manufacturing laid the foundation of Korea's industrialisation. The emphasis in the 1970s shifted to capital-intensive activities such as machinery, transport equipment, shipbuilding, steel, plant construction and engineering, petrochemicals and defence-related heavy industries. In the 1980s, more priority was given to high-technology industries.

Although the share of TCF (textiles, clothing and footwear) industries in manufacturing value added (MVA) declined, they are still a major activity

Table 9.3 Share in manufacturing value-added (%, producers' price)

Industries	1979	1985	1990	Growth rate (% 1980–91)
Food, beverage & tobacco	16.5	13.8	10.7	6.6
Textiles, clothing & footwear	19.6	16.5	11.9	6.2
Wood & furniture	2.4	1.5	1.8	8.8
Paper & printing	3.4	4.6	4.6	8.5
Chemicals	9.1	8.8	9.1	11.6
Petroleum & coal	2.7	4.5	3.4	12.6
Rubber, plastic, pottery, glass	11.4	10.1	10.7	8.4
Iron, steel & non-ferrous metal	11.7	11.8	12.5	12.2
Machinery	4.5	4.5	7.0	21.5
Electrical machinery	8.9	11.8	15.0	21.1
Transport equipment	6.0	9.1	10.4	20.7
Professional goods	1.0	1.0	1.1	14.4
Other industries	1.8	1.9	1.8	5.3

Source: UN, *Yearbook of Industrial Statistics* (various issues)

and Korea is the world's third largest exporter of textiles. The government announced a plan in early 1990 to develop the textile industry with a view to making Korea the world's leading textiles exporter by the turn of the century. During 1980–91, machinery, electrical machinery and transport equipment industries grew by more than 20 per cent, which is well over the average annual growth rate of 11.4 per cent for the entire manufacturing sector. Korea is now a leading producer of steel in the world and has overtaken Japan as the world's largest shipbuilder. In 1993 Samsung Electronics garnered nearly 11 per cent of the world's memory chip market and became the seventh largest semi-conductor chip producer in the world. In the same year Korea had a share of about 18 per cent of the world's semi-conductor market. The government initiated a program to increase Korea's share of the world electronics market from 5 per cent in 1989 to more than 12 per cent by the turn of the century.

External trade

Korea's phenomenal success in export expansion can be gleaned from the rise in exports from a meagre US$40 million in 1953 to US$82.3 billion in 1993. More than 90 per cent of Korea's exports are manufactured goods. By 1990, Korea became the 11th largest exporter in the world and the 7th largest trading partner of the US. Exports grew by more than 38 per cent in the 1960s and at a slightly lower rate in the 1970s. The slump in the world economy in the early 1980s slowed Korea's exports, but it recovered by 1986 and exports grew by 36.2 per cent and 28.4 per cent in 1987 and 1988 respectively. Exports growth has slowed down considerably since 1989, ranging between 2.8 per cent (1989) and 7.3 per cent (1993). This reflects the erosion of Korea's competitive advantage over other low-cost developing

Table 9.4 South Korea's major manufactured exports

Item	1980	1985	1990	1992
Clothing, woven textiles, textile yarn	28.6	22.5	22.5	18.8
Telecommunications, motor vehicles & ships	8.0	26.1	17.1	17.0
Electrical machinery & domestic electrical appliances	1.4	6.1	12.3	13.6
Iron & steel	3.5	1.9	2.9	2.9
Footwear	5.6	5.6	7.4	4.3
Recorders	1.4	2.6	5.0	4.1
Office machines	1.0	2.1	4.7	4.3
Machinery, n.e.s., non-electrical	1.0	1.0	2.2	2.5
Rubber products	3.2	1.7	1.7	1.6
Toys	2.1	2.4	2.1	1.3
Travel goods	1.7	1.7	2.0	1.3
Other	43.7	26.3	20.2	14.4

Source: APEG, *Asia-Pacific Profile, 1994*

countries, due mainly to rising labour costs. Korea is also increasingly facing growing protectionist measures in advanced countries.

As mentioned earlier, in anticipation of changing competitive advantage, Korea has restructured its industrial activities since the 1970s in successive stages. This is reflected in its changing export structure. For example, the share of more sophisticated items such as electrical machinery and domestic electrical equipment in total manufactured exports increased from 1.4 per cent in 1980 to 13.6 per cent in 1992. Similarly, the share of transport equipment (motor vehicles and ships) increased from 1.6 per cent in 1980 to 10.3 per cent. The restructuring of the manufacturing sector resulted in the rise of capital-intensive exports from 55.5 per cent in 1986–88 to about 72 per cent in 1993. During the same period, the share of labour-intensive exports declined from 39 per cent to around 24 per cent. The heavy industrial outputs, such as electronics, automobiles, steel and ships now dominate Korea's manufactured exports. The fastest growing export item in recent times has been semi-conductors and, as mentioned above, Korea accounts for about 18 per cent of the world's semi-conductors market.

Korea is the world's 10th largest importer. For every year between 1953 and 1985, imports exceeded exports, although the trade deficit as a proportion of exports decreased from 772.2 per cent in 1953 to 2.8 per cent in 1985. For the first time in 1986, Korea recorded a trade surplus of US$4.2 billion. The balance of trade became negative once again during 1990–92. In 1993, the trade account recorded a surplus of US$2.1 billion.

Machinery and other equipment dominate Korea's imports, accounting for nearly 35 per cent of total imports. Imports of mineral fuels account for about 15 per cent. The increase in the imports of capital goods mirrors closely the process of industrial restructuring that is occurring in Korea.

Table 9.5 South Korea's major trading partners (%)

Partner	1980	1985	1990	1993
ASEAN	6.5	5.0	7.7	16.8
	6.6	8.7	7.2	14.0
PRC, Taiwan and Hong Kong	5.9	5.7	8.1	15.1
	1.8	2.5	3.6	6.8
Japan	17.4	14.9	19.2	12.7
	26.3	24.3	26.4	22.7
USA	26.4	35.3	29.6	19.6
	22.0	21.1	24.1	17.6
European Union	15.5	10.6	13.5	12.5
	7.3	9.6	11.9	11.5
Rest of the world	28.3	28.5	22.0	23.3
	36.0	33.8	26.8	27.4

Source: Same as for Table 9.4
Note: 1st row = exports; 2nd row = imports

There is also an increasing trend in the import of consumer products which reflects the growing affluence of the Korean people.

The roles of both the US and Japan as Korea's main trading partners are on the decline. Korea is diversifying both its export market and the source of its imports. In particular, it is keen to reduce its technological dependence on Japan, the US and Europe. ASEAN and other Asian countries are becoming more important trading partners. Europe is supplying more to Korea's increasingly affluent domestic market.

Foreign direct investment

Unlike other East Asian NIEs, Korea has relied much less on foreign direct investment (FDI). For example, during 1965–84, FDI was less than 2 per cent of gross capital formation in Korea as opposed to more than 10 per cent in Singapore. Hill and Johns (1985: 358) described Singapore and Korea as two polar cases with respect to FDI. Until the early 1980s, Korea followed an extremely cautious policy which, according to Hill (1990: 25), was a result of a distrustful attitude towards FDI. Hill also noted that there were virtually no equity inflows between 1945 and 1962.

However, Korea's attitude towards FDI has changed significantly in recent years. To begin with, the number of areas open to foreign investors has been increased considerably and the aim is to raise to 95 per cent the areas open to foreign investment by January 1997. The only areas that will remain closed to foreign investment are those regarded as sensitive for national security and include mass media, real estate and energy. With a view to encouraging foreign investment in Korea, in late 1993 the government reduced the corporate tax rate on foreign-invested firms, relaxed regulations on foreign ownership of land and simplified the approval process. Foreign investors are also permitted to seek commercial loans from abroad to finance the purchase of capital goods. The government established a one-stop shop, the Korea Foreign Investment Service (KFIS), in 1994 for foreign investors in order to further simplify the approval procedure. Furthermore, the Korean stock market has been opened to foreign investment and the government increased the ceiling on foreign ownership of the stocks of listed companies to 12 per cent on December 1, 1994, with a target of raising it to 15 per cent in 1995. Japan is the major source of FDI in Korea, followed by the US and the EU. In 1989, their respective shares in FDI inflows stood at 61 per cent, 43.4 per cent and 21.1 per cent.

Korea began investment in overseas manufacturing in 1974. However, the annual outflow never exceeded US$39 million during the 1970s and the cumulative flow reached about US$126 million by 1980. In the 1980s, the cumulative flow increased to US$1.3 billion (Lee, 1994: 283). Korea's overseas investment in manufacturing increased rapidly from US$19.5

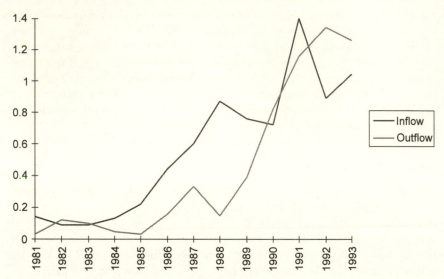

Figure 9.1 Foreign direct investment, South Korea (US$ bn)
Sources: OECD 1993; Trends in Foreign Investment, Ministry of Finance; Bank of Korea

million to US$530 million in 1990. The value of new Korean overseas investment reached US$1.3 billion in 1993.

Geographically, most Korean FDI went to North America and South East Asia. By 1990, North America and South East Asia accounted for 47.3 per cent and 30.6 per cent of cumulative Korean FDI, respectively (Lee, 1994: 283). Indonesia is the largest recipient among South East Asian countries of Korean FDI, followed by Malaysia. Lee (1994) cites rapid wage increases in excess of productivity growth, appreciation of Korean currency and rising protectionist barriers against Korean exports as three main reasons for Korean overseas investment, especially to labour-abundant South East Asian countries.

Labour market developments

The Korean labour market has become extremely tight in recent times, as the unemployment rate fell steadily from 5.2 per cent in 1980 to less than 3 per cent in 1993. As a result, wages were growing in Korea although the rate of growth has declined slightly since 1990 due to a strong government stance and increased flow of foreign workers. The total number of foreign workers was estimated at 76,400 (58,000 legal) in 1993 (APEG, 1994: 56). Furthermore, the Korean Federation of Trade Unions, the only official labour organisation, reached an agreement with the Korean Employers Federation in early 1994 to limit wages growth to between 5 and 8.7 per cent during the year.

Increased labour militancy and unionisation have also become a common feature in Korean. Between 1985 and 1990, union membership doubled to 1.9 million. Park (1991) attributed the growth of wages in excess of productivity gains to the increasing power of labour unions since the mid-1980s. According to Lee (1994: 286), there were virtually no strikes in Korea until 1984, but by 1987 there were 3,749 labour disputes, resulting in a loss of 7 million working days. As mentioned earlier, rises in wages over and above productivity gains are contributing to Korea's loss of international competitiveness and pushing Korean manufacturers to transfer production facilities to cheaper locations in South East Asia.

GOVERNMENT POLICIES

The Korean government has been the most interventionist among the East Asian NIEs. 'By means of planning, direct or indirect ownership and control of enterprises and financial institutions, control of foreign exchange, ...the Government has played a crucial role in adjusting the scale of the market, and incentives, in pursuit of its desired economic, social...objectives' (Chung, 1995: 483). It is widely believed that the successive five-year plans since 1962 significantly influenced the private sector and changed the course and pace of Korea's economic development.

Although the first long-range plan, popularly known as the Nathan Report, was produced by a US team in 1954, political conditions in Korea were not conducive to formal planning until the early 1960s. The First Five-Year Plan (1962–66) placed emphasis on the expansion of infrastructure such as generation of electricity, railways, ports and other communications. The first plan thus removed impediments to further investments as such infrastructure generates positive externalities and enhances returns to private investment. The Second Plan (1967–71) turned attention to the development of the manufacturing sector, based on the country's abundant supply of cheap and educated labour. Special attention was given to the electronics and textile industries. The Third Plan (1972–76) sought to restructure the industrial sector towards chemicals and other heavy industries. The plan provided for the construction of integrated steel works, the expansion and construction of petrochemical plants and the expansion of shipyards. The Fourth Plan (1977–81) had the objective of further industrial structuring towards skill- and technology-intensive activities. In addition, the Fourth Plan had the social objective of achieving a more equitable distribution of the fruits of economic expansion. Hence, there was increased expenditure on education, housing and public health.

As the economy transformed into a fully fledged NIE and became more complex, the government's role in the economy began to decline. Thus, the Fifth Plan (1982–86) incorporated programmes for liberalising the economy. The focus of the government also shifted to balanced regional development which was carried from the Fifth to the Sixth Plan (1987–91). The regional development component of the Sixth Plan sought to reduce the gap in the living standards between urban and rural people. The Seventh Plan (1992–96) was replaced with a new Five-Year Plan (1993–97) by President Kim. This plan envisages an average annual economic growth of nearly 7 per cent with a view to transforming Korea into an advanced economy and laying the foundation for the eventual unification of the two Koreas.

Recent policy developments

The new Five-Year Plan has given more emphasis to private-sector initiatives and reliance on market signals. President Kim has placed high priority on the internationalisation of Korea's economy and has taken steps to further liberalise trade and the financial sector. The government has also introduced legislation to reform agriculture and the services sector to bring Korea into line with the requirements of the World Trade Organisation (WTO). The new plan also envisages major institutional reforms, and Korea has already agreed to accept 27 of 178 OECD Acts in eight fields – trade, shipbuilding, steel, competition policy, education, maritime transport, science and technology and labour in order to bring its institutions into conformity with OECD countries.

Despite strong domestic political protests against the ratification of the Uruguay Round agreement, President Kim has shown his readiness to liberalise the Korean market. In April 1994, the government released details of the second stage of Korea's import liberalisation programme (1995–97) for 147 items. This is in addition to 137 items included in the first stage of the liberalisation programme (1992–94). The 147 items include 100 agricultural products, 46 fishery products and 1 silk yarn product.

In order to cushion the impact of the implementation of the Uruguay Round agreement, the government has undertaken an adjustment programme which includes the improvement of the agricultural marketing and distribution system, and mechanisation of agriculture. The programme also has a welfare net for people who would lose jobs during the adjustment.

The Uruguay Services Round outcome requires the opening of 78 business lines in eight areas to foreign participants. The government has a program to fully liberalise the distribution system by 1996. Foreign distribution companies have been allowed to increase domestic retail operations to a maximum of 20 retail shops, each of 3000 square metres. Foreign investors have been permitted to own shares in credit appraisal company stocks up to a level of 10 per cent from January 1995. Foreigners may also invest in trucking, power-generating, printing and filling station businesses up to a maximum of 50 per cent.

The government's programme to liberalise the financial sector is expected to be completed well ahead of schedule. Interest rates, including all lending rates and short-term deposit rates, were deregulated in November 1993. In addition to full liberalisation of current-account transactions, the plan is afoot to accelerate the liberalisation of capital accounts. The government has put a regulation in place restricting anyone from holding more than 4 per cent of the shares in any of the Seoul-based commercial banks in order to prevent market concentration in banking.

In August 1994, the government announced a comprehensive taxation reform programme. The aim of the programme is to establish a global income-tax system, with the taxation of domestic and foreign income combined. The reform is also expected to make the tax system compatible with international corporate tax standards and thereby enhance Korean corporations' competitiveness.

In addition to privatisation of most state-run corporations by 1998, the government of President Kim has proposed revising the Fair Trade Law to curb the monopoly power of the *chaebols* (Korean conglomerates). The revision calls for lowering the upper limit on subsidiaries of *chaebols* investing in other local firms from 40 per cent of their net worth to 25 per cent. It also suggests that each *chaebol* choose three main business lines where it is most competitive.

Chapter 10

Taiwan (The Republic of China)

HISTORY AND CULTURE

The Republic of China consists of the island of Taiwan (also known as Formosa), and some nearby smaller islands including the Penghu (Pescadores) group. The main island of Taiwan lies about 150 kilometres off the south-east coast of the Chinese mainland. It has a land area of 36,000 sq km, which is mostly mountainous, and only about 25 per cent of the land is cultivated. Taiwan has an estimated population of 21 million and an average density of 581.8 person per sq km, which is one of the highest in the world. The original inhabitants of Taiwan were tribes of Malayan origin.

Chinese settlement in Taiwan was established in the 14th century. It came into contact with Europeans (mainly the Portuguese, Spanish and Dutch) during the 17th century. The Dutch settled in the southern part in 1624, and in 1626 the Spanish occupied the northern part of the island. After driving the Europeans out of the island in 1661, the Chinese Ming loyalist Zheng Zheng Gong ruled Taiwan for 22 years. The Qing emperor, Kang Xi conquered the island in 1683 and Taiwan became a peripheral part of the Qing empire. This also marked the beginning of massive Chinese migration which ultimately changed the ethnic character of the island.

Taiwan was ceded to Japan after the 1894–95 Sino-Japanese War. It remained a Japanese colony until the defeat of Japan in the Second World War in 1945. During the colonial period, the Japanese landlords controlled a substantial part of the land and Taiwan served as a source of agricultural products, mainly food, to Japan. Japan made substantial investments in infrastructure, health and primary education. As a result, by 1920 Taiwan had 600 kilometres of public railways, 3,500 kilometres of roads and significant harbour facilities, whereas it had had almost no such infrastructure at the turn of the century. Also, by the end of the colonial rule, the primary school enrolment ratio stood at 71 per cent and the death rate had fallen from 33 to 19 per thousand between 1906 and 1940 (Ho, 1978, 1984). Despite significant reservations, most observers estimate that GDP during the colonial period grew by 3.5 to 4.5 per cent.

In 1945 Taiwan became a province of the Republic of China ruled by Gen. Chiang Kai-shek of the Kuomintang (KMT). After the communist victory on the mainland in 1949, Gen. Chiang Kai-shek moved his KMT regime to Taipei which later became the capital of the Republic of China. Gen. Chiang Kai-shek continued to assert that the Taipei regime of KMT was the rightful government of China in opposition to the People's Republic of China and vowed to recover control over the mainland. To legitimise its claim as an all-China government, Taiwan's legislative bodies had representatives from all the mainland provinces.

The year 1971 marked a turning point for the KMT government. In October Taiwan was expelled from the UN and the People's Republic of China replaced Taiwan at the UN Security Council. Under pressure from the People's Republic many countries broke off diplomatic relations with Taiwan and its membership of various international organisations, such as the IMF and the World Bank, was ended. However, a significant number of countries maintained some sort of quasi-diplomatic relations with Taiwan, and commercial relations continued to flourish.

The US government's anti-communist policy made it Taiwan's strongest ally. The US signed a mutual security treaty with Taiwan in 1954 with a pledge to protect it. Taiwan received significant economic and military aid from the US. Between 1951 and 1965, Taiwan received US$1.5 billion worth of economic aid and the US aid financed nearly 26 per cent of total value of capital formation during this period. The US aid also helped reduce an annual trade deficit of approximately US$100 million. Furthermore, the US aid officials pushed for land reform and adoption of policies aimed at mobilising domestic resources for investment. Taiwan enjoyed unrestricted access to the US market. The cumulative effects of massive US aid, unrestricted access to the US market and domestic reforms helped Taiwan launch on to a path of remarkable economic transformation.

Chiang Kai-shek, for whom Taiwan's economic development was a personal triumph over his military defeat at the hands of the communists, died in April 1976. His son, Chiang Ching-kuo, succeeded him as Chairman of the KMT and became President in May 1978. The Chiang dynasty ended when Chiang Ching-kuo died in January 1988. He was succeeded by the Vice-President, Lee Teng-hui, who served the remaining two years of Chiang's term of office. Lee was the first native Taiwanese to become the President of the Republic. He committed himself to political reforms and 'Taiwanisation' of the country's leadership.

GEOPOLITICAL DEVELOPMENTS

The wars in Indo-China and the Korean peninsula and the Cold War dominated geopolitical developments in the region during the 1950s and 1960s. However, the 1970s ushered in a new era of ascendancy of the People's Republic of China in the international arena. Following Taiwan's expulsion from the UN, the US decided to establish diplomatic relations with the People's Republic of China in February 1973. In December 1978, US-Taiwan relations reached its lowest point when the US withdrew its diplomatic recognition of Taiwan. Although the US maintained its commitment to protect Taiwan, it later terminated the mutual security treaty. In a joint Sino-US communique in August 1982, the US pledged to gradually reduce its arms sales to Taiwan.

Meanwhile, in October 1981, China offered suggestions of autonomy for Taiwan within the People's Republic which would have allowed Taiwan to retain its own armed forces. However, the proposal was rejected by the Taiwan leadership and a year later it implied that eventual reunification could be made possible by narrowing the economic gap between China and Taiwan over time. Encouraged by the softening of Taiwan's position, the paramount leader of China, Deng Xiaoping, indicated in 1983 that following unification Taiwan would be allowed to conduct international trade, have its own legal system, fly its own flag and issue passports and visas. Under the proposed framework, China would not send any military or civilian personnel to Taiwan. However, the People's Republic would represent all China in international affairs while Taiwan would be designated Chinese Taipei or China-Taiwan. After the Sino-British agreement on the transfer of sovereignty of Hong Kong, China proposed to Taiwan to accept a similar model of one country, two systems as a basis for unification. But Taiwan insisted that China renounce communism before any direct contact was established.

Despite the breaking of diplomatic relations and reduced military contacts with the US, the economic and trade links between the two countries continued. In 1984, President Reagan announced the US intention of continued support for Taiwan. The 1989 Tiananmen Square incident gave the US the opportunity to renew its commitment to Taiwan. President Bush announced the sale of 150 F-16 fighter planes to Taiwan in September 1992 and the US trade representative visited Taiwan in December. The US indicated in August 1994 that it might upgrade Taiwan's diplomatic status in order to facilitate official contacts. In May 1995, President Clinton decided to grant a visa to President Lee of Taiwan to allow him to attend an alumni ceremony at Cornell University where he was a student in the late 1960s. The improvement of relations between the US and Taiwan was strongly resented by the People's Republic which condemned the US decision to grant the visa to President Lee. As mentioned earlier, 1988 marked a turning point for Taiwan's domestic politics. With the growing influence of younger generations and native Taiwanese in domestic politics, the Taiwanese government took a more pragmatic approach to China. In April 1989, it was announced that Taiwan was considering a 'one China, two governments' formula for its future relationship with the mainland. The Finance Minister led a high-level team to a meeting of the Asian Development Bank held in Beijing in May 1989 under the name of 'Taipei,

China' and this marked a considerable relaxation of Taiwan's stance towards China. On April 30, 1991 Taiwan formally terminated its hostility towards the mainland by ending the 'period of mobilisation for the suppression of the Communist rebellion'. Later the existence, but not the legitimacy of the Government of the People's Republic of China was officially acknowledged by President Lee.

Lee's presidency also brought a new style in Taiwan's foreign policy. In March 1989, President Lee visited Singapore, ending 12 years of isolation. He also announced his intention to visit any country even if it had diplomatic relations with China. In February 1994, President Lee visited Indonesia, the Philippines and Thailand and in May he went to Nicaragua, Costa Rica, South Africa and Swaziland. In its diplomatic offensive and its attempt to assert its international position, Taiwan announced its intention to apply to rejoin the UN by September 1995, although the Secretary-General of the UN was quick to state that Taiwan could not be admitted. Taiwan also laid claim to the disputed Spratly Islands in the South China Sea and announced its intention to construct an airbase on one of the disputed islands.

Internal political developments

Taiwan's internal politics since the mid-1980s has been dominated by increased demand for democratisation and resentment against the domination of the old leadership from mainland China. In 1986, the ruling KMT bowed to political pressure from both outside and inside to discuss four controversial issues – the possible establishment of new political parties, the status of martial law, the structure of provincial government in Taiwan, and the question of the ageing political leadership. In September a new political party, the Democratic Progressive Party (DPP), was formed by leading opposition politicians, and in December the KMT announced its intention to withdraw martial law. The KMT began political reform with the suspension of martial law in February 1987. The reform included a retirement plan for the old guard and an eventual move towards full democratic elections for the legislative bodies.

The emergence of the DPP as the main opposition party marks an important turning point in Taiwan's internal politics. The DPP was formed on a platform of independence for Taiwan and it continues to refuse to declare its allegiance to the Republic of China as a precondition for registration as a political party. Despite the KMT government's repression of the DPP, its pro-independence stance is gaining wider support. In the first full elections, held in December 1992, the DPP obtained 31 per cent of popular votes and doubled its representation in the legislature to 50 seats.

There is also growing disquiet within the KMT. Younger and more liberal members are leaning more towards Taiwan's independence and openly opposing the conservative leadership. The rift between the liberals and the

conservatives culminated in May 1993 with the resignation of 30 conservative members from the KMT and the defeat of the government in the
legislature when a group of KMT deputies voted with the opposition to
approve legislation on financial disclosure requirements for elected and
appointed public officials.

The growing demand for independence and the popularity of the DPP
have been raising alarm on the mainland. Ironically, the People's Republic
would prefer to deal with its arch-enemy, the KMT, rather than having to
face the prospect of a DPP government in Taipei. This has injected a sense
of urgency into the unification efforts. Thus, it is not surprising that
Beijing's anger at the granting of the US visa to President Lee was being
largely directed at the US and not at Taipei. The event did not affect the
planned visit by a Chinese delegation to Taipei for reunification talks, but
the Chinese Defence Minister's visit to Washington was postponed.

Taiwan held its first direct presidential election in March 1996, marking
the completion of the democratic process. The election raised Sino-Taiwan
tension with China holding war-games with live ammunitions and threatening military intervention if Taiwan declared independence. Although no one
(especially the US) believed that a military conflict would ensue, it was
clearly designed to intimidate the pro-independence group. Ironically, the
Chinese posturing strengthened the resolve of the people of Taiwan to be an
independent nation and boosted President Lee's position as a strong advocate of national sovereignty. Soon after the election Taiwan offered to
resume talks with China while China continues to display a hard line, and
demands that Taiwan drop the issue of independence.

THE ECONOMY

Taiwan has all the trappings of a prosperous country. Its 21 million people
enjoy an annual average income of nearly US$12,000 a head. The govern-
ment envisages per capita income exceeding US$20,000, putting Taiwan into
the top league of the industrialised world by the turn of the century. It is the
14th largest trading economy in the world and boasts over US$90 billion in
reserves. Taiwan also tops the list of developing countries in terms of equity
in income distribution. Taiwan's basic macroeconomic indicators are presented in Tables 10.1 and 10.2.

Growth and Structural Change

Since taking off in the early 1960s Taiwan has recorded impressive growth
for nearly two decades. During the 1960s and 1970s, the GDP grew by an
average rate of 9 per cent per annum. Between 1960 and 1973, prior to the
first oil-price shock, Taiwan's real GNP increased more than threefold.
Estimates show that nearly half this increase originated from technical

progress, about 35 per cent from capital accumulation, and the remaining 14–15 per cent was accounted for by the growth in employment.

The second oil-price shock and the world recession in the early 1980s caused a deceleration of Taiwan's economic growth. However, it recovered faster than most other countries and economic growth peaked at 12.3 per cent in 1987, after which it began decelerating again. The annual GDP growth rate fell to 4.9 per cent in 1990. The economy is showing signs of maturity and has been growing at an average annual rate of 6–7 per cent since 1991; it must maintain this rate of growth if the target per capita GDP of US$20,000 is to be achieved by the year 2000.

Controlling inflation has always been a prime objective of Taiwan's macroeconomic policy, for the KMT leadership believed that the runaway inflation contributed to their loss of public support and eventual defeat at the hands of the communists (Lundberg, 1979). Thus, the high average inflation rate during the 1970s was predominantly due to two oil-price shocks. The rate of increase of CPI was only 0.5 per cent in 1987 when the annual GDP growth peaked. Although the growing labour shortage and the consequent rise in labour cost is putting pressure on prices, the authority has been able to cap the inflation rate at around 4 per cent.

The low inflation outcome was achieved largely by very conservative fiscal and monetary policy. The government is prevented from borrowing from the central bank by legislation and thereby the central bank is given considerable independence in its inflation control task. However, since 1991, the budget deficit has been increasing chiefly due to government's massive infrastructure project and a large purchase of defence equipment. There has also been a rise in expenditure on social security as demand for a better quality of life increased in recent years. The government has been issuing bonds and it is estimated that the central government debt will reach nearly 20 per cent of GNP in 1995. Given Taiwan's conservatism with regard to fiscal policy and long-held fear of inflation, this level of government debt has become a serious political issue and the government has been

Table 10.1 Macroeconomic indicators of Taiwan

	1971–80	1981–90	1992	1994
Real GDP growth rate (%)	9.3	8.5	6.6	6.4
Inflation rate (%, CPI)	11.1	3.1	4.5	3.8
Share in GDP (%)				
Gross domestic saving	32.1	32.9	26.7	27.3
Gross domestic investment	30.5	22.6	24.2	26.1
Current account	8.3	7.8	3.8	2.7
External debt servicing ratio (%, exports)[a]	4.3[b]	4.0[c]	0.3	0.2[d]

Sources: ADB, Outlook (various issues); ADB, Key Indicators (various issues)
Notes: a from APEG, Asia-Pacific Profiles, 1994; b 1980; c 1985; d 1993; e 1975

forced to legislate to limit the outstanding government debts (local and central) to 40 per cent of Taiwan's annual GNP.

Like other East Asian newly industrialising economies, Taiwan's labour-intensive industrialisation strategy has been remarkably successful in achieving full employment. The unemployment rate since 1988 has been below 2 per cent. Taiwan's other success lies in its export expansion which has consistently produced trade-account surplus since 1976. However, the growth in domestic demand has been responsible for the decline in the current-account surplus since 1988.

The shift from a dependency of the Taiwanese economy on agriculture to manufacturing accelerated in the 1950s following the implementation of the land reform programme during 1949–53. The government encouraged the former landlords to invest in urban enterprises by paying landlords a fair price for their land. The share of agriculture in GDP fell from about 36 per cent in 1952 to 3.5 per cent in 1993. During the same period, the share of the labour force employed in agriculture dropped from 56 per cent to only 11.5 per cent.

Manufacturing was the main force behind Tawian's 'economic miracle'. Manufacturing output grew by about 16 per cent in the 1960s and 15 per cent in the 1970s. Its contribution to GDP peaked at 39.5 per cent during 1986–87 from less than 20 per cent in 1952. Commensurate with its growth, the employment share of manufacturing rose from 17 per cent in 1952 to nearly 40 per cent in 1993. As the manufacturing sector reached its maturity, the growth rate declined to about 7 per cent in the 1980s.

In this matured phase of the economy, the growth in the services sector has been driving the economy. The value added in the services sector grew by more than 13 per cent in 1987 and then by about 11 per cent during 1988–89. The sector has been growing by 8–9 per cent since 1990. The share of the services sector in GDP stood at more than 55 per cent in 1993 compared with 42 per cent in 1952. The services sector accounted for nearly half the employment in 1993. However, due to over-regulation and formal and informal barriers, the services sector remains internationally uncompetitive, accounting for only about 13 per cent of Taiwan's total exports.

Tawian's manufacturing has undergone significant structural changes. In the 1950s, food processing, textiles and building materials were the major

Table 10.2 Sectoral contributions to Taiwan's GDP (%)

Sector	1975	1985	1993
Agriculture	11.3	6.2	3.5
Industry	39.2	46.5	40.6
Manufacturing	29.1	38.2	31.6
Services	49.5	47.2	55.9

Sources: ADB, Key Indicators (various issues)

manufacturing activities, while in the 1960s, labour-intensive assembling of consumer electronics, electrical products and plastic products flourished. In the 1970s, the government launched a major industrial restructuring pro-gramme and funded large-scale investment in basic and intermediate indus-tries, such as petrochemicals, iron and steel, machine tools and shipbuilding. Thus, the share of light industries in the net national output fell from 60 per cent in 1960 to 48 per cent in 1977. Further industrial restructuring oc-curred in the 1980s and there was massive expansion of Taiwan's machinery, electronics and information industries. The increases in labour and land costs have been responsible for the relocation of labour-intensive activities to the mainland and other low-cost countries, a trend also observed in the other Chinese economy of Hong Kong.

External trade

Export-oriented industrialisation is the hallmark of East Asian NIEs. These resource-poor economies depend almost entirely on imports for their industrialisation and hence must export to be able to finance their imports. Thus, Taiwan's total trade as a proportion of GDP stands around 70 per cent, exports accounting for nearly 40 per cent. In the 1950s, industrial output as a proportion of exports averaged less than 21 per cent, but by the early 1990s comprised more than 90 per cent. Manufactured exports them-selves have undergone changes. Taiwan's exports moved away from con-sumer goods towards more technologically advanced products. The extent of structural shift in Taiwan's manufactured exports can be gleaned from Table 10.3.

Table 10.3 Taiwan's major manufactured exports (%)

Item	1980	1985	1990	1992
Machinery	3.9	4.4	6.6	22.3
Electrical goods	20.5	23.3	28.1	17.9
Textiles and clothing	20.7	21.9	13.7	15.5
Rubber and plastic products	9.0	10.7	7.7	3.1
Transport equipment	4.3	4.6	5.3	4.0

Source: APEG, Asia-Pacific Profile, 1994: 124

Taiwan's imports are dominated by industrial raw materials and machin-ery. Table 10.4 shows that the composition of Taiwan's imports has changed more towards machinery which reflects its new industrial structure.

The US is still Taiwan's major export market although its importance is declining (Table 10.5). Taiwan traditionally enjoyed trade surplus with the US, but the surplus has declined in the 1990s. Taiwan's largest bilateral trade deficit is with Japan. In 1993, the Taiwan–Japan trade deficit stood at US$14.2 billion. This deficit is largely structural as Taiwan depends mainly on Japan for capital goods. However, the recent yen appreciation has improved Taiwan's competitiveness and for the first time in a decade the growth rate of Taiwan's exports to Japan exceeded that of its imports from Japan. Since 1992 Taiwan's competitiveness with major industrialised countries has also been rising.

Table 10.4 Composition of Taiwan's major merchandise imports (%)

Item	1980	1985	1990	1993
Electrical machinery	10.9	11.8	16.5	18.7
Machinery	10.3	10.4	13.5	12.6
Chemicals	7.0	8.8	10.7	9.8
Minerals	6.6	23.0	12.0	8.3
Iron and steel	5.7	3.4	6.1	8.5
Transport equipment	6.3	5.6	7.1	8.2

Sources: APEG, *Asia-Pacific Profile, 1994*: 125; Council for Economic Planning and Development, *Industry of Free China*, 82(2), August, 1994

Table 10.5 Taiwan's major trading partners (%)

Partner	1980	1985	1990	1993
ASEAN	7.9	6.0	8.6	9.4
	7.3	7.6	7.5	9.0
Hong Kong/China	7.9	8.3	20.5	21.7
	1.3	1.6	3.6	3.2
Japan	11.0	11.3	10.6	10.7
	26.7	27.5	29.1	30.0
European Union	14.6	8.8	13.7	13.3
	8.0	10.2	12.6	13.3
United States	34.3	48.4	27.8	27.6
	23.3	23.8	23.0	21.7

Source: APEG, *Asia-Pacific Profiles*: 126
Notes: 1st row = exports; 2nd row = imports

With the improvement of relations with China, the indirect trade with the mainland through Hong Kong has gone up dramatically. These China–Hong Kong exports accounted for nearly 22 per cent in 1993 as opposed to only 8 per cent in 1980. However, direct trade with China remains illegal and the government, worried about too much dependence on China, has put a limit at 10 per cent of total exports. In 1992, trade with the mainland increased by 27.9 per cent, followed by an increase of 17.8 per cent in 1993 to reach US$8.7 billion. Taiwan's Board of Foreign Trade believes that this figure underestimates the Taiwan–China trade by at least 20 per cent, once one takes account of trade through other points and smuggling. One study suggests that it is highly probable that more than half of Taiwan's exports to Hong Kong are destined for China (DFAT, 1995a: 20).

Foreign direct investment

Foreign direct investment played an import role in Taiwan's transformation into an NIE. In addition to contributing to capital formation, FDI has been a major vehicle for technology transfer. The flow of foreign investment peaked in 1989 (Figure 10.1) and accounted for approximately 25 per cent of gross capital formation.

The inflow of FDI into Taiwan declined quite sharply during 1991–93 due to depressed economic conditions in both Japan and the US. However, FDI inflows picked up in the first six months of 1994, especially from Japan, the US and Hong Kong.

There has been a rapid growth in outward investment from Taiwan since the mid-1980s. Rising labour and land costs, appreciation of the new Taiwan dollar and increased pressures from environmental groups, have all contributed to this surge in outward investment. Initially most of Taiwan's foreign investment went to South East Asia, in particular Malaysia. But with the easing of cross-Straits contact in 1987, Taiwanese investment in China increased dramatically. There has been a large-scale transfer of labour-intensive activity to the mainland and vertical integration with China has become a key feature of Taiwan's economy. This overdependence has caused anxiety among the Taiwanese leadership and the government is

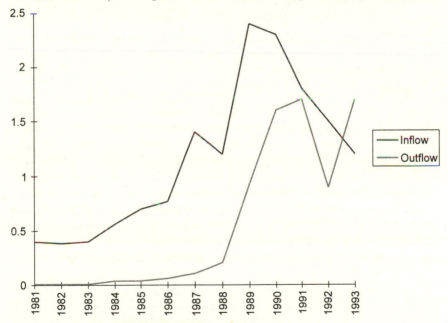

Figure 10.1 Foreign direct investment, Taiwan (US$ bn)
Sources: OECD 1993; Statistics on Overseas Chinese and Foreign Investment, Technical Cooperation, Outward Investment, Outward Technical Cooperation, Ministry of Economic Affairs, Taiwan

encouraging Taiwanese investors to diversify their investment in South East Asia.

Labour market developments

With full employment, labour shortage has become a major problem for Taiwan. The labour and skill shortage is felt most acutely in the emerging service industries. The severe labour shortage is fuelling rapid growth in wages. Although the growth in labour productivity picked up after 1987, wages grew at a faster rate, resulting in a rise in unit labour cost. In 1993, real labour cost grew by 3.5 per cent and was predicted to rise by 3 per cent in 1994. Average earnings in manufacturing exceed the legal minimum by nearly 50 per cent. According to government estimates, released in October 1994, labour costs in Taiwan's manufacturing were the highest in Asia outside Japan.

To ease the problem, the government has been allowing migrant workers in selected areas of manufacturing and construction since mid-1991. The number of workers hired legally by the end of 1993 stood at 135,000, representing an increase of 165 per cent over the previous year. The estimates for illegal workers vary from 50,000 to 100,000. Most of the migrant workers come from South East Asia. The government estimated that another 145,000 foreign workers would be needed in 1995 and raised the ceiling to 270,000 contract workers (FEER, 1995c: 56).

GOVERNMENT POLICIES

The KMT government always maintained a very strong presence in the economy, determined that the country should become strong economically. The KMT leadership committed its talent and energies to the promotion of economic development immediately following the retreat to the island of Taiwan. They set three objectives: control inflation, raise farm productivity and develop industries. Thus, foreign aid (mostly from the US) was used effectively to increase capital formation in manufacturing. The land reform programme was used both to raise farm productivity by giving the farmers the property rights and to induce landlords to invest their wealth in industry. Finally, in 1958, the government abandoned the import-substituting strategy and adopted policies to encourage manufacturing for export.

In the early 1960s, the government liberalised the financial sector by deregulating the interest rate. This, together with low inflation, produced a positive real interest rate. The reform was claimed to have been responsible for the rapid rise in Taiwan's domestic saving rate and the efficiency of investment. After the 1970s the government was also very active in industrial restructuring in anticipation of Taiwan's changing competitive advantage.

Recent policy developments

The government initiated a six-year development plan in 1991 for major infrastructure developments involving transport and communications, energy and water. The plan provided for over US$300 billion in public expenditure during 1991–96. However, after the mid-term review of the plan in 1993, the government reduced the number of planned projects from 775 to 632, and the planned outlay to US$229 billion.

As part of its commitment to industrial restructuring for maintaining Taiwan's competitive advantage, the government targeted 10 'strategic' industries for priority development in the 1990s. They include aerospace, communications, information technology, consumer electronics, semi-conductors, precision instruments and automatic machinery, new materials, specialty chemicals and pharmaceuticals, medical equipment and pollution control technology and equipment. The list was revised in 1994, targeting five key industrial technologies for development by local firms. These are technologies for manufacturing high-resolution colour-television cathode-ray tubes, integrated circuits, motor vehicle parts and accessories, liquid crystal devices and the organic chemical p-xylene. Transfer of technology, especially from Japan, is being encouraged since most of the imports from Japan are produced with these technologies.

The 1990 statute for upgrading industry offers tax incentives for investment in nominated 'functional areas', such as R&D, pollution control and automation. The incentives include provisions for accelerated depreciation of machinery and equipment and the deduction of between 5 and 20 per cent against business tax for upgrading the 'functional areas'. Other tax incentives are available for introducing energy-saving technology. The government also provides easy loans to encourage the development of high-technology ventures.

In 1992, the government announced its goal of developing Taipei as a regional centre for finance, communications and commerce, to benefit from Taiwan's advantages in dealing with China. The government therefore introduced reform programmes for the financial sector which include the admission of foreign banks and the lifting of restrictions preventing foreigners without official residency from opening local bank accounts. Foreign financial institutions have also been allowed to trade stocks on the local stock market. The ceiling for the total foreign investment on the Taiwan stock market was raised from US$5 billion to US$7.5 billion with a further US$2.5 billion limit allowed for funds raised from abroad by local investment trusts.

Chapter 11

Hong Kong

HISTORY AND CULTURE

The city economy of Hong Kong has an estimated population of 5.8 million. Over 98 per cent of the population are ethnic Chinese and the Cantonese form the largest community. About 60 per cent were born in Hong Kong and the rest are migrants, mostly from mainland China.

Hong Kong has a total area of 1078 km and is situated off the south-east coast of Guangdong Province of the People's Republic of China. The territory comprises the island of Hong Kong, the Kowloon peninsula and the New Territories and some 236 outlying islands and islets. The fine harbour of Hong Kong boasts one of the world's leading entrepôt ports.

British colonial rule over Hong Kong began in 1843 following the First Opium War (1840–42). In the war the Chinese authority in Guangzhou (Canton) seized and destroyed a large quantity of opium held by British traders in the city. The British demanded compensation and a commercial treaty to protect their trade. The hostility that ensued resulted in British occupation of the island of Hong Kong which was surrendered to the British in perpetuity by the Treaty of Nanjing (Nanking) in 1842.

However, disputes between the British and China over trade and shipping rights continued and a war broke out in 1856. The war ended in 1860 with the British annexation under the Convention of Beijing (Peking) of the peninsula of Kowloon on the mainland opposite the island. Following the defeat of China in the Sino-Japanese War of 1895, the British pressed for further concessions and obtained a 99-year lease on the mainland north of Kowloon and the adjoining islands.

Hong Kong enjoyed political stability under British rule and, attracted by its free-port status, the entrepôt trade between the West and China flourished until the Great Depression of the 1930s. Leading trading companies set up their regional headquarters, and banks, insurance companies and other commercial enterprises were established to serve the China trade. Also the colony experienced a huge influx of migrants between 1841 and 1939, leading to a rise in the population from 5,000 to over 1 million.

In 1938, Japanese forces occupied most of the Chinese Province of Guangdong and in 1941 overran Hong Kong. During the occupation Japan adopted a policy of mass deportation. Forced deportation as well as torture of civilians resulted in a decline in population during the Japanese occupation to about 600,000 (Miners, 1995: 270).

Japan surrendered in August 1945 and the colonial civil government was re-established in May 1946. The end of Japanese occupation encouraged all those who had earlier fled the island to return. The civil war in China which ended in communist victory in 1949 also resulted in a massive influx of refugees from the mainland. Thus, the population increased to about 2 million and the colony was forced to abandon its free access policy in 1950 with the closure of its border. The British garrison was heavily reinforced in 1949 in order to deter any possible Chinese attack and Britain recognised the new communist government in China in 1950.

Hong Kong's entrepôt status faced crisis during the Korean War in 1950 when an embargo on the export of strategic goods to China was imposed. This added to the problem of feeding the refugees. But the refugees constituted a pool of docile and hard-working labour. This later proved to be a great asset. Local business, especially those who had fled the mainland after the communist victory, utilised this pool of industrious workers and the commercial and financial infrastructure to turn Hong Kong's economy to manufacture for export.

The government embarked upon a massive housing programme following a devastating fire in 1953 at one of the shanty towns housing the refugees. By 1991 nearly half the population were living in government-provided housing and the housing program continued to be an important instrument for the government to fine-tune the economy.

The influx of refugees from Vietnam from 1976 onwards added pressure on the Hong Kong economy. In 1982, Hong Kong adopted a policy of confining all newly arrived Vietnamese in closed camps in order to deter further immigration, and in 1988 it abandoned the policy of automatically granting refugee status. When these policy changes failed to stop the influx of Vietnamese, it decided to repatriate the newly arrived refugees forcefully. After initial refusal to accept those classified as economic migrants, Vietnam finally agreed in 1992 to accept a limited programme of mandatory repatriation. This appears to have been successful in discouraging the Vietnamese to leave Vietnam and the plan is to close all detention camps by 1996.

GEOPOLITICAL DEVELOPMENTS

The year 1982 marked the beginning of a new era for Hong Kong when China and the UK started negotiations on the future of the colony. The uncertainty about the prospect after the Chinese take-over led to an increase in the outflow of both people and investment. This led to the collapse of the property market and economic difficulties. Confidence in the Hong

Kong economy returned after the signing of the Sino-British agreement in August 1984 which was subsequently ratified by the British Parliament in May 1985. Under this agreement, Chinese sovereignty over the whole of Hong Kong will be restored on July 1, 1997. A Sino-British Joint Liaison Group was formed to consult on the implementation of the agreement and to ensure a smooth transfer of sovereignty.

After 1997 Hong Kong will be reconstituted as a Special Administrative Region, designated 'Hong Kong China' and governed by its own inhabitants. Hong Kong will be allowed for 50 years to keep its own legal code, except in matters of foreign affairs and defence. It will retain its status as a free port and separate customs territory, and the Hong Kong dollar will remain a freely convertible currency. Existing land leases will be recognised and extended to the year 2047. With the continuation of its social and economic systems, Hong Kong and China will be 'one country, but two systems'.

In June 1985, China formed a Basic Law Drafting Committee (BLDC) with 59 members (25 from Hong Kong) to draft a new constitution (Basic Law) for Hong Kong in accordance with Article 31 of the Chinese Constitution, which provides for special administrative regions within the People's Republic. The Committee published the first draft of the Basic Law in April 1988 and, after public submissions, a revised version was published in February 1989. According to the final draft of the Basic Law, 20 out of 60 members of the 1997 legislature will be directly elected, 30 will be elected by functional constituencies and 10 by the electoral college. The Basic Law gives China the right to suspend the constitution by declaration of emergency and the right to station troops in the territory of Hong Kong.

The implementation of agreement on the transfer of sovereignty had been smooth until the Tiananmen Square massacre in 1989. That incident sent a ripple through the minds of the people of Hong Kong and raised doubts about China's intentions. The Hong Kong government's unwillingness to suppress local supporters of the democracy movement irritated China. There were also disagreements over Hong Kong's decision to build a new airport. China has accused Britain of violating the Memorandum of Understanding between the two countries in allocating extra funds for the airport without China's approval and saddling the post-1997 Hong Kong government with huge debts. The position of the Chinese government was that neither the Chinese government nor the future government of Hong Kong would be liable for any expenditure or debt incurred in building the airport, and all contracts approved by the Hong Kong government without China's consent would become invalid after July 1997. The difficulties were compounded by the emergence of a pro-Beijing political group which demanded a scaling down of the plan for the airport.

A more serious rift developed in 1993 over Governor Patten's proposal with regard to 1995 elections for the Legislative Council. The proposal includes lowering the voting age from 21 to 18, setting up one-person, one-vote electorates and abolishing appointments to local governments. The second phase of Governor Patten's reform allows the elected members of the Legislative Council to serve beyond the 1997 hand-over. Beijing has maintained that it would dissolve the legislature and other elected bodies after June 30, 1997 and all existing Hong Kong laws would be subject to review by the National People's Congress.

Despite diplomatic skirmishes between China and the UK, Hong Kong continues to enjoy relative stability as both sides are keen to maintain investor confidence. Beijing has a strong interest in ensuring that Hong Kong remains a stable and prosperous international business centre. However, a *FEER/Asia Business News* poll reveals that over 48 per cent of Hong Kong executives lost confidence in Hong Kong's future as they fear that the 1997 handover will accompany 'rough weather' (FEER, 1996a: 54). Many analysts believe that there will be a run on the Hong Kong dollar. Nonetheless, a good majority do not share this gloomy prediction. Their optimism rests on the expectations that business leaders will dominate the 400-member selection committee that will choose the first post-1997 chief executive. It is most likely that they will choose one among themselves for the position so as to ensure that Hong Kong's economic future remains 'in the hands that control its present' (FEER, 1996a: 55). This, of course, does not imply that the transition will be smooth, without any jitters or hurdles. One area which is almost certain to affect business is arbitration awards and cross-border court cases 'as many legal and tax-related issues have been left unattended because of Beijing's unwillingness to deal with the outgoing British administration' after Governor Patten's controversial 1992 political reforms (FEER, 1996a: 55).

THE ECONOMY

Hong Kong, now classified as a high-income economy by the World Bank, has per capita income higher than that of Australia and that of its colonial master, the UK. Despite political uncertainty regarding the 1997 change-over of sovereignty, the Hong Kong economy has been growing by 4–5.5 per cent per annum since 1991. The slowing of economic growth is a sign of its maturity rather than a lack of investor confidence. Its economic fundamentals remain sound and business confidence is high.

Growth and structural change

Being at the centre of regional and international economic activities, Hong Kong experienced high growth during most of its colonial period. After the disruptions caused by the Second World War and the Korean War, the gross domestic product (GDP) grew by 6–8 per cent per annum in the 1950s. The growth accelerated in the 1960s and GDP grew by an average annual rate of 9–10 per cent. The high economic growth continued through the 1970s, despite difficulties caused by the influx of refugees from Vietnam and international stagflation inflicted by two oil-price shocks.

The 1980s were volatile with GDP growth varying from –0.1 per cent in 1985 to 13.4 per cent in 1987. Besides the political uncertainty involving the talks on sovereignty between the UK and China, the rapid appreciation of the US dollar was responsible for the 1985 recession. After experimenting with floating exchange rate for a period of nine years (1974–83), Hong Kong reverted to a fixed exchange rate regime with the US dollar in 1983. When the US dollar appreciated in 1985, Hong Kong lost its competitiveness and its exports suffered. As the competitiveness improved with the decline of the US dollar following the 'Plaza Accord', growth rebounded and Hong Kong's GDP grew by 13.4 per cent in 1987.

Table 11.1 presents the basic macroeconomic indicators of the Hong Kong economy. As can be seen, inflation, although lower than in many Latin American and developing countries, remains a sore point. The tight labour market, budget deficits arising from increased infrastructure expenditure, and imported inflation from China will continue to exert pressure on inflation.

Table 11.1 Basic macroeconomic indicators of Hong Kong

Indicator	1971–80	1981–90	1992	1994
GDP growth rate (%)	9.3	7.2	5.3	5.5
Inflation rate (CPI, % change)	8.7	8.3	9.4	9.2
Share in GDP (%)				
Gross domestic saving	28.4	31.0	31.0	29.6
Gross domestic investment	27.8	28.2	29.1	29.5
Current account[a]	–4.7[b]	5.6[c]	2.0	–0.7[d]

Sources: ADB, *Outlook* (various issues)
Notes: a from APEG, *Asia-Pacific Profile 1994*; b 1980; c 1985; d 1993

However, the higher inflation rate in Hong Kong has had some beneficial impacts. The higher inflation rate compared with that in the US meant real appreciation of the Hong Kong dollar which is tightly linked with the US dollar. This has 'facilitated the shift of resources from the manufacturing to the services sector that would normally accompany current account surpluses and increasing prosperity (ADB, 1994: 66). In fact, the Hong Kong economy has undergone a significant structural change and, as mentioned earlier, is displaying signs of maturity where the dominant role of manufacturing has been replaced by the services sector. For example, the share of manufacturing in GDP fell from 25 per cent in 1980 to less than 14 per cent in 1992 (Table 11.2). Manufacturing is expected to account for less than 10 per cent of GDP in the near future. On the other hand, the services sector is growing at a rapid rate, having increased its share in GDP from 69 per cent in 1980 to 77 per cent in 1993. The wholesale, retail, import/export and restaurants and hotels sectors, together, contributed nearly 26 per cent to GDP in 1992. The combined contribution of financial, insurance, real estate and business services stood at 24.4 per cent. Tourism is the other fast-growing sector in Hong Kong.

Table 11.2 Sectoral contributions to Hong Kong's GDP (% at current factor cost)

Sector	1988	1990	1992
Agriculture and fishing	0.3	0.3	0.2
Manufacturing	20.1	17.2	13.8
Electricity, gas and water	2.5	2.3	2.2
Construction	4.8	5.6	5.3
Wholesale, retail, import/export, restaurants & hotels	23.8	24.3	26.1
Transport, storage and communication	9.2	9.4	9.5
Financing, insurance, real estate & business service	19.2	20.8	24.4
Community, social & personal services	14.6	15.0	15.4
Ownership of premises	10.5	10.8	10.8

Source: DFAT, 1994a: 33

One of the reasons for the decline in Hong Kong's manufacturing is increasing cost of labour and land. This is forcing a massive relocation of labour-intensive activities to southern China. About 30,000 of Hong Kong's factories are operating in China, employing 3 million people whereas man-ufacturing employment in Hong Kong itself has declined to less than 0.5 million (APEG, 1994: 95). As noted by OECD (1993: 41), 'the competitive position of Hong Kong with respect to its neighbours weakened : Korea, Singapore and Taiwan are providing better facilities required to develop a more sophisticated type of production, while low cost labour areas threaten its position as assembly centre'. The textile industry still occupies a domi-nant place (Table 11.3), although it is now more concentrated in the higher-value-added fashion end of the market. By moving up-market, the industry has avoided the restrictions of the Multi-fibre Arrangement and other national restrictions on exports.

External trade

Hong Kong is the eighth largest trading economy in the world (DFAT, 1994a: 12). It is an entrepôt for China and the region, and re-exports still dominate its trade structure. In 1993, re-exports accounted for more than 78 per cent of Hong Kong's total exports of goods and over 81 per cent in the 1st quarter of 1994. Re-exports grew by 19 per cent in 1993, compared with 13 per cent for the total exports. Table 11.4 shows the distribution of total exports by destination.

Table 11.3 Share in manufacturing value-added (in producers' price, %)

Industry	1979	1985	1990	Growth rate (1980–91, %)
Food, beverage & tobacco	4.6	6.4	8.2	3.1
Textiles, clothing & footwear	41.4	40.3	36.0	−0.4
Wood & furniture	1.8	1.3	1.0	−2.6
Paper & printing	5.2	6.7	9.6	2.2
Chemicals	1.6	1.6	1.8	3.5
Petroleum refining & coal	0	0	0.1	n.a.
Rubber, plastic, pottery & glass	10.2	10.4	7.5	3.3
Iron and steel	9.0	7.6	6.6	2.5
Machinery	2.0	3.6	8.9	3.5
Electrical machinery	14.0	11.4	10.0	1.3
Transport equipment	2.2	2.4	2.8	n.a.
Professional goods	4.5	4.4	4.5	n.a.
Others	3.4	3.8	3.6	3.5

Sources: UN, *Yearbook of Industrial Statistics* (various issues)

Table 11.4 Distribution of Hong Kong's exports by destination (%)

Country	Domestic exports 1990	1992	1994 (Jan.–Jun.)	Re-exports 1990	1992	1994 (Jan.–Jun.)
China	21	26	28.8	27	31	35.3
USA	29	28	11.4	21	21	21
Japan	5	5	4.8	6	5	5.5
Germany	8	7	5.7	6	5	4.5
United Kingdom	n.a.	n.a.	n.a.	3	3	2.9
Singapore	3	4	5.8	n.a.	n.a.	n.a.

Source: DFAT, 1994a: 40

As can be seen, China has overtaken the US as the major destination of both domestic and re-exports. Thus, growth and stability in China have become vitally important for Hong Kong's economic growth. If the Chinese economy falters, Hong Kong would be left with a wage and exchange rate level far too high to permit significant growth from domestic exports alone (Howe, 1995: 276).

China is also the single most important source of Hong Kong's imports, accounting for nearly 37 per cent of the total. The next most important source of imports is Japan which supplies about 17 per cent. Taiwan and Singapore, together, account for about 13 per cent of Hong Kong's imports.

Table 11.5 shows that, in line with its manufacturing structure, apparel and clothing (SITC 84) is still Hong Kong's main domestic export item. As mentioned earlier, Hong Kong does not have a comparative advantage in the production of electronic and other sophisticated items as do other East Asian newly industrialising economies and it is not expected to do as well in

Table 11.5 Hong Kong's domestic exports by major commodities (%)

Item	1991	1992	1993
Apparel & clothing accessories	32.7	33.0	32.2
Textile yarn, fabrics, made-up articles & related products	7.6	7.4	7.3
Electrical machinery, apparatus & appliances	8.3	8.6	10.2
Office machines & automatic data-processing machines	7.9	8.8	7.7
Photographic apparatus, equipment & supplies, optical	8.8	8.1	7.2
Miscellaneous manufactured articles	10.2	9.5	9.2

Source: DFAT, 1994a: 41

the export of these products. Hence, Hong Kong has to rely heavily on prompt delivery and other basic factors, such as after-sales service, to maintain its export markets. So far, the lower US dollar helped Hong Kong maintain its competitiveness due to the fixed exchange rate with the US dollar, but as the experience of 1985 shows, if the US dollar strengthens, Hong Kong will have serious economic difficulties.

Consumer goods dominate Hong Kong's imports, accounting for more than 40 per cent of the total. The next most important items are raw materials and semi-manufactured goods with a share of over 30 per cent. Imports of capital goods contribute about 18 per cent to the total import bill.

Financial sector

Hong Kong serves as an important regional financial centre. There are 172 banks and 1,500 bank branches in Hong Kong. These include branches of some of the 142 foreign banks which have representative offices in Hong Kong. There are also 57 restricted-licence banks (formally known as 'licensed deposit-taking companies') and 142 'deposit-taking' companies. More than half of the assets and liabilities of the Hong Kong banks are foreign (Howe, 1995: 277). Since the end of 1993, Hong Kong banks have been subject to Banking Ordinance, designed for prudential regulation.

Prudential regulation of the stock market has also been the focus of the government in the 1980s. The Stock Exchange Unification Ordinance of 1980 provided for the establishment of one exchange in place of the previous four, and the new Stock Exchange of Hong Kong started operating in 1988. All members of the existing exchanges were invited to apply for shares in the new exchange. By the end of June 1994, the total stock market capitalisation was HK$2,241 billion. A watchdog body for the stock exchange, the Securities and Futures Commission, began operation in 1989.

Since 1993 mainland Chinese companies have been allowed to list on the Hong Kong Stock Exchange. New regulations were designed in order to avoid problems associated with the difference in accounting procedures and alleged financial mismanagement in the mainland companies. Under these regulations, the Hong Kong (H) shares must have a three-year record and acceptable accounts. The H shares must account for 10 per cent of a company's total capitalisation and the minimum market size is HK$50 million. Dividends must be paid in Hong Kong dollars and mainland companies wishing to list on the Hong Kong Stock Exchange must find a 'sponsor'.

Foreign direct investment

Hong Kong welcomes foreign investment. However, Hong Kong does not offer any special inducement and does not discriminate between foreign and domestic investment. Hong Kong's policy towards foreign investment is best summarised by OECD (1993: 22) as follows:

> Hong Kong stands out among the DAEs [dynamic Asian economies] as having a regime of total freedom in which FDI is subject to virtually no regulation or restriction concerning establishment or foreign participation. The Hong Kong Government has sought first and foremost to create a favourable climate for investment by providing the necessary infrastructures together with a simple tax regime, and applying no discrimination between foreign and local investors.

Although one can expect the above policy framework to be quite attractive to foreign investors, it is difficult to ascertain its success as the Hong Kong government does not officially publish any data on foreign investment. However, the estimates by the OECD (1993) show that the inflow of foreign investment has been very volatile in the 1980s (Figure 11.1). At the end of 1990, fixed assets at book value plus working capital of manufacturing companies known to have foreign interests stood at US$3 billion, compared with US$0.5 billion in 1980. The OECD estimates also show that the US was the main source of foreign investment in the early 1980s, but Japan overtook the US during 1986–90 and accounted for 46 per cent of total inflow of foreign investment. Interestingly, the flow of investment from Asian countries dropped from 28 per cent during 1980–85 to 12 per cent in the second half of the 1980s. The electronics industries received the largest share of foreign investment in Hong Kong from the mid-1980s.

As for other East Asian newly industrialising economies, investment abroad has become crucial for Hong Kong, both to maintain cost competitiveness and to sustain economic growth. Hong Kong's overseas investment started following the highly restrictive national multi-fibre agreement (MFA) quotas imposed on exports of textiles and garments. Hong Kong is by far the largest investor among DAEs. Asian countries, in particular China, Taiwan and South-East Asia, receive the bulk of Hong Kong's overseas investment. It is estimated that about 80 per cent of Hong Kong's overseas investment went to China during 1986–87. Recently, Hong Kong

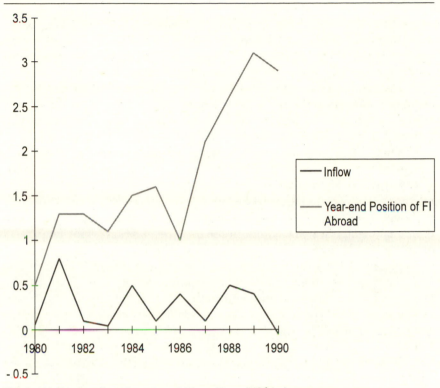

Figure 11.1 Foreign direct investment, Hong Kong (US$ bn)
Source: OECD 1993

has been diversifying its overseas investment and South-East Asia and Pacific island countries, such as Fiji, are increasingly attracting more funds. Hong Kong's overseas investment is concentrated mainly in export-oriented light manufactured products, such as seasonal novelty items, toys and clothing.

Labour market developments

In line with Hong Kong's structural change, employment in manufacturing is declining while that in the services sector is growing. For example, manufacturing employment fell by nearly 14 per cent during 1993–94 and employment in the services sector rose by 9 per cent. Employment in the two fastest growing services areas – (a) the wholesale, retail, import/export trades and (b) finance, insurance, real estate, business services – grew by 13 and 11 per cent respectively.

Despite the structural shift, unemployment remains very low at less than 2 per cent. Thus, it appears that workers losing jobs in the manufacturing sector are finding jobs elsewhere without much difficulty. Skilled professionals are also finding better jobs on the mainland where Hong Kong manufacturing are being relocated. An estimated 55,000 white-collar workers left Hong Kong in 1989–90. There are in fact serious shortages of professional, managerial, clerical, sales and service workers.

The government has attempted to alleviate the problem by raising the ceiling on migrant workers. In 1994, a quota of 25,000 was set for foreign workers in occupations where there were critical shortages. This ceiling was expected to rise to 30,000 in 1995.

The tight labour market is fuelling wages growth. Average nominal earnings in both manufacturing and services rose by 10 per cent during 1993–94. The wages would have risen at a much faster rate had it not been for migrant (legal and illegal) workers who come mostly from the mainland. Although foreign workers are to be paid the local average wage – the minimum being HK$9,880 a month for unskilled workers – the employers often pay much less than the legal minimum. This has been a major cause of unemployment for some 6,700 local construction workers (FEER, 1995a: 59). There are also about 15,300 underemployed workers. A survey by the Hong Kong Construction Industry Employees General Union reveals that 14 per cent of local construction workers work fewer than 10 days a month and half of them can find work for only about half of every month (FEER, 1995a: 59). The unemployment and underemployment of local workers have been exerting community pressure against further expansion of the government's labour importation scheme.

GOVERNMENT POLICIES

Hong Kong is often cited as a shining example of a *laissez-faire* economy where business thrives in an environment where the government is limited to its basic functions of maintaining law and order, guaranteeing property rights and the provision of infrastructure. However, contrary to popular belief, the Hong Kong government has always had a large stake in the economy. The government has been responsible for very large flows of spending, both recurrent and capital. During the 1970s, for example, government expenditure accounted for 22 per cent of aggregate demand (Howe, 1995: 274).

As a matter of fact, the government in Hong Kong is very much Keynesian in nature and has never shied away from using its public expenditure programme to fine-tune the economy. For example, when uncertainty following the Tiananmen incident hit Hong Kong, the government used its spending power to boost demand and increased public-sector wages. As a result, the public-sector share of GDP increased sharply from 15 per cent in 1987–88 to 17 per cent in 1992–93, and is expected to peak at 20 per cent in 1995–96.

The skill shortage has also prompted the Hong Kong government to be more activist. In 1991, the government set up the City Polytechnic and the

University of Science and Technology in order to strengthen technological education and the skill level of the economy. The plan is to increase first-year first-degree places by 50 per cent by the mid-1990s. The government-sponsored Hong Kong Productivity Council was expanded in the 1980s and is providing a wide range of technical support to industry.

However, where the Hong Kong government remains minimalist is in the area of sector- or industry-specific interventions. For example, Hong Kong adheres to free trade and tariffs are set at zero for all products other than tobacco, alcoholic beverages and hydrocarbon oils, which are subject to some indirect taxes. There is no protection for domestic industries, nor are there any special incentive packages for foreign investment.

Chapter 12

Singapore

HISTORY AND CULTURE

One of the 'miracle economies' of South East Asia, the city state of Singapore has an area of only 641.4 sq km. It is situated off the southern tip of the Malay Peninsula in the South China Sea. Between the island and the mainland are the Johor Straits and it is joined with Johor (Malaysia) by a 1.2 km causeway.

Singapore is a multicultural and multilingual society. Of an estimated population of 2.8 million, about 78 per cent are Chinese, 14 per cent Malays and 7 per cent are Indians. There are four official languages, Mandarin Chinese, Malay, Tamil (Indian) and English. However, the Chinese speak many dialects, chiefly Fukien, Cantonese, Teochew, Hakka and Hainanese. English is the language of the government. The government has been very successful in maintaining racial harmony and is keen to protect the traditional Eastern values against the influence of individualistic Western philosophy. It promotes core values of Confucian morality, family loyalty, placing society before self, frugality, and regard for education.

Singapore, or the local name Singapura, is from the Sanskrit for 'the city of the lion'. The popular story surrounding the naming of the island involves the sultan (king) once seeing some strange animal which looked like a lion and naming the island Singapura. Prior to then, the island had been known as Temasek. In the 14th century Temasek was a prosperous trading centre and was a centre of rivalry between the expanding empires of Ayudhya (Thailand) and Majapahit (Java). Attacks and counter-attacks eventually destroyed Temasek towards the end of the 14th century. The rulers fled the island and it was left deserted for almost 400 years, except for a few tribes who lived by fishing, piracy and minor trading. The island remained nominally under the rule of the Sultan of Johor.

Being far off the Dutch-dominated main maritime trading route through the Sunda Straits (separating Sumatra and Java) between Europe and East Asia, Singapore was an isolated backwater until the early 19th century. Its commercial and strategic importance began to change as the East India Co.

sought to protect its trade with China and challenge the Dutch domination. In 1819 Sir Stamford Raffles, an official of the East India Co. obtained permission from the Sultan of Johor and the local chief to establish a trading post at the mouth of the Singapore River. In 1824, the island was leased to the East India Co. in perpetuity in return for monetary payments and pensions.

The East India Co. united Singapore with its two other dependencies, Penang and Malacca, in 1826 to form one administrative unit, called the Straits Settlements, to be administered from India. The port of Singapore being free of customs duties and restrictions, and, protected by the East India Co., soon began attracting traders from all over the region. Migrants from China, India and the nearby region began their settlement as the trading activity grew.

When the East India Co. lost monopoly of the China trade in 1833, the laxed and inefficient administration of the city made the European traders in Singapore increasingly unhappy. In 1857, when the Indian Mutiny broke out, Singapore's traders demanded that the administration of the Straits Settlements be separated from India and brought under direct British rule. The Straits Settlements became a crown colony in 1867.

The opening of the Suez Canal in 1869 and the signing of mutual protection treaties between the British and the Malay sultans in 1874 gave new impetus to Singapore's development (Turnbull, 1995: 914). After the commissioning of the Suez Canal, the India–Malacca Straits route became the main trading route between Europe and the Far East, replacing the Sunda Straits route. Being placed strategically on the new maritime highway, Singapore's commercial importance grew rapidly. As the maritime trade grew with the coming of steamships and the invention of telegraphs, the natural sheltered harbour of Singapore became the hub of international trade in South East Asia. It became a vital link between the chain of British ports and developed into a commercial and financial centre for the entire region.

On the other hand, the 1874 mutual protection treaties raised Singapore's political importance. Under these treaties, the Malay sultans agreed to accept British political Residents at their courts. Singapore, being the base of the Straits Settlements' Governor, who was also the Commissioner of the Malay States and the chief of authority for the three British-protected Borneo states, Sarawak, North Borneo and Brunei, became the political focal point as the Malay States were effectively brought under the British rule.

The continued stability and economic prosperity of the city attracted migrants from the troubled Guangdong and Fujian provinces of southern China, who increasingly took up residence in Singapore. Immigration peaked in 1927 when an estimated 360,000 Chinese arrived in Singapore (Turnbull, 1995: 914). However, a quota on immigration of men was imposed during the Great Depression of the 1930s.

Singapore fell to Japan in 1942. The Japanese renamed it Syonan, meaning 'Light of the South'. With a view to making it a focal point in its proposed 'Greater East Asia Co-Prosperity Sphere', Japan wanted to keep Singapore as a permanent colony and military base. However, the Japanese occupation army destroyed Singapore's economy and unleashed horrific torture on the local people, especially the Chinese who regarded Japan as an enemy because of Japan's invasion of China. On the other hand, a small number of the Indian community collaborated with Japan on the assurance that Japan would help liberate India from British rule. Singapore became the regional headquarters of the Indian National Army and the Indian Independence League. The Japanese occupation ended almost abruptly with the surrender of Japan in August 1945 immediately after the dropping of atomic bombs on Hiroshima and Nagasaki.

GEOPOLITICAL DEVELOPMENTS

As British rule was re-established, the Straits Settlements Colony was broken up into the Malayan Union and Singapore Crown Colony. The Malayan Union included all the Malay States, Penang and Malacca. Singapore was kept outside the Union because of its importance as a port and military base. The decision to separate Singapore from the Union provoked local opposition which led to the formation of Singapore's first political party, the Malayan Democratic Union (MDU). Singapore was also kept outside the reconstituted Federation of Malaya which replaced the Malayan Union in 1948 because the Malays were worried about the influence of predominantly Chinese Singapore.

In preparation for self-rule, elections were held in 1948 for a six-member Legislative Council but they were boycotted by the communist-dominated MDU. In the meantime, the poverty-stricken people were increasingly being attracted by the communist movement and in 1948 there was a communist insurgency in Malaya. A period of severe repression of radical politics in Singapore followed and eventually the Malayan emergency was brought under control. Later, when Singapore gained independence, the oppressive legislation put in place during the Malayan emergency became handy for the new administration in banishing opposition politics and taking a more authoritarian style of governance.

In 1957, the British granted independence to the Federation of Malaya. In the same year, terms were agreed for full internal self-rule for Singapore and, accordingly, elections were held in 1959 in which the People's Action Party (PAP), led by Lee Kuan Yew, scored a landslide victory. The new government of Lee Kuan Yew had an agenda to achieve full independence within its four-year term through a merger with the Federation of Malaya. The union with the Malayan Federation was seen as vital for Singapore's survival both militarily and economically.

The Malays who had been reluctant in the past to take Singapore into the Federation to maintain their racial majority, now had to face a new reality of having to deal with the prospect of an emerging near-communist country. In order to neutralise the communist threat, the first Prime Minister of the Federation of Malaya, Tunku Abdul Rahman, drew up a plan for the Federation of Malaysia to include Singapore in it. But to prevent the Chinese from becoming a near-majority, the proposed Federation would include Sarawak and Sabah (North Borneo) when they had gained independence. The proposed merger of Singapore with the Federation was endorsed by the people in a referendum in 1962 despite opposition from the socialist front, Barisan Sosialis; and the Federation of Malaysia was formed in 1963.

However, the conservative Malay politicians were always suspicious of Singapore's membership of the Federation, and their suspicion grew as the PAP wanted to participate in the 1964 general election. The ruling Alliance Party in Malaysia objected to the PAP's decision and the crisis deepened when Lee Kuan Yew attempted to unite all Malaysian opposition parties. This led to the expulsion of Singapore from the Federation on August 9, 1965.

Thus, Singapore became an independent state in its own right, against the wishes of its leaders and perhaps those of the majority of its people, who saw this as a serious blow to their economic and political survival as the country was shut off from its hinterland and its market. Singapore became a member of the United Nations in September 1965 and of the Commonwealth of Nations in the following month. It became a republic on December 22, 1965. Although the internal administration was not affected much by this sudden break, it was a very big task for a tiny new state to establish its international presence.

The episode also meant that Singapore could no longer follow an inward-looking development. It thus took the very bold step of opening up the country to foreign investment and multinationals with attractive fiscal incentives. The PAP rejected its party platform of socialism and adopted the policy of a mixed economy. In 1968, the government passed far-reaching industrial relations legislation curbing trade union activity and giving employers wide-ranging powers over labour with a view to achieving industrial peace and making the island state attractive to multinationals.

The passage of such repressive legislation was made easier by the situation that arose from the British decision in 1966 to withdraw from its bases 'east of Suez'. When in 1968 the British decided to accelerate the withdrawal, the Singapore economy was threatened, as the bases accounted for nearly 16 per cent of employment and 20 per cent of Singapore's GNP (Regnier, 1995: 919).

As the Vietnam War became protracted and the US involvement deepened, there were various attempts by the South East Asian countries to form a regional defence alliance against communist aggression. Besides internal and external communist threats, there were expectations of sizeable economic aid from the West, in particular the US, which provided the impetus for such alliances. These attempts culminated in 1967 in the formation of the Association of South East Asian Nations (ASEAN). It marked the beginning of a new era of regional co-operation, by providing an effective forum to defuse the tension surrounding the formation of the Malaysian Federation. Singapore together with Malaysia joined their former adversaries, Indonesia, the Philippines and Thailand, in promoting regional security and economic prosperity.

Singapore enjoys remarkable political stability and the PAP is likely to rule the country for the foreseeable future. However, there is now an increasing demand for openness and political freedom. Some limited success of the Opposition and a drop in popular support for the government in recent elections are some indications of the changing expectations of the people.

THE ECONOMY

Singapore had its initial success as an entrepôt, providing the doorway for the regional hinterland to wider international trade. The sudden and forced break with the Malaysian Federation in 1965 turned out to be a blessing in disguise for Singapore. The re-orientation of its trade and industrialisation policies following independence in 1965 produced an unprecedented growth of GDP by nearly 10 per cent per annum during the rest of the decade which ended with an average annual growth rate of 8.8 per cent. Estimates by Tsiang and Wu (1985) show that Singapore took off towards emerging as a newly industrialising economy within a year of separating from Malaysia to become an independent country. Singapore's per capita GNP stood at US$17,133 in 1993 and it has a vision of achieving the Swiss standard of living by the year 2000. The World Bank and the UN now classify Singapore as a high-income economy. There is a strong possibility that it will become a member of the Organisation for Economic Co-operation and Development (OECD) before 2000 (Regnier, 1995: 919).

Growth and structural change

In 1960, after a year of self-rule, Singapore had an unemployment rate in excess of 10 per cent and GDP was growing by roughly 5 per cent. But, between 1968 and 1974, the economy recorded an average annual growth rate of 12 per cent. The two oil-price shocks of the 1970s hit Singapore's petroleum-refining activity and inflicted serious macroeconomic problems. Yet Singapore managed to record nearly 8 per cent average annual growth rate of GDP over 1971–80. The only other occasion Singapore had economic difficulties (a mild recession) was in 1985–86 when GDP declined by about 2 per cent. The recession in major industrialised countries in the early 1990s was responsible for slower growth during 1991–92. Strong growth resumed in 1993 when GDP grew by 10 per cent. Despite the maturing of the economy, the strong growth is expected to continue.

Except for the period affected by the two oil-price shocks, inflation remained well under control. Exchange rate is the main instrument with which Singapore fights inflation (Lim *et al.*, 1988). The Monetary Authority of Singapore remains vigilant against any rise in underlying inflation.

The strong growth of the economy helped reduce the unemployment rate from about 10 per cent in 1970 to 3 per cent in 1980. The unemployment rate fell to 1.7 per cent in 1990 and stood at less than 3 per cent in 1993.

Table 12.1 presents the basic macroeconomic data for Singapore. As can be seen, Singapore has a very high domestic saving rate, a result, to a large extent, of the compulsory provident fund scheme. The high national savings finally turned Singapore's current account into a surplus since 1988.

Table 12.1 Basic macroeconomic Indicators of Singapore

Indicator	1971–80	1981–90	1992	1994
Real GDP growth rate (%)	7.9	6.3	5.8	10.1
Inflation rate (%, CPI)	7.4	2.3	2.3	3.5
Share in GDP (%)				
Gross domestic saving	30.0	42.6	47.1	45.0
Gross domestic investment	41.2	42.2	40.8	41.5
Current account	−13.7[a]	−0.8[b]	6.4	2.8

Sources: ADB, *Outlook* (various issues)
Notes: a 1980; b 1987

Singapore never had a significant agriculture sector and due to the predominance of trade and commerce, its service sector was always relatively large. In 1975, the share of agriculture in GDP was only 1.5 per cent whereas that of services was 61.3 per cent. In 1993, these figures stood at 0.2 per cent for agriculture and 63 per cent for services. The contribution of manufacturing to GDP has hovered around 27 per cent since 1975, although it did reach 29.5 per cent in 1990. Thus, the conventional index of structural change (in terms of shares in GDP) cannot fully capture the huge structural change that has occurred in Singapore over the past three and half decades.

The rapid structural change that transformed Singapore into a newly industrialising economy happened within the manufacturing and services sector rather than through transfer between sectors. In the 1960s, the economic strategy focused on the expansion of low-skill, labour-intensive manufacturing activities. The focus shifted in the 1970s to the diversification of the manufacturing sector to higher skill levels and higher value added activities. For the services sector the focus shifted from simple re-export and entrepôt activities to developing Singapore into a regional and international financial centre. Emphasis was placed on the development of the tourist industry, transportation, warehousing, and financial and insurance services.

Following the launching of the second industrial restructuring programme in 1979, the 1980s witnessed further movement of the manufacturing sector into more sophisticated and high value-added activities (Chowdhury and Kirkpatrick, 1987). These included petrochemicals, aerospace, biotechnology and information technology. Table 12.2 presents the share of various industries in manufacturing value added (MVA). As can be seen, the share of petroleum-refining, which dominated in the 1970s, declined significantly as other countries in the region, notably Indonesia and Malaysia, developed their own refineries. The chemical sector grew by 13 per cent compared with 6.8 per cent average annual growth rate for the entire manufacturing sector, resulting in the rise of its share in MVA from 4.8 per cent in 1979 to 10.4 per cent in 1991. The electrical machinery sector, which grew by an average annual rate of 7.3 per cent in the 1980s, has the largest share in MVA. Electronics goods accounted for 46 per cent of MVA in 1993. Singapore is a leading producer of disk drives, other computer parts and peripherals, consumer electronics, printed circuit boards, semi-conductors and telecommunications products. Singapore accounts for about half the world's output of disk drives.

In 1993, the financial and business services sector grew by 13 per cent and contributed roughly 29 per cent to GDP. Commerce and tourism continued to grow after a slowdown during 1991–92. The number of international visitor arrivals topped the 6 million mark in 1993, registering an increase of 7.3 per cent.

The telecommunications industry grew by 9.6 per cent in 1993 and container throughput by 20 per cent to reach a staggering 9 million boxes (TEUs). Singapore is now the second busiest container port after Hong Kong.

Table 12.2 Share of manufacturing in value-added (%, factor cost)

Industry	1979	1985	1991	Growth rate (%, 1980–91)
Food, beverages and tobacco	5.7	6.0	4.3	5.0
Textiles, clothing and footwear	6.1	4.0	2.9	−3.6
Wood and furniture	4.3	2.1	1.1	−4.5
Paper and printing	4.5	6.5	6.0	3.9
Chemicals	4.8	8.3	10.4	13.3
Petroleum refining	14.1	8.2	8.6	4.7
Rubber, plastic, pottery, glass	6.6	5.5	4.8	−3.2
Iron and steel	7.0	7.5	7.4	5.8
Machinery	8.1	7.6	6.0	5.5
Electrical machinery	22.9	31.6	38.4	7.3
Transport equipment	12.3	10.0	7.3	5.5
Professional goods	2.0	1.8	1.7	n.a.
Other	1.6	1.2	1.0	−0.2

Sources: UN, *Yearbook of Industrial Statistics* (various issues)

Financial sector

Singapore's geographical location, excellent infrastructure, and economic and political stability are ideal for its development as an international financial centre. The incentive package, relative ease of entry and deregulation of restrictive practices were instrumental in the rapid growth of the banking sector (both local and foreign). In 1994, there were 138 commercial banks (13 local and 125 foreign) and 54 representative offices in Singapore. Of these banks 89 have 'offshore' banking licences. The Singapore International Monetary Exchange (SIMEX) began operation in 1984 and the average daily volume of exchange on the foreign exchange market increased from US$82,000 million in 1992 to US$85,000 million in 1993.

The Asian Dollar Market (ADM) is the focal point of Singapore's development as an international financial centre. It was established in 1968 to facilitate countries in the region carrying out intermediate transactions involved with foreign currency loans and deposits. The market functions through Asian Currency Units (ACUs) which are separate divisions of participating banks and financial institutions. The combined assets of the ADM increased at an average annual rate of 77.5 per cent over 1969–79. In 1993, the total assets increased to US$386,000 million through both increased interbank lending and loans to non-bank customers. A complementary Asian Dollar Bond Market was established to enhance the market's development into an effective instrument for mobilising funds for long-term development.

The government is also promoting off-shore fund management services. Tax exemptions are made available for off-shore fund management. Exemptions are also extended to investments in the local stock market and approved fund managers without ACU licences.

External trade

Re-export continues to be an important component of Singapore's external trade. Its share in total merchandise exports stands at around 38 per cent. In 1993, the share of merchandise exports in GDP was 140.2 per cent reflecting significant re-export activities. The total merchandise exports recorded a strong growth (10 per cent) in 1993 as the world economy came out of recession. In 1994, exports grew by 23 per cent and imports by 14 per cent. However, merchandise imports continue to outstrip exports producing a trade account deficit of US$2.3 billion in 1994. The trade deficit in 1993 was US$11.5 billion. But thanks to the services account which consistently help turn out current account surplus since 1988, the current-account surplus increased from US$8.4 billion in 1993 to US$18.3 billion in 1994 (FEER, 1995b: 93).

In line with its industrialisation strategy, Singapore's exports are dominated by petroleum products, disk drives, computer parts and peripherals, office machinery, other electrical components, and radio and television receivers. The combined share of electronic products in total exports rose from 38 per cent in 1988 to 49 per cent in 1993. Table 12.3 shows the commodity composition of Singapore's exports.

Machinery dominates Singapore's imports. In 1993 machinery accounted for 52 per cent of the total imports bill. The shares of mineral fuel and chemicals stood at 11 and 7 per cent, respectively.

Table 12.3 Composition of Singapore's exports (% of total)

Items	1980	1985	1990	1992
Office machines, electrical machinery, telecommunications equipment, electrical power machinery, switches	43.1	57.7	53.7	55.3
Machinery (non-electrical)	8.8	9.9	7.6	7.6
Clothing and textiles	5.4	6.3	5.5	5.0
Plastic materials	1.0	2.7	2.3	2.0
Sound recorders	1.8	2.4	4.4	4.9
Organic chemicals	1.0	3.2	2.3	2.9
Ships and boats	4.2	1.7	1.0	1.3
Instruments, apparatus	1.4	1.7	2.1	2.3
Veneers, plywood	2.2	1.7	1.0	1.0
Chemical n.e.s.	1.0	1.2	1.4	1.3
Aircraft	1.5	3.7	1.1	1.0
Road motor vehicles	2.0	1.2	1.1	1.0
Others	26.9	6.4	16.7	15.3

Source: Asia Pacific Economic Group, Asia-Pacific Profile, 1994: table 10.5

The US still remains the single most important destination for Singapore's exports, accounting for nearly 20 per cent. Malaysia is the next most important export market with a share of 14.2 per cent out of the ASEAN total of 22.4 per cent. The European Union (EU) accounts for roughly 12 per cent of Singapore's exports. Table 12.4 gives the share of major export markets and import sources.

Japan is the single most important source of Singapore's imports. Nearly 20 per cent of Singapore's imports come from Japan, and the USA supplies about 14 per cent. ASEAN as a bloc is also a major supplier, accounting for nearly 20 per cent of total imports.

Singapore's dollar remains very strong and has appreciated 10 per cent against the US dollar since 1993. The Singapore dollar also appreciated against neighbours' currencies although, on a trade weighted basis, it weakened against those of Japan and Germany (FEER, 1995b). Singapore's competitiveness against major industrialised countries in terms of real exchange rate has declined since 1989.

Since 1989 Singapore has no longer qualified for the US Generalized System of Preferences (GSP) scheme. It also continually faces actions of anti-dumping and countervailing duty from the US, and, more recently, from Australia and New Zealand. In 1993, Singapore's exports to Australia attracted the highest number of anti-dumping actions (Regnier, 1995: 921). Singapore faces similar protectionist actions from the EU. In order to counteract the protectionist trends, Singapore's Trade Development Board has been trying to develop new markets by promoting international purchasing offices and new international trading activities such as futures contracts in metals, coffee and petroleum. Singapore also took steps to keep its trade options as open as possible.

Table 12.4 Singapore's major trading partners (% of total)

Partner	1980	1985	1990	1993
ASEAN	25.7	24.6	23.5	22.4
	24.7	22.8	19.9	21.4
PRC, Taiwan and Hong Kong	10.4	9.1	12.5	15.2
	6.4	13.0	11.1	10.1
Korea	1.4	1.2	2.1	3.5
	1.0	1.5	2.9	4.6
Japan	7.7	9.1	8.3	5.7
	16.3	16.1	17.4	19.9
EU	12.2	10.2	13.9	12.3
	10.2	10.7	12.7	10.1
USA	11.9	20.4	20.5	18.9
	12.8	14.3	15.9	14.2
Others	30.7	25.4	19.2	22.0
	28.7	21.6	20.6	19.7

Source: Asia Pacific Economic Group, Asia-Pacific Profile, 1994: table 10.6
Notes: 1st row = exports; 2nd row = imports

Foreign direct investment

Multinationals and foreign investment have played a crucial role in Singapore's industrialisation. And, even today, multinationals supply more than 80 per cent of investment in the manufacturing sector. Over 3,000 multinationals operate in Singapore and many of the world's biggest companies such as Shell, General Electric, Hewlett Packard, NEC, Philips, ICI, Du Pont, Exxon and Hitachi have their regional headquarters in Singapore.

Singapore's political and economic stability, its strategic location in the region and the availability of sophisticated infrastructure continue to attract foreign investment. There was, however, a big drop in foreign investment in 1985 when the government pushed its high-wage policy too far in order to force investment in priority sectors. The rise in real wage and the consequent decline in profitability were diagnosed as the main factors behind the drop in foreign investment which eventually led to the 1985–86 recession (Kirkpatrick, 1988).

In recent years, more and more foreign investment has been going to financial and business services. For example, 18 per cent of foreign equity

investment went to financial and business services in 1980. But the proportion of foreign equity investment in the financial and business sector in 1991
stood at 44 per cent. The main areas that are attracting most foreign investment are information-technology-related services and medical, engineering
and hosting regional headquarters of international companies (headquarters
services). There is also a trend for new companies to move beyond mere
manufacturing into design and engineering, as well as research and development activities, especially in the electronics, precision equipment, precision
tools and dies, and metal engineering industries (Regnier, 1995: 922).

The US, the EU (in particular the UK and the Netherlands) and Japan are
the major sources of foreign direct investment (FDI) in Singapore. Together
they accounted for 62 per cent of cumulative FDI in 1991. The US investment grew more significantly in the petroleum refinery and aerospace
industries. Japanese firms are increasingly investing in headquarters services.

The government is encouraging Singaporean firms to exploit the opportunities in the region. In 1993, Singapore was the biggest foreign investor in
Indonesia with total investment of US$1.3 billion. Singapore companies
invested US$0.2 billion in Malaysia, making it the fourth largest source of
foreign investment in 1993. Singapore is the fifth largest foreign investor in
both China and Vietnam and is reportedly the largest in Myanmar (DFAT,
1994b: 29). By the end of 1994, Singapore's cumulative overseas investment
stood at US$37.3 billion, representing a rise of 29 per cent over the previous

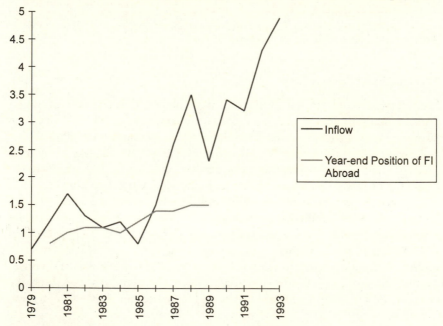

Figure 12.1 Foreign direct investment, Singapore (US$ bn)
Sources: OECD 1993; Key Indicators, Asian Development Bank (various issues)

year. According to the official estimates, Singapore's investment in the region by late 1995 stood at nearly US$36 billion (FEER, 1996b: 59). China, with US$17.3 billion, topped the list, followed by Malaysia (US$7.3 billion). The next largest recipients are Hong Kong (US$4.6 billion) and Indonesia (US$3.5 billion). Thailand and Vietnam received US$1.7 billion and US$1.52 billion respectively. Singapore investors are also looking at the increased opportunities offered by liberalisation in India. In 1995, Singapore ranked eighth among countries investing in India.

Labour market developments

Singapore has invested heavily in human resource development since the mid-1970s and Singapore's major resource endowment is its well-trained and highly motivated labour force. Singapore enjoys a high level of industrial peace. The National Trade Union Congress (NTUC) holds a symbiotic relationship with the government and is an active party in the tripartite National Wages Council (NWC) which formulates annual wage guidelines for the economy and ensures 'orderly wage developments'.

Singapore's labour market is extremely tight, with unemployment rate as low as 2.6 per cent. The median duration of unemployment is only 5.2 weeks. Singapore, thus, depends quite heavily on a large pool of both skilled and unskilled foreign workers, which represents about 20 per cent of the labour force (FEER, 1996b: 58).

The tight labour market exerted considerable pressure on wage rates which rose by 6.7 per cent in 1995 (FEER, 1996b: 58). The unit labour cost has risen by nearly 30 per cent since 1988. However, a strong productivity growth since 1993 has been responsible for a slight decline in unit labour cost (Table 12.5).

Table 12.5 Indices of unit labour cost in Singapore (1988 = 100)

Year	Overall Economy		Manufacturing	
	Index	Annual Change (%)	Index	Annual Change (%)
1984	112.4	4.0	112.2	6.4
1985	113.5	1.0	119.8	6.8
1986	100.8	−11.2	101.7	−15.1
1987	96.7	−4.1	96.2	−5.4
1988	100.0	3.4	100.0	4.0
1989	108.9	8.9	111.4	11.4
1990	118.1	8.5	122.3	9.8
1991	126.4	7.0	131.5	7.5
1992	129.6	2.5	140.3	6.7
1993[a]	129.0	−0.5	135.8	−3.2

Source: Government of Singapore, Ministry of Trade and Industry, *Economic Survey of Singapore, 1994*
Note: a provisional

GOVERNMENT POLICIES

In the early stages, when you try to bring up a very low level of economy to catch up with others, the government must be an activist, and catalyst to growth. But once the business got going, they would become too complex and specialised for any government to be involved. Hence private entrepreneurs and companies must be encouraged to take over.

(Lee Kuan Yew, 1991)

The above quote from the architect of modern Singapore, Lee Kuan Yew, epitomises the role of government in Singapore. Despite its open foreign investment policy and liberalised trade regime, the Singapore government exercises considerable influence on the processes and direction of industrialisation. The Economic Development Board (EDB) is the main body through which the government influences industrialisation by laying down its priorities and channelling both private and foreign investment to priority sectors in anticipation of changes in Singapore's comparative advantage. In addition, the Singapore government has either direct or indirect control over a substantial amount of national savings accumulated in the Central Provident Fund (CPF), the Post Office Savings Bank and the Development Bank of Singapore. In the early stages of development, the government made substantial investment in industrial activities, such as shipbuilding, oil refineries and the iron and steel industry. Also, through numerous statutory boards and state and semi-state companies, organised under wholly government-owned holding companies, the Singapore government entered into a wide range of economic activities from air and sea transport to the provision of utilities.

Recent policy developments

As the economy matured, the government policy since 1987 has been gradual privatisation. Thus, the government reduced its equity in a number of government-linked companies such as Singapore Airlines and it also floated Singapore Telecom. The government has also announced a plan to privatise the Public Utilities Board and the Singapore Broadcasting Corporation.

With the rise in labour cost, scarcity of land and the lack of natural resources acting as constraints on further expansion of traditional manufacturing sectors, government policy is focused on the concept of the 'dual engines of growth' – financial and business services, and high-technology manufacturing activities. Thus, the government is promoting Singapore as a regional and global hub for finance, shipping, air transport, telecommunications and information technology. At the same time, the government is strengthening Singapore's capabilities in 'core' industries such as electronics and is nurturing local enterprises.

As the limitations of further domestic expansion are becoming more and more acute, Singapore is also actively seeking to develop an 'external wing'. In a speech to business leaders, Prime Minister Goh said: 'Building an external economy is a national imperative... Investing in the region... is part of our long-term strategy to climb up the economic ladder' (FEER, 1996b: 58). The government is encouraging and offering incentives to Singapore companies to work and invest abroad, particularly in the high-growth countries of the region. It has introduced new tax incentives and will increase public-sector support for local companies seeking to 'go regional'. The government has established a US$100 million venture fund to invest in local companies which are either regional or have potential to go regional. It has also set up a US$250 million Asian Infrastructure Fund (AIF) to channel investment into major Asian infrastructure projects. Half of the AIF's target of US$761 million up to the year 2005 is expected to be invested in China. The rest will go to Indonesia, Malaysia, Thailand, the Philippines and Taiwan. Recently, Singapore's Senior Minister Lee Kuan Yew told Parliament that the government would itself invest in higher-growth Asian countries, starting with 2–3 per cent of its foreign reserves and eventually reaching 30 per cent.

Senior Minister Lee Kuan Yew also announced a number of new initiatives for boosting Singapore's attempt to make it a regional financial centre. These include measures that give fund managers and investment bankers in Singapore greater access to a very large pool of funds, estimated at US$80 billion, currently in the hands of Government Linked Companies (GLC) and statutory boards, the Government Investment Corporation and the Central Provident Fund. These measures are expected to provide greater depth and breadth to Singapore's capital markets.

Singapore continues to actively court foreign investment and places no restriction on repatriation of profit. The government provides tax incentives to attract foreign investment into selected priority or core industries. Companies investing in selected core industries are entitled to tax exemptions for five to ten years under the Pioneer Status Scheme. There are also schemes that provide double deductions for approved R&D expenditure, concessional tax rates for approved operational headquarters and expansion incentives.

With a view to reducing government's dependence on income and corporate tax, a comprehensive goods and services tax was introduced in April 1994. The rate was set at 3 per cent and will be held for at least five years. While most goods and services are included in the scheme, businesses with an annual turnover of less than US$1 million are exempt and exports are zero-rated. As part of the taxation reform, corporate and personal tax rates were reduced by 3 percentage points. The taxation reform package is expected to improve Singapore's competitiveness.

Singapore has only a limited range of products which attract tariff, primarily for social reasons. These include tobacco, alcohol, motor vehicles and petroleum products. Almost all goods can be imported into Singapore without restrictions provided they comply with health and safety conditions. There is no duty on exports from Singapore. To make Singapore attractive as a regional and global trading hub, the government offers a wide range of tax incentives under different schemes. They include the Approved Oil-Trader Scheme, Approved International-Trader Scheme, Approved International Shipping Enterprise Scheme and Pioneer Status Scheme for counter-trade.

Singapore is an active member of APEC (Asia-Pacific Economic Co-operation) and ASEAN Free Trade Area (AFTA). In order to fulfil its obligations under AFTA, Singapore reduced tariff rates for 373 lines to zero for imports from the ASEAN countries. Products for which tariff was reduced include sugar, confectionary, chocolate, pastries and articles of apparel and clothing.

In an attempt to encourage Singapore companies to 'go regional' and ally their fears about the chaotic nature of the region, the government is establishing industrial parks in areas such as Suzhou in China and Bangalore in India. It has set up government-to-government bodies such as the China–Singapore Joint Steering Council in order to enable Singapore officials to raise specific problems Singapore firms face with their counterparts in host countries. The EDB now has a director for international business development, according to whom Singapore emphasises quality rather than quantity when it comes to overseas investment. The international business development wing of EDB helps identify opportunities or resources as well as help companies solve policy issues. The government-linked companies are taking 'a leading role in jump starting big projects' which are often boosted by high-profile visits by Prime Minister Goh and Senior Minister Lee Kuan Yew.

Chapter 13

Indonesia

HISTORY AND CULTURE

Indonesia, a country consisting of 17,000 islands, lies along the Equator between northern Australia and the south-eastern tip of the Asian mainland. These islands vary widely in size and geographical characteristics, and only 6,000 are inhabited, with nearly two-thirds of Indonesia's population living in Java (Jawa), Madura and Bali. The south and west coasts of Indonesia face the Indian Ocean, and to the north lie the Straits of Malacca and the South China Sea. The Pacific Ocean lashes the remote northern coast of Irian Jaya.

Indonesia came into contact with the broader world of civilisation by participating in the spice, resins and fragrant woods trade along Asia's great maritime trade route, linking China, India and South East Asia in about AD 100 (Cribb, 1995: 358). Its geographical position on the trading route and rich endowment of natural resources attracted traders from Arabia, India, China and Europe. These traders brought with them their culture and religion, and Indonesia's present population represent a rich diversity of culture, language, religion and ethnicity. Indonesia has one of the largest Chinese communities in South East Asia. Although nearly 90 per cent of Indonesia's estimated population of 190 million is Muslim, their practices vary widely from strict Islamic principles; they are influenced by age-long traditional practices and local culture. There is a significant number of Hindus, largely concentrated on the island of Bali, and Christianity remains dominant in the eastern part of the country.

Although the official national language is Bahasa Indonesia, there are about 25 languages and 250 dialects in Indonesia. Bahasa Indonesia is a modernised version of what is commonly known as 'market Malay' – the lingua franca of traders during the colonial era.

The Dutch East Indies Company began colonisation of Indonesia in the early 16th century and Indonesia was converted into a formal Dutch colony in 1799. Dutch rule was interrupted briefly by British rule in 1811–16 under Sir Stamford Raffles, and by the Japanese occupation of 1942–45. After the

Japanese surrender in 1945, Sukarno, a nationalist, declared independence, and established the Republic of Indonesia with himself as its President. This led to a protected guerilla war with the Dutch colonial government which eventually succumbed to international pressure, notably of the USA, and sovereignty was formally transferred to the authority of the Republic of Indonesia on December 27, 1949.

POLITICAL DEVELOPMENTS

Indonesia's brief experience with parliamentary democracy during 1950–57 was chaotic. The First Parliament was not elected and the members occupied their positions based on their roles in the war of independence. As a result, the government was a coalition of diverse political and social groups that participated in the struggle against colonial rule. The government was rendered largely ineffective by political infighting and corruption. The lack of physical infrastructure and human resources also made it difficult for the government to deliver its promises to fulfil the expectations of independence. This made the people disgruntled and the country experienced civil strife and unrest.

In response, Sukarno declared martial law in 1957 and replaced the parliamentary system with what he called 'guided democracy'. In the new system, the legislature became an appointed one and the cabinet was chosen by and responsible to the President. The martial law restricted political activities and during this period the military became deeply involved in the administration and the economy.

Sukarno was seen increasingly being influenced by the Indonesian Communist Party as he used the rhetoric of 'continuous revolution' of the poor and oppressed to legitimise his so-called guided democracy. This made the conservative elements within the army deeply worried. As the ideological conflict was deepening amidst declining economic conditions, a group of young left-leaning junior army officers staged a pre-emptive coup on September 30, 1965 against the conservative hierarchy of the military. However, the coup was crushed by the senior command led by General Suharto. Sukarno remained nominally in power until March 1966 when Suharto formally assumed power and became President.

President Suharto immediately abandoned the ideology of guided democracy and the continuous revolution of the poor. He called his administration 'New Order' and sought to restore political stability and promote economic growth. Suharto received considerable support from the US as a means for stopping a communist take-over.

In an attempt to legitimise his regime, Suharto elevated the national symbol of *pancasila* – five principles of belief in God, national unity, humanitarianism, social justice and democracy which had been expounded by Sukarno during the war of independence. By doing so, Suharto was able to occupy a desirable middle ground away from religious and other ideological extremes. 'The pancasila was held to prescribe a society modelled on the traditional family, in which individual interest was subordinate to the well-being of the community' (Cribb, 1995: 360). Thus, it emphasised the primal role of authority and thereby reinforced Suharto's presidency.

Under international and domestic pressure some limited democracy was restored in 1971 with the presidential election and elections for the parliament, the People's Consultative Assembly. Under the new system, elections are held every five years. But political activities remain restricted and the minor parties are forced to amalgamate under two umbrella parties. There is no 'official' political party of government. The government candidates come from functional groups, of anti-communists, known as *Golkar*. The President and Vice-President are elected by the People's Consultative Assembly which has 1,000 members of whom 600 are effectively appointed by the outgoing President. This ensures the President's re-election and political stability. The latest elections were held in early 1993.

The military became increasingly a dominant player in the New Order administration. The armed forces expounded the concept of *dwifungsi* (dual role), namely that they have the responsibility of maintaining both national security and good government. For example, the candidates in the elections to the People's Consultative Assembly are screened by security officials before being permitted to stand and the armed forces have representation in the parliament itself. The new legislation introduced in February 1988 re-affirmed *dwifungsi* and the military played an important role in the selection of Indonesia's Vice-President.

However, with growing economic prosperity and rising middle-class expectations, there is increasing pressure for political liberalisation. As the President is ageing, there is also growing uncertainty about his succession.

THE ECONOMY

Indonesia is a resource-rich country with sizeable deposits of petroleum, natural gas and other minerals. Yet it was a relatively poor country until very recently. It achieved the status of a 'middle-income' country by World Bank criteria only in 1981 when its national income per capita exceeded US$500 after a sustained period of rapid growth in the 1970s. Its GDP per capita stood at US$665 in 1993.

Growth and structural change

The basic macroeconomic indicators of the Indonesian economy are presented in Table 13.1. As can be seen, spectacular growth rates have been recorded since the early 1970s. The economy grew at an average annual growth of 7.7 per cent during 1971–80. The collapse of oil prices in the

Table 13.1 Basic macroeconomic indicators of Indonesia

Indicator	1971–80	1981–90	1992	1994
Real GDP growth rate (%)	7.7	5.5	6.4	7.0
Inflation rate (%, CPI)	17.5	8.6	7.5	9.6
Share in GDP (%)				
Gross domestic saving	21.6	31.8	37.3	38.7
Gross domestic investment	19.3	30.4	34.6	33.9
Current account	1.7[a]	−2.1[b]	−2.9	−2.4
Debt servicing ratio (% exports)	12.7[a]	24.9[b]	32.1	27.5

Sources: ADB, *Outlook* (various issues)
Notes: a 1980; b 1985

mid-1980s and the resultant austerity measures were primarily responsible for the reduction in the average annual growth rate of real GDP to 5.5 per cent during the 1980s. The growth rate picked up in the late 1980s and the year-on-year growth rate of real GDP has been hovering around 7 per cent since 1989. The high growth rate has been underpinned by high domestic saving and investment rates.

However, the impressive growth record was dented by double-digit inflation. The average annual inflation rate, as measured by changes in consumer price index, was 17.5 per cent during 1971–80. Nonetheless, the Indonesian government was able to bring down the average annual inflation rate to 8.6 per cent in the 1980s. Another weak spot is the deterioration of current account of the balance of payments. From a surplus of US$1.3 billion in 1980, the current account recorded a deficit of US$1.8 billion in 1981 and rose to 3.5 per cent of GDP in 1991. The current-account deficit shows that despite a relatively high gross domestic saving rate, Indonesia still has a resource gap. The average short-fall between gross domestic and gross national saving rates due to outflows of net factor income and servicing of debt ranges from 4 to 5 per cent of GDP. However, this gap is declining because of a steady rise in gross domestic savings and relatively stable outflows of net factor income.

The rapid growth of the Indonesian economy has been accompanied by significant structural changes in the 1980s. As can be seen from Table 13.2, the roles of agriculture and the resource sector have declined and manufacturing is becoming a major activity. In 1993, agriculture contributed only 18.4 per cent to GDP, which is about half its 1975 contribution. Mining and quarrying activities now contribute only about 9 per cent as opposed to more than 25 per cent in 1980. On the other hand, the share of manufacturing has increased rapidly from only 11 per cent in 1975 to more than 22 per cent in 1993. Since the late 1980s, manufacturing output has grown at an average annual rate of more than 10 per cent as opposed to agriculture's average annual growth rate of only 2.5 per cent and about 3 per cent annual growth rate of the mining sector.

Table 13.2 Sectoral contributions to Indonesia's GDP (%)

Sector	1975	1980	1985	1990	1993
Agriculture	36.8	24.8	22.7	21.5	18.4
Industry	27.3	43.4	39.7	39.4	39.1
Manufacturing	11.1	11.6	15.8	20.0	22.4
Mining & quarrying	10.8	25.7	14.0	13.3	8.9
Services	35.9	31.8	37.6	39.1	42.6

Sources: Asian Development Bank, Key Indicators (various issues)

Although the manufacturing sector grew quite rapidly in the 1980s, its structure did not change much, except for the rise in the shares of wood products, iron and steel and metal products (Table 13.3). The production of wood products grew at an average annual rate of 11 per cent, resulting in the rise in its share in manufacturing value added (MVA) at factor costs from 7 per cent in 1980 to nearly 13 per cent in 1989. Iron and steel was the fastest growing sector in the 1980s, registering an average annual growth rate of nearly 15 per cent and its share in MVA rose from 3 per cent in 1980 to 8 per cent in 1989. The production of other metal products grew at a rate of more than 7 per cent and its share in MVA rose from 3.5 per cent to 6.6 per cent.

Table 13.3 Share in manufacturing value-added (at factor costs, %)

Industry	1980	1985	1989	Growth rate (%) 1981–89
Food products	11.1	13.4	11.8	5.0
Textiles	12.4	10.6	12.5	8.0
Wood products	7.0	9.4	12.8	10.7
Industrial chemicals	4.3	6.6	4.6	6.1
Other chemicals	7.1	6.0	4.1	5.4
Iron and Steel	3.1	7.2	8.3	14.7
Metal products	3.5	4.3	6.6	7.6
Machinery	1.6	1.2	1.0	n.a.
Electrical machinery	5.3	3.8	2.7	3.3
Transport equipment	6.4	5.1	6.9	7.2

Sources: UN, Yearbook of Industrial Statistics (various issues)

The private sector is increasingly playing an important role in Indonesia's industrialisation. For example, most consumer goods such as processed foods, beverages, tobacco, textiles and garments, motor vehicle components and assemblies, and electrical appliances are produced predominantly by the private sector, often in joint ventures with foreign companies. The production of capital and intermediate goods, such as fertilisers, cement, chemicals and machinery remains primarily in the public sector.

External trade

Until the mid-1980s, Indonesia's export trade was dominated by crude petroleum and natural gas. Together they accounted for nearly three-quarters of total export revenue in the first half of 1980. This made Indonesia's export earnings highly dependent on the vagaries of the international oil and gas markets with serious implications for the government budget. For example, the slump in oil prices in 1986 resulted in a sharp decline in government revenue and the contribution of oil and gas to government revenue fell from about 70 per cent in 1980 to about 40 per cent. This led to the adoption of wide-ranging measures to boost non-oil exports, and since 1986 the composition of Indonesia's exports has changed significantly. The share of oil and gas in total exports declined from over 75 per cent in 1980 to about 25 per cent in 1994 and non-oil exports now play a much more important role.

Table 13.4 Major Indonesian exports (% of total export value)

Item	1989	1992	1994[a]
Oil and gas	39.2	31.5	24.7
Agricultural products	8.8	6.5	6.3
Mining products	2.3	4.3	4.2
Non-oil industrial	49.8	57.7	64.8
Wood & plywood	15.5	12.3	14.7
TCF	10.2	21.7	15.1
Electronics	0.9	3.2	5.7

Source: DFAT, 1994d
Note: a First half of 1994

As can be seen from Table 13.4, exports of wood products including plywood and TCF (textiles, clothing and footwear) products have increased since the second half of the 1980s. Electronics and electrical products are also emerging as important export items.

Intermediate and capital goods continue to dominate Indonesia's imports. Chemicals (industrial and other) and machinery, for example, constitute nearly 75 per cent of imports. This is not surprising given Indonesia's industrialisation drive. Table 13.5 gives the composition of Indonesia's imports by SITC product type.

Until the early 1980s the export growth, usually outstripped import growth, producing a surplus in the trade account. However, in recent years, due to the growth in domestic demand, imports have been growing at a much faster rate than exports. For example, in the first half of 1994, the value of imports grew by more than 10 per cent as opposed to only 2.5 per cent increase in the value of exports. In the past, the surplus in merchandise trade account was more than enough to offset a consistent deficit on

invisible items consisting of interest payments on external debt and repatriation of profit. However, the trend in the growth of imports and exports
since the mid-1980s is adding to the current account deficits.

Table 13.5 Indonesia's imports (% of total import value)

SITC product type	1989	1992	1994[a]
0 Food, animals	5.6	4.7	5.6
1 Beverage, tobacco	0.2	0.3	0.4
2 Raw materials	10.2	8.8	8.9
3 Energy resources	7.7	7.7	6.9
4 Fats, non-fuel oils	0.9	0.5	0.4
5 Chemical products	17.6	13.8	15.0
6 Industrial chemicals	16.0	17.1	16.5
7 Machinery, equipment	37.8	42.9	42.7
8 Other industrial goods	3.9	4.0	3.7
9 Other goods	0.1	0.1	0.0

Source: Same as for Table 13.4
Note: a First half of 1994

Table 13.6 Indonesia's major trading partners (% total exports
            and imports)

Country	1989	1992	1994[a]
Japan	42.1	31.7	27.8
	23.0	22.0	24.3
USA	15.8	13.0	14.8
	13.6	14.0	10.9
Singapore	8.2	9.7	10.6
	6.9	6.1	5.4
Korea, Taiwan, China	11.9	16.6	17.5
Hong Kong	13.5	15.1	17.1

Source: Same as for Table 13.4
Note: a First half of 1994; the first row is exports to and the second row is
imports from

Japan, the USA and Singapore together account for more than 75 per cent
of Indonesia's exports and more than half of imports. Table 13.6 shows the
distribution of Indonesia's exports and imports among its major trading
partners. As can be seen, Japan is the most important trading partner of
Indonesia. In 1993, 30 per cent of Indonesia's exports went to Japan while
22 per cent of imports came from Japan. Indonesia's competitiveness with
Japan, measured in terms of real exchange rate, has been increasing since
1990, and the overall competitiveness against major industrial country
trading partners has been maintained. However, there has been a slight
decline in Indonesia's competitiveness with East Asia in recent years.

Foreign investment

The assumption of power by President Suharto in 1965 was marked by a significant policy shift towards foreign investment. In order to attract foreign investment, the 'New Order' government of President Suharto enacted the Foreign Investment Law of 1967 which granted investors a high degree of protection and a wide range of incentives. The investment co-ordinating board, Badan Koordinas Penanaman Modal (BKPM), approved foreign investment projects worth about US$85 billion between January 1967 and July 1994. This amount, however, excludes investments in the oil and gas and financial sectors which are outside the jurisdiction of the BKPM. Figure 13.1 shows that the inflow of direct foreign investment accelerated after 1990 but declined in 1993. The decline in foreign investment in 1993 prompted the government to relax foreign investment regulations, as discussed later.

The manufacturing sector received nearly 60 per cent of total approved and 61 per cent of implemented investment by the end of 1993. Approximately 10 per cent of approved and 18 per cent of implemented foreign investment went to the mining sector. The tourism and agriculture sectors received the bulk of the remaining funds (Hobohm, 1995: 371).

Japan is the major source of foreign investment, followed by Hong Kong. The share of Japan in the cumulative approved foreign investment between

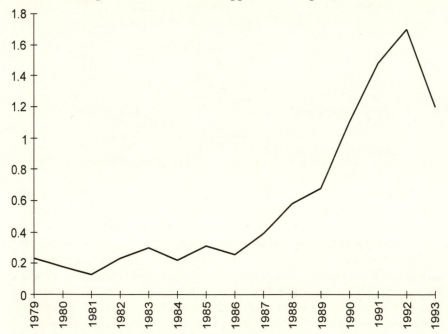

Figure 13.1 Foreign direct investment, Indonesia (US$ bn)
Sources: Key Indicators, Asian Development Bank (various issues)

1967 and July 1994 stood at 18 per cent and that of Hong Kong at 13.5 per cent. If foreign investment in the petroleum and gas industries were included, Japan's share would be much higher. There has been some increase in foreign investment in Indonesia from the US and the East Asian NIEs since 1990.

Labour market developments

Indonesia has an estimated labour force of around 80 million which is growing at an annual rate of nearly 3 per cent. More than 50 per cent of the labour force is engaged in agriculture with employment in manufacturing accounting for only 10–11 per cent. Although the measured unemployment rate is around 2–3 per cent, there is a high incidence of underemployment or disguised unemployment, as is very common with a large agricultural labour force. According to one estimate, the current underemployment rate is around 40 per cent (DFAT, 1994d: 27).

A significant number of unskilled Indonesian labourers work abroad, mainly in Malaysia's plantation and construction sectors. Many of these workers do not possess legal work permits. In 1992, Indonesia received US$184 million from workers' remittances.

The great majority of the labour force have a low level of education, although there have been some improvements in the past decade. In 1980, 68.5 per cent of the population aged 10 years and over and 67 per cent of the labour force had either no education or had not completed primary school. These figures had been reduced to 47.5 and 45.6 per cent respectively by 1990.

Despite government's efforts to enhance human resources, the skill level and educational attainment of this large pool of Indonesian labour remains very low compared with other ASEAN countries. According to the United Nations' *Human Development Report* (UNDP, 1993) Indonesia has only 10.1 scientists and technicians (1.7 R&D scientists and technicians) per 1,000 population and only 11 per cent of graduates have a science degree. Between 1989 and 1994, the government had hoped to train approximately 6 million workers: 2.1 million as production personnel, 1.76 million as sales personnel, 1.38 million as agricultural workers and about 76,000 for other services. However, qualified workers, especially in key technical and managerial positions, are expected to remain scarce in the remaining years of the 1990s.

Although there is a large pool of underemployed workers, many of whom are willing to accept wages below the official minimum wage rate, the legislated minimum wages have been increased by over 20 per cent. Batam island, which forms the growth triangle with Singapore and Johor (Malaysia), has the highest minimum wage. As a result of government efforts to increase the enforcement of minimum wage payments and workers' demand for better conditions, Indonesia has experienced rises in labour costs in recent times.

There are also increasing pressures for reforms in industrial relations from labour activists and semi-organised labour groups. There was a wave of large strikes and demonstrations in 1994 in support of demands to open the industrial relations system to independent trade unions outside the official umbrella trade union SPSI. The officially recorded number of strikes by mid-1994 was double the number in 1993 and stood at 370. Although the government is prepared to make some concessions, the demand for faster and wider reforms will continue to cause tensions.

GOVERNMENT POLICIES

The government plays a very active role in Indonesia through its Four Year Plans, known as REPELITA. However, there is a significant difference between the Indonesian approach to planning and those of many other developing countries in the sense that these plans do not 'constitute comprehensive proposals for thorough-going state-controlled change with fixed sectoral targets' (Hobohm, 1995: 365). Rather they represent 'guidelines for public-sector investment projects' (Hobohm, 1995: 365). In line with the 'New Order' government's liberal attitudes towards foreign investment, initially there was a very high dependence of REPELITA projects on foreign aid and funds. This has changed considerably over time and it has been projected that only 6.7 per cent of the REPELITA-VI (1994/95–1998/99) would require foreign funding.

The first of the Four Year Plans, REPELITA-I, which covered the period 1969/70–1973/74 involved expenditure of US$2 billion aimed at achieving an average annual GDP growth rate of 4.7 per cent. Its emphasis was on the development of agriculture and infrastructure. The manufacturing investment was weighted towards the production of intermediate goods such as cement, fertilisers and equipment for the production and processing of agricultural products (Hobohm, 1995: 365). REPELITA-I can be regarded as largely successful as most of the targets were either fulfilled or surpassed and the real GDP grew at more than 8 per cent per annum.

REPELITA-II (1974/75–1978/79) gave a high priority to employment generation and equitable distribution of the benefits of economic growth. Thus it sought to avoid capital-intensive projects and urban bias while agricultural and infrastructural development continued to receive attention. It also emphasised the role of both the private and public sectors and provided a blueprint for a mixed economy.

While REPELITA-III retained the main objectives of the previous two plans, and continued to encourage the development of a mixed economy, the launching of REPELITA-IV in April 1984 marked a clear re-orientation towards export-oriented manufacturing. It also sought to promote sectors other than oil and gas. The private sector was identified as the prime mover and was expected to provide 45 per cent of total investment. In order to encourage the private sector and export, an extensive liberalisation programme, involving the taxation system, financial institutions, customs and port-handling formalities and licensing procedures for private investment, was initiated.

REPELITA-V, launched in April 1989 gave more emphasis to the private sector which was expected to contribute 55 per cent to total investment. The private sector was envisaged as playing a much greater role in the export-oriented manufacturing sector. Human resource development also received greater attention and the public sector was designated to play a greater role in education, rural development and infrastructural development such as communications and electricity generation.

REPELITA-VI, introduced in April 1994, constitutes the first phase of the Second 25-Year Long-Term Development Programme which aims to transform Indonesia into a modern industrialised economy. The private sector is expected to account for more than 70 per cent of total investment while the government will continue to concentrate on education and the development of infrastructure.

Recent policy developments

The oil-price slump and the international debt crisis in the early 1980s prompted the Indonesian government to embrace a wide-ranging liberalisation programme. In October 1988, the government introduced a series of financial sector reforms involving the removal of interest rate controls and relaxation of regulations on foreign banks opening branches outside Jakarta. The other changes in the banking sector included permission for domestic banks to form joint ventures with foreign financial institutions with representation in Indonesia, the removal of the upper limit on offshore borrowing by commercial banks, and relaxation of licensing requirements for dealing in foreign exchange. Private banks were also allowed to compete with state-owned banks for deposits from state corporations. By 1993, there were 144 commercial banks and 39 foreign and joint-venture banks operating in Indonesia.

In order to encourage private-sector capital formation, measures were introduced to invigorate the Indonesian Stock Exchange. This included various incentives for domestic firms to float on the Jakarta Stock Exchange, equalisation of tax rates on bank-deposit interest rates and dividends on equity holdings and partial opening of the Stock Exchange to foreign institutional investors. There were also measures to encourage 'foreign joint-ventures into the leasing, factoring, venture capital, securities tradings, credit-card and consumer finance industries' (Hobohm, 1995: 372).

With a view to further encouraging private investment, the Indonesian government initiated a major deregulation programme in 1993. It has also

embarked upon the reform of legal and administrative procedures to enhance the efficiency of the public sector. More than 400 laws are under
review, some of them dating back to the colonial period. As Low and Toh
(1994: 45) note, 'The review of laws is an urgent measure that has to be
instituted as the region is increasingly becoming a trans-border investment
zone. It is also a necessary feature in Indonesia's attempts to diversify its
export base and enhance industrial competitiveness.'

Low and Toh (1994: 45) have listed the following changes to regulatory
measures introduced in 1993:

- exemption from import duties, surcharges, and value-added tax for
  materials imported to be used entirely for exports;
- increasing the allowance for the companies operating in bonded zones to
  sell in the domestic market from 12 per cent to 25 per cent;
- reduction of the number of business areas where new investment is
  restricted or banned;
- improving the licensing procedures, the stock exchange, and deregulating
  the pharmaceutical industry;
- streamlining the investment approval procedures;
- waiving visa requirements for businessmen from 45 countries.

The government introduced further regulatory changes in June 1994.
They include:

- reduction in tariffs on 739 products taking average Indonesian tariffs to
  well below Indonesia's 40 per cent Uruguay Round binding;
- removal of non-tariff barriers on 27 products and surcharges on 108 items
  covering raw materials and intermediate goods used in the livestock
  industry, textile machinery and components, agricultural machinery,
  foreign-assembled passenger cars, semi-trailer parts and components of
  heavy duty equipment;
- removal of the entitlement to any tariff escalation for new projects;
- removal of the prohibition on leasing of machinery and equipment by
  companies in bonded and special export zones to companies operating
  outside such zones.

The June 1994 announcement also included significant changes in regulations governing foreign investment. The major changes are as follows:

- an increase in the level of permissible foreign capital participation in joint-
  venture companies from 80 to 95 per cent;
- lifting of the foreign-ownership restriction on Indonesian companies to
  allow ownership by foreign individuals;
- extension of the period of operation of licence fees from 20 to 30 years;
- abolition of the requirement of a minimum capital investment of
  US$250,000 on foreign investors;

- easing of the divestment requirement for fully owned foreign companies so that divestment of a token proportion of as little as 1 per cent need only be carried out within 15 years of the commencement of commercial production, and this can be done by float rather than finding a suitable local partner;
- opening up the previously off-limit areas such as ports, electricity generation and distribution, telecommunications, shipping, airways, drinking water, railways, nuclear power and mass media to joint ventures;
- easing of operating conditions for foreign companies to allow them to establish subsidiaries and acquire other foreign and domestic forms.

The tax system has also been overhauled. The new tax bill introduced in October 1994 reduced the rates of the presently existing income brackets and increased the annual tax-free income from 0.96 million to 1.72 million rupiahs. It has also reduced the top rate to 30 per cent for companies as well as individuals. It allows for special tax incentives for companies to invest in priority sectors and reinvest their after-tax earnings in Indonesia.

Although many of the changes have not been fully implemented yet, there are signs of growing investor confidence in the Indonesian economy. The Indonesian government continues to reiterate its commitment to tariff reductions and reform of its laws to achieve GATT consistency by 1997. However, this does not mean that there will not be any attempt at seeking protection by some industries, as revealed by the petrochemical complex Chandra Asri's application for tariff protection. While supporting the tariff protection, President Suharto in his budget speech on January 5, 1995 has set down clear guidelines. Any 'protection "must meet certain conditions" ... First, it must be given only for a limited period and gradually reduced – "the sooner the better". Second it should not be contrary to international agreements nor stifle downstream industries' (FEER, 1995d).

Chapter 14

Malaysia

HISTORY AND CULTURE

Modern Malaysia came into existence after gaining political independence from British rule on August 31, 1957. It consists of 11 states in Peninsular Malaya and 2 states on the island of Borneo. However, its historical roots lie in the founding of the Malacca sultanate (kingdom) in 1400. Malacca was a vigorous trading and cultural centre which influenced the shaping of political institutions and traditional Malay culture through the succeeding centuries (Brown, 1995a: 543). Malacca was captured by the Portuguese in 1511 and subsequently by the Dutch in 1641. The colonial powers attempted to prevent the rise of another Malay state in the peninsula which could rival the power of Malacca. By the mid-18th century the modern geopolitical pattern of Malay states had emerged in the peninsula beyond the influence of the European-fortified entrepôt of Malacca.

In an attempt to secure the trade route to China through the Straits of Malacca, the British captured the island of Penang in 1786 and Malacca in 1795. Following the establishment of a trading post in Singapore in 1819 the British formed a single administrative unit, the Straits Settlements, comprising Penang, Malacca and Singapore, in 1826. The Straits Settlements were administered from British India until 1867 when the administration was transferred to the Colonial Office in London.

Although initially the British did not want to become involved in the Malay states, the rivalry among Malay rulers following the discovery of major tin deposits in Perak and other mining activities slowly drew the Straits Settlements into closer political and economic ties with the hinterland. As the Malay rulers fought among themselves, often using the secret societies of migrant Chinese workers to control newly found wealth, there was a total collapse of law and order by the late 1860s. The local Chinese and European merchants urged the Straits Settlements to intervene and restore order. In 1873 the British government agreed to intervene in the fear that the chaos would give the rival German colonial power an opportunity to capture the peninsula, threatening British commercial interests. Over the period

1874–88, the British entered into agreements with the Malay rulers of Perak, Selangor, Negri Sembilan and Pahang, which required the sultans to accept a British Resident whose advice 'must be asked and acted upon on all questions other than those touching Malay religion and custom'. The sultans were allowed to keep all their privileges and the splendour of the Malay ceremonial court. This agreement effectively turned the Malay rulers into figureheads while the executive powers rested on the British Resident.

The Federated Malay States (FMS) with the four signatory states was established in 1896 and Kuala Lumpur became its capital. By 1914 the four northern states of Kedah, Perlis, Kelantan and Trengganu and the southern states of Johor accepted permanent British advisers. Although these five states remained outside the FMS and became collectively known as Unfederated Malay States (UMS), the acceptance of permanent British resident advisers effectively allowed British rule to extend throughout the Malay peninsula.

British rule was interrupted by Japanese occupation during 1942–45. After the Japanese surrender, the British began negotiations with a new political force, the United Malays National Organisation (UMNO), and the Malaya rulers formed a unified administration of the Malayan Union, combining FMS, UMS, Penang and Malacca. This eventuated in the formation of the Federation of Malaya in February 1948. The new constitution of the Federation maintained the sovereignty of sultans and granted citizenship to the Chinese and Indian settlers.

The restrictive citizenship requirements for the Chinese and Indians angered the non-Malay settlers; in particular the Chinese regarded the Federation as a betrayal of the loyalty they had shown to the British during the Japanese occupation. This strengthened the hardliners in the Communist Party of Malaya (CPM) which launched a guerilla warfare against colonial rule. However, the CPM did not enjoy much support among the Malays and by the mid-1950s the communist insurgency had died down.

By then, however, the British had decided to grant self-government to the Federation and worked towards finding a consensus among the various ethnic groups. The negotiation among the various groups resulted in a compromise whereby the Malays retained the political power and in exchange allowed the Chinese to continue their economic functions with the understanding that in time more equality would be achieved among the races in both the economic and political spheres. The new constitution also had the provision for a single nationality, with citizenship open to all those in Malaya who qualified either by birth or by fulfilling requirements of residence and language. Independence was proclaimed on August 31, 1957 and the UMNO president, Tunku Abdul Rahman, became the first Prime Minister. The government was formed by the coalition of major ethnically oriented parties: UMNO, the Malayan Chinese Association (MCA) and the Malayan Indian Congress (MIC).

Singapore joined the Federation of Malaya in 1963 when it gained full independence. But, in order to prevent the Chinese becoming the numerical majority with Singapore's entry, Sarawak and North Borneo (renamed Sabah) were also taken into the Federation to form the Federation of Malaysia. However, Singapore's membership was always an uneasy one due to its more radical politics and Lee Kuan Yew's intention of participating in the politics of the mainland. Singapore was, therefore, expelled from the Federation in 1965.

The formation of the Federation of Malaysia was not taken very easily by Indonesia or the Philippines which had laid its territorial claim to North Borneo (Sabah). In 1963 both Indonesia and the Philippines broke off diplomatic relations with Malaysia and Indonesia launched a series of military confrontations. However, after the failed coup in Indonesia in 1965 and Suharto's accession to presidency, the tension eased.

Malaysia is a multicultural society where the indigenous Malays have interacted with the Chinese, Indian and other cultures ever since the spice trade flourished along the prosperous maritime trade route linking China and India thorough South East Asia. Arab traders brought Islam and the majority of Malays are now Muslims. The Chinese and Indians migrated mainly during the colonial period to work in plantations and mines. In Peninsular Malaysia, the Malays constitute about 59 per cent of the population, the Chinese 31 per cent and Indians 10 per cent. In Sabah and Sarawak, the Chinese populations comprise about 14 per cent and 29 per cent respectively. Despite a long history of interaction among the Malays, Chinese and Indians, a common culture did not emerge and each group maintained more or less its own distinct ethnic and cultural identity. The division of economic functions along ethnic lines was largely responsible for mutual distrust and perhaps prevented cultural integration to some extent.

POLITICAL DEVELOPMENTS

Malaysia is a parliamentary democracy with a figurehead monarch and an executive parliament elected by popular votes. The conference of independent Malay rulers (sultans) elects the monarch (*Yang di-Pertuan Agong*) from among themselves.

Political developments in Malaysia are driven primarily by ethnic tensions and compromises. Malaysia since independence has been ruled by a government of coalition between UMNO, MCA and MIC – the three major parties representing Malays, Chinese and Indians, respectively. The compromise that was hatched between the coalition partners at the eve of independence has failed to fulfil the rising expectations of younger generations. The new generation of Malays wanted more and quicker economic gains and the non-Malays (in particular the Chinese) were unhappy with their lack of political power. The resentment culminated in a bloody race riot in May 1969.

The reassessment of earlier compromise following the riot led to the formulation of the New Economic Policy (NEP) to be implemented over 20 years to 1990. Its primary objectives were eradication of poverty among all races and of the identification of race with economic function. The latter was designed to give the Malays a greater share in economic wealth with specific target of raising the share of Malays and other indigenous people (*bumiputra*) to 30 per cent of commercial and industrial capital by 1990. It was also recognised that for the maintenance of racial harmony the increase in Malay shares in wealth should not be achieved at the expense of other races. The NEP's role in economic growth with distribution in Malaysia is discussed later.

New legislation was also introduced immediately after the 1969 riot, to remove from public discussion such sensitive matters as the powers and status of sultans, Malay special rights, the status of Islam as the official religion and citizen rights. Under the leadership of the new Prime Minister, Tun Abdul Razzakt, the ruling UMNO–MCA–MIC coalition was reorganised as Barisan National (National Front) which included other major opposition parties. This was designed to prevent public discussion of sensitive issues which was made seditious, but allowed the bargaining of communal interests to take place in a more discreet manner within the government.

As the economic growth rate declined during the early 1980s due to global economic recession, a new element surfaced in Malaysian politics. Intra-racial politics became dominant in the 1980s as coalition partners, especially UMNO and MCA, faced growing discontent among their own constituencies. The Malays, Chinese and Indians became disillusioned and blamed their respective parties in the ruling coalition for not doing enough. This resulted in the formation of new opposition parties by disaffected members who left UMNO or MCA. However, the ruling alliance managed to fend off opposition attacks and scored victory in successive elections. The resounding victory of BN and its dominant partner UMNO, especially in opposition heartlands, in the 1995 election has strengthened the leadership of Dr Mahathir against the opposition both within and outside his own party.

The 1980s also witnessed growing tensions between the executive government of Dr Mahathir who became Prime Minister in 1981 and the traditional Malay rulers. Dr Mahathir won public support for his attempt to restrict the powers and privileges of sultans which shows the weaning off traditional values in a modernising society where public tolerance for the excesses of feudal rulers declines. A new code of conduct was agreed in July 1992 with the sultans outlining the parameters of their involvement in both politics and commerce. The constitutional amendments in February 1993 further curbed the powers of sultans by restricting their personal legal immunity.

THE ECONOMY

Malaysia is the star economy in South East Asia, posting an average annual growth of over 8 per cent during 1988–95. It is rich in natural resources with extensive deposits of hydrocarbons, natural gas, tin, copper, bauxite, coal and uranium. Malaysia is the leading exporter of palm oil, a major exporter of tropical hardwoods and a major producer of rubber. It has an estimated population of about 19 million. Malaysia aspires to reach a developed country status in the year 2020.

Growth and structural change

Table 14.1 presents the basic macroeconomic indicators of the Malaysian economy. The global recession in the early 1980s and the collapse of the international tin market in 1985 on top of the slump in oil prices were primarily responsible for a decline in GDP by roughly 1 per cent. However, Malaysia successfully came out of recession with a real GDP growth of 5.4 per cent in 1987. Real GDP grew at about 9 per cent in the subsequent four years.

As can be seen from the table, the inflation rate, measured in terms of changes in consumer price index, has been kept in check. After a slight increase in the inflation rate, it has fallen to 3.7 per cent. This was largely achieved by cuts in import duties and other statutory charges.

The economic growth and the compulsory employee provident fund contributed largely to a rapid rise in the savings rate. This helped reverse the general trend and merchandise exports grew at a faster rate than merchandise imports in 1992 and 1993. However, the economic buoyancy in 1994 caused imports to grow at a faster rate (32 per cent) than exports (26 per cent). As a result, the trade surplus shrank from US$8.2 billion in 1993 to US$3.7 billion in 1994. The adverse trade balance did not cause much damage to the current account because of the relatively smaller deficit in the services account (FEER, 1995e).

Table 14.1 Basic macroeconomic indicators of Malaysia

Indicator	1971–80	1981–90	1992	1994
Real GDP growth rate (%)	7.8	5.2	7.8	8.7
Inflation rate (%)	6.0	3.2	4.7	3.7
Share in GDP (%)				
Gross domestic saving	29.1	33.0	35.5	33.0
Gross domestic investment	24.9	30.7	33.8	34.5
Current account	−1.2[a]	−1.9[b]	−2.8	−1.3
Debt servicing ratio (% exports)	4.6[a]	29.0[b]	6.3	5.0

Sources: ADB, *Outlook* (various issues)
Notes: a 1980; b 1985

Table 14.2 Sectoral contributions to Malaysia's GDP (%)

Sector	1975	1980	1985	1990	1993
Agriculture	27.7	22.9	20.7	18.7	15.9
Industry	26.8	37.0	36.7	38.5	44.7
Manufacturing	16.4	19.8	19.7	26.9	40.0
Mining & quarrying	4.6	10.1	10.5	9.7	10.3
Services	45.5	40.1	42.6	42.8	39.4

Sources: ADB, *Key Indicators* (various issues)

Table 14.2 shows the rapid structural change of the Malaysian economy during the past two decades. Manufacturing, which contributed only 16.4 per cent to the GDP of a predominantly agricultural and primary producing country, now accounts for 40 per cent of the total output in the economy. Manufacturing grew by an average annual rate of 10 per cent during the 1970s and 9.4 per cent over 1980–91. The average growth rate of manufacturing was 12–13 per cent per annum during 1991–94. On the other hand, agriculture grew by an annual average rate of around 5 and 4 per cent in the 1970s and 1980s, respectively.

As can be seen from Table 14.3, most manufacturing activities could hold on to their position in terms of their shares in manufacturing value added (MVA) during the 1980s. The big losers, though, were food, beverage and tobacco (ISIC 31), wood and furniture (ISIC 33), and rubber products, whereas chemicals (ISIC 351, 352), electrical machinery (ISIC 383) and transport equipment (ISIC 384) registered gains. Electrical equipment which includes television receivers, video cassette recorders, air-conditioners,

Table 14.3 Share in manufacturing value-added (at factor costs, %)

Industry	1979	1985	1989	Growth rate (%) 1980–91
Food, beverage & tobacco	25	21	13	2.8
Textiles, clothing and footwear & leather products	7	5	6	8.2
Wood products & furniture	12	6	7	n.a.
Paper & printing	5	5	5	n.a.
Chemicals	6	16	11	7.6
Petroleum & coal	4	4	2	8.1
Rubber	10	5	6	5.0
Plastic, pottery, glass & non-metal products	7	9	9	8.9
Iron and non-ferrous metals	6	7	7	8.7
Machinery	3	2	4	n.a.
Electrical machinery	12	15	22	18.8
Transport equipment	4	4	6	11.9
Professional equipment	1	1	1	n.a.
Other	1	1	1	n.a.

Sources: UN, *Yearbook of Industrial Statistics* (various issues)

personal computers, typewriters and domestic refrigeration was the fastest growing area. Its average annual growth rate of about 19 per cent was nearly 10 percentage points higher than the overall growth of the manufacturing sector during 1980–91. This helped its share in MVA to rise from 12 per cent in 1979 to 22 per cent in 1989.

External trade

The rapid structural change during the past two decades has transformed Malaysia from a primary producing country to a next-tier newly industrialising economy. This is reflected in its external trade. The share of agricultural products in total merchandise exports dropped from nearly 44 per cent in 1980 to about 13 per cent in 1993. Similarly, the importance of petroleum and other mineral products declined sharply from 34 per cent in 1980 to about 14 per cent in 1993. On the other hand, manufacturing's share in total merchandise exports rose from 22 per cent to 74 per cent during the same period. Since 1990, manufacturing exports have grown on average by 30 per cent per annum.

The composition of manufacturing exports, too, changed significantly. For example, the share of electrical machinery in manufacturing exports dropped from 40 per cent in 1980 to 22 per cent in 1992. This drop was taken up almost entirely by telecommunications equipment whose share rose from 3 per cent to 19 per cent. Tape recorders and office machines also increased their shares from less than 1 per cent to 7 and 9 per cent, respectively during 1980–92.

Malaysia's industrialisation process depends highly on imported capital and intermediate products. Together, they account for nearly 80 per cent of Malaysia's imports. The rapid industrialisation and economic growth have been generating import demands, and merchandise imports grew by 36, 30 and 26 per cent in 1989, 1990 and 1991, respectively. In the first seven

Table 14.4 Major Malaysian exports (% of total export value)

Item	1989	1992	1994[a]
Manufactures	54.7	69.8	78.3
Crude petroleum	11.0	8.7	4.5
Palm oil	6.7	5.2	4.5
Sawn logs	6.3	3.7	1.7
Rubber	6.5	2.2	1.6
Liquefied natural gas	3.0	2.3	1.7
Tin	1.8	0.7	0.4
Other commodities	10.0	7.4	7.3

Source: Dept. of Foreign Affairs and Trade, *Country Economic Brief, Malaysia*
Note: a January–July

Table 14.5 Malaysian imports by types of use (% of total)

Item	1990 (Jan.–Aug.)	1992 (Jan.–Dec.)	1994 (Jan.–July)
Investment goods	36.4	42.0	40.8
Intermediate goods	41.3	41.3	43.9
For manufacturing	31.8	32.1	n.a.
Consumption goods	21.5	16.1	14.7
Imports for re-exports	0.8	0.6	0.5

Source: Same as for Table 14.4

months of 1994, imports of investment goods rose by 29 per cent and of intermediate goods by 35 per cent. Total merchandise imports grew by 32 per cent in 1994. Table 14.5 presents the composition of Malaysian imports by types of use.

The high dependence on foreign investment for industrialisation and the consequent repatriation of profits and dividends resulted in consistent deficits on services trade. Freight and insurance payments also place a significant strain on the services account. This is offset to some extent by increased international tourism revenues.

Singapore, Japan, the US and the European Union are Malaysia's major trading partners. Together they account for more than 65 per cent of exports and 70 per cent of imports. The Asian NIEs are also becoming important trading partners. Malaysia's competitiveness with Japan, measured in terms of real exchange rate, has registered a sharp increase in recent years, as the yen continues to strengthen. Its competitiveness with East Asia has also been increasing, albeit slowly. But there is a sign of declining competitiveness with industrial countries taken together.

Table 14.6 Malaysia's trading partners (% of total)

Partner	1989 (Jan.–July)	1992 (Jan.–Dec.)	1994 (Jan.–July)
Singapore	19.2	23.3	20.7
	13.7	15.9	14.4
United States	17.8	18.6	21.2
	16.5	16.9	17.1
Japan	16.5	13.2	12.1
	24.3	25.9	27.0
Other ASEAN	5.8	6.5	6.6
	5.4	4.7	4.6
European Union	14.9	14.8	12.6
	13.7	12.6	12.6
Asian NIEs and China	5.3	3.4	10.4
	4.7	8.0	10.4
Others	20.5	20.2	16.4
	21.7	16.0	13.9

Source: Same as for Table 14.4
Notes: 1st row = exports from; 2nd row = imports to

Table 14.6 shows the geographical distribution of Malaysia's exports and imports. The discrepancy in the shares of exports to and imports from Japan and the US is a reflection of the fact that Japan is increasingly using Malaysia as a production platform for labour-intensive and medium-tech products for exports to the US.

Foreign investment

Malaysia's policy of wooing foreign investment through a combination of attractive incentive packages and the provision of infrastructural support in the export-processing zones has been extremely successful in attracting multinationals. According to the World Bank, Malaysia was one of the top five recipients of foreign direct investment (FDI) in the developing world during 1987–91 (DFAT, 1995b: 15). Strong economic growth, political and macroeconomic stability, availability of trained manpower and good physical infrastructure attracted high levels of much needed foreign investment. Figure 14.1 shows that inflow of FDI increased rapidly after 1989. In response to government policy changes, FDI rebounded in 1994 after a drop in the previous year. In the first nine months of 1994, the Ministry of Trade and Industry approved 457 projects with foreign investment components of US$9.61 million, compared with 390 projects worth

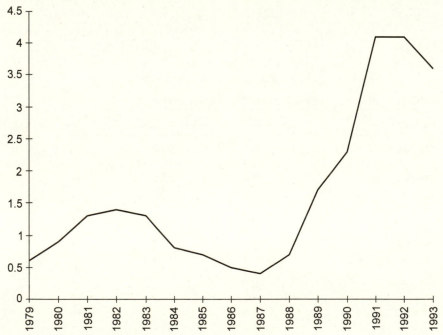

Figure 14.1 Foreign direct investment, Malaysia (US$ bn)
Sources: Key Indicators, Asian Development Bank (various issues)

US$3.23 million in the corresponding period of 1993. In addition to attractive tax incentives, appreciation of the yen and the merger and acquisition activities of multinational corporations also contributed to the high inflow of foreign capital. However, Malaysia will continue to face competition from other low-wage countries.

Taiwan, Japan, the US, the EU and Singapore are the major sources of FDI into Malaysia. In 1990, Taiwan and Japan accounted for 35.8 per cent and 24 per cent of FDI, respectively. Taiwan's share in FDI in 1994 stood at 24.1 per cent and that of Japan at 20.4 per cent. Among the other major sources of FDI, in 1994, the US supplied 11.6 per cent, Singapore 9.5 per cent and Hong Kong 8.2 per cent.

Manufacturing received the bulk of FDI, with concentration in electronic and electrical activities. Chemicals, coal and petroleum products, mechanical equipment and textiles also attracted substantial FDI.

Malaysia is trying to reduce its dependence on multinationals and has a target of a 60 : 40 ratio between domestic and foreign investment. The ratio has increased from 40 : 60 in 1993 to 46 : 54 in 1994. In order to accelerate the achievement of the target, the government has set up a US$1 billion domestic investment fund in the 1995 budget. This will be supplemented by an allocation of US$71.6 million to develop basic infrastructure for small and medium-sized industries.

In line with the general trend observed in other NIEs, Malaysia is turning into a capital exporting country (OECD, 1993). In 1990, FDI outflow from Malaysia stood at US$205 million. The major recipients of Malaysian FDI were Papua New Guinea, Singapore, Thailand and the UK. However, recently the aviation industry in the US and the Japanese services sector have been attracting Malaysian funds. ASEAN as a whole received 23 per cent of Malaysian investment between 1988 and 1993. About 35 companies invested in China, and Malaysian investors are concentrating on the regional niche markets, such as Vietnam and Cambodia, and on raw-material-based industries in which they possess management skills (ADB, 1994: 107). In order to encourage Malaysian overseas investment, a new statutory board, the Malaysia Trade Development Corporation, was set up in 1993, and the 1995 budget has fully exempted income remitted from abroad from tax.

Labour market developments

The continued buoyancy in the economy has resulted in a steady decline of the unemployment rate from 4 per cent in 1992 to 2.9 per cent in 1994. The market for the skilled workforce, particularly in manufacturing and construction, is extremely tight. There is also a shortage of plantation workers. As a result, Malaysia has been forced to rely on foreign migrant workers. According to Asian Development Bank estimates, at least half a million of the total labour force of eight million are foreign workers (ADB, 1994: 103).

Another estimate shows that there are about 200,000 illegal foreign workers in Malaysia (APEG, 1994: 150).

The government imposed a ban on further recruitments of foreign workers on January 8, 1994 to allow the police to complete a crackdown on illegal migrants. The ban was lifted in the middle of the year and the manufacturing and construction sectors were allowed to recruit skilled and semi-skilled foreign workers and to hire from the pool of foreign workers already within the country (ADB, 1994: 104).

Education and training have received the largest ever allocation in the 1995 budget as a response to skill shortage. A host of tax incentives are also offered to the private sector for implementing technical or vocational training programmes or automation projects.

The tight labour market is fuelling wages growth. The wages in the manufacturing sector grew at a rate of 11–12 per cent in 1993 and 1994. Labour productivity growth, on the other hand, lagged behind. According to the Malaysian Institute of Economic Research, the productivity gap is about 6 per cent (DFAT, 1995b: 32).

There is no legislated minimum wage in Malaysia. Industrial relations are governed by the Employment Act of 1995. The industrial system operates mainly on enterprise bargaining. In response to an increase in industrial accidents, the government has introduced an Occupational Safety and Health Act.

The government discourages the formation of national unions and only about 10 per cent of the labour force is unionised. The key private-sector unions are the Malaysian Trade Union Congress (MTUC) and the Malaysian Labour Organisation (MLO).

GOVERNMENT POLICIES

Malaysian development and the role played by the state owe much to the ethnic 'settlement' that was bargained among the Malays, Chinese and Indians at the time of independence in 1957. The leaders of the three ethnic groups agreed at independence to a *modus vivendi*: recognition by the Chinese and the Indians of the primacy of Malay political power and of special rights and privileges for Malays, in return for full citizenship rights and a voice in government. This bargain also meant that the Chinese would continue to have economic dominance as long as they did not challenge the political dominance of the Malays (Bowie, 1988: 54; Alamgir, 1994: 70).

This broad agreement between the three ethnic groups regarding the separation of roles severely limited the state's ability to act autonomously. The *laissez-faire* economic policy in the 1960s can largely be explained in this light. According to Bowie (1991: 74),

Malay leaders, recognizing that Chinese and Indian political acceptance of UMNO hegemony was conditional on the state's not interfering in private commerce and industry, beyond the performance of its traditional regulatory functions, were constrained from imposing any particular vision of Malaya's industrial future on the private sector. Moreover, all parties to the settlement shared a common interest in suppressing claims to special treatment (i.e. state promotion of particular manufacturing industries over others).

Thus, the communal settlement of 1959 contributed to Malaysia's economic growth in the first decade of her independence in at least three ways. First, and most significantly, it ensured that the Chinese economic dynamism was not interrupted. Second, it shielded the state from rent-seeking activities during the import-substituting industrialisation phase of the 1960s. Third, it provided the stability which many decolonised nations like India and Pakistan did not enjoy. This made Malaysia attractive to foreign investment at a time when multinationals were looking for off-shore production platforms. It must also be mentioned that being constrained in its policy towards the industrial sector, the government's development efforts during the 1960s focused primarily on the rural–agricultural sector. As a result, the rural and agricultural sector received the bulk of public investment. Agricultural and rural development spending accounted for 17.6 per cent of public investment during 1961–65 and 26.3 per cent during 1966–70 as opposed to 2.5 per cent and 3.3 per cent for industrial development during the corresponding periods (Bowie, 1991: 69). The focus on the rural and agricultural sector also matched with UMNO's concern to establish its legitimacy with the Malay population, the majority of whom lived in rural areas. The heavy infrastructural development in rural areas contributed significantly to the growth of agricultural output.

The race riot of 1969 and New Economic Policy

Although the *laissez-faire* approach to commerce and industry was found to be congenial to economic growth as it favoured Chinese economic dynamism, it perpetuated 'separate and unequal' development of the three ethnic communities. As expected, most of the benefits of economic growth accured to the Chinese community. This widened the gap between the Malays and Chinese. The small number of new-generation Malay entrepreneurs felt the Chinese competitive edge and began to question the validity of the 1957 bargain. At the same time, the non-Malays were resentful of Malay 'special rights' and felt a keen sense of discrimination (Sivalingam, 1988: 39). The growing ethnic tension culminated in the violent race riot of May 13, 1969.

The events of 1969 represent a major watershed in Malaysia's economic and political history. As mentioned earlier, politically the riot meant an end of the earlier communal settlement on the separation of economic and political roles along ethnic lines. In economic terms, it ended the *laissez-faire* approach to commerce and industry. The Malay political leadership

responded to the riot with the New Economic Policy (NEP) which provided the state with a vehicle for a more active role in economic affairs.

The primary thrust of the NEP was to 'accelerate the process of restructuring Malaysian society to correct economic imbalance, so as to reduce and
eventually eliminate the identification of race with economic function'
(Government of Malaysia, 1971: 1). The state became the main instrument
for this economic reorganisation. With a view to increasing the Malay share
in business and employment a large number of state corporations were set
up along with the introduction of quotas on enrolments for different ethnic
groups in public educational institutions. The government also used a
preferential credit system to channel funds to Malay business and to preferred industrial sectors.

NEP: a recipe for disaster?

According to neo-classical political economy, the expanded role of the state
as proclaimed in the NEP is a recipe for disaster as it distorts the price
signals. In addition, the interventionist state becomes a fertile ground for
rent-seeking and directly unproductive activities by vested interest groups,
which in this case clearly means the Malay ethnic community. One can, in
fact, cite numerous examples where state interventions went wrong. According to Balassa (1991: 148), over half the state enterprises posted loss in 1986.
Among them is the most notorious example of the US$2.5 billion loss by
Bumiputra Malaysia Finance which revealed the corruption and personal
interests of the management (Bowie, 1988: 64). The government's heavy
industries initiatives of the early 1980s were also largely regarded as disappointing (UNDP/World Bank, 1985; MIDA/UNDP, 1985). In particular,
the rapid growth of public enterprises such as Heavy Industries Corporation
of Malaysia (HICOM) resulted in the 'crowding out' of private-sector
industry. These public enterprises have enjoyed preferential access to finance
and the government has not allowed private industries to compete freely
with state enterprises. The public corporations have also enjoyed advantages
in procuring government contracts (Bowie, 1988: 63).

The NEP's education policy and the push for Malay human resource
development has also been responsible for graduate unemployment. For
example, a survey in 1983 found that some six months after graduation 35.5
per cent of graduates who were on government scholarships were still
unemployed (Mehmet, 1987: 89). Yet the bonded nature of scholarships
prevented them from seeking jobs in the private sector. The distortion in the
allocation of skilled human resources is also reflected in the fact that more
than 80 per cent of graduates work for the government and statutory bodies.

There were also macro-level distortions. For example, under the NEP, the
budget deficit increased by 120 per cent from US$476 million in 1970 to
US$1.0 billion in 1971.

Between 1979 and 1981 the Malaysian government had to rely heavily on deficit budgets to sustain the NEP's high economic-growth targets in the face of adverse international economic trends. It could not deviate from its course of high public investment in favour of Malays (Alamgir, 1994: 73). As a result, the federal government debt as a proportion of GNP rose from 10 per cent in 1980 to 30 per cent in 1985.

Malaysia's external debt, too, increased quite alarmingly. In 1983, the total external debt as a proportion of GNP was 49 per cent, well above the developing country average of 36 per cent. The public external debt in the same year was 39 per cent of GNP. The external debt rose to 56 per cent in 1985. (See Jomo, 1987: 124–30.)

Nevertheless, the Malaysian economy has grown remarkably during the past two decades (except for a period in the mid-1980s). It is poised to graduate into a newly industrialising economy. What role did the NEP play in the transformation of the Malaysian economy? Can we regard the NEP as a recipe for disaster?

NEP: a formula for growth with distribution

Although the NEP changed the nature of the inter-communal settlement, in the core of it was the objective of maintaining national unity and political stability. In the words of one of the architects of the NEP, the present Prime Minister, Dr Mahathir (1976: 9)

> [The NEP's] formulation was made necessary by the economic needs of the nation as much as its politico-social needs. There can be no economic stability without political stability and social stability. Thus the NEP is also a formula for economic growth.

Therefore, the most important catalyst role the NEP played in the economic growth of Malaysia was the provision of social and political stability. The NEP proclaimed the uplifting of Malay fortunes as one of the fundamental prerequisites for social stability. It was argued that a more equitable distribution of wealth and a more balanced participation of all ethnic communities in the modern sector of the economy is 'a sine qua non, an indispensable condition for a united Malaysian nation in the longer run and an essential requisite for political survival and stability in the shorter term' (Musa, 1986: 6).

It was also realised by the Malay political leadership that while short-term political and social stability can be achieved through redistribution of wealth and appeasing the Malays, a zero-sum distributional policy would mean longer-term disaster. Thus, the redistribution of wealth was perceived within a growing economy. As stated in the *Second Malaysia Plan, 1971–75* (Government of Malaysia: 1, emphasis added):

The New Economic Policy is based upon a rapidly expanding economy which offers increasing opportunities for all Malaysians as well as additional resources for development. Thus, in the implementation of this policy, the Government will ensure that *no particular group will experience loss or feel any sense of deprivation.*

Thus, the NEP represented a Pareto optimal solution to social and economic problems in so far as the distributional objective was pursued within the context of an expanding pie. It became almost imperative for the Malay dominated government to pursue growth-oriented policies if it were to maintain racial harmony and draw support from all Malaysians. Thus, although the Malaysian state is captured by one particular ethnic community, the ethnic imperatives curtailed the state's ability to pursue narrow distributional objectives at the cost of long-term growth. This conclusion is in sharp contrast with Bowie's (1988: 53) pessimistic view of the Malaysian state that 'in fragmented societies, short-run policies favouring wealth redistribution will take precedence over policies promoting long-run economic growth'.

The NEP's explicit objective of wealth redistribution within a growing economy continued to dominate Malaysia's five-year plans. For example, the *Third Malaysia Plan, 1976–80* (Government of Malaysia, 1976: 7, emphasis added) was formulated

to eradicate poverty among *all Malaysians* and to restructure Malaysian society so that the identification of race with economic function and geographic location is reduced and eventually limited, *both objectives being realised through the rapid expansion of the economy over time.*

Malaysian Industrial Policy Studies and the Industrial Master Plan

As the completion year of the NEP drew nearer, the government commissioned two studies to evaluate the achievements of NEP and formulate policies to ensure that NEP targets are met. The first is the Malaysian Industrial Policy Studies (MIPS) and the second, the Industrial Master Plan (IMP) covering the period 1986–95. The MIPS examined tax and tariff incentives for industrialisation and recommended reductions in the rate of protection. The IMP emphasised 12 key industries and gave details of how linkages and diversification of the manufacturing base could be achieved.

Following the recommendations of the IMP, the government introduced a series of pieces of legislation to encourage foreign investment. These included the relaxation of foreign equity rules in 1986, the freeing of credit restrictions in 1987, and the withdrawal of proposals to abandon tax incentives for foreign firms. The government also introduced the New Investment Fund in 1985 and the Industrial Adjustment Fund in 1987 to encourage domestic private investment.

New Development Policy and recent policy developments

In June 1991, the government announced the New Development Policy (NDP) to succeed the NEP. The NDP replaced the racially based economic and social policy by one of national unity. Although the 30 per cent target for *bumiputra* corporate ownership was retained, no specific deadline was set for its achievement. It was considered that the shortage of Malays with relevant management and technical qualifications was an impediment to the achievement of the *bumiputra* ownership target. Thus, the NDP emphasises human resource development as is reflected in the Sixth Malaysian Plan (1991–95). The Seventh Malaysian Plan (1996–2000) will continue to place strong emphasis on technical and vocational skills training and investment in R&D capabilities in order to reduce dependence on foreign investment and technology.

As a means of reducing the dependence on multinationals, the NDP targeted the development of small and medium-sized industries (SMIs). The Domestic Investment Initiative (DII) was launched with a view to encouraging domestic value-added production, strengthening SMIs and improving the accessibility of the local capital market.

The NDP forms the basis of the Prime Minister Dr Mahathir's 'Vision 2020', named for the date by which he intends Malaysia to attain developed country status. The NDP's macroeconomic and social targets are contained in the Outline Perspective Plan for 1991–2000. According to the Outline Perspective Plan, the real GDP is projected to grow at an average annual rate of 7 per cent and the share of manufacturing in exports is projected to increase to more than 80 per cent.

Although the Malaysian government is very pro-active in its industrial and economic policy, close co-operation between the government and the private sector is an important aspect of the NDP's economic policy agenda. It envisages that the private sector in the new era will play a more leading role. Thus, the government has one of the most comprehensive and broad-ranging privatisation programmes in the region (DFAT, 1995b: 16). The government had privatised 103 entities by May 1994 and over 15 previously government-owned companies which include the national energy company, Tenaga Nasional, Heavy Industries Corporation of Malaysia (HICOM) and Telekom, have been listed on the Kuala Lumpur Stock Exchange. Under the Rolling Action Privatisation Plan 1994/95, 78 projects were identified for privatisation, followed by 77 projects in 1995. The 1994 programme includes the development of seaports in Penang, Johor and Kelang, the commissioning of independent power producers and the development of a new television station. Aspects of the new Kuala Lumpur International Airport, the ports of Kuantan and Kemaman, the National Savings Bank and the housing loan division of the Ministry of Finance were earmarked for privatisation in 1995.

Foreign companies are allowed to participate in these projects provided relevant local expertise is not available, local capital is insufficient and the participation is necessary for export promotion. Foreign equity is, however, restricted to 25 per cent of share capital.

Export-oriented industrialisation remains the main vehicle for achieving the Vision 2020. Government policy is encouraging core dynamic industries that are capable of competing internationally without significant protection. Thus, the government has embarked on an ambitious trade liberalisation program. In 1994, tariff duties on 600 items were cut and the 1995 budget targeted over 2,600 products, most of them food and consumer goods, for tariff reductions. However, the agricultural sector as a whole and some key manufacturing activities such as automobiles, paper and plastic resins and a range of processed agricultural products continue to receive high protection. There is also limited protection for some key service-sector activities.

Although the government wants to reduce the dependence on foreign investment and achieve a 60 : 40 ratio between domestic investment and FDI, it still actively seeks FDI. In order to remain competitive with emerging low-cost countries in Indochina, and with China, in October 1993 the Malaysian government introduced attractive incentive packages which included reductions in corporate taxes and import duties on a wide range of items.

Chapter 15

The Philippines

HISTORY AND CULTURE

The Philippines consists of some 7,100 of the northern most islands of the Malay Archipelago. This island group extends nearly 1,166 km east–west and about 1,916 km north–south between Borneo and Taiwan. While some of these volcanic islands are summits of a partly submerged mountain mass, all are mountainous, and only about 800 of them are inhabited. The two largest islands are Luzon in the north and Mindanao in the south: together they cover roughly 66 per cent of the territory. Another 26 per cent is accounted for by the nine next largest islands, Samar, Negros, Palawan, Panay, Midoro, Leyte, Cebu, Bohol and Masbate.

The indigenous population of the Philippines were pygmy Negritos. The present 'Filipino' people are descendants of the Malays and are divided according to language, religion and ethnic groups. Numerically the two most important ethnic groups are the 'Visayans' who live mainly in the central portion of the archipelago, and the 'Tagalos', in central Luzon. The third largest group, 'Ilokanos', live mostly in the Cagayan valley on Luzon. The southern portion of the archipelago, in particular Mindanao, Sulu and Palawan, is inhabited mostly by the Moro and Samal Muslim groups. Spanish and Chinese descendants constitute the main non-Malay groups. Christianity is the most dominant religion with 83 per cent belonging to the Roman Catholic Church and 10 per cent being members of various Protestant denominations. Only about 7 per cent of the population is Muslim.

The Philippines lacks a common language and about 80 languages and dialects are spoken in the islands. However, Filipino, a Malay dialect, is the official language of the republic. Both Spanish and English are widely used for government and commercial purposes.

Unlike other South East Asian nations, the fragmented nature of the archipelago could not sustain any great indigenous empire or powerful traditional kingdom to lay the foundation for the modern nation-state (Brown, 1995b: 872). Thus, the European settlement in the 16th century did not face much resistance. The only conflict during that period was between the Spanish and the Portuguese who had established themselves in Malacca. The Portuguese threat was entirely eliminated after 1580, when King Philip also became the king of Portugal. However, towards the end of the 16th century other European nations, notably the British and Dutch, began their attempts to acquire a foothold in the Philippines.

The Philippines became a hub of international trade and commerce as the ports of Manila, Iloilo and Cebu were opened to unrestricted commerce, irrespective of nationality, in 1834, 1855 and 1873, respectively. Other Westerners were also allowed to engage in domestic agriculture and manufacturing. These initiatives turned the Philippines into an important producer and exporter of sugar, coconuts and tobacco, and these crop-based businesses still remain the Philippines' major economic activity. There was also a rise of a vigorous entrepreneurial class, mainly of Chinese ethnicity.

In the late 19th century, however, the Philippines was troubled with both internal and external threats. The indigenous middle class that emerged with economic expansion sought reform of the harsh colonial rule. They received support from the masses who became increasingly impoverished due to loss of land to plantations. This led to an attempt at revolution during 1886–87.

The US declared war on Spain in 1898 following the sinking of the USS *Maine* in the harbour of Havana and, under the Treaty of Paris, Spain surrendered the Philippines to the US for the payment of US$20 million.

The US, in collaboration with the leader of the earlier failed revolution, Aguinaldo, established the Philippine Republic on January 23, 1899 and Aguinaldo was sworn in as President. Aguinaldo initially opposed the US occupation, but later took an oath of allegiance.

The US domination of the republic continued until the Great Depression of the 1930s. The US was always uncomfortable with its presence in the Philippines as its people found it difficult to reconcile the ideal of freedom with the acquisition of empire. The US farming lobby also became opposed to the continued occupation of the Philippines as they blamed the importation of crops from the colony for their losses which became worse because of the depression.

Thus, there was a build-up of domestic pressure in the US to leave the Philippines. On March 24, 1934, President Rossevelt signed the Tydings–McDuffie Act under which the Philippines was to achieve full independence in July 1946. The treaty also stipulated a 10-year transition period of internal self-government during which the Philippines would remain under the US control with regard to foreign relations and defence.

Japanese occupation forces landed in the Philippines in December 1941 and Manila fell in early January 1942. On October 14, 1943, the Japanese declared the Philippines as an independent republic within the 'Greater East Asia Co-Prosperity Sphere'. The following year, in October, US forces under General MacArthur landed on Leyte island and they entered Manila in early February 1945; the interim Commonwealth rule was re-established on February 27th.

GEOPOLITICAL DEVELOPMENTS

In the presidential election of April 1946, Manuel Roxas defeated Osmena who had headed the interim Commonwealth government. Immediately after becoming President, Roxas attempted to secure the Philippines' economic relations with the US. After considerable domestic resentment, the Philippine legislature ratified the clauses of the Bell Trade Relations Act. Under this Act, which was passed in the US Congress in 1946, the US allowed, subject to quotas, duty-free entry of Philippine exports into the US market until 1954, and from then on the tariff would rise and quotas fall to reach the US tariff level in 1974. In exchange, the Philippines was required to maintain a fixed rate for the peso with respect to the US dollar and was not allowed to impose export duties. The Act also provided for equal standing of US interests with those of Filipinos in the exploitation of the country's natural resources. The US and the Philippines entered into agreement in March 1947 on the use of military bases and the US received a 99-year lease on 23 bases. Later, the lease was, however, shortened to 25 years.

In 1954, the Philippines became a founder member of the US-sponsored defence organisation, South-East Asia Treaty Organisation (SEATO). The agreement to grant parity to US interests in the exploitation of natural resources was extended in 1956 to cover all economic activities until 1974.

Diosdado Macapagal was elected President in 1961, defeating Carlos Garcia whose presidency had been riddled with corruption, graft and financial scandals. Macapagal introduced far-reaching economic reforms encouraged by the US and the IMF. In 1963, the Philippines lay claim to Sabah when it was included in the Federation of Malaysia and then broke off relations with Malaysia.

The civil unrest that led to the 'revolution' in the late 19th century never died down completely. Philippines society remained deeply divided as the gap between the poor and the rich widened. Initially, it was the *Huks*, an armed group formed against the Japanese, who took up the cause of the masses and agitated, often with violence, against successive governments. When the *Huks* were marginalised, the poverty-stricken people turned to the Communist Party which was waging an armed struggle to overthrow the government. In the late 1960s, during Ferdinand Marcos's second term in office, Philippines society became extremely polarised between the right and the left and there was an alarming increase of political violence and intimidation. The situation became even more volatile when the Moro separatists in the South took up arms.

The Marcos presidency sagged amidst allegation of widespread corruption by his family and friends. But Marcos utilised the political situation to his advantage by proclaiming martial law on the pretext that the country was facing communist threat. Marcos's oppressive and corrupt regime continued in pseudo-democratic form until he was overthrown in 1986 by a civil–military revolt that followed the mysterious assassination of his main political opponent Benigno Aquino on his return from exile in the US.

The 'people's power revolution' swept Benigno Aquino's wife, Corazon to power on February 25, 1986. The Aquino government initiated a new constitution which was ratified in a plebiscite on February 1987 and returned the Philippines to constitutional government, with a US-style bicameral legislature and an executive presidency. Aquino also sought to establish peace with both the National Peoples' Army (of the Communist Party) and the Moro National Liberation Front against the wishes of the armed forces who wanted a military solution.

Although Aquino enjoyed considerable public support, she had to deal with a number of attempted coups by defence personnel and revolts from her own supporters. Following the abortive coup in December 1989, the Congress granted Aquino emergency powers to deal with the economy. This enabled her to impose price controls on basic commodities and temporarily close businesses that overpriced their products.

In late August 1991, the Aquino government and the US provisionally agreed to a treaty regarding the US military bases. This included the withdrawal from Clark Air Base by September 1992 and a new 10-year lease on Subic Bay Naval Base for which the Philippines would receive compensation of US$550 million in 1992 and US$203 million annually thereafter. The US also pledged other economic aid and improved trade opportunities. The armed forces and business lobbied for the ratification of the treaty by the Senate on the ground that the US bases were crucial to the economy. But there was mounting pressure from the people for the closure of the US bases and the Senate rejected the treaty by 12 votes to 11. On September 30, 1992, the US military started vacating the bases, ending the long US military presence in the islands.

In May 1992, Gen. Ramos, who had sided with Aquino during the mass uprising against Marcos, was elected President. He immediately moved to establish peace with the rebels and offered a general amnesty. President Ramos created a National Unification Commission to help frame the government's peace and amnesty strategy. Hope for a peaceful political settlement rose as the NPA's position softened due to its internal conflict and the MNLF dropped its demand for secession. The government signed a cease-fire agreement with the MNLF, which was brokered by Indonesia under the auspices of the Organisation of Islamic Conference. But smaller splinter groups still remain a threat, however minor it may be.

The 1995 congressional elections have considerably strengthened President Ramos against his political opponents. He is now in a position to take bolder steps for both political and economic stability.

THE ECONOMY

The islands of the Philippines are richly endowed with minerals and forest resources. Gold, copper, iron, chromite, manganese and coal are the major minerals. There are also deposits of silver, lead, mercury and uranium. The Philippines boasted a vibrant economy based on free trade and commerce in the 19th century and was the first country in South East Asia to embark on industrialisation. However, it has failed to take off as a full-fledged industrialised country and agriculture still plays a dominant role.

Growth and structural change

The Philippines' GDP is the lowest among the ASEAN countries. In 1993, the Philippines' GDP stood at US$53.3 billion, and per capita GDP at US$824. Between 1981 and 1990, the Philippines economy grew at an average annual rate of only 1 per cent. A number of internal and external factors were responsible for economic recession during 1983–85. GDP declined by 6 per cent in 1984 and by 4.3 per cent in 1985. The economy recovered and grew by 6.4 per cent in 1988. However, the recovery could not be sustained. In 1991, the economy contracted by 0.7 per cent and GDP growth remained virtually flat during 1992. The economy picked up again and GDP grew by 4.5 per cent in 1994 and was expected to grow by more than 5 per cent in 1995.

Table 15.1 Macroeconomic indicators of the Philippines

Indicator	1971–80	1981–90	1992	1994
Real GDP growth rate (%)	6.0	1.0	0.1	4.5
Inflation rate (%, CPI)	14.8	13.3	8.9	9.6
Share in GDP (%)				
Gross domestic saving	26.5	22.3	14.7	15.0
Gross domestic investment	27.8	21.9	22.2	25.0
Current account	−6.0[a]	−0.6[b]	−1.9	−2.0
Debt servicing ratio (% of exports)	13.5[a]	19.5[b]	27.7	23.4

Sources: ADB, *Outlook* (various issues)
Notes: a 1980; b 1985

The Philippines also performed very poorly in terms of inflation. In the 1970s and 1980s, the average annual inflation rate was approximately 14 per cent. However, the inflation rate fell dramatically from nearly 19 per cent in 1991 to 7.6 per cent in 1993, although it rose to 9.6 per cent in the following year.

The low national saving rate is a ramification of the Philippines' continued macroeconomic instability. Its gross domestic investment rate is also considerably lower than in other ASEAN countries.

Table 15.2 Sectoral contributions to the Philippine GDP (%)

Sector	1975	1980	1985	1990	1994
Agriculture	24.7	23.5	24.6	22.4	21.9
Industry	38.1	40.5	35.1	35.7	33.1
Manufacturing	26.0	26.2	25.2	25.4	23.2
Services	36.9	36.0	40.4	41.6	41.3

Sources: ADB, *Key Indicators* (various issues)

However, the economic reform programmes put in place as a result of an agreement with the IMF in 1994 are expected to restore macroeconomic stability. There are signs of increased investor confidence, resulting in high levels of capital inflow. The Philippines also received a pledge for increased assistance from donor countries and obtained a rescheduling of its debts.

The Philippines having been an early starter in industrialisation, manufacturing's share in GDP reached 24–5 per cent by the 1960s. However, the Philippine economy has not undergone much structural change in the past three decades (Table 15.2). In 1994, the share of manufacturing still stood at approximately 23 per cent. An important reason 'behind manufacturing's underperformance and the lack of dynamism is the high level of protection it has received over many years' (ADB, 1994: 110). Agriculture contributed about 22 per cent to GDP in 1994 and provides work for roughly 55 per cent of the labour force.

Although the manufacturing sector in general stagnated, some sectors grew quite rapidly. For example, in 1994, electrical machinery recorded a growth rate of 29.5 per cent and machinery except electrical grew by 16 per cent. Other activities that grew at a reasonable rate are non-metallic minerals

Table 15.3 Share in manufacturing value-added (%, in producer prices)

Industry	1979	1985	1988	Growth rate (%) 1980–91
Food, beverages & tobacco	32.7	37.4	37.2	14.2
Textiles, clothing and footwear	14.8	6.6	10.9	13.0
Wood & furniture	5.8	3.1	4.2	13.2
Paper & printing	7.1	4.2	4.0	12.3
Chemicals	11.0	8.9	12.9	14.1
Petroleum & coal	2.5	2.1	6.0	13.4
Rubber, plastic, pottery, glass	9.2	3.3	7.8	15.1
Iron, steel & non-ferrous metals	4.6	7.0	7.5	29.7
Machinery	2.0	1.0	1.0	15.0
Electrical machinery	4.2	4.5	5.5	20.8
Professional equipment	0.01	0.01	0.01	n.a.
Other	1.0	1.0	1.0	15.0

Sources: UN, *Yearbook of Industrial Statistics* (various issues)

(14 per cent), petroleum (18 per cent), tobacco products (6 per cent), basic metals (5.5 per cent), publishing and printing materials (6 per cent) and food (4.4 per cent). Table 15.3 shows the changing shares of manufacturing activities in manufacturing value added (MVA).

External trade

As a legacy of import-substituting industrialisation, Philippines exports were dominated by agriculture until the early 1980s. For example, in 1980, agriculture accounted for nearly 42 per cent of total merchandise exports. Manufacturing for the export market was encouraged only in the 1970s by offering tax and duty exemptions and establishing export-processing zones where 100 per cent foreign ownership was permitted, and companies did not have to follow the minimum wage legislation. This resulted in a rapid expansion of labour-intensive textile and electronics industries. Further liberalisation measures in the 1980s saw the share of manufacturing in merchandise exports rise from 36.8 per cent (in 1980) to 73 per cent (in 1992). Table 15.4 shows that electronics is the single largest export item, followed by textiles and apparel.

Table 15.4 Commodity composition of Philippine exports (%)

Item	1989	1992	1994 Jan.–June
Semi-conductors	8.2	9.0	10.0
Electrical products & parts	3.5	4.9	5.2
Electronic microcircuits	4.7	3.9	5.2
Apparel of textile	2.4	3.5	3.0
Garments	9.7	11.1	10.6
Coconut oil (crude/refined)	4.4	4.9	2.4
Copper metal	4.1	2.2	2.0
Shrimps & prawns	3.1	2.1	1.9
Others	59.9	57.9	59.7

Source: DFAT, 1994e.

The Philippines' imports structure is dominated by manufactured products, mainly industrial raw materials and capital equipment. The other large item is petroleum and petroleum products. The composition of Philippines imports remained stable during the 1980s. Table 15.5 shows the commodity composition of Philippines imports.

The USA and Japan are the Philippines' major trading partners. However, due to the recent US decision to increase quotas for sugar and garments from the Philippines, the importance of the US has increased. Japan's share declined from more than 19 per cent in 1980 to approximately 15 per cent in 1994 (Table 15.6). However, Japan has maintained its position as a source of imports. The East Asian NIEs are also becoming important as reflected in

Table 15.5 Composition of Philippine imports (%)

Items	1989	1992	1994 Jan.–June
Producer goods	91.4	92.4	91.0
Semi-processed raw materials	44.0	40.1	38.7
Machinery & equipment	23.2	26.4	25.7
Supplies	16.4	20.4	20.3
Unprocessed raw materials	7.7	6.5	6.3
Consumer goods	8.6	8.6	9.0

Source: Same as for Table 15.4

Table 15.6 The Philippines' major trading partners (% share)

Partner	1980	1990	1994 Jan.–June
US	36.5	37.8	38.0
	19.3	20.3	18.4
Japan	19.7	19.7	15.4
	18.3	18.4	18.4
EU	17.7	17.7	16.8
	11.2	11.6	10.4
East Asian NIEs	12.3	12.3	15.9
	19.1	18.9	22.8
Others	13.8	12.5	13.9
	32.1	30.8	30.0

Source: Same as for Table 15.4
Note: East Asian NIEs are Hong Kong, South Korea, Singapore and Taiwan

the rise in their shares both as export markets and sources of imports. However, trade with ASEAN has declined. The depreciation of the peso against major currencies (dollar, yen and European currencies) in 1993 resulted in a slight rise in the Philippines' competitiveness.

Foreign direct investment

The peso's depreciation at the end of 1994 sent a ripple through foreign investors who saw a parallel with the Mexican currency crisis. However, government officials were quick to assure the investors that the Philippines was not Mexico and the central bank moved to tighten domestic credit which pushed the interest rate up. This appears to have averted any major capital flight and cumulative foreign investment rose from US$231.6 million in the first five months of 1993 to US$602.6 million for the same period in 1994.

The Netherlands, the US, the UK and Japan are the major sources of new foreign investment. Most of the foreign capital went to the manufacturing sector and public utilities, in particular communications (receiving roughly

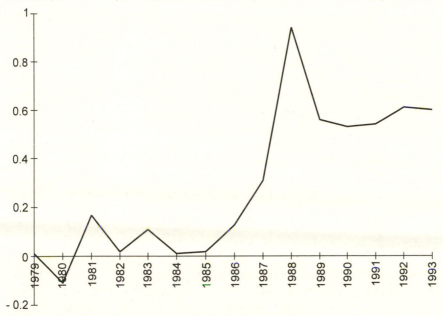

Figure 15.1 Foreign direct investment, the Philippines (US$ bn)
Sources: Key Indicators, Asian Development Bank (various issues)

one-third each). The energy sector received 8.3 per cent of foreign funds. Figure 15.1 shows that the cumulative foreign direct investment (FDI) into the Philippines rose very sharply after 1985, peaking in 1988. It has remained stable at around US$600 million since 1989.

Labour market developments

Both unemployment and underemployment remain high in the Philippines as a result of stagnation in the 1980s. As of July 1994, unemployment rate was 9.7 per cent compared with 9.3 per cent in 1993. The underemployment is estimated at more than 20 per cent.

The general slack in the labour market has kept the wage rate low and there has been no rise in the minimum wage since 1993. The number of industrial disputes also fell. The level of unionisation is very low, as in other ASEAN countries: only 5–10 per cent of the labour force is unionised. In an interesting development, the four largest labour unions forged an alliance in May 1994 under a Caucus for Labour Unity. This alliance aims to minimise disputes and maintain industrial peace.

The Philippines' labour productivity is low and has not increased significantly since 1970 (World Bank, 1990: 76). The low expenditure on science and technology education and R&D has resulted in a shortage of key skills necessary to increase value-added in the economy. This has also held up the Philippines' transition to more sophisticated manufacturing. The Philippines has the lowest number of scientists and engineers per 1,000 of population and the lowest percentage share of R&D expenditure in GNP among the ASEAN countries (World Bank, 1990: 76).

A high proportion of the Filipino labour force works overseas. The workers' remittances form an important source of foreign exchange and help finance current-account deficits. The remittances increased from US$201.7 million in 1980 to US$320 million in 1992. However, out-migration of labour has affected the market for skilled labour (World Bank, 1990: 74). The political fallout arising from the execution of a Filipino maid in Singapore did not spin out of control. Both the private sector and the government are now working to protect the rights of the Filipinos working overseas.

GOVERNMENT POLICIES

The political instability prevented the Philippines from pursuing vigorous economic policies. After the imposition of martial law in the early 1970s, Marcos increased state control of the economy and the management of the economy was carried out essentially by various presidential decrees and 'letters of instruction'. The government set up marketing monopolies for the coconut and sugar industries and special privileges such as subsidised and preferential credit were awarded to companies owned by Marcos associates, known as 'cronies'.

In response to economic crisis, precipitated by political instability, the IMF approved credit facilities and the Philippines was to undertake economic reforms. After the fall of Marcos, the reform programmes were pursued with greater commitment and the sugar and coconut monopolies were abolished. Non-performing assets were removed from the portfolios of the government banks, their operations were rationalised and they were placed on the same footing as other private banks. Government corporate holdings as well as six government-owned commercial banks were listed for privatisation. The government also undertook investment in infrastructure, especially in the energy sector (see World Bank, 1989a, 1990 for policy reforms in the 1980s).

Recent policy developments

President Ramos has launched his vision, 'Philippines 2000' by which he wants to transform the Philippines into a newly industrialising economy. He is continuing the reform programme introduced in the 1980s. In 1993, Ramos removed a major element of macroeconomic instability by legislating the establishment of a new independent monetary authority, the Bangko Sentral, to replace the Central Bank of the Philippines. The legislated independence of the Bangko Sentral will impose some fiscal discipline as well as give the central bank more flexibility in its pursuance of anti-inflation policies. Furthermore, President Ramos has undertaken a major taxation reform programme, including a tougher stance on tax evasion and computerisation of the tax department to enhance the efficiency of tax collection. He also introduced legislation on expanded value added tax.

The Congress passed legislation in May 1994 to allow the entry of up to ten new foreign banks over the next five years. Prior to this legislation, there were only four foreign banks operating in the Philippines. The new legislation also broadened the scope of the foreign banks' operations.

President Ramos also accelerated the pace of privatisation. The government approved the privatisation of its 123 corporations. By the first half of 1994, 28 of them had been sold completely and 72 partially.

Despite strong domestic resistance the trade liberalisation programme is still alive. In July 1994, President Ramos reduced tariff rates on capital equipment from an average of 20–30 per cent to 3–10 per cent. The Tariff Review Board began hearings in March 1994 to address the distortions created by previous Executive Orders pertaining to tariff and quotas and to assess the Philippines' obligations arising from the successful conclusion of the Uruguay Round and the agreement on acceleration and expansion of tariff cuts under the ASEAN Free Trade Area. The Ramos administration aims to achieve a four-tier tariff regime as follows:

(a) 3 per cent for critical raw materials and capital equipment not produced locally;
(b) 10 per cent for other raw materials and capital equipment produced locally;
(c) 20 per cent for intermediate goods;
(d) 30 per cent for finished goods.

The government's stated objective is to have an average tariff level of 5 per cent by 2001.

With a view to encouraging foreign investment, the Ramos administration broadened the Foreign Investment Act of 1991 by removing foreign equity restrictions in enterprises exporting at least 60 per cent of their total products. Under the changed regulation 100 per cent foreign ownership in enterprises serving the domestic market is also allowed, except in areas identified in the 'negative list'. The 'negative list' is reviewed continuously and the areas of exemption are reduced. The government is also planning to remove the current minimum capital requirement for foreign investors and to open up retail trade.

Chapter 16

Thailand

HISTORY AND CULTURE

Thailand, 'land of the free', lies in a central position of the South East Asian mainland. To the north-east lies Laos, to the south-east are the Gulf of Thailand and Cambodia and to the West is Myanmar (Burma). Peninsular Thailand extends southwards to Malaya between the Andaman Sea on the west and the Gulf of Thailand on the east. The Kingdom of Thailand (Siam) once covered parts of Laos and Cambodia in the east and Malaysia in the south.

The indigenous Thai people came from the mountainous areas of Yunan province of China and gradually spread southward into the present-day Laos, the northern part of Vietnam, and northwards into Myanmar and northern Thailand. The first Thai kingdom was established along the river Chao Phraya in AD 1238 and was called the Kingdom of Sukothai. The religion of Sukothai was Hinayana (Theravada) Buddhism, as it still is for the majority of indigenous Thai people. The standard Thai writing system was derived from Indian scripts. In present-day Thailand, there are about 700,000 Malay Muslims in the far south, a smaller number of Cambodians in the east and an estimated 300,000 scattered hill peoples, mainly in the far north and west. The largest minority, apart from the Laotians, are the ethnic Chinese most of whom have assimilated into the Thai culture (Demaine, 1995: 973).

Thailand has a unique history. It is the only country in South East Asia which was not formally colonised by any European power. This was achieved by internal reforms and considerable concessions to European interests. It had to concede to France's claims over Laos and western Cambodia and surrender the northern Malay states of Kedah, Perlis, Kelantan and Trengganu to the British.

The Thai King Ramkamheng (1283–1317) established the Thai power as a major element in the South East Asian political system. In the 15th century, a new centre of Siamese power, called Ayudhya, was established by King Trailok (1448–88). He made the first progress towards a centralised bureaucratic structure, codified the customs into laws and thereby strengthened the Siamese state organisation.

'Ayudhya's position on the central river [the Chao Phraya river], near enough to the sea to become involved in the developing trade between Europe and the Far East, gave it a particular advantage in the accumulation of power' (McVey, 1995: 974). During the 17th century, it became increasingly involved in the rivalries of the European powers, in particular, the Portuguese and French. Finally, King Narai (1657–88) accepted a French military mission to end instability. However, after the death of King Narai, there was considerable reaction against the involvement with foreigners which led to a long period of isolation. This ultimately reduced Ayudhya's resources and power, and the city was laid waste by the Burmese in 1767.

A Chinese war-lord, Taskin, founded a new Siamese state centre at Thonburi, near the mouth of the Chao Phraya river after the fall of Ayudhya, but it was soon overthrown by the house of Chakri in 1782. This marked the beginning of a modern Thai state. The Chakris moved the capital across the river to Bangkok which remains the capital of modern Thailand.

The Chakri kings rebuilt Siamese military power and strengthened the central administration in a bid to counter the Burmese and European threats. They extended their kingdom to Laos, western Cambodia and the northern Malay states. The Chakri kings also improved the efficiency of internal revenue collection by replacing the old tributary system with farming tax. This was made necessary by the imposition by the British in 1855 of the Bowring Treaty which deprived the Thai kings of income from tolls and monopolies on foreign trade. Under this treaty, Thailand agreed to allow free trade in almost all products, to keep tariffs at or below 3 per cent and to limit export duties (Robinson et al., 1991: 5).

The Kingdom of Siam (Thailand) prospered most during the period it suffered unequal relationships with the European powers (McVey, 1995: 974). Thailand had to sign treaties, similar to Bowring, with other Western powers. These treaties, although they meant a substantial surrender of the nation's sovereignty, turned Thailand into an almost completely open economy. The development of the international rice trade, especially after the opening of the Suez Canal in 1869, provided the major source of revenue for the state. Rice exports increased some 25-fold between 1850 and the 1930s and comprised about 30 per cent of world trade in rice (Robinson et al., 1991: 5). Settlement grew rapidly throughout the central Thai plain as rice cultivation extended inland and Bangkok became a major trading centre.

The Chakri kings Mongkut (Rama IV, 1851–68) and Chulalongkorn (Rama V, 1868–1910) had developed keen interests in Western technology and systems. Chulalongkorn was later able to reorganise the state by introducing a modern centralised bureaucracy and fiscal system. The bureaucracy consisted of people drawn from the old nobility and partly of commoners who participated in the rapidly expanding Western education system. The new bureaucratic elite influenced by Western ideology found it increasingly difficult to accommodate royal absolutism and a group of young Western-educated officers attempted to stage a coup in 1912 to overthrow King Wachirawut (Rama VI, 1910–25) in favour of a republic. The king responded by identifying royalty with the new force of nationalism and 'Nation, Religion, King' became the central patriotic slogan. However, a bloodless coup in 1932 brought to an end the absolute power of the king.

GEOPOLITICAL DEVELOPMENTS

Ever since the '1932 revolution', the military have been dominant in Thai politics. The country has been riven by coups and counter-coups since the Second World War. The three officers who led the 1932 coup had varied backgrounds. Pridi was influenced by French utopian socialism and Phibun was a radical compared with Phahon. Pridi's programme of land nationalisation and abolition of private trade was not received very well by the military and a conservative government was established under Phahon. He banned the Communist Party and imposed press censorship.

In 1938, Phibun became Prime Minister and took fascism as his model. He was fiercely anti-Chinese and anti-West, and encouraged Japan to counter the Chinese and Western powers. To mark the new beginning, Phibun changed the name of the country from Siam to Thailand in 1939 and, like Kemal Ataturk in Turkey, imposed dress codes and introduced new words of greetings which he regarded as modern. In order to achieve self-sufficiency, especially in basic military hardware, Phibun undertook state-sponsored industrialisation and oppressed his opponents ruthlessly.

With Japanese help, Phibun attacked French Indo-China in 1940 and acquired Laotian territory west of the Mekong river as well as the north-western provinces of Cambodia. On December 8, 1941 Japanese troops landed in peninsular Thailand from where they marched towards south Malaya. Phibun, now a Japanese ally, declared war on the United Kingdom and the USA in January 1942. As a reward, Thailand got two of the Shan states from British Burma and four southern Malay states which were surrendered by British Malaya.

Although as an ally Thailand did not suffer the worst of treatment by the Japanese, the alliance was not popular with the independent-minded Thai people. The Thai ambassador to the US, Seni Pramoj, always opposed the alignment with Japan and so too did Pridi. The National Assembly formally deposed Phibun in August 1944 and Seni Pramoj became Prime Minister in September.

Under Seni Pramoj, Thailand had a very brief period (1945–47) of civilian rule. The civilian leaders allied the country with the US in order to avoid extensive British demands for reparations. However, the civilian leadership was unable to establish discipline and there was widespread corruption and mismanagement. In November 1947, the army staged a coup which brought Phibun back to power in April 1948. Pridi tried to make a comeback in a failed coup in February 1949 and went into exile in China. In November 1951, Phibun completed his hold on power by a bloodless coup. He ended all that was left of Thai democracy by abrogating the constitution, banning all political parties and ruthlessly suppressing leftist elements. Although Phibun had been an adversary during the war, now, with changed international circumstances, he became an ally of the West against the communists. In 1954, Thailand became a member of the US-led anti-communist alliance, the South-East Asia Treaty Organisation (SEATO). Thus, Phibun managed to receive substantial US military and economic aid.

During Phibun's second dictatorship (1948–57), the military became increasingly involved in the economy and Phibun found it difficult to defend his position against the ambitious generals, in particular the Bangkok army chief, General Sarit. Phibun tried to strengthen himself by drawing popular support and gave elections in 1957. The election was discredited for corruption and the confusion that followed gave Sarit the opportunity to seize power.

Sarit urged the restoration of traditional values and appealed for loyalty to the king. Conservative Sarit had a conviction that Thailand should be open to foreign investors for rapid industrialisation and he removed limits on landholding. When the US became involved in the Vietnam War, Sarit seized the opportunity to take Thailand much closer to the US. He offered Thailand to be used as a US military base and Bangkok became a rest and recreation centre for US troops.

Thailand benefited enormously as the US military built roads and communication facilities across the country. The monetisation of the Thai economy progressed rapidly with increased US military expenditure. There was also expansion of education.

After the death of Sarit in 1963, General Thanon and General Praphat took up the leadership. Although they were less dynamic, the economy continued to boom as a new phenomenon was added to the Thai economy. Japanese began investing heavily in Thai agri-business as well as in trade and manufacturing. In 1968, Generals Praphat and Thanom tried to broaden their power base by restoring constitutional democracy, but in the face of opposition from the conservative Thai military, they had to revert to autocratic rule.

The suspension of the constitution in 1971 caused much public anger. The political unrest was amplified as the economic boom was drying up with the US decision to withdraw from Vietnam. The social and economic upheaval eventually led to the overthrow of the military regime in October 1973 as the military refused to back Thanom and Praphat and the king withdrew his support for them. However, the civilian leadership failed once again to contain the situation. There was growing chaos and disorder. The brief sunshine of democracy ended with the seizure of power by a military-dominated National Administrative Council in October 1976.

Although there were changes within the military leadership and some political liberalisation, the regime largely failed to formulate any viable economic programme. Then came two good fortunes. The first was the discovery of oil and gas in the Gulf of Thailand towards the end of the 1970s which helped restore some confidence in the economy. The second was Vietnam's invasion of Cambodia in the early 1980s. By maintaining its strong anti-communist stance, the regime was able to restore US economic and military aid. The renewed US military involvement was crucial for restoring the confidence of foreign investors. As one observer puts it, 'The involvement of the USA both supplemented foreign investment and boosted the confidence of investors' (Dixon, 1995: 982).

As elsewhere, with economic expansion in the 1980s and growth of the middleclass, there was a growing demand for political liberalisation. Democracy was restored in 1992 and Thailand is now ruled by an elected coalition government. However, the military establishment still remains a powerful force.

THE ECONOMY

An inward-looking Thailand has become increasingly integrated with the regional and world economy since the mid-1980s. The share of Thailand's total trade in GNP has almost doubled since the mid-1970s and stood at 85 per cent in 1993. Export-propelled growth helped raise GDP per capita from US$1,434 in 1990 to US$2,358 in 1994. Thailand is now a major economic player in South East Asia and is vying to become a newly industrialising economy (NIE) by the turn of the century.

Growth and structural change

The Thai economy grew by an estimated rate of 8.5 per cent in 1994 and was predicted to maintain a growth rate above 8 per cent in 1995. As can be seen from Table 16.1, this high growth rate has come on the back of sustained growth of GDP at an average annual rate of nearly 8 per cent for the past two and half decades. In fact, the economy grew at 9.0, 13.2, 12.0 and 11.6 per cent in 1987, 1988, 1989 and 1990, respectively. The driving force behind this exceptional economic expansion was twofold. First, there was a boom in manufacturing exports, which grew by 29 per cent per annum in volume terms. Second, there was the surge in private investment, especially foreign direct investment in the export-oriented manufacturing sector (Robinson *et al.*, 1991, 10).

Table 16.1 Basic macroeconomic indicators of Thailand

Indicator	1971–80	1981–90	1992	1994
Real GDP growth rate (%)	7.9	7.8	7.5	8.5
Inflation rate (%, CPI)	10.0	4.4	4.1	5.4
Share in GDP (%)				
Gross domestic saving	22.2	24.6	33.1	35.0
Gross domestic investment	25.3	26.9	36.7	41.0
Current account	−7.4[a]	−4.0[b]	−6.3	−5.8
Debt service ratio (% of exports)	14.5[a]	25.1[b]	10.5	11.0

Source: ADB, *1994*
Notes: a 1980; b 1985

However, by late 1989, the Thai economy faced infrastructural bottle-necks, especially in transport, port capacity, and water and electricity sup-ply. At the same time, a shortage of skilled manpower also emerged as a constraint to further economic expansion. Furthermore, large inflows of foreign capital increased balance of payment surpluses and resulted in accelerated growth of money supply. Thus, there was inflationary pressure as well as deterioration of the current account.

The main challenge for the Thai policy-makers was, therefore, how best to sustain the economic growth without overheating the economy in the short run and to eliminate infrastructure bottlenecks in the longer term. Policy measures introduced in early 1990 to reduce excess liquidity and dampen credit demand, appear to have been successful in containing in-flation. From the peak of 6 per cent in 1990, the inflation rate dropped to around 4 per cent in 1992 and 1993. However, it rose again in 1994.

There was also a marked improvement in the fiscal position. The public-sector deficit of 5 per cent of GDP in 1984–85 was eliminated by 1987–88 and turned into a surplus of nearly 5 per cent of GDP by 1989–90. The improvement in public-sector savings resulted in a substantial increase in the domestic saving rate, despite a decline in private savings. However, the national savings still fall short of the investment needs for continued growth of the economy. According to the Bank of Thailand's estimate, the current-account deficit in 1994 was nearly 20 per cent higher than in the previous year. Although, the financing of current account has not been a serious problem as foreign investment inflows continue to surpass the deficit, continued sterilisation of balance of payments surplus remains problematic given the limited availability of monetary instruments. The government has recently introduced measures to further boost savings. These include the development of new saving instruments such as negotiable certificates of deposits, tax incentives for private provident funds and contractual savings for education and housing (ADB, 1994: 118).

Thailand's economic growth rates of 8.3 and 7.9 per cent in the 1960s and 1970s are easily comparable with the average annual growth rate of East

Asian NIEs during the same periods. However, what makes it different is that there was not much structural change in the Thai economy in that period. Unlike the East Asian NIEs, the growth in the Thai economy was driven mainly by a limited range of primary products and not by manufacturing. However, the limited structural change in the 1970s reduced the share of agriculture in GDP from 30 per cent in 1970 to 24 per cent in 1980, and the share of primary products in exports dropped from 85 per cent to 70 per cent during this period. Although the share of agriculture has declined substantially, it still remains the major source of employment. In 1991, 58 per cent of the labour force was employed in agriculture. The pace of structural change accelerated in the 1980s (Table 16.2).

Table 16.2 Sectoral contributions to Thailand's GDP (%)

Sector	1975	1980	1985	1990	1993
Agriculture	24.8	23.9	19.1	13.6	12.1
Industry	27.3	30.8	31.6	35.2	39.4
Manufacturing	19.9	n.a.	22.5	27.2	29.5
Services	47.9	45.3	49.4	51.2	48.5

Sources: ADB, *Key Indicators* (various issues)

The economic crises precipitated by the 1979–80 oil-price shocks and the subsequent collapse of non-oil commodity prices forced Thailand to seek Structural Adjustment Loans (SAL) totalling US$225 million and from the IMF which granted a loan of US$596.6 million. As conditions for loans, the World Bank and the IMF imposed some structural reform measures for the Thai economy and recommended stringent monetary and fiscal policies. Although very little of these programmes was implemented, the crises of the early 1980s made the Thai leadership realise the limitations of import-substituting industrialisation and the vulnerability of an agriculturally based economy. Thus, in 1986, Thailand began re-orienting its economy towards export-based manufacturing, and devalued its currency to improve its competitiveness.

As a result of policy changes, the manufacturing sector experienced rapid growth. It grew by 16 per cent in 1989 and 1990, and posted an 11 per cent growth rate in 1993. Labour-intensive electronics and electrical appliances assembling became the most rapidly growing export-oriented manufacturing in Thailand from 1986. The next most important manufacturing activity is textiles and garments which accounted for 24.4 per cent of GDP in 1990. The government is now 'devoting an increasing share of its resources to facilitating the technological upgrading of the industrial base' in a bid to move towards higher-valued manufacturing (ADB, 1994: 117). As a result, technologically more sophisticated products like vehicle parts and accessories, transformers, generators and motors, and optical appliances and instruments are emerging as important activities. The industrial policy also emphasises the creation of backward linkages in the Thai economy (Kunnoot and Chowdhury, 1994).

External trade

As mentioned earlier, until the mid-1980s, Thailand's exports were dominated by a range of agriculture-based products. Thailand is still a major world exporter of rice. After the opening of the Japanese rice market, rice exports from Thailand rose by 80 per cent in 1993–94. With its agricultural exports, Thailand is well poised to exploit the opportunity presented by the successful conclusion of the GATT negotiations.

Starting from a limited array of labour-intensive manufacturing, such as textiles, manufacturing rapidly increased its share of Thailand's exports. In 1993, manufacturing accounted for 75 per cent of exports, whereas its share was only 50 per cent in 1986. Table 16.3 shows the commodity composition of Thai exports. Manufacturing exports grew by 14 per cent in 1993 and in the first quarter 1994 posted an increase of 18 per cent. Among manufactures, exports of plastic products grew by 158.2 per cent, vehicle parts and accessories by 89.4 per cent, transformers, generators and motors by 60 per cent, and optical appliances and instruments by 54.5 per cent.

Table 16.3 Commodity composition of Thailand's exports (%)

Items	1989	1991	1993
Food	33.6	26.5	21.5
Beverages & tobacco	0.3	0.5	0.4
Crude materials	6.8	5.1	4.3
Mineral fuels & lubricants	0.7	1.0	1.0
Chemicals	1.3	1.9	2.2
Manufactured goods	18.1	16.7	19.0
Machinery	17.8	24.2	30.0
Miscellaneous manufactured goods	20.0	22.6	19.1
Miscellaneous transactions & commodities	1.2	1.2	1.0
Re-exports	0.2	0.3	0.2

Source: DFAT,1994c

Thailand depends almost entirely on imports for capital and intermediate goods for its industrialisation. For example, 90 per cent of raw-material needs of the textiles industry were imported in 1991. Imports of capital goods increased by nearly 15 per cent in 1993 and there were significant rises in the imports of integrated circuits and electrical machinery and parts. The rapid growth of the economy has also been fuelling imports of consumer goods. In 1993, the imports of consumer goods increased by almost

9 per cent. Overall, the value of imports increased by 13 per cent in 1993. Table 16.4 shows the commodity composition of Thailand's imports.

Table 16.4 Commodity composition of Thailand's imports (%)

Items	1989	1991	1993
Food	4.5	4.4	3.6
Beverages & tobacco	0.5	0.6	0.5
Crude materials	6.8	6.2	6.0
Mineral fuels & lubricants	9.0	9.1	10.1
Animal & vegetable oils & fats	0.1	0.1	0.1
Chemicals	11.2	9.2	10.0
Manufactured goods	23.0	24.6	20.5
Machinery	37.9	40.5	46.0
Miscellaneous manufactured goods	4.4	3.0	3.2
Miscellaneous transactions & commodities	2.2	1.8	2.4
Gold	0.4	0.5	0.6

Source: Same as for Table 16.3

The US is the largest market for Thai exports, followed by Japan, the EU and ASEAN. In 1993, the US accounted for more than 21 per cent of Thailand's exports. The share of exports going to Japan and the EU in the same year stood at 17 and 16.7 per cent respectively. Whereas no single country within the EU is a dominant market for Thai products, Singapore is the single largest market for Thai exports within ASEAN. In 1993, Singapore accounted for 12.1 per cent (ASEAN 15.5 per cent) of Thailand's exports.

Japan is the main source of Thailand's imports, accounting for 33.3 per cent in 1993. The strong link between capital goods imports and foreign direct investment, both dominated by Japanese companies, has been an important factor in the growth of imports from Japan (Robinson *et al.*, 1991: 35). The second largest supplier of imports is the EU with a 1993 share of nearly 15 per cent. Imports from the US constituted 11.7 per cent and Singapore and Malaysia together supplied roughly 12 per cent of Thailand's imports in 1993. Table 16.5 shows the major trading partners of Thailand. Although there is much emphasis on regional trade, involving Thailand, Burma, Laos, Cambodia and Vietnam, the Indo-Chinese trade remains insignificant. Among the East Asian NIEs, both South Korea and Taiwan feature prominently as sources of imports, and Taiwan features more prominently as an export market.

Thailand maintains a crawling-peg exchange rate system against a basket of currencies. The basket is kept secret in order to prevent any speculative attacks on the currency. However, the nominal effective exchange rate tracks the US dollar closely. In 1994, the Thai currency (baht) appreciated against the US dollar by about 2 per cent and depreciated against the yen and Deutsche Mark by approximately 10 per cent.

Table 16.5 Thailand's major trading partners (% of total)

Partner	1989	1991	1993
USA	21.7	21.3	21.6
	11.3	10.6	11.7
Japan	17.0	18.1	17.0
	30.0	29.4	30.3
EU	19.1	20.7	16.7
	13.9	13.9	14.8
ASEAN	11.5	11.8	15.5
	12.4	12.5	11.8
China, Taiwan, Hong Kong,	9.8	9.7	11.8
Indo-China and South Korea	11.6	13.1	12.6
Middle East	6.2	5.2	4.6
	4.6	3.3	3.3
Others	14.7	13.2	12.8
	16.2	17.2	15.5

Source: Same as for Table 16.3
Notes: 1st row = exports; 2nd row = imports

Foreign direct investment

Although Gen. Sarit significantly opened up towards foreign investment during the 1960s, foreign direct investment (FDI) in Thailand was relatively small until about 1988 (Figure 16.1). However, in the past few years, Thailand has emerged as the third largest recipient of FDI in ASEAN and an Asian Development Bank study notes that Thailand is becoming the fastest growing nation in the region in terms of FDI (DFAT, 1994c: 28). In addition to attractive incentive packages, the rising labour cost in the NIEs and the rising yen are the main factors behind this rise in FDI in Thailand.

Japan is the largest source of FDI in Thailand, accounting for more than 36 per cent of net FDI during 1987–92. FDI from Hong Kong, Taiwan and Singapore accounted for nearly 36 per cent during the same period. In 1993, the proportion of net inflow of FDI from Japan, Hong Kong and Singapore stood at 23.7, 11.2 and 14.9 per cent, respectively. The USA accounted for 19.9 per cent and the UK for 10.6 per cent in 1993.

Manufacturing is the main recipient of FDI. Its share in FDI increased from 20 per cent in 1983 to 53 per cent in 1993. Again, the bulk of FDI went to the electronics and electrical equipment sector and its share rose from 14.3 per cent in 1983 to 44.6 per cent in 1993.

Although Thailand is a capital shortage country, it is taking advantage of business opportunities in the emerging markets. Preliminary figures show that Thai foreign investment abroad more than doubled during 1993. The bulk (about 45 per cent) of Thai foreign investment went to ASEAN. Thai investment in former French Indochina increased by nearly 180 per cent

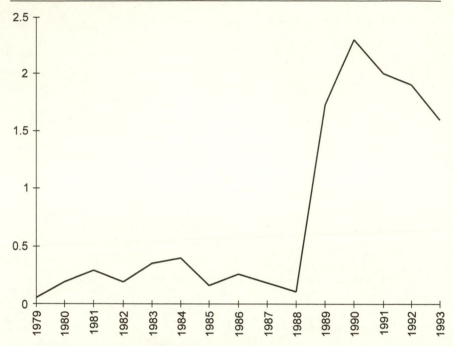

Figure 16.1 Foreign direct investment, Thailand (US$ bn)
Sources: Key Indicators, Asian Development Bank (various issues)

during the first six months of 1993 compared to the same period in the previous year. Thailand is also a major investor in India, holding the fourth largest position in 1993.

Labour market developments

Despite the decline of agriculture, it still remains the main employer. Nearly 60 per cent of Thailand's 33 million labour force find employment in agriculture. However, non-agricultural employment is increasing rapidly and in 1993 grew by 4.2 per cent as opposed to 0.3 per cent in agriculture. The largest employment growth occurred in the construction, manufacturing and transportation sectors.

The unemployment rate fell from a peak of 5.8 per cent in 1987 to 3.2 per cent in 1993 and the tight labour market is exerting pressure on wages. The manufacturing-sector wage increased by 12.6 per cent in 1992 and by more than 6 per cent in 1993. The minimum wage was adjusted upward by 8.7 and 5.5 per cent in 1993 and 1994, respectively. There was also an increase in industrial disputes.

Thailand suffers from skill shortage. Only 20 per cent of the labour force has completed secondary education and Thailand has 15 engineers/scientists per 10,000 of the population. The present government has given priority to skill development, in particular secondary education.

A significant proportion of the Thai labour force works abroad and their remittances are an important source of foreign exchange for Thailand. Over 20,000 workers left Thailand in the first two months of 1994 for overseas employment, representing an increase of nearly 85 per cent over the same period in 1993. The number of workers going to the Middle East and Japan has fallen sharply in recent years. On the other hand, the number of Thai workers going to Taiwan increased more than fourfold.

GOVERNMENT POLICIES

Ever since the Phibun regime introduced state-sponsored capitalism in the 1950s, the state and the Thai military establishment have played an important role in Thailand's industrialisation. The main instrument through which the government directs the economy is that of Thai National Plans. However, since the mid-1980s, the government has been encouraging the private sector to take a leading role as it embarked on a programme of privatisation. Thus, the Seventh National Plan (1992–96) is aimed at reducing government's 'role as the "principal economic stimulator" by limiting public expenditure and encouraging private investment, and becoming the "co-ordinator, adviser and facilitator to the private sector"' (Dixon, 1995: 982).

The government has used a variety of measures such as deregulation, joint ventures, contracting and divestment to privatise Thailand's 47 state enterprises. The private sector is allowed to operate in the rail and mass-transit sector as well as in telecommunications. In addition, the Telephone Organisation of Thailand has entered into joint ventures for mobile phones, fibre-optic communication networks and pagers. From 1996, the government will allow the private sector to meet 50 per cent of the projected growth in demand for electricity. The government also plans to list the Electricity Generating Authority of Thailand and its subsidiary, the Electricity Generating Company, on the Stock Exchange.

As Thailand moves from import-substituting to export-oriented industrialisation, it is also reforming its trade regime. Since the early 1980s, considerable progress has been made in reducing non-tariff barriers, including the proportion of goods subject to import restrictions. The use of specific import surcharges by the Board of Investment to protect domestic industries has also declined sharply.

Tariff changes announced in October 1982 were aimed at reducing the sectoral variation in effective rates by lowering nominal rates to a maximum of 60 per cent. However, the imposition of a special surtax on imports to offset potential revenue losses due to reductions in tariffs on capital and intermediate goods was responsible for the average effective rate of protection (ERP) as well as its variance across sectors remaining high (World

Bank, 1989b: 57–8). The import surtax was removed in 1984 following the devaluation of the baht. Major tariff changes were introduced in April 1985. The most significant of these changes were the reductions of tariffs on electrical and electronic goods as well as inputs into these products. In addition to introducing preferential trading arrangements with ASEAN, Thailand adopted a 'harmonised' tariff code in January 1988. This was designed to make the tariff code more explicit.

In the 1990s, tariff reform has become more important in the Thai liberalisation programme. To begin with, in October 1990, tariffs on capital goods were reduced from 20 per cent to 5 per cent. A second package of tariff reductions on raw materials, intermediate products and certain capital goods, and some finished goods was introduced in 1991. Thailand will introduce further reforms to tariff and non-tariff barriers to trade in agricultural and industrial products, to the protection of intellectual property rights, to regulations governing trade in services, and to trade-related investment measures under the Uruguay Round outcome.

Financial-sector reforms are also in place to complement the reforms in the real and external sectors (see Lian, 1994). These included deregulation of interest rates, abolition of exchange controls and a more realistic pricing of the baht, and reforms of the oligopolistic banking sector and the removal of entry barriers, in particular, for foreign banks. With a view to enhancing savings, steps were also taken to increase the depth of the financial market, and the government is considering introducing new savings instruments such as provident funds and other forms of contractual saving schemes. A mutual-fund industry has emerged as an important competitor for savings deposits. Regulations were put in place for prudential supervision of the banking sector and the functioning of the capital market. The government is also actively encouraging the development of the bond market in order to improve financial intermediation. Thailand has launched its first Export–Import Bank to provide and develop financial support for export growth.

In recognition of the need for FDI, the procedure regarding the approval of foreign investment was simplified in the mid-1980s and applications were guaranteed a decision within 90 days. During 1992 and 1993 the Board of Investment (BOI) introduced very generous incentive packages for FDI to encourage investment in 57 provinces outside Bangkok and its neighbourhood. The whole country is divided into three zones : zone 1 is Bangkok and neighbouring provinces, zone 2 is the central provinces and zone 3 is all outlying provinces. Projects located in zone 3 receive the maximum incentive. They include permanent exemption from import duties on machinery and a three-year exemption on raw-material imports, an eight-year exemption from corporate income tax, tax deductibility of water, electricity and transport, and 25 per cent of installation costs for ten years. The new guidelines for FDI also accord priority to investment in agriculture, animal husbandry, fisheries, mineral exploitation and mining, manu-facturing and services.

Thailand 2000

The Thai government's vision for the the economy at the turn of the century is contained in the National Economic and Social Development Board's 'Thailand 2000' statement released in 1993. Among the projections are:

- double the GDP from US$123 billion in 1993 to US$250 billion in the year 2000;
- increase per capita income from US$2,112 in 1993 to US$3,860;
- raise the share of manufacturing in GDP to 35 per cent and manu-facturing to account for 83 per cent of total exports.

Chapter 17

The People's Republic of China

HISTORY AND MAJOR EVENTS

China covers an area of 9,561,000 square kilometres, slightly larger than that of the United States. After the disintegration of the Soviet Union, China now shares borders with fourteen countries, namely, North Korea, Mongolia, Russia, Kazakhstan, Kirgizstan, Tajikistan, Afghanistan, Pakistan, India, Nepal, Bhutan, Myanmar, Laos and Vietnam.

Relative to its estimated population (at the end of 1993) of 1.89 billion, China's arable land per person is well below the world average. Both China's greatest resource and greatest problem is its huge population. Indeed, the 1.2 billionth baby was born in February 1995 and the 1.3 billionth will come along in just five years' time for, despite a tough family planning programme since 1971, the population has still been growing at a rate of 17 million people per year. The labour force is rising by an estimated 14 million people a year (Perkins, 1994: 30).

The Han Chinese form nearly 92 per cent of the population, and most of the population inhabit the eastern coastal side of the country. Nearly 300 million people in China live in cities or towns, but the other 74 per cent live in rural areas.

With per capita GNP of less than US$400, China ranks 23rd from the bottom among the world's 40–43 poorest countries and the World Bank classifies China as a low income country. However, when GNP is converted into purchasing power parity value, China turns out to be the third largest economy after the US and Japan (IMF, 1993). If the current double-digit growth continues, 'there is every likelihood of it moving into first place within the next three decades' (Yusuf, 1994: 71).

China boasts a very rich civilisation, dating back thousands of years (at least to 1500 BC). There arose in China various schools of philosophy – Confucian, Daoist, Moist and Legalist. However, since about the time of Confucius' death in 479 BC, China has been the centre of conflicts between contending kingdoms (Fitzgerald, 1995).

In 221 BC, the Qin dynasty unified China and imposed a harsh Legalist code of laws and administration. Qin law glorified war and despised art and literature. It promoted agriculture as the foundation of military strength. The Han dynasty replaced the Qins in 206 BC and ruled until AD 221. Unlike the Qins, the Hans promoted art and culture, and during Han rule the use of paper and ink began. The Hans also replaced the feudal system, filled the civil service with educated people, and accepted Confucianism as the state philosophy.

After the confusion and split of the country due to Tartar invasion, the Tang dynasty reunified the empire in AD 618. The Tangs introduced a bureaucracy recruited by public examination open to all literates. It was a highly developed administrative system, and art and literature flourished during the Tang rule.

The Mongol conquered China in AD 1280 in a most destructive war. It was the most oppressive regime and during the Mongol rule huge depopulation occurred, turning great areas of fertile land into wilderness. The Mongol rule ended in AD 1368 with the foundation of the Ming dynasty.

The Mings expanded the limits of the empire and incorporated Manchuria in the north and Yunnan in the south. The Ming rule was autocratic and it sent naval expeditions to South East Asia, the Indian coast, the Persian Gulf, the Red Sea and East Africa. The Ming dynasty fell in 1644 to an internal rebellion, which led to the foundation of the Manzhou or Qing dynasty. The Qings ruled until 1912. It was during the Qing rule that the infamous Opium War was fought and lost, leading to the Treaty of Nanjing which established the Treaty Ports. After that, Qing rule became weakened by internal feuds. Foreign powers took advantage and Russia, France and Japan seized parts of China. The monarchy was finally abolished in 1911 following a revolt of the army at Wuhan.

The erosion of Chinese sovereignty in the face of growing influence of foreign powers, and the despotic monarchy were deeply resented by the people. Dr Sun Yat-sen, a Western-educated physician inspired young intellectuals to revolutionary ideas. He built up a nationalist party and maintained an unceasing effort for radical transformation of China. Although Dr Sun Yat-sen was largely unsuccessful, he became increasingly influential among the young educated Chinese. A student riot broke out on May 4, 1919 in Beijing to protest against the government's secret deal with Japan to hand over the former German port of Qingdao in Shandong. The riot quickly turned anti-Western, in particular against the British. Dr Sun Yat-sen gradually aligned himself with the Soviet Union, and gained considerable support in arms and money. His army and party regained control of Guangzhou in 1923.

The formation of the Chinese Communist Party (CCP) in 1921 marked an important turning point. The two parties (Nationalist KMT) and CCP, initially co-operated with each other, but in 1935 the CCP under the leadership of Mao Zedong organised the 'Long March' to oust the KMT government. The KMT was forced to cease hostility with CCP in 1936 as its own army mutinied, and when Japan invaded China in July 1937 both CCP and KMT armies fought unitedly against Japan.

The People's Republic of China was founded on October 1, 1949 after the victory of the Communist Party led by Mao Zedong over the Nationalists backed by the United States in China's civil war which had broken out immediately after the defeat of Japan in the Second World War. Ever since the establishment of the new government on the mainland, the 'Long March' generation of senior communists have played the major role in national politics and economic policy-making.

Initially, the Soviet Union provided aid and technical support, and played the role model for China, but the two great socialist countries became suspicious of each other over the Korean War. Mao also started doubting the heavily bureaucratic Soviet style of development. He introduced the idea of the 'Great Leap Forward' in 1958 as his favoured approach to economic development. The essence of this approach was to unleash the enthusiasm of the masses, under the leadership of politically inspired cadres of the CCP, rather than controlled by bureaucracy.

The two communist countries eventually broke off relations on ideological grounds after the death of Stalin and the assumption of power by Khrushchev in the late 1950s. The Soviets withdrew their technical aid and experts from China in 1960, forcing China into a very painful adjustment. This, however, turned out to be a blessing in disguise as China did not have to face the kind of adjustment problems that the East European countries encountered after the sudden breakdown of the Soviet Union and the Eastern bloc common market.

Although the CCP mounted a strong ideological attack on the Soviet party, political struggle between hardliners and reformists (revisionists) developed within the Chinese party itself. Very soon, the 'hundred flowers' movement, which was introduced in 1957 and allowed open criticisms of the CCP's methods, was banished by the hardliners. The power struggle culminated in the Cultural Revolution (1966–76) which saw the rise and fall of President Liu Shaoqi and purging of Deng Xiaoping and his followers.

Deng Xiaoping made a dramatic comeback after the death of Mao Zedong in 1976. Two years later, under the leadership of Deng, the Communist Party Plenum in December 1978 adopted the policy of economic reform. The reform leaders strongly believed that Mao's bias against foreign technology and trade had severely hurt China's modernisation.

The younger generations of Chinese who tasted economic freedom following the market-oriented reforms became thirsty for political freedom. Premier Zhao Ziyang emerged as the champion of the democratic movement within the Communist Party. The demand for more political freedom and democracy culminated in the 1989 Tiananmen Square protest which was brutally crushed by the hardliners, apparently with the blessing of China's paramount leader, Deng Xiaoping. Following the massacre, Premier Zhao and his followers were purged and the one-time reformist (revisionist) Deng looked more conservative in the shadow of Mao Zedong. The event looked very similar to the one that purged Deng himself at the height of Cultural Revolution.

However, what made the difference was that the leaders of the Cultural Revolution (the 'gang of four') had been ideological demagogues, whereas Deng is a pragmatist who believes that without economic strength, no lasting socialist state can be built. Deng Xiaoping pointed out that the market mechanism could be a useful tool for China's economic development and, hence, consistent with socialist ideology. Deng's view was formally endorsed in October 1992 by the 14th National Congress of the Chinese Communist Party. The concept of establishing a socialist market economy was enshrined in China's constitution during the first session of the 8th National People's Congress in March 1993.

POLITICAL DEVELOPMENTS AND ADMINISTRATIVE STRUCTURE

The latest version of China's constitution, which was promulgated in 1982 and amended in 1993, describes China as a socialist state of the dictatorship of the proletariat led by the working class, and based on an alliance of workers, peasants and intellectuals. Thus, China's basic political structure remains that of an authoritarian one-party government. Party and government functions are still intertwined. The Party delegates much of the running of China's affairs to a government machine which is organised separately but is subordinate to it. A party committee keeps watch within every institution of government at every level. The Party has not only enforced social control and political discipline through the pervasive role of party branches, but has also claimed absolute command of China's military forces.

By 1994, the Chinese Communist Party (CCP) had about 52 million members, roughly 4.3 per cent of the population of China. Party membership is a benefit in material and professional life, and, in some government bodies, is in effect a prerequisite to advancement.

One has to bear in mind that the ideological breakthrough for a legitimate role for the market was made when the two concepts of 'building the economy' and 'building socialism' were officially accepted in the early 1990s. However, the disappearing border between socialism and capitalism is having serious implications for the CCP – 'its rule has become arbitrary, and hence intrinsically more fragile' (*Economist*, 1995). CCP has never been prepared to lose its absolute power over the changed society. The Tiananmen Square massacre on June 4, 1989 was an example of this determination.

According to the constitution, the supreme organ of state power is the National People's Congress. It makes legislation and treaties, nominates the executive and approves the constitution. It has roughly 3,000 members, indirectly elected from the lower-level People's Congresses every five years. A plenary session of two to three weeks is normally held each spring in Beijing.

The country's administration is run by the State Council (the cabinet) whose members are chosen by the National People's Congress acting on recommendations from the Communist Party. Li Peng is the current Prime Minister and on his second five-year term since 1992.

The first layer of administration comprises twenty-two provinces, five autonomous regions and three municipalities (Beijing, Shanghai and Tianjin). The names of the autonomous regions reflect the concentration of non-Han peoples. The next layer of administration includes 151 rural prefectures and 187 prefecture-level cities, under which there are about 289 county-level cities and 1894 counties.

In addition, four Special Economic Zones (SEZ) were established in 1980 in the southern provinces. Hainan province was later declared as the fifth SEZ. The SEZs enjoy considerable financial autonomy, and preferential treatment for foreign investors.

Hong Kong and Macau will become Special Administrative Regions after their reversion from British and Portuguese rule in 1997 and 1999, respectively. The Chinese government has also offered a similar model to Taiwan upon reunification.

THE ECONOMY

In a nutshell, the most remarkable feature of China's economy for the past 15 years has been rapid economic growth; the real annual rate has averaged close to 10 per cent since 1978, making China the world's fastest growing economy (Jefferson and Rawski, 1994: 47). Furthermore, although the initial 'reform efforts that began as experimental changes aimed at improving performance rather than...establishing a Western-style market system' (Jefferson and Rawski, 1994: 47), they have been responsible for fundamental structural changes and put China firmly on the road to a market economy. The reform operations have become more systematic and sweeping in every part of Chinese society since 1993.

Productivity gains due to reforms have permitted substantial improvements in real incomes and living standards, and notable progress has been made in reducing poverty. In 1987, the proportion of population living in absolute poverty was over one in four. Since then the proportion has fallen to one in twelve, or about 100 million in a population of 1.2 billion. Meanwhile workers' real earnings have doubled or tripled, and in comparison to 1987, China's GDP quadrupled in 1994. Tables 17.1–5 highlight some basic features of China's recent economic performance and structural change.

Table 17.1 Selected macroeconomic indicators (annual percentage changes)

Indicator	1980	1984	1988	1992	1993
Real GNP	7.9	14.7	11.3	13.0	13.4
Real gross industrial output	9.3	16.3	20.8	22.0	21.1
Real gross fixed investment	2.9	22.7	10.4	28.2	22.0
Retail prices (period average)	6.0	2.8	18.6	5.3	13.0
Merchandise exports (US$)	33.7	15.4	18.2	18.6	8.0
Merchandise imports (US$)	24.8	27.6	27.4	26.2	29.0
Foreign debt (US$ billion)	n.a.	n.a.	n.a.	69.3	72.5
Debt service ratio (% of exports)	n.a.	n.a.	n.a.	13.2	13.2
Current account (% of GNP)	0.3	0.8	−1.0	1.8	−2.5
Overall budgetary balance (% of GNP)	−3.3	−1.5	−2.4	−2.5	−2.1

Sources: State Statistical Bureau, *China Statistical Yearbook*, various issues; IMF, *International Financial Statistics*, various issues

Table 17.2 Comparative economic indicators, 1993

Indicator	China	India	USA	Japan
GDP (US$ billion)	544.6	227.4	6,378.0	4,223.0
GDP per capita (US$)	459.5	256.0	24,700.0	33,850.0
Manufacturing % GDP (Including utilities)	51.7	26.9	18.3	27.9
Agriculture % GDP	21.2	32.3	2.3	2.2
Exports of goods (US$ bn)	75.7	24.1	456.8	351.3
Imports of goods (US$ bn)	86.3	25.1	589.2	209.8
Foreign trade % GDP	29.7	21.6	16.4	13.3

Sources: National sources; Economist Intelligence Unit

Table 17.3 Sectoral contributions to China's GDP (%)

Sector	1989	1990	1991	1992	1993
Agriculture	26.3	28.3	26.1	23.8	20.1
Industry	39.0	37.4	38.2	40.6	41.0
Construction	4.8	4.8	5.0	5.8	6.6
Transport	3.4	4.5	4.4	4.0	3.6
Commerce	8.8	6.5	8.4	8.9	8.1

Source: State Statistical Bureau, *China Statistical Yearbook*, 1994

Table 17.4 Industrial enterprises by ownership, end-1993

	000s	% of total
Total	9911.6	100.0
State-owned	104.7	1.1
Collectives	1803.6	18.2
Township-owned	209.8	2.1
Village-owned	777.3	7.8
Privately owned	7971.2	80.4

Source: Same as for Table 17.3

Table 17.5 Growth rate of gross value-added of industry output by ownership

	1990	1991	1992	1993	Average annual growth (1980–92)
State-owned	2.7	8.3	13.1	9.1	7.8
Collectives	6.2	18.4	32.3	40.2	18.4
Private	47.4	40.7	51.8	64.3	64.9[a] 37.2[b]

Sources: Department of Foreign Affairs and Trade, *Country Economic Brief: China, 1984; Economic Daily*, May 12, 1995 and Jefferson and Rawski, 1994
Notes: a private firms employing less than 8 workers; b private firms with more than 8 employees

Observers attribute China's impressive growth performance in GDP, exports and investment predominantly to reforms (see Perkins, 1994; Jefferson and Rawski, 1994; IMF, 1993). However, there were other favourable factors. To begin with, the pre-reform Chinese economy was more decentralised, being dominated by small-scale enterprises rather than large-scale industrial organisations, and had a weaker planning bureaucracy than the other command economies of the former Soviet Union and Eastern Europe (Hussain and Stern, 1995: 161). Secondly, China did not have to struggle with stabilisation as, unlike East European countries, China enjoyed relative macroeconomic stability (Hussain and Stern, 1995: 162); it had no foreign debt to pay off in 1978 and inflationary pressure was largely absent in the early 1980s (Table 17.1). Furthermore, China did not have to find new export markets, as most East European countries did after the break-up of the Council for Mutual Economic Assistance (Comecon). The Chinese connections with Hong Kong and Taiwan also helped China in attracting foreign investment, and expanding manufacturing and trade (Hussain and Stern, 1995: 162). According to Chen *et al.* (1992), the financial, commercial and technical capabilities of Chinese communities in Hong Kong, Taiwan, and throughout the Asia-Pacific region, magnified the impact of China's open-door policy. Perkins (1994: 33–4) puts the impact of Chinese connections more succinctly as: 'connections with Hong Kong probably account for much of China's success.... In effect, the formidable marketing talents of Hong Kong and Taiwan are being grafted onto the manufacturing capacity of the mainland.' (See Jones *et al.*, 1993 for a good discussion of economic integration between China, Taiwan and Hong Kong.)

In addition to the rise in the share of manufacturing and the decline in the share of agriculture, an important feature of structural change of the Chinese economy is the rise of the non-state private sector. Putterman (1992) calls this 'nonstate–nonstaple' third sector. As can be seen from Table 17.4, by the end of 1993 more than 80 per cent of enterprises were privately owned. Their share in national output increased from less than 1 per cent in 1980 to 14 per cent in 1992, while the share of state-owned enterprises (SOEs) dropped from 76 per cent to 48.4 per cent. The index of output of privately owned enterprises grew by 64.9 per cent annually during 1980-92 as opposed to an average annual growth of only 7.8 per cent for SOEs and 18.4 per cent for collectives (Table 17.5). In 1994, employment in SOEs and collective enterprises dropped by 300,000 and 1.82 million, respectively, whereas employment in other forms of enterprise rose by 2.12 million.

In sum, the above shows that the Chinese reforms have been largely successful in enhancing economic performance and accelerating structural change towards a market economy.

ECONOMIC REFORMS

China's economic reform process is 'gradual' as opposed to what is termed 'shock therapy' or 'big bang' in the context of East European economic reforms. The Chinese leaders named their reform method 'crossing the river by feeling the stones underfoot'. According to Naughton (1994), China's reform path is more akin to 'growing out of the plan'. Since Deng Xiaoping and his reformist associates had no economic reform blueprint other than a strong desire to turn China into a wealthy and powerful state, 'they were willing to try almost anything if it worked' (Perkins, 1994: 23). In such circumstances, 'a gradual approach to economic reform was inevitable' (Perkins, 1994: 23).

Most of the reforms were undertaken initially on an experimental basis. If they went wrong, the government was quick to bury them. However, in most cases, the pilot reform measures were further fine-tuned and re-introduced in a more sophisticated fashion. After 15 years, this gradualism is still favoured in China. What China has achieved since it embarked on economic reforms in 1978 can be attributed to its attention to the following points:

1 The end justifies the means. Today's reform in China is a continuous and gradual process as it required the destruction of one system ('growing out of the plan') and the building of another. The slowness and some confused moments are exactly the price for China to complete the transition and to minimise the suffering for people caught out in the quiet revolution.

2 An entire new social infrastructure has to be built and introduced to a people who know very little about it. In moving away from the old system to a new system, a lot of interim arrangements have to be made, but there could be more corruption during the life of such interim policies. The hiccups witnessed by many in the reform of China's price system, taxation system and foreign exchange are just a few examples.

3 The removal of an ideological barrier which has been in place for a generation is a problem peculiar to China and not to be observed in other developing countries. Answers to questions like 'why the Communist Party has to adopt an economic system from capitalism' may appear more apparent today, but were very difficult to handle, say 10 years ago.

4 Sequencing the reform measures according to the most binding constraints. For instance, at the beginning, the rural and foreign sectors were selected for reforms as per capita grain output stagnated and it was believed that Mao's bias against foreign technology and products had hurt the economy most. Later when the reforming SOEs faced difficulties, the financial sector and the welfare system as well as the infrastructure were identified for further reforms.

5 Finally, to regard economic reform as a dynamic programme in which non-profitable activities will be squeezed out by more vibrant sectors. For example, instead of a large-scale privatisation programme or bankruptcy of SOEs, the reduction in the role of SOEs was achieved by letting the dynamism of the private sector grow while SOEs struggled to survive (see Table 17.5).

Rural-sector reforms

Inspired by the Soviet forced collectivisation of agriculture, the Chinese state used artificially low farm prices and forced extraction of farm products as a means of keeping real state wages and state-sector profit and accumulation rates high (Putterman, 1992: 474). In other words, the rural sector was called upon to bear the burden of capital accumulation in the name of 'comrades' voluntary contributions'. The most damaging result of this policy was the stagnation of the agricultural sector. For example, per capita grain production in 1978 had remained almost the same since the mid-1950s.

The twin components of Chinese rural reforms were gradual decollectivisation and freeing of the agricultural markets. In the late 1970s and early 1980s the huge collective farms began to be broken up. Land remained in theory in state ownership, but was leased out to farmers, initially for 15 years. The term of lease has recently been extended to 30 years. Since the early 1990s, buying and selling of long-term land leases (especially for factory use) have been allowed; this has typically involved guaranteeing a basic grain ration to those giving up their land-use rights.

Under the 'household responsibility system' which replaced the collectives, farmers grow grain and other staples under contract to the state which also extracts taxes calculated as a percentage of the harvest. Once these obligations are fulfilled, farmers may grow what they want, selling excess grain or cash crops at market prices. About 60 per cent of agricultural commodities were transacted on competitive markets by the second half of the 1980s, compared with only 8 per cent at the start of reforms in 1978. By 1990, about half of all grains, 75–80 per cent of fruit and vegetables, and 80 per cent of all agricultural commodities were bought and sold on 'free' markets. Recently, there has been talk of freeing up agricultural prices altogether.

The rural reforms produced spectacular results. Grain production rose from a trough of 150m tonnes in 1960 to a record of 456m in 1993 (*Economist*, 1995). This success provided the foundation from which other reform programs were launched.

External-sector reform

The external-sector reforms introduced in 1979 were aimed primarily at facilitating exports of manufactured products. The measures included various export subsidies, devaluation of the currency and the establishment of SEZs (export-processing zones). The reform measures also allowed foreign investment for the first time. (See Fukasaku and Wall, 1994, Nicholas, 1992 and Cheng, 1992 for details of China's external-sector reforms.)

The SEZs offer foreign investors a variety of incentives which include:

- an enterprise tax of just 15 per cent and possible tax exemption for up to 10 years of continuous operation;
- no income tax on the portion of profits being remitted;
- income tax on dividends, interests, rents, royalties or other incomes to non-residents not having operations in China reduced to 10 per cent;
- exemption from consolidated industrial and commercial taxes on building materials, production equipment, raw materials, parts and components, transportation vehicles, and office equipment imported for their own use;
- exemption of export customs duties on all export products, except those restricted by the state;
- exemption of customs duties on household goods and personal vehicles imported by foreign investors and their staff and technicians for their own use;
- same priority treatment for export-oriented enterprises employing advanced technologies in the supply of water, power, and transportation and communication services that domestic state-run enterprises enjoy;
- special permission in Pudong Zone for foreign businesses to open financial institutions, departmental stores, supermarkets, and other service enterprises.

The results of external-sector reforms were once again dramatic. China's exports grew at an average annual rate of 16 per cent and its imports at 15 per cent, transforming a fundamentally inward-looking country into one of the world's ten largest trading nations. Between 1982 and 1994, China signed investment protection agreements with 65 countries, and over the past decade has attracted more than US$90 billion of foreign direct investment (FDI). Foreign-owned and joint-venture firms accounted for 27.5 per cent of China's exports in 1993, and for all of the growth in its exports over 1992 (*Economist*, 1995). Thus, the economy has become more open and integrated with the rest of the world through trade and investment (Tseng *et al.*, 1994: 1).

Table 17.6 China's main trading partners, 1993

Exports to	US$ (m)	Share
Hong Kong & Macau	22,063.9	24.0
USA	16,964.0	18.5
Japan	15,779.4	17.2
Germany	3,968.5	4.3
South Korea	2,860.2	3.1
Russia	2,691.8	2.9
Singapore	2,245.0	2.4
UK	1,928.6	2.1
Netherlands	1,608.8	1.8
Taiwan	1,461.8	1.6

Imports from	US$ (m)	Share
Japan	23,253.3	22.4
Taiwan	12,933.1	12.4
USA	10,688.1	10.3
Hong Kong	10,472.7	10.1
Germany	6,039.8	5.8
South Korea	5,359.9	5.2
Russia	4,987.4	4.8
Italy	2,737.4	2.6
Singapore	2,645.6	2.5
Australia	1,949.0	1.9

Source: State Statistical Bureau, *China Yearbook*, 1994

Table 17.6 shows the importance of Hong Kong and Taiwan for China's trade and industrial expansion. The emergence of a so-called growth triad of the three Chinese economies becomes clearer when foreign investment flows are considered. Table 17.7 presents distribution to FDI in China by source.

Table 17.7 Foreign direct investment in China, 1979–93

Source	US$ bn	Share %
Hong Kong & Macau	150.9	68.0
Taiwan	28.4	8.3
USA	14.4	6.5
Japan	8.9	4.0
Singapore	3.0	2.2
UK	3.0	1.4
Thailand	2.1	0.9

Source: Ministry of Foreign Trade and Economic Cooperation, reported in *China Economic News*

As can be seen, Hong Kong and Macau and Taiwan account for more than 75 per cent of accumulated FDI in China. The Economist Intelligence Unit estimates that percentage of foreign capital in China of overseas Chinese origin is 78.5 per cent and believes that if ethnic Chinese investors from the USA, Canada, Thailand and Australia are included, this figure would be even higher (EIU, 1995).

Hong Kong has had an enormous part in introducing foreign capital into China, especially southern China. In more recent years, however, a sizeable but unknown proportion of mainland Chinese money has been invested in China through Hong Kong as foreign investment. In order to qualify for tax exemptions, and to make it easier to take capital out of the country, a large number of Chinese investors have established Hong Kong shelf companies (unofficial subsidiaries) and posed as 'foreign investors'. Through these companies, billions of dollars of Chinese money have left the country, mostly to be parked in Hong Kong. A large proportion of this money is then reinvested in China, as foreign investment, a phenomenon which EIU (1995) terms 'round-tripping'.

During 1986-93, China maintained a dual exchange rate system. The official rate was adjusted periodically while a more depreciated market rate was determined in the Foreign Exchange Adjustment Centres (the swap market). A new unified exchange rate system was introduced on January 1, 1994, and is determined in an interbank market. On April 1, 1994, the China Foreign Exchange Trading System (CFETS) became operational. CFETS is situated in Shanghai, and it is a nationally integrated electronic system for foreign exchange trading. It has largely eliminated the fragmentation of the foreign exchange market. Any financial institution wanting to participate in the new system must become a member of CFETS. More than 200 financial institutions had become CFETS members by May 1994. However, not all local banks and their branches are allowed to buy and sell foreign currencies among themselves on their own account. Foreign banks and other financial institutions may sell foreign currencies or trade among themselves only on behalf of their customers.

Recently the State Administration of Exchange Control (SAEC) has expressed concerns regarding some discrepancies in foreign exchange policies between the 13 'bonded zones' and other areas which have 'resulted in some management problems'. While business activities in the bonded zones can be settled in foreign currency, the circulation of foreign currency outside the zones is restricted. But an increasing number of institutions in other areas have been buying large quantities of foreign currency from inside firms as a way of skirting the restrictions. To overcome this problem, the SAEC issued new regulations effective from January 1, 1996, strictly prohibiting enterprises in the bonded zones from selling foreign exchange earnings to financial institutions outside. Under the new system domestic and foreign firms in the bonded zones can open foreign exchange accounts without approval, but they can only have one principal account, which must be held with a bank in the same zone. Since China still strictly controls the capital accounts, domestic and foreign firms will receive the same treatment on their current account, but not on their capital account.

The unification of its two-tier exchange rate system and effective devaluation of the renminbi by approximately 33 per cent helped China raise its export competitiveness. Exports rose by 30 per cent to US$120 billion in 1994 as opposed to a 10 per cent rise in imports, turning a balance of payments deficit of US$12.2 billion in 1993 to a surplus of US$5.3 billion. The inflow of FDI also jumped to US$28.8 billion in 1994 from US$27.5 billion in 1993. As a result of improved trade performance and increased FDI flows, the official foreign exchange reserve rose sharply from US$22.4 billion at the beginning of the year to US$49 billion at the end of November 1994.

Thus, just as with rural reforms, the slow reform experiment in the external sector became pervasive, and, by 1993, the role of planning in external trade became quite limited. For example, mandatory export planning was abolished in 1991 and budgetary subsidies to Foreign Trade Corporations for exports were eliminated. Likewise, by 1992, planning for imports accounted for about 18 per cent of total imports and covered only 11 broad product groups. The scope for mandatory import planning was further reduced in 1993 to cover only five broad product groups (Tseng *et al.*, 1994: 1). Since October 1993, the Ministry of Foreign Trade and Economic Cooperation has published 93 documents governing trade and has rescinded 744 internal documents. The Foreign Trade Law was enacted and became effective on July 1, 1994. The exchange rate reform of 1994 and liberalisation measures included in the Foreign Trade Law are designed to meet GATT's principles.

State-owned enterprise (SOE) reform

In 1978, just before the reforms programme was introduced, SOEs accounted for 78 per cent of China's industrial output. These enterprises operated under strict planning guidelines set out by the state economic bureaucracy, and managers had hardly any authority over investment planning and production scheduling, raw-materials purchase, research and development or marketing. The wage structure and employment levels, too, were dictated by the state planning machinery.

The reform of SOEs was sequenced to follow the rural- and external-sector reforms, and the first tentative attempt at SOE reform was made in 1980. The program allowed enterprises to retain a modest share of profits and transact any output over and above the mandatory targets on decentralised semi-markets. These measures, which supplemented the 'open-door policy' towards international trade and investment, were designed to give some incentives to managers in order to improve SOEs' performance.

A more systematic effort to reform SOEs began in 1984. Like the rural reforms, the SOE reform package also involved two innovative measures. The first is dual pricing and the second, the enterprise contract responsibility system. The dual pricing system gave a more formal structure to the emerging market trend that followed once the SOEs were allowed to engage in market transactions for surplus output. Under this system, output supplies are partitioned into plan and market components and SOEs are increasingly responding to the market signals, resulting in the reduction of the planned component. As SOEs' production decisions become increasingly market-driven, less and less inputs (materials) are being allocated by plan. For example, in 1978 about 700 kinds of producer goods were allocated by plan, but, by 1991, the number had fallen below 20. At the same time, bank loans are replacing budgetary allocations as the chief source of external funding. Thus, both production decisions and allocation of resources have become increasingly market-based.

Under the contract responsibility system, the people involved in the running of an enterprise – managers and the workforce – agree to fulfil specific obligations in return for extensive control over the operation of the enterprise and retention of a substantial portion of (or the entire) excess profit. The contractual obligations typically involve targeted profits, delivery of profits to the state, and productivity increases.

The industrial reform produced some dramatic results. For example, between 1980 and 1992 the real output in industry grew at an annual average rate of 13.1 per cent, resulting in nearly a fivefold increase in industrial output (Burki, 1995: 163). As mentioned earlier, there has been a striking change in the pattern of ownership of industrial assets. While there was no privately owned industry in 1980, private enterprises accounted for 7 per cent of industrial output by 1992 (Burki, 1995: 161).

Although SOE reforms have been responsible for moving China's industrial sector towards a market system, by any measure – productivity, profitability, returns on assets – the state sector remains vastly inferior to the non-state firms. Even after the introduction of the reform package, both the scale and the volume of SOEs' losses are moving upward. According to the State Statistics Bureau's 1994 report, of 72,400 SOEs, 28,300 suffered loss. Many SOEs are chronically overstaffed. About 70 per cent of China's industrial workers are still employed by the state. Indeed, employment in the state sector has risen by 25 per cent since 1985.

Why has a very similar reform package been largely successful in vastly improving rural performance, but largely failed in the case of SOEs? According to Perkins (1994), the answer lies in the more complex nature of the industrial sector. Unlike the small-scale rural sector, large industrial enterprises are tied with other institutions such as the banking system and the tax system, and require much clearer legal and property rights at the core of the incentive structure. Therefore, the full realisation of the benefits of industrial reforms depends crucially on reforms of these interlocking sectors.

Furthermore, the Chinese SOEs are an integral part of the social welfare system as roughly a quarter of the population depend on the health and housing benefits derived from SOE employment. An estimated 30–40 per cent of SOE employees would lose their jobs if the SOEs were forced to operate on strictly commercial basis. As the experience of Eastern Europe shows, the human cost of wide-scale privatisation and bankruptcies before putting in place some social safety net would be enormous. As Burki (1995: 165) puts it, 'The leadership is unwilling to risk social instability in order to improve enterprise efficiency'.

One of the reasons for the gradualism in their approach to reforms, is the Chinese leadership's understanding of the above complexities. No matter how slow the Chinese reform may appear, it will continue, and the 1990s will witness the gradual reform of the other related sectors. (See Broadman, 1995 for a comprehensive discussion of challenges facing China's enterprise reform.)

REFORMS IN THE 1990s

In an effort to revitalise and restructure the economy, the reform leaders in China have focused on reforms of banking, public finance, the legal system and the social welfare system.

Financial reform

Under the old system, the People's Bank (central bank) performed both central and commercial banking functions. Bank loans were allocated on the basis of directives received from the economic bureaucracy in line with planned targets. There was no effective control of money supply as both the state and any sick SOEs could borrow from the bank almost without limit.

Although the People's Bank of China was formally entrusted with central banking functions in 1984, its control over the money supply was weak. In the face of intense demand for financing from provincial governments which became increasingly powerful, bank credit expanded rapidly at an annual average rate of 23.6 per cent during 1987–92 (Yusuf, 1994: 86). The People's Bank put up minimal resistance to breaching of annual credit targets as governments at all levels and SOEs pursued their aggressive development strategies.

The process of thoroughly overhauling the banking system began in 1993. The program included the transformation of the People's Bank into a kind of Chinese Federal Reserve. A very bold attempt was made at the National People's Congress in March 1995 to make the People's Bank of China independent from the executive arm of the government and to remove it from the political influence of the Communist Party. However, in the face of strong opposition, a compromised central bank law was passed. The new law renders local branches of the People's Bank independent of local governments.

The separation of the central and commercial banking functions began in 1987 when nine banks, led by the Bank of Communications, formed commercial banks. There are now eight 'comprehensive' banks authorised to engage in commercial operations. Although the banks are still granting loans for reasons of government policy, pressure is growing to make their operations based on commercial considerations. In order to ease the financing pressure on the commercial banks, the government established the State Development Bank (SDB) in 1994. The SDB is mandated to finance priority projects with long payback periods, particularly large-scale infrastructure schemes. In addition, two other policy banks, the Import & Export Credit Bank and the Agriculture Development Bank, have been set up to take over policy loans held by existing state-owned banks with the expectation that it would allow existing state-owned banks to operate in a genuine commercial environment. There are also two more specialised banks, the Industrial and Commercial Bank and the Construction Bank. It is expected that the setting up of these specialised policy banks would allow increased transparency and accountability in lending for large state-sponsored projects. Foreign banks are also being allowed to operate and 118 foreign banks with total assets of over $13 billion are coming to China. The flow chart (Figure 17.1) depicts the banking sector in China.

Funding government deficits by 'printing money' (borrowing from the central bank) was a prime cause of the inflation which began to surge in 1993. It was also felt that the old practice of coercing state employees to buy government bonds through payroll deductions was deeply unpopular. It was quite easy to attract savings which are generally 'kept under the mattress' by offering attractive returns. This led to the development of a secondary capital market, and the government began issuing bonds underwritten by financial institutions in 1990. Since then, the secondary capital market has developed very rapidly. Government treasury bond issuance increased tenfold between 1990 and 1994 and a record issue of more than Rmb 113 billion (renminbi) was disposed of in 1994 without much difficulty.

In 1990, two stock exchanges were opened in Shanghai and Shenzhen. Although the markets have been extremely volatile, by the end of 1994, the stock capitalisation had reached US$43.5 billion and there were over 300 listed companies (Spencer, 1995: 28). There are two categories of shares: category 'A', denominated in renminbi, are open to Chinese investors and 'B' shares, denominated in foreign currency – US dollars in Shanghai and Hong Kong dollars in Shenzhen – are intended for foreigners. However, the distinction between 'A' and 'B' shares is unlikely to last for long as joint ventures

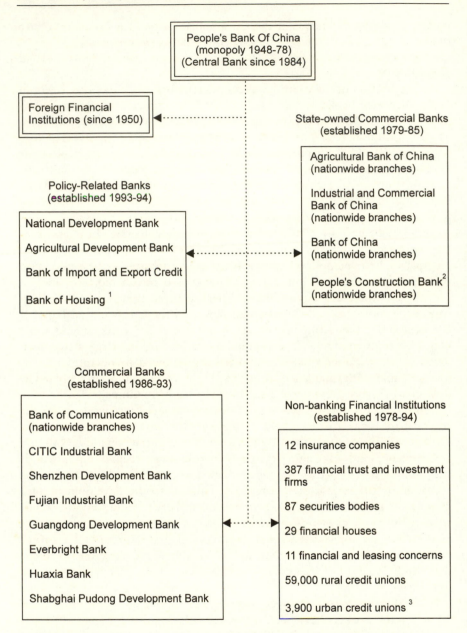

Figure 17.1 Flow chart for China's banking industry in 1994
Notes:
1 This bank is still debated and only two such regional banks have been in operation since 1988
2 From March 1, 1996, the name has been changed to China Construction Bank
3 Towards the end of 1995, these urban credit unions formed a new bank

between foreign finance houses and Chinese institutions are allowed to invest in 'A' shares (EIU, 1995). Foreign-currency-denominated shares issued to foreigners and listed on foreign exchanges are categorised as 'H' shares.

The Chinese authorities are very anxious about orderly development of the securities markets and want to ensure a certain minimum quality of issues to protect novice investors from fraud and market manipulation. The reform leaders believe that there must be some controls in order to reduce the possibility of scandals that might turn popular sentiment against the future development of these markets. Thus, not all firms wishing to raise capital from the stock market are allowed to issue securities based on their own evaluation. Rather the central government sets an aggregate quota for A share listings and decides which firms will be permitted to issue shares. Instead of relying on market information, the government decision is based on the State Assets Bureau and State Land Administration's valuation of firms' land and other assets. Although there is no quota for B shares, the approval process is more complicated and more tightly controlled. The firms must prove, at the very least, that they need foreign exchange. The H share issues are not subject to any quota but are entirely controlled by the central government.

Another area of concern for the authorities is the relationship between the banking and securities industries, especially the use of bank credit to finance securities activities. Until early 1993, banks were heavily involved in the securities markets as most securities firms were bank subsidiaries. The mixing of banking and securities activities was responsible for the diversion of funds from the productive sector with adverse impacts on industry performance as bank financing still remains the main source (over 80 per cent) of external finance for industry. Moreover, the banks were exposed to new sources of risks about which they had no prior knowledge. Therefore, regulations were introduced providing for a complete separation of the two industries. Banks closed down or sold off their securities subsidiaries and called in loans made to securities firms and investors.

With the aim of further strengthening orderly development, a national company law was passed in late 1994. This law formalised such basic concepts as limited liabilities and the definition of a joint-stock company. The regulatory mechanism was also centralised when the China Securities Regulatory Commission (CSRC) became operational in April 1993. The CSRC is primarily responsible for implementing regulations and for supervising securities firms and markets.

Fiscal reform

The taxation system in China was irrational. The burden of taxation was not rationally shared between enterprises even within the same industry.

For example, the same production materials could be taxed as high as 20 per cent or as low as 3 per cent rate depending on the type of ownership. Furthermore, the nature of 'soft budget constraint' faced by the SOEs, meant that they could negotiate the rate and amount of tax. This has been a major source of revenue loss for the government. For example, one estimate shows that the loss of tax revenue was Rmb 100 billion, enough to wipe out the entire accumulated government deficit for the past 12 years (*Economist*, 1995).

In addition to the drain of tax revenue through the SOEs, the fiscal decentralisation, introduced in 1981, enabled provinces to retain and allocate more of the tax revenues collected instead of passing them on to the centre (Yusuf, 1994: 75). The central government increasingly lost revenue to local governments which became adept at constructing tax exemptions to attract new investment. For example, the proportion of fiscal revenues fell from 31 per cent of GDP in 1978 to 13 per cent in 1993, and the share of tax revenue going to the central government dropped from 60 per cent to 40 per cent during the same period. Thus, the reform of the taxation system became essential for both improving the central government's fiscal position and hardening the SOEs' budget.

A comprehensive tax reform programme was introduced in 1994. The main plank of the tax reforms is a value added tax (VAT) at a uniform rate of 17 per cent, replacing other turnover taxes. The split of VAT revenues between the national and local governments is in the ratio 3:1. The tax on corporate profit is standardised at 33 per cent. The basic features of the 1994 tax reforms are summarised below:

1 A unified corporate tax of 33 per cent. The foreign companies in SEZs continue to enjoy tax benefits.
2 VAT replacing the old consolidated commercial and industrial tax (CICT). The rate for most goods is 17 per cent, for agricultural products 13 per cent and for small-scale business, a flat rate of 6 per cent.
3 A sliding scale for income tax ranging from a top rate of 45 per cent for those earning more than Rmb 100,801 per month to a minimum of 5 per cent for those earning between Rmb 800 and Rmb 1,301.
4 A capital gains tax on both property and stock transactions. Property developers are subject to three types of tax: a 5 per cent business tax, capital gains tax and corporation tax. Residential property developers making a profit of less than 20 per cent are exempt.
5 Luxury items, including alcohol, tobacco and cars, are subject to a separate sales tax on a sliding scale of rates up to 45 per cent.
6 A business tax for services instead of VAT, ranging from 3 per cent to 20 per cent.

The Economist (1995) believes that if all goes well, the tax reform would push back the central government's share of tax revenue and by the turn of the century net transfer would be made from the central government to the local governments, reversing the present balance, and giving the centre more influence over the regions' economic policies. Furthermore, the central government would have the opportunity to reduce its deficit.

The major differences between the old and new taxation system are summarised in Table 17.8.

Table 17.8 Major differences between China's old and new taxation systems

Old taxation system	New taxation system
1 Narrowly defined areas for VAT	1 VAT applies to production, wholesale, retail and imports
2 VAT is implicitly included in price	2 VAT is charged explicitly – no confusion between profits and costs
3 VAT applies only to domestic enterprises whereas foreign-funded enterprises pay CICT, causing inequality in tax burden	3 Both domestic and foreign-funded enterprises are taxed the same VAT
4 Too many tax categories and calculation methods are not unified	4 Simplifies the range of VAT from previously 11 steps (8–45%) to 3 steps (6–17%)
5 Invoices are not unified, causing frauds and accounting confusion	5 VAT invoice rectifies many of the problems of the earlier system

Legal reforms

An incomplete legal framework without clearly defined property rights or accounting system was a major impediment to the successful operation of markets in China. A new phase of China's economic reform thus aims at something closer to a rule of law. The speed at which the government is moving is reflected in the number of laws and regulations passed since 1993. Table 17.9 presents a summary of major legislation.

In addition to the legilsations and regulations listed in Table 17.9, a number of new rules have been implemented since the beginning of 1996. For example, a new Chinese standard for the labelling of food showing food name, a list of ingredients in descending order of quantity, net content, production date and the use by date has become mandatory in April, 1996. The rules of the China International Economic and Trade Arbitration Commission (CIETAC) dealing with disputes involving foreign enterprises have also been amended, defining the jursidiction of CIETAC, composition of the tribunal and the process. Some other regulations are Auditing Law, Civil Aviation Law and Food Hygiene Law. The Standing Committee of the National Peoples' Council has set a target of 152 new laws by the turn of the century. Of these, 35 laws will cover financial and economic issues, such as bankruptcy, state-owned property, 'solely-funded' enterprises and rural enterprises.

The Chinese government is also emphasising law enforcement. At the moment there are only about 75,000 lawyers and 6,000 law firms across China. A dozen foreign law firms have established offices in China recently.

Welfare reforms

One of the major obstacles to SOE reforms is that SOEs have traditionally been the main provider of welfare services. Employees usually get not just their pay, but their housing and health benefits through their employment at SOEs. The government is forced to tolerate SOEs' inefficiency as many SOEs lose money due chiefly to their burden of paying surplus workers. It is estimated that 20 million out of 100 million industrial workers might otherwise be unemployed if SOEs operated on the basis of strict market principles (*Economist*, 1995).

Table 17.9 Major economic legislation passed since 1993

Legislation	Date of Promulgation
Science & Technology Law, Agriculture Law	March 31,1993
Anti-Unfair Competition Law, Amendments to Economic Contract Law	September 2,1993
Consumer Right Protection Law, Amendments to Personal Income Tax Law	October 31,1993
Company Law, Amendments to Accounting Law	December 29,1993
Taiwan Investment Protection Law	March 5,1994
Government Budget Law	March 22,1994
Foreign Trade Law, National Compensation Law	May 12,1994
Labour Law, Urban Real Estate Management Law	July 5,1994
Arbitrage Law, Auditation Law	August 31,1994
Amendments to Taxation Management Law	February 28,1995
People's Bank (Control) Law	March 18,1995
Commercial Banks Law, Commercial Documents Law	May 10,1995
Co-operative Joint Venture Rules	September 4,1995
Secured Interests Law	October 1,1995
Insurance Law	October 1,1995
Measures and Implementation Rules on Statististical Reporting of International Payments	January 1,1996
Law on links with the internet	January 23,1996
Electricity Law	April 1,1996
Prevention and Control of Solid Wastes Pollution	April 1,1996
Regulations on the Management of Foreigner's Employment in China	May 1,1996

Reform of the welfare system has also become essential because of the ageing population. It is estimated that the proportion of elderly increased from 9.4 per cent in 1982 to 10.5 per cent in 1990, and the aged population has been growing at 3.37 per cent per annum since 1991. Traditionally, the elderly Chinese depended on their children and this is one of the reasons why rural families found China's 'one-child' policy so harsh. Table 17.10 presents the sources of old-age income in China.

Table 17.10 Sources of income for old people, 1994

	Family	Employment	Pension	Social Security	Others
Proportion of the old (%)	57.07	24.83	15.82	1.22	1.04

Source: Economic Daily, May 3, 1995: 1

As part of the welfare reforms, the Ministry of Labour is working on a 'Basic Pension Coverage Scheme' which will extend the current pension system covering only SOEs and partial collective-owned enterprises to all types of enterprises. The main features of this scheme are unified regulation, unified stance, unified management and unified transfer funds. The time target is that coastal and major cities will have to establish the basic framework within three years and other locations must have this system in place within five years. Details of the implementation will vary according to specific conditions in regions.

Thirty-five big and medium-sized cities have finalised their housing reform plans by May 1995. In order to encourage tenants to purchase their flats, rents for public housing are being raised. The target is to increase rent to 15 per cent of household income by 2000.

Migrant workers

China has strict internal migration regulations. It does not allow rural people to settle in urban areas at will. However, the industrialisation in the urban centres is very much dependent on the surplus rural labour in the classic Lewsian sense. A survey conducted in 1994 showed that there were about 1.7 million 'non-residential' people working in Shanghai. Nearly 800,000 construction workers were from outside Shanghai. Of workers in the Shanghai textile industry 40 per cent came from outside. An estimated 30,000 non-resident women work as housemaids in Shanghai.

In response to such a large pool of rural people, the term 'floating population' was coined. The floating population includes all those who had migrated to the cities to work but were not formally classified as urban residents. These people could not get food ration coupons and before 1978 public security officials would quickly deport them back to the countryside (Perkins, 1994: 30). However, by the mid-1980s, the security officials largely ignored the problem and the floating population could buy their own food from the market.

There is now a suggestion that migrant workers be issued one-year, two-year or three-year residency permits. They may be given permanent residency in cities after five years of residence. China's stated policy is to reduce the proportion of people living in the countryside from 87 per cent to 50 per cent by 2040.

EDUCATION, RESEARCH AND TECHNOLOGY POLICY

China's adult literacy rate of 73 per cent, although reasonably high compared with that of many developing countries, is still far short of the East Asian NIEs or even the ASEAN countries which range from 96 per cent (Korea) to 82 per cent (Indonesia). At the top end of the education spectrum, only 0.5 per cent of the population in the corresponding age group had tertiary degrees during 1987–90. This compares very poorly with countries such as Singapore (5.8 per cent), Thailand (5 per cent) and the Philippines (6.7 per cent). China also has a very small pool of scientists and technicians. According to the Human Development Report, 1995 of the United Nations, there were only 8.5 scientists and technicians per 1,000 people in China during 1986–90 compared with 47.3 in Korea, 23.6 in Singapore and 110 in Japan. Thus, both mass education and skill development are vital for China's modernisation drive.

One major step in encouraging technological progress was initiated in April 1985 when the Patent Law became effective. Protection measures for intellectual property rights were largely responsible for an average yearly 22 per cent increase in patent applications. In 1985, the number of patent applications was 14,000, and this rose to 77,000 in 1994. The recent agreement between the Chinese and American governments to protect US intellectual property rights is another step in the right direction.

To promote communications technology, China has joined the Internet facility and opened Chinanet in late 1994. Its aim is to install 100 million telephones in China in the next five years.

R&D input in China's large and medium-sized enterprises accounts for a relatively small percentage of their revenue, 1.4 per cent. But of 17,000 large and medium-sized enterprises, 62.4 per cent are capable of conducting R&D involving 370,000 researchers and technicians.

The government's emphasis on R&D has intensified in recent times. There are now about 1,000 tertiary institutions and 120 research institutes under China's Science Academy, and 5,000 specialised research institutes at or above county level. By 1993, the government had designated 52 high-technology development districts employing more than 600,000 people. The Chinese government's emphasis on higher education can be ascertained from Table 17.11.

The result of increased emphasis on technological education and research is being reflected in the number of scientific papers published internationally by Chinese scholars. For example, China's ranking in terms of scientific papers published in international journals increased from below 20th in

1985 to 12th in 1993. For every 100 scientific papers published in the world, 1.1 is done by mainland China's scientists. Furthermore, between 1981 and 1994, China signed up 2,393 export contracts for technology licence, technology service or complete systems of equipment, worth US$8.8 billion, while in the 1970s China's technology export barely existed.

Table 17.11 Educational attainment of the population at two censuses (% of total)

Level	1982 census	1990 census	% change
University	0.6	1.4	131.2
Senior middle	6.8	8.0	18.6
Junior middle	17.9	23.3	30.5
Primary	35.2	37.1	5.2
Illiterate and semi-literate	22.8	15.9	−0.3

Source: State Statistical Bureau, China Yearbook, 1994

INFRASTRUCTURE

Inadequate infrastructure such as roads and railways has been a concern. The Chinese government has taken major steps to develop nationwide infrastructure. One such project involves the construction of north–south railway links, bisecting the existing coastal route via Shanghai and the inland route that crosses the Yangtze at Wuhan. A specialised State Development Bank was established, in particular, to finance infrastructure projects. There has also been deregulation of the airline industry: the national flag carrier CAAC ceased to operate as an airline in 1988 and became a regulatory authority, and there are now about 30 Chinese airline companies.

REGIONAL INEQUALITY

Regional equality was one of the main objectives of Chinese industrialisation under Mao. But one of the adverse impacts of the recent industrial drive has been increased regional imbalance. It is a concern that the benefits of increased growth are not shared by all regions and people. For example, of the 11 coastal provinces and municipalities, all but 2 have incomes above the national average. On the other hand, of the 19 inland provinces and regions, all but 3 have incomes below the national average (Economist, 1995). Furthermore, the average urban income in the mid-1980s was barely double the average rural income. But the urban average income has become three times the rural average in the past 10 years. According to the Far Eastern Economic Review (June 1, 1995), 'people in the countryside now earn 39 per cent of what their city cousins get, down from 59 per cent in 1984'. To make the situation worse, the rural people have less social wages in the form of housing and welfare benefits.

In order to gauge the situation, China began publishing a social development index (SDI) in 1991. The SDI is calculated by using ten indicators, such as environment, population, basic economic figures, income distribution, employment, social security, public health and medicare, education and science, culture and sports, and crime rate. The 1993 SDI is presented in Table 17.12.

The table shows that although overall SDI for China increased by 6 points between 1992 and 1993, there was a wide disparity between regions. The largest increase in SDI occurred in Beijing. Only 14 regions experienced any improvement. The rest either stagnated or declined. The growing regional disparity is going to be a major concern for Chinese policy-makers.

Table 17.12 Spread of social development indices for regions, 1993

Ranking	Region	SDI (1992 = 100)
	China (National)	106
1	Beijing (Municipal city)	181
2	Shanghai (Municipal city)	174
3	Tianjin (Municipal city)	167
4	Liaoning (Province)	132
5	Guangdong (Province)	129
6	Jiangsu (Province)	127
7	Jilin (Province)	123
8	Zhejiang (Province)	121
9	Hainan (Province)	120
10	Helongjian (Province)	119
11	Shangdong (Province)	118
12	Fujian (Province)	113
13	Hebei (Province)	113
14	Shanxi (Province)	103
15	Hubei (Province)	100
16	Inner Mongolia (Autonomous region)	100
17	Shaanxi (Province)	97
18	Hunan (Province)	97
19	Guangxi (Autonomous region)	96
20	Anhui (Province)	92
21	Henan (Province)	92
22	Xinjian (Autonomous region)	90
23	Jiangxi (Province)	84
24	Ningxia (Autonomous region)	83
25	Sichuan (Province)	82
26	Qinghai (Inner region, Province)	74
27	Yunnan (Province)	73
28	Gansu (Province)	73
29	Guizhou (Province)	52
30	Tibet (Autonomous region)	n.a.
31	Taiwan	n.a.

Source: Outlook, No 2, January 9, 1995

Thus, contrary to fears that China may revert back to the 'iron curtain' era, it seems that despite China's gradual and stop–go approach to economic reform, its journey towards a market economy is irreversible. However, this does not mean that a complete *laissez-faire* economy will emerge. What is likely to happen is an economy with a heavy presence of government, perhaps on the pattern of South Korea or Taiwan (Perkins, 1994: 44). This, therefore, requires careful development of an institutional framework which would minimise government failures. Independence of the central bank and the government budget law restricting its deficit-making capacity are steps in the right direction. Most importantly, as long as China follows an open door policy, the government has to behave responsibly.

References for Part II

ADB (1994) *Asian Development Outlook, 1995*, Manila: Asian Development Bank

Alamgir, J. (1994) 'Formula and Fortune: Economic Development in Malaysia', *Journal of Contemporary Asia*, 24(1): 67–80

Asia Pacific Economic Group (1994) *Asia-Pacific Profile, 1994*, Canberra: Australian National University

Balassa, B. (1991) *Economic Policies in the Pacific Area Developing Countries*, New York: New York University Press

Bowie, A. (1988) 'Redistribution with Growth? The Dilemma's of State Sponsored Development in Malaysia', in Clark, C. and Lemaco, J. (eds) *State and Development*, Leiden: E.J. Brill

Bowie, A. (1991) *Crossing the Industrial Divide: State, Society and the Policies of Economic Transformation in Malaysia*, New York: Columbia University Press

Broadman, H.G. (1995) 'Meeting the Challenge of Chinese Enterprise Reform', *World Bank Discussion Papers* 283, Washington DC: World Bank

Brown, I. (1995a) 'Malaysia – History', *The Far East and Australasia, 1995*, 26th edn., London: Europa Publications

Brown, I. (1995b) 'The Philippines – History', *The Far East and Australasia*, 26th edn. London: Europa Publications

Burki, H. (1995) 'Comment on "How Industrial Reform Worked in China: The Role of Innovation, Competition, and Property Rights" by Jefferson and Rawski', *Proceedings of the World Bank Annual Conference on Development Economics, 1994*: 163–6

Chen, K., Jefferson, G. and Singh, I.(1992) 'Lessons from China's Economic Reform', *Journal of Comparative Economics*, 16: 201–25

Cheng, H.S. (1992) 'China's Foreign Trade Reform, 1979–91', *Pacific Basin Working Paper Series* No. PB92–01, Center For Pacific Basin Monetary and Economic Studies, Reserve Bank of San Francisco

Chowdhury, A. and Kirkpatrick, C. (1987) 'Industrial Restructuring in a Newly Industrializing Country: The Identification of Priority Industries in Singapore', *Applied Economics* 19(7): 915–26

Chung, J. (1995) 'Republic of Korea – Economy', *The Far East and Australasia*, 26th edn, London: Europa Publications

Cribb, R. (1995) 'Indonesia – Economy', *The Far East and Australasia*, 26th edn, London: Europa Publications

Demaine, H. (1995) 'Thailand: Physical and Social Geography', *The Far East and Australasia* 26th edn, London: Europa Publications

DFAT (1994a) *Country Economic Brief, Hong Kong*, Department of Foreign Affairs and Trade, Government of Australia, October

DFAT (1994b) *Country Economic Brief, Singapore*, Department of Foreign Affairs and Trade, Government of Australia, October

DFAT (1994c) *Country Economic Brief, Thailand*, Department of Foreign Affairs and Trade, Government of Australia, October

DFAT (1994d) *Country Economic Brief, Indonesia*, Department of Foreign Affairs and Trade, Government of Australia, November

DFAT (1994e) *Country Economic Brief, Philippines*, Department of Foreign Affairs and Trade, Government of Australia, November

DFAT (1995a) *Country Economic Brief, Taiwan*, Department of Foreign Affairs and Trade, Government of Australia, January

DFAT (1995b) *Country Economic Brief, Malaysia*, Department of Foreign Affairs and Trade, Government of Australia, January

Dixon, C. (1995) 'Thailand – Economy', *The Far East and Australasia* 26th edn, London: Europa Publications

Economist (1995) 'China Survey', *The Economist*, March 18, p. 62

EIU (1995) *Country Profile 1994–95 China*, Economist Intelligence Unit

FEER (1995a) 'Building Asia: What Shortage?', *Far Eastern Economic Review*, May 25:59

FEER (1995b) 'Economic Monitor – Beyond Expectations', *Far Eastern Economic Review*, May 18: 93

FEER (1995c) 'Cover Story – Give and Take', *Far Eastern Economic Review*, May 25: 54–9

FEER (1995d) 'Middle Ground', *Far Eastern Economic Review*, January 19: 48

FEER (1995e) 'Economic Monitor: Malaysia', *Far Eastern Economic Review*, April 20: 74

FEER (1996a) 'Here Come the Jitters', *Far Eastern Economic Review*, April 25: 54–6

FEER (1996b) 'It's a Jungle Out There', *Far Eastern Economic Review*, April 25: 58–61

Fitzgerald, C.P. (1995) 'The People's Republic of China: History up to 1966', *The Far East and Australia*, London: Europa Publications

Fukasaku, K. and Wall, D. (1994) *China's Long March to an Open Economy*, Paris: Development Centre of the OECD

Government of Malaysia (1971) *Second Malaysia Plan*, 1971–75, Kuala Lumpur: Government Printer

Government of Malaysia (1976) *Third Malaysia Plan*, 1976–80, Kuala Lumpur: Government Printer

Government of Malaysia (1981) *Fourth Malaysian Plan*, 1981–85, Kuala Lumpur: Government Printer

Hill, H. (1990) 'Foreign Investment and East Asian Economic Development', Asian-Pacific Economic Literature, 4(2): 21–58

Hill, H. and Johns, B. (1985) 'The Role of Direct Foreign Investment in Developing East Asian Countries', *Weltwirtschaftliches Archiv*, 121(2): 355–81

Ho, S.P.S. (1978) *Economic Development of Taiwan*, New Haven, Conn. and London: Yale University Press

Ho, S.P.S. (1984) 'Colonialism and Development: Korea, Taiwan, Kwantung' in Myers, R.H. and Petrie, M.R. (eds) *The Japanese Colonial Empire, 1895–1945*, Princeton, NJ: Princeton University Press

Hobohm, S.O.H. (1995) 'Indonesia – Economy', *The Far East and Australasia, 1995*, 26th edn, London: Europa Publications

Howe, C. (1995) 'Hong Kong – Economy', *The Far East and Australasia, 1995*, London: Europa Publications

Hussain, A. and Stern, N. (1995) 'Comment on "How Industrial Reform Worked in China: The Role of Innovation, Competition, and Property Rights" by Jefferson and Rawski', *Proceedings of the World Bank Annual Conference on Development Economics, 1994*: 157–62

International Monetary Fund (1993) *World Economic Outlook*, Washington DC: IMF

Jefferson, G. and Rawski, T. (1994) 'Enterprise Reform in Chinese Industry', *Journal of Economic Perspectives* 8(2), Spring: 47–70

Jomo, K.S. (1987) 'Economic Crisis and Policy Response in Malaysia', in Robinson, R., Hewison, K. and Higgot, R. (eds) *Southeast Asia in the 1980s: The Politics of Economic Crisis*, London: Allen & Unwin

Jones, R., King, R. and Klein, M. (1993) 'Economic Integration between Hong Kong, Taiwan and the Coastal Provinces of China', *OECD Economic Studies*, Spring, No. 20: 115–44

Kirkpatrick, C.H. (1988) 'Real Wages, Profits and Manufacturing Performance in the Small Open Economy; the Case of Singapore', mimeo

Kunnoot, S. and Chowdhury, A. (1994) 'Export-Oriented Industrialization and Industrial Deepening: An Input–Output Perspective', *Economic Bulletin for Asia and the Pacific*, 43(1): 52–62

Lee, C.H. (1994) 'Korea's Direct Foreign Investment in Southeast Asia', *ASEAN Economic Bulletin*, 10(3): 280–96

Lee, K.Y. (1991) In *The Straits Times*, September 15

Lian, D.C.B. (1994) 'Gradual Financial Reform in Action – The Case of Thailand, 1979–92', ASEAN Economic Bulletin, 10(3): 297–315

Lim, C., Chowdhury, A., Islam, I. *et al.* (1988) *Policy Options for the Singapore Economy*, Singapore: McGraw-Hill

Low, L. and Toh, M.H. (1994) 'Economic Outlook: ASEAN 1994–95', *Regional Outlook: Southeast Asia 1994–95*, Institute of Southeast Asian Studies, pp. 35–54

Lundberg, E. (1979) 'Fisacal and Monetary Politics', in Glenson, W. (ed.) *Economic Growth and Structural Change in Taiwan*, Ithaca, NY: Cornell University Press

Mahathir bin Mohammad (1976) 'Speech by Y.A.B. Dr. Mahathir Mohammad, Deputy Prime Minister/Education Minister', delivered at the opening of the *Federation of Malaysian Manufacturers Seminar on the Third Malaysian Plan*, Kuala Lumpur, August 26

McVey, R. (1995) 'Thailand – History', *The Far East and Australasia*, 26th edn, London: Europa Publications

Mehmet, O. (1987) 'The Malaysian Experience in Manpower Planning and Labour Market Policies', in Amjad, R. (ed.) *Human Resource Planning: The Asian Experience*, New Delhi: ILO-ARTEP

MIDA/UNDP (1985) *Medium and Long Term Industrial Master Plan Malaysia 1986–95*, Kuala Lumpur: Government Printer

Miners, N.J. (1995) 'Hong Kong – History', *The Far East and Australasia*, 26th edn, London: Europa Publications

Musa, H. (1986) 'Keynote Address' delivered at the *Conference on Malaysia*, Tufts University, Medford, Mass., 18–20 November

Nahm, A.C. (1995) 'Republic of Korea – History', *The Far East and Australasia*, 26th edn, London: Europa Publications

Naughton, B. (1994) *Growing out of Plan: Chinese Economic Reform, 1978–1993*, New York: Cambridge University Press

Nicholas, L. (1992) *Foreign Trade and Economic Reform in China, 1978–1990*, Cambridge: Cambridge University Press

OECD (1993) *Foreign Direct Investment Relations between the OECD and the Dynamic Asian Economics*, Paris: OECD

Park, F. (1991) 'Emerging Issues of Labor Markets and Industrial Relations in Korea', in Lee, C.H. and Park, F. (eds) *Emerging Issues of Industrial Labor Markets in Developing Asia*, Seoul: Korea Development Institute

Park, Y.C. (1983) 'Inflation and Stabilization policies in Korea, 1960–80', in *Conference on Inflation in East Asian Countries*, Chung-Hua Institution for Economic Research, Taipei

Perkins, D. (1994) 'Completing China's Move to the Market', *Journal of Economic Perspectives*, 8(2), Spring: 23–46

Putterman, L. (1992) 'Dualism and Reform in China', *Economic Development and Cultural Change*, 40(3): 467–94

Regnier, P. (1995) 'Singapore – Economy', *The Far East and Australasia*, 26th edn, London: Europa Publications: pp. 918–24

Robinson, D., Byeon, Y., Teja, R. and Tseng, W. (1991) *Thailand: Adjusting to Success – Current Policy Issues*, Washington DC: IMF

Sivalingham, G. (1988) 'The New Economic Policy and the Differential Economic Performance of the Races in West Malaysia, 1970–85' in Nash, M. (ed.) *Economic Performance in Malaysia; The Insider's View*, New York: Professors World Peace Academy

Spencer, M. (1995) 'Securities Market in China', *Finance and Development*, June: 28–31

Tseng, W. *et al.* (1994) 'Economic Reform in China: A New Phase', *IMF Occasional Paper*, November

Tsiang, S.C. and Wu, R.I. (1985) 'Foreign Trade and Investment as Boosters for Take-off: The Experience of Four Asian Newly Industrializing Countries', in Glenson, W. (ed.) *Foreign Trade and Investment: Economic Development in Newly Industrializing Countries* Madison: Wisconsin University Press

Turnbull, C.M. (1995) 'Singapore – History', *The Far East and Australasia*, 26th edn, London: Europa Publications

UNDP (1993) *Human Development Report 1993*, New York: United Nations

UNDP/World Bank (1985) *Final Report: Malaysian Industrial Policy Studies Project*, Kuala Lumpur: Government Printer

World Bank (1989a) *Philippines: Towards Sustaining the Economic Recovery, Country Economic Memorandum*, Washington DC: World Bank

World Bank (1989b) *Thailand: Country Economic Memorandum, Building on the Recent Success – A Policy Framework*, Washington DC: World Bank

World Bank (1990) *The Philippines, Country Economic Memorandum: Issues in Adjustment and Competitiveness*, Washington DC: World Bank

Yusuf, S. (1994) 'China's Macroeconomic Performance and Management during Transition', *Journal of Economic Perspectives*, 8(2), Spring: 71–92

Index